J. B. (John Bennet) Lawes, J. Henry Gilbert

On the sources of the nitrogen of vegetation

with special reference to the question whether plants assimilate free or uncombined nitrogen

J. B. (John Bennet) Lawes, J. Henry Gilbert

On the sources of the nitrogen of vegetation
with special reference to the question whether plants assimilate free or uncombined nitrogen

ISBN/EAN: 9783337374310

Printed in Europe, USA, Canada, Australia, Japan

Cover: Foto ©Lupo / pixelio.de

More available books at **www.hansebooks.com**

THE SOURCES OF

THE

NITROGEN OF VEGETATION;

WITH SPECIAL REFERENCE TO THE QUESTION WHETHER PLANTS ASSIMILATE FREE OR UNCOMBINED NITROGEN.

BY

JOHN BENNET LAWES, F.R.S., F.C.S.,

JOSEPH HENRY GILBERT, PH.D., F.R.S., F.C.S.,

AND

EVAN PUGH, PH.D., F.C.S.

From the PHILOSOPHICAL TRANSACTIONS.—PART II. 1861.

LONDON:

PRINTED BY TAYLOR AND FRANCIS, RED LION COURT, FLEET STREET.

1862.

S

XXIII. *On the Sources of the Nitrogen of Vegetation; with special reference to the Question whether Plants assimilate Free or uncombined Nitrogen.* By John Bennet Lawes, *F.R.S., F.C.S.*, Joseph Henry Gilbert, *Ph.D., F.R.S., F.C.S.*, and Evan Pugh, *Ph.D., F.C.S.*

Received June 21,—Read June 21, 1860.

Contents.

PART FIRST.

GENERAL HISTORY, AND STATEMENT OF THE QUESTION.

PART SECOND.

EXPERIMENTAL RESULTS OBTAINED AT ROTHAMSTED, DURING THE YEARS 1857, 1858, AND 1859.

APPENDIX.

PLATES XII. XIII. XIV. and XV.

PART FIRST.

GENERAL HISTORY, AND STATEMENT OF THE QUESTION.

Section I.—INTRODUCTION, AND EARLY HISTORY.

The facts at the present time generally accepted regarding the ultimate composition, and the sources of the constituents, of plants, have, for the most part, received their preponderating weight of proof within the limits of the present century. But it is to the century preceding it that we must look for the establishment of much that was essential as the foundation of those advances which have since been made.

Whatever may be the value at present attached to the particular views of Hales regarding the composition and the sources of vegetable matter. we must accord to his labours, in the early part of the eighteenth century, the merit of having been guided by a proper spirit of experimental inquiry. Nor did he fail in applying to good account, and even in extending, the then existing knowledge of the material things around him which were apparently involved in the mysterious processes of vegetable growth.

With our present knowledge, however, of the general composition of plants, and of the sources of their constituents, it is easy to see how essential was a proper understanding of the chemistry of the air, and of water, to any true conceptions of the material changes involved in the vegetative process. It can, indeed, hardly excite surprise, that what may be called the germs of our present knowledge of the chemistry of plant-growth came forth almost simultaneously with the now adopted views of the composition of those universal, though not exclusive, media of vegetation—*air*, and *water*.

Accordingly, it is between the dates of 1770 and 1800 that we find Black, Scheele, Priestley, Lavoisier, Cavendish, and Watt establishing for us the facts that common air consists chiefly of nitrogen and oxygen, with a little carbonic acid, that carbonic acid itself is composed of carbon and oxygen; and that water is composed of hydrogen and oxygen; and it is within the same period that Priestley and Ingenhousz, Sennebier and Woodhouse, laboured to show the mutual relations of these bodies and vegetable growth.

But the observers last mentioned seem to have had more prominently in view the question of the influence of plants upon the media with which they were surrounded, than that of the influence of these media in contributing materially to the increased substance of plants themselves. Following closely on their footsteps, both in point of time and in general plan of research, came De Saussure. His labours were conducted towards the end of the last century and in the beginning of the present one; and their results, and the arguments he founded upon them, published by him in 1804, may be said to have indicated, if not indeed established, many of the most important facts with which we are yet acquainted regarding the sources of the constituents stored up by the growing plant. To De Saussure we owe the experimental, and even quantitative, illustration of the fact, that plants in sunlight increase in their amounts of carbon, hydrogen, and oxygen, at the expense of carbonic acid and of water. It is remarkable, too, that, in the case of the main experiment he cites on the point, he, with his very imperfect methods, found the increase in carbon and in the elements of water to be almost identically in the proportion in which these are known to exist in the so-denominated carbo-hydrates. He further maintained the essentialness of the so-distinguished "mineral" constituents of plants; and he pointed out, in opposition to previous views, that they were derived from the soil, and were not the result of a creative power exercised by the living plant. He also called attention to the probability that the incombustible or mineral constituents derived by plants from the soil, were the source of those found in the animals which are fed upon them.

Besides carbon, hydrogen, oxygen, and the more peculiarly mineral constituents, plants had already been shown to contain *nitrogen*. PRIESTLEY and INGENHOUSZ thought they had observed that plants absorbed the free nitrogen of the confined atmospheres in which they were placed in their experiments. SENNEBIER and WOODHOUSE arrived at an opposite conclusion. DE SAUSSURE, again, did not find that plants took up appreciable quantities of the nitrogen supplied to them in the free and gaseous form. On the other hand, he thought that his experiments indicated rather an evolution of that element at the expense of the substance of the plant, than any assimilation of it from gaseous media. On this point he further concluded that the source of the nitrogen of plants was, more probably, the nitrogenous compounds in the soil, and the small amount of ammonia which he demonstrated to exist in the atmosphere.

From his results, as a whole, DE SAUSSURE concluded that air and water contributed a much larger proportion of the dry substance of plants, than did the soils in which they grew. In his view, the fertile soil was the one which yielded liberally to the plant nitrogenous compounds and the incombustible or mineral constituents; whilst he attributed to air and water, at least the main part of the carbon, hydrogen, and oxygen of which the greater portion of the dry substance of the plant was made up.

Up to the present time, carbonic acid and water are admitted to be the chief sources of the carbon, hydrogen, and oxygen which constitute the great proportion of vegetable produce. Nor is it questioned that ammonia, and especially ammonia provided within the soil, is at least an important source of the nitrogen of such produce. But the experiments of DE SAUSSURE—however sagacious his conclusions—were less satisfactory as to the source of the nitrogen, than as to that of the carbon, hydrogen, and oxygen, of vegetable matter.

It will not be supposed, from what has just been said, that there remain no questions, of vast scientific as well as of practical interest, to be yet solved, regarding the conditions under which our different crops take up their carbon, hydrogen, and oxygen. At the same time, those who devote themselves to the subject of Agricultural Chemistry soon find that the explanation of the chemical phenomena of agricultural production awaits much more for a further elucidation of the sources, and of the modes of assimilation, of the *nitrogen* than of the other, so-called, organic elements of our crops—carbon, hydrogen, and oxygen.

In 1837, BOUSSINGAULT took up the subject of the sources of the Nitrogen of plants, where DE SAUSSURE had left it more than thirty years before. To the investigations and conclusions of BOUSSINGAULT, and others, in connexion with this question, from the date above mentioned up to the present time, we shall have to refer pretty fully further on. It may here be mentioned, however, that already at that early period BOUSSINGAULT had so far advanced in his inquiries into the chemical statistics of certain agricultural practices on the large scale, as to be apparently led by them to see the importance of investigating much more closely the sources of the Nitrogen periodically yielded by a given area of land, over and above that which was artificially supplied to it.

We fully admit the pertinence of the considerations, and the sagacity of the observations adduced on this head, more than twenty years ago, by BOUSSINGAULT. It will, nevertheless, be well to preface the discussion of our own experimental evidence regarding the sources of the nitrogen of plants, by the statement of a few prominent and striking facts, established by investigations conducted here, at Rothamsted, illustrative of the amounts of nitrogen yielded by different crops over a given area of land, and of the relation of these amounts to certain measured, or known, sources of it. Of these points, however, we profess to speak only in a very brief and summary manner on the present occasion. The discussion in detail, of the evidence relating to them, would indeed itself exhaust the limits of our Paper. Moreover, we have already treated of this subject in a separate form, elsewhere*; and it is our intention to consider it much more fully at some future opportunity.

SECTION II.—ANNUAL YIELD OF NITROGEN PER ACRE, IN DIFFERENT CROPS†.

A.—*Yield of Nitrogen per acre when the same Crop is grown year after year on the same Land.*

The following Summary Table shows the average annual amounts of nitrogen yielded per acre, in the crops enumerated, when each was grown for a number of years consecutively on the same land, without manure.

TABLE I.

Description of Crop.	Dates of the Experiments.	Number of Years.	Average Annual yield of Nitrogen per acre, without Manure.
			lbs.
Wheat	1844—1859 inclusive	16	24·4
Barley	1852—1859 inclusive	8	24·7
Meadow Hay..........	1856—1859 inclusive	4	39·4
Beans	1847—1858 inclusive	12	47·8

There were obtained, then, in each of the Cereal crops (wheat and barley) about 24½ lbs. of Nitrogen per acre, per annum, without manure. In the case of each of the crops the land was, in an agricultural sense, exhausted at the commencement of the

* British Association for the Advancement of Science, Leeds Meeting (1858), Section B.

† The results given in this Section have been revised, and in some cases the periods over which the estimates are taken extended, since the reading of the Paper.

experiment; that is to say, it had been brought to such a condition by previous cropping, that, in the ordinary course of practice, it would be deemed necessary to supply manure to it before growing another corn-crop. It may be further remarked that in the case of the wheat there is as yet little, but in that of the barley more obvious indication of progressive decline in the annual yield.

The meadow-land yielded nearly 40 lbs. of Nitrogen per acre, per annum, or above one-half more than the exclusively Graminaceous crops, wheat and barley. The heterogeneous produce, meadow-hay, contained, however, a good deal of Trifolium, and other Leguminous plants, intermixed with the Grasses. To this fact is to be attributed, at least in great part, its comparatively high amount of Nitrogen. It should be observed, too, that the average is as yet taken over only four years.

The Leguminous crop (beans) has given, over a period of twelve years, an average of nearly 48 lbs. of Nitrogen per acre, per annum. The yield of Nitrogen in this *Leguminous* crop was, therefore, nearly twice as great as in the *Graminaceous* corn-crops. The bean and allied crops are, however, very subject to disease, especially when grown too frequently on the same land. It is, at least in part, owing to this circumstance, that the average annual yield over the twelve years was so much less than would be the yield of the crop when grown in suitable alternation with others in a season of average adaptation for its healthy development. In fact, so great was the deterioration in the character and amount of produce in the experiments in question, due to the continuous cropping, that whilst the average annual yield of Nitrogen over the first six of the twelve years was 70 lbs., that over the concluding six years was only 26 lbs. Nor did the addition of nitrogenous manure in the form of ammonia-salts, together with liberal mineral manuring, obviate this deterioration in any material degree more than did mineral manures alone.

In further illustration of the larger amount of Nitrogen obtained over a given area of land in Leguminous crops than in Graminaceous ones, some remarkable results with *clover* may be cited. Red clover was grown in three out of four consecutive years, the intermediate crop being wheat—all without manure. The following amounts of Nitrogen were obtained per acre:—

TABLE II.

Season.	Crop.	Nitrogen per acre.
		lbs.
1st Year, 1849	Clover.	206·8
(2nd Year, 1850 ...	Wheat.	45·2)
3rd Year, 1851	Clover.	29·3
4th Year, 1852	Clover.	111·9
Average of the three years Clover		116·0

All further attempts to grow clover year after year, on this land, have, however, failed. Neither ammonia-salts, nor organic matter rich in carbon as well as other constituents, nor mineral manures, nor a mixture of all has availed to restore the clover-yielding capabilities of the land. On the other hand, it should be particularly observed that, after taking 206·8 lbs. of Nitrogen from an acre of land in the clover-crop of the first year, the wheat-crop of the second or succeeding year, compared with that of the same season in the adjoining experimental wheat-field where the crop is grown year after year on the same land, was about double that obtained from the plot which had there been unmanured for a series of consecutive years, and fully equal to that from a plot which had for the same period received annually a dressing of farm-yard manure. It should be added that, after failing to get any crop of clover at all in 1853 and in 1854, and getting a very poor one in 1855, the land was allowed to lie fallow for two years; that after this, in 1858, there was obtained an over-luxuriant and laid crop of barley, more than twice as great as the average annual produce of eight years of the successive growth of the crop without manure in the same field; yet, after resowing with clover in the spring of 1859, and getting a small cutting in the autumn of the same year, the plant has again died off during the winter of 1859–60. This was the case notwithstanding that it was a perennial variety that was last sown.

Again, eight consecutive crops of *turnips* (four "White Globe" and four "Swedish") gave an average annual yield, per acre, of about 40 lbs. of Nitrogen, without the supply of any in the manure. In the case of these turnips, however, the land received annually certain "mineral" manures. In fact, turnips grown year after year without manure of any kind, yielded, after a few years, only a few hundred-weights of produce per acre; but the *percentage* of Nitrogen in these diminutive unmanured turnips was very unusually high. It will be observed that the average annual yield of Nitrogen per acre, in the turnips grown by mineral manures (containing no Nitrogen), was considerably more than that in the unmanured Cereal grain-crops. And, in connexion with this point, it is worthy of remark, that, on barley, without manure, succeeding on the land from which these eight mineral-manured turnip-crops had been taken, the produce was only about three-fourths as much as that obtained, in the same season, where barley was grown for the second year in succession without manure, in another field; and it was only about three-fifths as much as that obtained, also in the same season, where barley was grown as the second crop of the second course, in a series of entirely unmanured four-course Rotation-crops.

It may be mentioned that, in the case of the purely Graminaceous crops, there has been but very little gain in the annual yield of Nitrogen per acre by the use of mineral or non-nitrogenous manures. But in the case of the Leguminous crops, as in that of the root-crops just referred to, there has been much more Nitrogen harvested over a given area, within a given time, when mineral manures were employed, than when no manure at all was used.

It has thus far been seen, then, that the Leguminous crops yield much more Nitrogen over a given area than the Graminaceous ones, and, further, that the amount of Nitrogen harvested in the former is increased considerably by the use of "mineral" manures, whilst that in the latter is so in a very limited degree. It is, nevertheless, a well-known agricultural fact, that the growth of the *Leguminous* crops, which *carry off* such a comparatively large amount of Nitrogen, is one of the best preparations for the after-growth of wheat. On the other hand, it is equally true that *fallow*—one important effect of which is to *accumulate* within the soil the available Nitrogen of two or more years for the growth of one—and *adding nitrogenous manures*, have each much the same effect in increasing the produce of the Cereal crops.

B.—*Yield of Nitrogen per acre when Wheat is grown in alternation with Beans, or with Fallow.*

The striking and interesting fact, that the growth (and removal from the land) of a highly nitrogenized Leguminous crop, and fallow, have each the effect of increasing the amount of produce, and with it the yield of Nitrogen per acre, of a succeeding Cereal crop, is briefly illustrated by the summary of direct experimental results given in the following Table:—

TABLE III.

Showing the Amount of Nitrogen obtained per acre, in Wheat grown consecutively, in Wheat alternated with Beans, and in Wheat alternated with Fallow.

Period of Experiment ten years, 1850—1859 inclusive.

		Nitrogen per acre, lbs.	
		Total.	Average annual.
Beans—10 crops consecutively	without Manure	346·9	34·7
	with Mineral Manure	510·6	51·1
Wheat—without Manure	10 Crops consecutively	234·0	23·4
	5 Crops alternated with Fallow	219·3	43·9 or 21·9
Wheat without Manure	5 Crops alternated with Beans	225·8	45·2 or 22·6
Beans without Manure	5 Crops alternated with Wheat	244·5	48·9 or 24·5
Wheat with Mineral Manure	5 Crops alternated with Beans	207·0	41·4 or 20·7
Beans with Mineral Manure	5 Crops alternated with Wheat	227·2	45·4 or 22·7

It is seen, then, that ten consecutive crops of beans, without manure of any kind, gave an average annual yield of Nitrogen, per acre, of 34·7 lbs.; and ten consecutive crops with "mineral" but without nitrogenous manure gave an average annual yield, per acre, of 51·1 lbs.

During the same period, ten consecutive crops of wheat without manure of any kind gave annually 23·4 lbs. of Nitrogen, or less than half as much as the beans with mineral but without nitrogenous manure. Again, extending over the same series of years, five crops of wheat *alternated with fallow* gave, taking the average of the five years under crop, 43·9 lbs., and on the average of the ten years, 21·9 lbs. per acre, per annum, of Nitrogen. That is to say, the wheat alternated with fallow gave, taking the average of the five years of its growth, nearly twice as much Nitrogen annually as the wheat grown after wheat in the same seasons. The total Nitrogen obtained, per acre, over the ten years, was, however, pretty much the same in the two

Note.—At page 439, line 3 from bottom, *after* "…. average annual amount, per acre, of 42·6 lbs." *insert* The second and third courses gave, however, much less than the first, and hence a less average per annum than that stated for the twelve years.

cases,—namely, 234 lbs. in the ten crops of wheat grown consecutively, and 219·3 lbs. in the five crops of wheat alternated with fallow.

Again, five crops of wheat *alternated with beans* gave 45·2 lbs. of Nitrogen per acre, per annum, over the five years—equal half that amount, or 22·6 lbs., averaged over the ten years. The total amount of Nitrogen obtained during the ten years was, in the ten crops of wheat grown consecutively, 234 lbs., in the five crops of wheat alternated with fallow, 219·3 lbs., and in the five crops of wheat alternated with beans, 225·8 lbs. —or not very materially different in the three cases. But, notwithstanding that the land has thus yielded in wheat, over ten years, almost as much total Nitrogen in five crops alternated with beans, as in ten crops grown consecutively, and rather more than in five crops alternated with fallow, the five intermediate crops of beans have, in addition to this, themselves carried off more than the same amount of Nitrogen as the wheat—namely, 244·5 lbs.

The general result is, then, that pretty nearly the same amount of Nitrogen was taken from a given area of land in wheat, in ten years, whether ten crops were grown consecutively, five crops in alternation with fallow, or five crops in alternation with beans. In fact, the crop of wheat was increased fully as much when it succeeded *beans*, which carried off a large amount of Nitrogen, and of mineral matters also, as when it succeeded *fallow*, which conserved the stores both of Nitrogen and of mineral matter.

It will be seen, by the illustrations given in the next sub-section (C.), that the experimental results thus far adduced are perfectly consistent in character with those obtained under circumstances more nearly allied to those of ordinary farm practice.

C.—*Yield of Nitrogen per acre when crops are grown in an actual course of rotation.*

In Boussingault's experiments, he obtained, taking the results of six separate courses of rotation, an average of between one-third and one-half more Nitrogen in the produce than had been supplied in the manure. He found, moreover, that the largest yields of Nitrogen were in the Leguminous crops, and, further, that the Cereal crops were the larger when they next succeeded upon the removal of the highly nitrogenized Leguminous crops.

For our own experiments at Rothamsted upon an actual course of rotation, a piece of land was selected which was, in an agricultural sense, exhausted; that is to say, it had grown a course of crops since the application of manure, and would, under ordinary practice, have received a new supply before growing another crop. On this land the four-course rotation of Turnips, Barley, Leguminous crop (or Fallow), and Wheat, in the order of succession here enumerated, and *without manure*, has now been followed for twelve years—that is, through three separate courses. The yield of Nitrogen during these twelve years, or three courses, has been determined; and the result shows an average annual amount, per acre, of 42·6 lbs. This, it will be remembered, is nearly twice as much as was obtained in either wheat or barley when these crops were, respectively, grown year after year on the same land. The greatest yield of Nitrogen obtained in the Rotation experiment was in the case of a clover-crop, grown once during the twelve years, and which constituted the Leguminous crop of the first course. After both this clover-crop (in which was removed such a large amount of Nitrogen) and beans which replaced it in the second and third courses (but which gave a very small yield of Nitrogen), the wheat-crop was about double as much as the average where wheat has been grown succeeding wheat, and it was about equal to the average per crop when wheat was grown after fallow, or after beans, in the experiments already referred to.

It has been seen, then:—that even Cereal crops grown, year after year, on the same land, gave an average of about 24½ lbs. of Nitrogen per acre, per annum; that, under similar circumstances, Leguminous crops gave much more; that, nevertheless, the produce of the Cereal crop was nearly doubled when it was preceded by the more highly nitrogenized Leguminous crop; that the produce of the Cereal crop was also nearly doubled when it was preceded by fallow; and lastly, that in an actual rotation of crops, though entirely without manure, there was also an average annual yield of Nitrogen nearly twice as great as that obtained in the continuously grown Cereal.

It has been incidentally mentioned, too, that the highly nitrogenous Leguminous crops are comparatively little benefited by the direct application of nitrogenous manures (ammonia-salts). It has also further been stated, on the other hand, that, notwithstanding the comparatively small amount of Nitrogen harvested in a Cereal crop, and that both the crop and its Nitrogen are very much increased when succeeding upon the growth and removal of a highly nitrogenous Leguminous crop, yet the application of nitrogenous manures is also one of the surest means of increasing the produce, and the yield of Nitrogen, of a Cereal crop.

D.—*Relation of the increased yield of Nitrogen in the produce, to the amount supplied, when nitrogenous manures are employed.*

Not only do we harvest in our crops (particularly the Leguminous ones) a large amount of Nitrogen, the source of which, it will afterwards be seen, is by no means fully explained, but, when we increase their growth (particularly that of the Cereals) by the direct application of nitrogenous manures, it is found that, over a series of years, a considerable proportion of the so-supplied Nitrogen is not recovered in the increase of crop.

Thus, when a certain amount of ammonia-salts (in addition to a complex mineral manure) was applied, year after year, for the growth of wheat, the result, taken over a period of six years, was, that the increased yield of Nitrogen in the crop was only equal to about 43 per cent. of the Nitrogen which had been supplied in the manure. When double the amount of ammonia-salts was employed, by which the crop was still further increased, the proportion of the supplied Nitrogen which was recovered as increase was almost identically the same; but with more still, the proportion was less.

Again, when the smaller amount of ammonia-salts was applied annually, for six years, to barley, the increased yield of Nitrogen corresponded to only about 42 per cent. of the

Nitrogen supplied in the manure; and when the double amount of the manure was employed for barley, over the same series of years, only about 43 per cent. of the supplied Nitrogen were recovered as increased yield.

To the statement of these facts it should be added that the Nitrogen (equal in amount to, say 60 per cent. of that supplied in the manure) which is not obtained as increased yield in the immediate crop does not appear to exist in the soil availably for an immediately succeeding crop. Thus, when by the use of nitrogenous manures an increased yield of Nitrogen has been obtained in the first succeeding wheat-crop, equal in amount to about 40 per cent. of the Nitrogen supplied in the manure, the increased yield obtained in the second crop, without any further supply, is equal to little more than one-tenth of the remainder.

In connexion with this subject it may be mentioned that, so far as our experiments with *meadow-grasses* at present show, it does not appear that the increased yield of Nitrogen in the crop on the use of nitrogenous manures bears a much higher proportion to the amount supplied in their case than in that of either wheat or barley. In the case of the Leguminous corn-crops, the proportion of the increased yield to the amount supplied appears to be even less than in that of the Cereal grains. Root-crops, on the other hand, would seem to gather up an increase of Nitrogen bearing a larger proportion to the quantity directly supplied in the manure.

On the assumption that the relation of the immediately increased yield of Nitrogen to the amount supplied in manure represents really or approximately the proportion of the directly supplied Nitrogen which is actually recovered in the immediate crop, the following questions seem to suggest themselves:—

Is the unrecovered amount of supplied Nitrogen, or at any rate a considerable proportion of it, drained away and lost?

Are the nitrogenous compounds transformed within the soil, and their Nitrogen, in some form, evaporated?

Does the missing amount for the most part remain in some fixed combination in the soil, only to be yielded up, if ever, in the course of a long series of years?

Is ammonia itself, or Nitrogen in the free state, or in some other form of combination than ammonia, given off from the surface of the growing plant? Or, lastly,

When Nitrogen is supplied within the soil for the increased growth of the Graminaceous crop, is there simply an unfavourable distribution of it, considered in relation to the distribution of the underground feeders of the crop?—the Leguminous crop, which alternates with it, gathering from a more extended range of soil, and leaving a residue of assimilable Nitrogen within the range of collection of a next succeeding Cereal one?

But other and wider questions than those just enumerated present themselves on a careful review, as a whole, of the Nitrogen-statistics of field-produce to which attention has briefly been directed. For the moment, all may be asked in one—namely, What are the sources of all the Nitrogen of our crops beyond that which is directly supplied to the soil by artificial means? This brings us to a consideration of the next Section of our subject.

SECTION III.—GENERAL VIEW OF THE VARIOUS ACTUAL OR POSSIBLE SOURCES OF THE NITROGEN OF OUR CROPS.

The following actual or possible sources of the Nitrogen obtained in our crops, beyond that supplied in manure, may be enumerated:—

1. The Nitrogen in certain constituent minerals of the soil, especially the ferruginous and aluminous; and certain nitrides.

2. The combined Nitrogen annually coming down in the aqueous depositions from the atmosphere:—

   (*a*) As ammonia.
   (*b*) As nitric acid.
   (*c*) As organic corpuscles, &c.

3. The accumulation by the soil of combined Nitrogen from the atmosphere:—

   (*a*) By surface absorption aided by moisture.
   (*b*) By the chemical action of certain mineral constituents of the soil.
   (*c*) By the chemical action of certain organic compounds in the soil.

4. The formation of ammonia in the soil, from free Nitrogen, and nascent Hydrogen (the so-formed ammonia either remaining as such, or being oxidated into nitric acid).

5. The formation of nitric acid from free Nitrogen:—

   (*a*) By electric action.
   (*b*) With common Oxygen, in contact with porous and alkaline substances.
   (*c*) Under the influence of Ozone, or nascent Oxygen.

6. The direct absorption of combined Nitrogen from the atmosphere, by plants themselves.

7. The assimilation of free Nitrogen by plants.

A careful consideration of the above actual or possible sources of the Nitrogen of the vegetation which covers the earth's surface will show, in regard to some of them, that they at least are quantitatively inadequate to supply the amounts of Nitrogen which direct experiment has shown to be removable in various crops from a given area of land.

(1) The combined Nitrogen that may be due to certain of the constituent minerals of the débris of which our soils are made up cannot be supposed to be an adequate source of the nitrogen annually carried off in the vegetable produce of the land.

(2) The combined Nitrogen which comes down from the atmosphere in the various aqueous deposits of rain, hail, snow, mists, fog, and dew—whether it be merely the return from previously existing generations of plants or animals elsewhere, or whether in part the product of a new formation—undoubtedly does contribute materially to the

annual yield of Nitrogen in our crops. The amount of Nitrogen derivable from these sources is, moreover, perhaps more readily quantitatively estimated than that from any of the other sources enumerated. Accordingly, much labour has, of late years, been bestowed in determining the amounts of ammonia and nitric acid in these several aqueous deposits.. Extensive series of observations have been made on these points by BOUSSINGAULT, BARRAL, WAY, and two of ourselves; and others have experimented on a more limited scale. It may be stated, generally, that the rain of the open country has indicated an average of very nearly the same amounts of ammonia in the hands of BOUSSINGAULT in Alsace, and of WAY and ourselves in England. The most numerous and reliable determinations of the amount of nitric acid in rain-water are probably those of Mr. WAY.

By the aid of numerous determinations of the ammonia by ourselves, and of both the ammonia and nitric acid by Mr. WAY, we are enabled to form an estimate of the total amount of Nitrogen coming down as ammonia and nitric acid in the total rain, hail, and snow, and in some of the minor aqueous deposits, during the years 1853, 1855, and 1856, here at Rothamsted, where the experiments relating to the acreage yield of Nitrogen in the different crops were made. The result was, that in neither of the three years did the Nitrogen so coming down as ammonia and nitric acid amount to 10 lbs. per acre.

Supposing the combined Nitrogen coming down in the direct aqueous deposits were to be estimated, in round numbers, at 10 lbs. per acre, per annum, this amount would supply less than half as much Nitrogen as was annually removed in the continuously grown wheat and barley crops. It would amount to only about one-fourth of that which was obtained in the hay, and in the turnips; to a less proportion of that obtained in beans; and to a still less proportion of that obtained in the clover. Lastly, it would amount to only about one-fourth as much as was obtained per annum, over twelve years of ordinary Rotation, but without manure of any kind either during that period or for some years previously.

We are driven, then, to seek for other sources of the Nitrogen of our crops, than that which comes down as ammonia and nitric acid in the more direct and more easily measurable aqueous deposits from the atmosphere. Nor does it appear, so far as can be judged from the results of BOUSSINGAULT on this point, that the amounts of combined Nitrogen deposited by dew are such as to lead to the supposition that our approximate estimate would require any material modification, were as large a proportion of dew included in our collected and analysed aqueous deposits as is probably received by the soil itself or the vegetation which may cover it.

(3) With regard to the amounts of combined Nitrogen accumulated by the soil from the atmosphere by virtue of surface absorption, or chemical action, it is probable that they constitute no inconsiderable proportion of that which is annually available for vegetation over a given area of land. Numerous investigations have indeed been undertaken during the last few years, both by ourselves and others, to determine the actual or relative capacities for absorption of different soils, or constituents of soils. Unfortu-

nately, however, even quantitative results established by laboratory methods do not admit of very direct and certain application in accounting, quantitatively, for the amount of combined nitrogen that may be so fixed, to a given depth, over a given area of land, within a given time. We hope, however, to treat of this subject in some detail on some future occasion.

(4 & 5) The circumstances of the formation of ammonia, or nitric acid, from gaseous, dissolved, or nascent Nitrogen, are at present involved in too much obscurity, and are the subject of too much conflicting statement for their consideration to serve us much in our present inquiry. The various assumed actions are, as yet, by no means all clearly established in a merely qualitative way; and still less, quantitatively. Moreover, as in the case of absorption, so in that of the formation of ammonia, or of nitric acid, there would be considerable difficulty and uncertainty in applying the results of laboratory experiments to the estimation of the probable amount of the Nitrogen of vegetation due to such sources. To some of the questions involved, we shall, however, have to refer more or less in detail in discussing the conditions of the experiments which will form the subject of the second part of the present Paper.

(6) With regard to the direct absorption of ammonia or nitric acid from the air by plants themselves, we have little of either qualitative or quantitative evidence of any kind to guide us. Still, a few observations may be usefully hazarded, in passing, which may bear more or less directly upon the point.

In our ripened Cereal crops, we find 1 part of Nitrogen to somewhere about 30 parts of carbon; and in our Leguminous crops, 1 part of Nitrogen to about 15 or fewer parts of carbon. It is supposed that the atmosphere, on the average, contains 1 part (or rather more) of carbon in the form of carbonic acid to 10,000 parts of air. We may perhaps assume, as an extreme amount, that the atmosphere contains only 1 part of Nitrogen in the form of ammonia to about 12,000,000 parts of air. Adopting these assumptions, there would obviously be, instead of only 30 or 15 times less Nitrogen than carbon (as in the respective crops), 1200 times less Nitrogen in the ambient air in the form of ammonia, than of carbon in the form of carbonic acid in the same medium.

If, however, we were to adopt as more nearly the amount of ammonia in the air that found by M. G. VILLE (namely, only about one-fifth as much as we have assumed above), it would then appear that there were 6000 times less of Nitrogen in the air in the form of ammonia, than of carbon in that of carbonic acid.

Taking the former or more favourable assumption of the two, the result would be, that the ambient atmosphere contained Nitrogen as ammonia, to carbon as carbonic acid, in a proportion 40 times less than that of Nitrogen to carbon in the Cereal produce, and 80 times (or more) less than that of Nitrogen to carbon in the Leguminous produce. Adopting M. G. VILLE's estimates, on the other hand, the proportion of the so-combined Nitrogen to the so-combined carbon, in the air, would be 200 times less than that of the Nitrogen to the carbon in the Cereal crops, and about 400 times less than that of the Nitrogen to the carbon in the Leguminous crops.

Looking, therefore, at the subject from the point of view of *actual quantity merely*, the ammonia in the atmosphere would appear very inadequate to yield Nitrogen in a degree at all corresponding to the yield of carbon by carbonic acid. It would appear too, from the observations hitherto recorded bearing upon the point, that the amount of Nitrogen existing in the atmosphere as nitric acid is very much less than that existing as ammonia. Hence, the inclusion, in the estimate of the combined Nitrogen in the atmosphere, of the amount existing as nitric acid would, in point of quantity, by no means materially affect the question.

But it is worthy of remark, in reference to the question of the proportion of Nitrogen as ammonia to carbon as carbonic acid, that may be available to vegetation from atmospheric sources, that, although the actual amount of Nitrogen as ammonia in the atmosphere is very small compared with that of the carbon as carbonic acid, yet, a given amount of water would absorb very much more Nitrogen as ammonia, or dissolve very much more Nitrogen as carbonate of ammonia, than it would absorb of carbon in the form of carbonic acid under equal circumstances. In illustration, it may be mentioned that water at 60° F. (about 15°·5 C.) would at the normal pressure absorb about 850 times as much Nitrogen in the form of ammonia as it would of carbon in the form of carbonic acid; and, under equal circumstances, very many times more Nitrogen as carbonate or even as bicarbonate of ammonia would be dissolved, than there would be of carbon as carbonic acid absorbed. There would appear to be, then, a compensating quality for the small actual amount of Nitrogen as ammonia in proportion to carbon as carbonic acid in the atmosphere, in the greater absorbability or solubility of the compounds in which Nitrogen exists than of the carbonic acid in which the carbon is presented. How far, however, the compensating quality here suggested may really influence the proportion of the Nitrogen to the carbon available from the atmosphere, in the combined form, under the actual conditions involved in vegetation, is a question the numerous and intricate bearings of which we do not profess here to enter upon.

Before passing from this question of the direct absorption of Nitrogen in the combined form from the atmosphere by plants themselves, one or two further observations may yet be made which are suggested by the actual facts of agricultural production. It is undoubtedly the case that the Graminaceous crops depend very materially upon combined Nitrogen *within the soil*, to determine the amount of their produce. They seem, however, to be comparatively independent of carbonic acid yielded by manure within the soil. The Leguminous crops, on the other hand, appear to be much less benefited by direct supplies of characteristically nitrogenous manures. It would hence seem that they are more able to avail themselves of Nitrogen supplied in some way by the atmosphere, possibly by the aid of their green parts. But it can hardly be to a greater *mere extent of surface above ground* that the property which the Leguminous plants possess of acquiring a greater amount of Nitrogen than the Graminaceous ones, over a given area of land, and under otherwise equal circumstances, is to be attributed.

A bean and a wheat crop may yield equal amounts of dry matter per acre, whilst the bean produce would contain from two to three times as much Nitrogen as the wheat. Nevertheless some attempts at approximate measurement have indicated that the wheat-plant offers a greater external superficies in relation to a given weight of dry substance, than does the bean. The wheat-plant would, of course, show a still higher relation of superficies to a given amount of Nitrogen fixed. If, therefore, the larger amount of Nitrogen yielded per acre by a bean than by a wheat crop be due to a larger assumption of it directly from atmospheric sources in some form, it is obvious that the result must be due to *character*, and *function*, and not to mere extent of surface above ground. In connexion with this point it may be observed, more particularly with reference to the crops that are grown for their ripened seed, that the Leguminous ones generally maintain their green and succulent surface in relation to a more extended period of the season of active growth and accumulation than do the Graminaceous ones.

(7) *Assimilation of free or uncombined Nitrogen by Plants.*—It has been seen, in the course of the foregoing brief review of the various sources of combined Nitrogen to plants, that those of them which have as yet been quantitatively estimated are inadequate to account for the amounts of Nitrogen obtained in the annual produce of a given area of land beyond that which may be attributable to the supplies by previous manuring. It must be admitted, too, that the sources of combined Nitrogen which have been alluded to as not yet even approximately estimated in a quantitative sense (if indeed they are all fully established qualitatively) offer many practical difficulties in the way of any such investigation of them as would afford results directly applicable to our present purpose. It appeared, therefore, that it would be desirable to settle the question, whether or not that vast storehouse of Nitrogen, the atmosphere, in which the vegetation which covers the Earth's surface is seen to live and flourish, be of any measurable avail to the growing plant, so far as its *free* or *uncombined Nitrogen* is concerned.

The settlement of this question (whether affirmatively or negatively) would at any rate indicate the degree of importance to be attached to the remaining open points of inquiry. Indeed, were it found that plants generally, or some of those we cultivate more than others, were able to fix Nitrogen from that presented to them in the free or uncombined form, we should, in this fact, have a clue to the explanation of much that is yet clouded in obscurity in connexion with the chemical phenomena of Agricultural production. We should establish for vegetation, the attribute of effecting chemical combinations with an element at once the most reluctant to associate itself with other bodies in obedience to laboratory processes and at the same time apt to rid itself of connexions once formed in the most violent manner—as the explosive character of many Nitrogen compounds forcibly illustrates. We should further be able, much more satisfactorily than we are at present, to account—by processes established to be going on under our own observation—for the actually large total amount of combined Nitrogen which we know to exist and to circulate, in land and water, in animal and vegetable life, and in the atmosphere.

But another and potent reason for investigating the relation of plants to the free or uncombined Nitrogen of the atmosphere is to be found in the fact, that the question has, of late years, been submitted to an immense amount of research by numerous experimenters, and from the results obtained very opposite conclusions have been arrived at. Thus, M. BOUSSINGAULT concludes that plants do not assimilate the free or uncombined Nitrogen of the atmosphere. M. G. VILLE maintains, on the contrary, that the assimilation of free Nitrogen does take place, and further, that, under favourable circumstances, a considerable proportion of the Nitrogen of a plant may be derived from this source. Others have experimented in connexion with the subject on a more limited scale; and various explanations have been offered of the discrepant results and conclusions of M. BOUSSINGAULT and M. G. VILLE.

Before entering upon the discussion of our own experimental evidence in regard to the question of the assimilation of free or uncombined Nitrogen by plants, it will be desirable to pass in review the methods, results, and conclusions of M. BOUSSINGAULT and M. G. VILLE, and also of some other experimenters, who seem to have been led to take up the subject by a consideration of the contrary opinions arrived at by BOUSSINGAULT and VILLE.

SECTION IV.—REVIEW OF THE RESEARCHES OF OTHERS, ON THE QUESTION OF THE ASSIMILATION OF FREE NITROGEN BY PLANTS, AND ON SOME ALLIED POINTS.

It has already been mentioned that, in 1837, BOUSSINGAULT took up the question of the sources of the Nitrogen of Plants where DE SAUSSURE had left it more than thirty years before. DE SAUSSURE and his predecessors had sought to solve the question, among others, whether plants assimilated the free or uncombined Nitrogen of the atmosphere, by determining the changes undergone in the composition of limited volumes of air by the vegetation of plants within them. BOUSSINGAULT pointed out that the methods which had been adopted were not sufficiently accurate for the determination of the point in question. The general plan instituted by himself, and adopted with more or less modification in most subsequent researches, was:—

To set seeds or plants, the amount of Nitrogen in which was estimated by the analysis of carefully chosen similar specimens.

To employ soils and water containing either no combined Nitrogen, or only known quantities of it.

To allow the access, either of free air (protecting the plants from rain and dust), of a current of air freed by washing from all combined Nitrogen, or of a fixed and limited quantity of air, too small to be of any avail so far as its compounds of Nitrogen were concerned. And finally—

To determine the amount of combined Nitrogen in the plants produced, and in the soil, pot, &c., and, so, to provide the means of estimating the gain or loss of Nitrogen during the course of the experiment.

A.—M. Boussingault's Experiments.

1. M. Boussingault's *experiments in* 1837 *and* 1838, *in which the plants were allowed free access of air, but were protected from rain and dust.*

In 1837* Boussingault grew, in burnt soil, watered with distilled water, and with the access of free air, a pot of Trifolium for two months, and another for three months; also a pot of Wheat for two months, and another for three months.

The total Nitrogen in the seeds sown in the two experiments with *Trifolium*, amounted to 0·224 gramme. The Nitrogen in the produce, soil, pot, &c., amounted to 0·276 gramme. There was a gain, therefore, of 0·052 gramme of Nitrogen = nearly 20 per cent. of the total Nitrogen of the products. The development of vegetable matter, implying, of course, the assimilation of carbon, hydrogen, and oxygen, was, however, in a much greater proportion; the dry matter of the produce in the two experiments amounting to nearly three times that of the seed sown.

In the two experiments with *Wheat*, the total Nitrogen in the seed was estimated at 0·100 gramme. The Nitrogen in the products was exactly the same amount. In the case of the Wheat, there was, therefore, no gain of Nitrogen indicated. Nevertheless the *dry matter* of the produce amounted to nearly double that of the seed.

In 1838†, Boussingault, in a similar manner, sowed *Peas* containing 0·046 gramme Nitrogen. The plants obtained; yielded flowers and ripe seed, and their dry matter was more than four times as much as that of the seed sown. The Nitrogen of the total products amounted to 0·101 gramme. Here again, therefore, the *Leguminous* plants seemed to gain Nitrogen from some undetermined source.

Boussingault made experiments in the same year (1838), with Trifolium, and with Oats. In these cases, he commenced with carefully selected plants instead of with seeds. The *Trifolium* nearly trebled its total vegetable matter during growth; and it gained 0·023 gramme of Nitrogen out of 0·056 gramme in the total products. The *Oat*, on the other hand, indicated only 0·053 gramme Nitrogen in the total products, whilst it was estimated that there was 0·059 gramme contained in the plants taken for the experiment. The total vegetable matter was, however, doubled.

The substance of M. Boussingault's conclusions from the above experimental results, may be stated as follows:—That under several conditions, certain plants seem adapted to take up the Nitrogen in the atmosphere; but that it was still a question, under what circumstances, and in what state, the Nitrogen was fixed in the plants. He submitted —that the Nitrogen might enter directly into the organism of the plant, provided its green parts were adapted to fix it; that it might be conveyed into the plant in the aërated water taken up by its roots; that, as some physicists suppose, there may exist in the atmosphere an infinitely small amount of ammoniacal vapour. He further suggested that the gain of Nitrogen beyond that supplied in manure, which he had observed in agricultural production on the large scale, and which he thought evidently

* Ann. de Chim. et de Phys. sér. 2. tome lxvii. 1838.

† Ibid. tome lxix.

came from the atmosphere, might be partly due to Nitrate of Ammonia produced by electrical action and brought down by rain.

2. M. Boussingault's *experiments in* 1851, 1852, *and* 1853, *in which the plants were confined in limited volumes of air* *.

Boussingault resumed the subject of the sources of the Nitrogen of vegetation in 1851. His object was, apparently, to settle more definitely, whether plants assimilated Nitrogen from any other source than the combined forms of it.

In his experiments in 1851 and 1852, Boussingault confined his experimental plants under a glass shade of about 35 litres capacity, which shut off the free access of external air by resting in a lute of sulphuric acid. Tubes passed under the shade for the supply of carbonic acid, and water, as they might be needed. Pumice-stone, coarsely powdered, washed, ignited, and cooled over sulphuric acid, served as soil. To this, at the commencement, some of the ash from farm-yard manure, and also from seed of the kind to be sown, was added.

In 1851, a Haricot was grown under these conditions, the seed of which, when sown, was estimated to contain 0·0349 gramme of Nitrogen. After two months of growth, flowers being formed, the dry substance of the plant was more than double that of the seed sown; and the total products yielded only 0·0340 gramme of Nitrogen. There was, therefore, apparently a slight loss of Nitrogen, which amounted, however, to less than a milligramme. In 1852, two Haricots, sown respectively in separate pots, contained, together, 0·0455 gramme Nitrogen. They were each allowed to grow for three months, during which time the dry substance was nearly doubled; and in one instance open flowers were formed. The products of both experiments taken together yielded to analysis only 0·0415 gramme of Nitrogen. There was an apparent loss, therefore, in the two experiments, of 4 milligrammes of Nitrogen. It is seen, then, that in these new experiments with *Leguminous* plants, in which the free circulation of atmospheric air was not permitted, there was not the apparent gain of Nitrogen that had been met with in Boussingault's early experiments (in 1837 and 1838), in which free access of air into the enclosing apparatus was allowed.

In 1851, ten seeds of Oats, and in 1852 four, were experimented upon in a similar manner. In both cases there was an apparent very slight loss of Nitrogen. In the first case the Oats vegetated for two months, and in the second for 2½ months; and in the latter, the plant arrived at the point of shooting forth the ear.

In 1853, the apparatus adopted by Boussingault consisted of a large globe, or carboy, of white glass, having a capacity of 70 or 80 litres. At the bottom of this vessel, a matrix of pumice-stone (or burnt brick) and ashes, prepared as in the last series, was placed to serve as soil. This was watered with distilled water, and then the seeds were sown. The neck of the vessel was then closed with a cork, through a perforation in which, a flask of carbonic acid was inverted, whose aperture, opening into the globe, was

* Ann. de Chim. et de Phys. sér. 3. tome xli. 1854.

somewhat contracted. Finally, access of air from without was excluded by bandages of caoutchouc, which were so secured as to render the whole apparatus air-tight.

In such an apparatus, BOUSSINGAULT made five separate experiments with White Lupins. In all he sowed thirteen seeds, which were estimated to contain, together, 0·2710 gramme of Nitrogen. The experiments extended over periods varying from six to eight weeks. In one instance, burnt brick instead of pumice-stone was used as the soil; and in this case, as well as in one where pumice was used, bone-phosphate as well as ashes was added as manure. The dry matter of the produce was about three times as much as was contained in the thirteen seeds sown. The Nitrogen in the total products of the five experiments amounted to 0·2669 gramme. There was, therefore, a loss, in the five experiments taken together, of about 4 milligrammes of Nitrogen. In two of the cases there was a slight gain of Nitrogen, but in neither instance did it amount to 1 milligramme.

In a similar apparatus, two experiments were made with Dwarf Haricots, a single seed only being sown in each case. One of the experiments extended over two months, and the other over two and a half months. In both instances flowers were formed, and in one of them seed. The dry matter of the produce was three to four times as much as that of the seed sown. Taking the two experiments together, the Nitrogen contained in the seed was estimated at 0·0652 gramme; and that found in the products amounted to 0·0637 gramme. There was a loss, therefore, of 1½ milligramme of Nitrogen.

There was, then, in this third series of experiments with *Leguminous* plants, again rather a loss than a gain of Nitrogen,—the supplies of it in this case being confined to the combined Nitrogen contained in the seeds sown, and to the free or uncombined Nitrogen in the fixed and limited volume of air within the apparatus.

Still in the same apparatus, BOUSSINGAULT sowed Garden Cress. Thirteen seeds were sown, all of which germinated, but three plants only survived. The growth of these extended over three and a half months; and flowers and seed were produced. The Nitrogen in the products amounted to precisely as much as was estimated to be contained in the thirteen seeds sown.

The last experiment in this closed globular apparatus was as follows: Two White Lupins were sown to grow; and eight others were applied as manure, after treatment with boiling water to destroy their powers of germination. The experiment continued for a period of between four and five months. The dry matter of the produce was nearly twice as much as would be contained in the ten seeds involved in the experiment. The whole ten seeds were estimated to contain 0·1827 gramme of Nitrogen; whilst the total products yielded only 0·1697 gramme. The loss of Nitrogen was here, therefore, 13 milligrammes; or about one-fourteenth of the whole amount involved in the experiment. BOUSSINGAULT considered that the loss was probably due to free Nitrogen being given off in the process of decomposition of the organic matter employed as manure.

In order to ascertain whether the limitation of growth in the foregoing experiments was due to the limitation in the amount of air, or to a deficiency of available Nitrogen in the matters used as soil, BOUSSINGAULT sowed Cress in a good soil, placed the vessel in a limited atmosphere, and supplied carbonic acid. The result was, that the plants thus grown, in a limited atmosphere, but in a good soil, were even more luxuriant than a parallel set, grown in a similar soil, in the open air. In both cases a large quantity of seed was produced.

3. M. BOUSSINGAULT'S *experiments in* 1854, *with a current of washed air* *.

In this series of experiments, BOUSSINGAULT supplied his plants with a *current* of air, previously washed by passing first through vessels containing pumice-stone saturated with sulphuric acid, and then through water. He also supplied carbonic acid from bicarbonate of soda acted upon by sulphuric acid,—the gas evolved being passed first over chalk, then through a solution of carbonate of soda, and lastly over pumice-stone saturated with a solution of carbonate of soda. The enclosing apparatus consisted of a metal-framed glass case of 124 litres capacity, which was cemented down upon a polished iron plate, upon which the experimental pots were placed. Across one side of the case was a metallic joint-bar, in which were apertures for the insertion of tubes for the admission of the washed air, and for the supply of water and carbonic acid. On the opposite side was a similar joint-bar, to an aperture in which, a tube was attached connecting the case with an aspirator of 500 litres capacity. By this apparatus, therefore, the plants could be supplied with a current of air freed from ammonia, with water, and with carbonic acid, at pleasure. During the experiment, the atmosphere in the Case generally contained from 2 to 3 per cent. of carbonic acid. Lastly, by means of one of the apertures any withered leaves were removed as they fell from the plants; and they were then dried and preserved for analysis with the remainder of the products.

One of the experiments made in this apparatus was with a single Lupin, which was allowed to grow for two and a half months. The dry matter of the produce was more than six times that of the seed. The Lupin sown was estimated to contain 0·0196 gramme of Nitrogen. The Nitrogen found in the products amounted to 0·0187 gramme. There was a loss, therefore, of nine-tenths of a milligramme of nitrogen.

Four experiments were made with Dwarf Haricots, in three of which single seeds, and in the fourth two seeds, were sown. One experiment lasted over two and a half months, and the plant flowered; one over three months, and the plant seeded; one over three and a half months, in which case also the plant seeded; and another over three and a quarter months. The dry substance of the produced plants was from three to four times as much as that of the seed sown. The total Nitrogen in the five seeds employed in the four experiments was estimated at 0·1672; the Nitrogen found in the total products amounted to 0·1661 gramme. There was therefore, upon the whole, a loss of 0·0011 gramme of Nitrogen. In two of the experiments there was a loss of 1 milligramme each of Nitrogen; and in the other two a gain, amounting to less than 1 milligramme in each case.

In the next experiment, one Lupin seed was sown to grow, and another was steeped in hot water and applied as manure. The dry matter of the produce from the one seed amounted to nearly three times that of the two seeds employed in the experiment. The

* Ann. de Chim. et de Phys. sér. 3. tome xliii. 1855.

total Nitrogen in the two seeds was estimated at 0·0355 gramme. That found in the products was 0·0334 gramme. There was a loss, therefore, of 0·0021 gramme Nitrogen.

Lastly, forty-two seeds of Cress were sown, twelve of which served as manure. Many of the plants seeded. The dry matter of the produce was more than five times that of the seed. The Nitrogen in the forty-two seeds was estimated at 0·0046 gramme. That found in the products amounted to 0·0052 gramme. There was a gain, therefore, of 0·0006 gramme, or little more than half a milligramme of Nitrogen.

The whole of these experiments in 1854, in which a current of air was supplied to the plants, taken together, indicated a slight loss of Nitrogen. This was the case, notwithstanding that all the plants, excepting the Cress, were of the *Leguminous* family.

4. M. BOUSSINGAULT's *experiments in* 1851, 1852, 1853, *and* 1854, *in which the Plants were allowed free access of air, but were protected from rain and dust**.

Contemporaneously with the several series of experiments above described, BOUSSINGAULT grew plants simply covered with a case, in such a manner as to exclude any material amount of dust, but so as to allow of the free access of the external air.

Single Haricots were grown in the manner here described, in the seasons of 1851, 1852, 1853, and 1854, respectively. All four plants flowered; one podded; and one seeded. The Nitrogen in the seed of the four experiments amounted to 0·1173 gramme. That found in the vegetable produce, soil, &c., was 0·1238 gramme. There was a total gain of Nitrogen, therefore, under these circumstances, of 0·0065 gramme. In one case there was an apparent loss of Nitrogen of a little more than 2 milligrammes; in the three others the gain was about equal. The dry matter in the produce amounted to from three to four times as much as that in the seeds sown.

In the seasons of 1853 and 1854, three experiments of the same kind were made with White Lupins. The dry matter of the produce was from three to four or more times as much as that in the seed. The Nitrogen in the seed of the three experiments taken together amounted to 0·0780 gramme. That in the total products was 0·0873 gramme. Here again, therefore, there was a gain of Nitrogen—amounting in this case, in all, to between 9 and 10 milligrammes.

Under similar conditions, Oats were grown in 1852 which yielded seed. The Nitrogen sown was 0·0031 gramme. That in the products was 0·0041 gramme. There was a gain, therefore, of 1 milligramme of Nitrogen.

In like manner, five seeds of Wheat were sown in 1853. The dry matter of the produce was more than three times that of the seed. The Nitrogen in the seed was estimated at 0·0064 gramme. That in the products was 0·0075 gramme. The gain was, therefore, 0·0011 gramme.

Lastly, 210 seeds of Cress were sown in 1854. Many of the plants seeded; and there was, of course, a considerable gain of dry matter. The Nitrogen in the seed was 0·0259 gramme. That in the products amounted to 0·0272 gramme. There was a gain, therefore, of 0·0013 gramme.

* Ann. de Chim. et de Phys. sér. 3. tome xliii. 1855.

Taking all these experiments together, in which the plants were shaded from rain and dust, but still allowed free access of air, the total gain of Nitrogen was 0·0192 gramme upon 0·2307 gramme supplied in the seed sown. There was a gain of Nitrogen, therefore, equal to about one-twelfth of that sown in the seed. BOUSSINGAULT considered that part of the gain was due to organic corpuscles, and part to the ammonia in the atmosphere. He also considered that, bearing in mind the circumstances of the experiment, the gain was not sufficiently great to justify the conclusion that there had been any assimilation of the free or uncombined Nitrogen of the air.

5. M. BOUSSINGAULT'S *collateral experiments to control and explain his results* *.

In order to ascertain the amount of Nitrogen that might be introduced into the materials under experiment when the matter used as soil, &c. was not excluded from the air whilst cooling after ignition, or when free access of air was allowed during the whole period of vegetation, BOUSSINGAULT instituted the following experiments.

Sand, powdered brick, powdered bone-ash, and wood-charcoal were each exposed to the air for two or three days after being ignited, and then the Nitrogen determined in them. The result was that, after this exposure, a kilogramme of sand gave 0·5 milligramme, a kilogramme of powdered brick 0·5 milligramme, a kilogramme of powdered bone-ash 0·84 milligramme, and a kilogramme of wood-charcoal 2·9 milligrammes of ammonia.

In order to test the influence of the organic corpuscles of the atmosphere, a pot of burnt sand, with ashes, the whole moistened with water, was so arranged under a shade as nevertheless to allow free access of air, and it was so exposed for two and a half months. At the end of this period small spots of cryptogamic vegetation were visible on the surface of the sand; but the whole yielded only 0·74 milligramme of Nitrogen.

Again, BOUSSINGAULT found that unless the ashes used as manure were burnt until nearly all apparent traces of carbon were destroyed, they were liable to retain more or less and sometimes material amounts of Nitrogen. In some imperfectly burnt ashes cyanides, and in some, ferrocyanides were found; in others the Nitrogen seemed to exist in neither of these conditions.

With regard to the much larger gain of Nitrogen indicated in his early experiments in free air (1837 and 1838) than in those made more recently, BOUSSINGAULT remarks that the result may be partly due to the comparatively defective methods of analysis at the early date, and partly also to the distilled water used for watering the plants containing some ammonia. For, at the time of his first experiments, he was not aware of the fact, since learned in his analyses of rain and other waters, that water distilled from that which contained minute quantities of ammonia did not come over free from it until about two-fifths of the whole had been drawn off.

It will be observed that, in most of the experiments of BOUSSINGAULT thus far passed in review, he limited the supply of Nitrogen to the plants to that contained in the seed sown, and to that which they could obtain from the atmosphere, either washed or un-

* Ann. de Chim. et de Phys. sér. 3. tome xliii. 1855.

washed, in which they grew. In no case among those experiments in which the modern refinements of analysis were had recourse to did he find, either with Leguminous or with other plants, such a gain of Nitrogen beyond that supplied in the seed, as could lead to the conclusion that the free or uncombined Nitrogen of the atmosphere had been assimilated. In many of the instances the plants yielded not only flowers but seed; and hence it might be concluded that the conditions provided were adequate for the performance, by the plant, of the complete course of its natural functions of growth. Still it might be objected that the vigour of growth was somewhat limited, and that, under these circumstances, the plant might well refuse to perform the, perhaps, difficult office of assimilating a very refractory elementary body. In a few instances, seeds whose germinating power had been destroyed were supplied as manure. In these cases the amount of Nitrogen assimilated by the plants was much greater than that contained in the living seed sown; and the luxuriance of growth was consequently comparatively great. Nevertheless, instead of a gain, there was generally a loss in the total amount of combined Nitrogen, which was considered to be due to the evolution of free Nitrogen by the decomposing manurial matter. To get increased vigour of growth—to avoid, if possible, a loss of Nitrogen such as is above supposed—and, at the same time, to determine whether or not the Nitrogen of Nitrates were really assimilable by plants—BOUSSINGAULT has latterly made some experiments in which Nitrates were employed as manure, a brief notice of the results of which should be here given.

6. M. BOUSSINGAULT'S *experiments in which he supplied combined Nitrogen in the form of Nitrate of Potash, or Soda**.

In 1855 BOUSSINGAULT made one experiment with Helianthus in which he supplied no nitrate to the soil, and another in which a small known quantity of Nitrate of Potash was employed. In a third experiment Cress was grown in a manured soil, in a fourth in a soil destitute of combined Nitrogen, and in a fifth in a soil to which a known quantity of Nitrate of Soda was added. In the case of the manured soil, and in the two cases where Nitrate was employed, there was a very considerable increase in the assimilation of carbon; and there was also much more Nitrogen assimilated than was supplied in the seeds sown. The increased assimilation of Nitrogen where Nitrate was used, did not, however, exceed that supplied in the manure. BOUSSINGAULT concluded that the gain of Nitrogen was to be attributed to the Nitrogen of the Nitrate.

Lastly in regard to BOUSSINGAULT'S experiments: In 1858† he resumed the question of the action of Nitrates upon vegetation. He grew two separate pots of Helianthus, two seeds being sown in each pot. The soils were composed of sand and quartz well washed from saline matter and ignited. To one pot Nitrate of Potash containing 0·0111 gramme of Nitrogen, and to the other Nitrate containing 0·0222 gramme Nitrogen, was added. In the first case, he did not get back, in the plant, soil, and pot, the Nitrogen of the seed and Nitrate by 0·0014 gramme. In the second experiment the loss of Nitrogen amounted to just 1 milligramme. BOUSSINGAULT found, however, that there remained

* Ann. de Chim. et de Phys. sér. 3. tome xlvi. 1856.

† Compt. Rend. tome xlvii. 1858.

in the soil an amount of carbonate of potash very nearly corresponding in potash to the amount of nitrate of potash which would represent the observed loss of Nitrogen. He concluded that nitrate had been decomposed in the soil, by the organic matter of the débris of the seeds and of the roots, and that Nitrogen had been evolved. If we clearly understand this explanation of the loss of Nitrogen of the nitrate, we would suggest that it would seem to require for its validity that the plant should have assimilated potash from the nitrate exactly corresponding in amount to the Nitrogen it fixed from the same source.

From the results of these experiments with nitrate, BOUSSINGAULT drew the following conclusions:—

1. That there was no assimilation of free Nitrogen.

2. That there was a loss of supplied Nitrogen, either from the soil, or by the plant.

3. That, in the two cases, the amount of carbon assimilated bore a close relation to that of the Nitrogen taken up by the plant.

It is seen, then, that the results of the laborious investigations of BOUSSINGAULT, extending at intervals over a period of more than twenty years, have led him to conclude that, neither *Leguminous* plants, nor the others experimented upon, were able, either when their supplies of combined Nitrogen were limited to that contained in the seed sown, or when their vigour of growth was stimulated by artificial supplies of combined Nitrogen, to assimilate the free or uncombined Nitrogen of the atmosphere.

B.—M. G. VILLE'S EXPERIMENTS*.

1. M. G. VILLE'S *determinations of the Ammonia in the atmosphere.*

M. G. VILLE, of Paris, commenced his investigations, on the subject of the assimilation of Nitrogen by plants, in 1849. He first sought to determine the proportion of Ammonia in the atmosphere. To this end, he aspired known quantities of air through acid, and determined the amount of ammonia absorbed. He operated upon very much larger volumes than previous experimenters had done. His results show, moreover, a much smaller proportion of ammonia in the air than those of others.

The air of Paris, during part of 1849 and part of 1850, gave a mean of only 0·0237 part by weight of ammonia, to 1,000,000 parts by weight, of air; and that of the suburbs of Paris, during some period of 1852, gave 0·0211 parts of ammonia, to 1,000,000 parts of air.

2. M. G. VILLE'S *general plan of experimenting on the question of the assimilation of Nitrogen by plants.*

M. G. VILLE employed specially-made porous flower-pots, and used, as soil, washed

* Recherches Expérimentales sur la Végétation, par M. GEORGES VILLE. Paris, 1853.

and ignited sand, sand and brick, or sand and charcoal, with the addition of the ash of the plant to be grown. He planted seeds or plants, the composition of which was estimated by the analysis of parallel specimens. Several pots were for the most part enclosed in an iron-framed glazed case of 150 litres (or more) capacity, through which a current of air equal in amount to several times the volume of the vessel was aspired daily. Carbonic acid and distilled water were supplied as needed. In some cases the air admitted into the apparatus was only previously freed from dust; and then the amount of atmospheric ammonia that would be brought in was calculated according to the determination of the proportion of ammonia in the air, above alluded to. In other cases the aspired air was previously freed from ammonia by washing. In some experiments, ammoniacal gas was passed, in known quantities, into the air of the apparatus. Lastly, others were made, in which combined Nitrogen was added to the soil in the form of nitrate, or of ammonia salts; and in these cases the plants were allowed to grow in free air, only shaded from rain and dust.

3. M. G. VILLE's *experiments in* 1849 *and* 1850, *in which the plants were supplied with a current of unwashed air.*

In 1849, sand was used as soil; three pots of plants were grown for two months; namely, one of Cress, one of large Lupins, and one of small Lupins. The air admitted into the apparatus was not previously deprived of its natural ammonia. The dry substance of the produced Cress plants amounted to more than sixteen times that of the seed sown. The Nitrogen in the Cress seeds amounted to 0·026 gramme; that in the products to 0·147 gramme. The Nitrogen in the products was, therefore, between five and six times as much as that in the seed; and the actual gain of it amounted to 0·121 gramme. In the case of the large Lupins, the dry matter of the produce was about 3½ times as great as that of the seeds sown; but there was neither gain nor loss of Nitrogen. The small Lupins gave 2½ times as much dry substance in the produce as was supplied in the seeds; and of the Nitrogen of the seeds sown, there was an apparent loss of rather more than one-fourth, during the experiment.

The total gain of combined Nitrogen in the apparatus, taking the three experiments together, was 0·103 gramme. The Nitrogen in the ammonia of the current of unwashed air, was, however, estimated at only 0·001 gramme. M. G. VILLE concluded, therefore, that the Cress had appropriated a considerable quantity of the free or uncombined Nitrogen of the atmosphere.

The plants experimented upon in 1850, were Colza, Wheat, Rye, and Maize. In the case of the Colza, the experiment commenced with young plants, but in the other cases with seed. The four pots were placed in an apparatus similar to that used before, and the conditions supplied were also the same as in 1849.

The dry matter of the produced Colza plants amounted to between forty and fifty times as much as that of the young plants when taken for experiment. The Nitrogen was also increased more than forty-fold. The dry matter of the Wheat plants was about four times that of the seed sown; and the Nitrogen in the total products was nearly double that in the seed. The dry substance of the produced Rye plants was five times, and their Nitrogen nearly three times that of the seed. In the experiment with Maize, the dry matter increased only about three times, but the Nitrogen nearly 4½ times.

The actual gain of Nitrogen in the total products of the four experiments, was 1·1803 gramme. The whole admitted in the form of atmospheric ammonia was estimated at 0·0017 gramme, or less than 2 milligrammes. M. VILLE remarks, moreover, that an examination of the distilled water before being used to water the plants, and of the water afterwards removed from the apparatus, showed more ammonia in the latter than in the former. The conclusion from this second series of experiments also was, therefore, that a considerable quantity of free or uncombined Nitrogen had been assimilated.

4. M. G. VILLE's *experiments in* 1851 *and* 1852, *in which the plants were supplied with a current of air washed free from ammonia.*

In 1851, one pot of Sun-flower, from seed, and two pots of Tobacco, starting from plants transplanted from good soil, were grown together, under circumstances similar to those of the preceding experiments, with the exception that now the air was deprived of its ammonia by passing over pumice-stone saturated with sulphuric acid, and also through a solution of bicarbonate of soda, previous to entering the apparatus.

The Sun-flowers gave 95 rudimentary grains; but the Tobaccos did not flower. However, taking the three experiments together, the dry matter increased nearly 200-fold, and the Nitrogen increased nearly 40-fold, during a period of growth of three months. The total gain of Nitrogen in the apparatus was 0·481 gramme.

In 1852, the conditions of the apparatus were the same as in 1851. The selection of plants was as follows:—One pot of Autumn Colzas, starting with young plants; one of Spring Wheat, from seed; one of Sun-flower, from seed; and two of Summer Colzas, from plants.

In every case the dry matter of the produce was many times that of the young plants or seed. In the case of the Sun-flower, it was more than 100 times that of the seed. In each experiment, there was of Nitrogen, also, much more at the conclusion, than at the commencement. In the experiment with Autumn Colzas there were 4·7 times, in that with Spring Wheat 2·2 times, in that with Sun-flower 26·5 times, in one with Summer Colza 3·4 times, and in the other with Summer Colza 6·7 times as much Nitrogen in the total products as in the original plants or seeds. The total amount of Nitrogen gained in the five experiments, was 1·624 gramme, which was 5·3 times as much as was contained in the total original plants and seeds.

To show the degree of luxuriance of growth of the different descriptions of plant, it may be mentioned that the Winter Colzas flowered, but gave no seed; the Sun-flower gave 412 rudimentary grains; and the Wheat seeded completely, giving 47 grains. The Summer Colzas had little tendency to go to seed, but developed a great deal of leaf; and hence it was, it was supposed, that they gained large actual amounts of Nitrogen.

5. M. G. VILLE'S *experiments in which known quantities of Ammonia were admitted into the atmosphere of the enclosing apparatus.*

In each of the three seasons 1850, 1851, and 1852, M. G. VILLE had a duplicate apparatus, enclosing, in each case, similar plants to those in the other, but with this difference in the conditions—that ammonia was supplied to the atmosphere of the second apparatus. As might be expected, the increase, both in dry substance, and in Nitrogen, was much the greater, in relation to the amounts of them contained in the seed or young plants, when ammonia was thus employed. In no case, however, did the plants take up Nitrogen equal in amount, much less exceeding, the whole of that supplied to the air in the combined form, as ammonia. The results have not, therefore, so direct a bearing on the question of the assimilation of free or *un*combined Nitrogen, as to require that we should quote them in any detail. Their chief interest was in showing the influence of ammoniacal supply, not only upon the vigour and luxuriance of growth generally, but upon the order, or course of development, of the plants, according to the stage of growth at which the application was made.

6. *Comparison of* M. G. VILLE'S *results with those of* M. BOUSSINGAULT *up to* 1853 *inclusive.*

It will be remembered that, up to 1853 inclusive, M. BOUSSINGAULT'S experimental plants had been grown either in *free air*—in which case they had fixed, from some source, slightly larger amounts of Nitrogen than were contained in the seed,—or in fixed and *limited volumes* of air (carbonic acid being added), in which cases no gain of Nitrogen was observed. The gain of Nitrogen in the free air was, moreover, considered to be too small to indicate, under all the circumstances, any assimilation of free or uncombined Nitrogen. On the other hand, M. G. VILLE'S experiments up to the same period had indicated an enormous gain of Nitrogen. The Nitrogen in the products, indeed, sometimes amounted to more than forty times that contained in the seed.

Results so strikingly contradictory could hardly fail to excite great attention and interest among Chemists and Vegetable Physiologists. But M. VILLE'S plants had been grown in a *constant current of renewed air*, and not in only a *fixed and limited volume* of it. This fact, and some other points, were alleged to account for the difference in result. At any rate, on the one hand, M. BOUSSINGAULT commenced in 1854, to experiment with a *current of air*; whilst, on the other, a Commission, composed of Members of the Academy of Sciences of France, was appointed to superintend the conduct of a new set of experiments by M. G. VILLE. It has already been shown, that M. BOUSSINGAULT'S new experiments in which a *current of air* was employed, did not indicate any assimilation of free or uncombined Nitrogen, any more than did those in which the plants had grown in limited volumes of air only.

7. M. G. VILLE's *experiments conducted under the superintendence of a Commission comprising* MM. DUMAS, REGNAULT, PAYEN, DECAISNE, PELIGOT, *and* CHEVREUL.

These experiments were conducted at the Muséum d'Histoire Naturelle, Jardin des Plantes, Paris, in the autumn of 1854. M. CLOEZ was appointed to assist M. VILLE; and M. CHEVREUL reported on behalf of the Commission, in 1855*.

In an apparatus similar to that employed in the experiments of M. VILLE which have been already described, three pots of Cress were placed. The soil consisted of ignited brick and sand, to which was added some of the ash of the plant. Carbonic acid was supplied artificially; and the plants were watered with distilled water. The Cress in one of the pots did not thrive well; and, in this case, analysis showed a loss of 2 milligrammes of Nitrogen. In one of the other cases, there was a gain of 0·0492 gramme of Nitrogen, upon 0·0038 gramme supplied in the seed; and in the other, there was a gain of 0·0071 gramme of Nitrogen, upon 0·0039 gramme contained in the seed.

At the suggestion of one of the members of the Commission, a smaller vessel was also attached to the aspirator, in which one pot sown with Cress was placed. The soil being duly watered with distilled water, the apparatus was then closed, and not opened (as the other frequently was) until the conclusion of the experiment. In this case also, there was a considerable gain of Nitrogen indicated, namely, 0·0287 gramme gain, upon 0·0063 gramme in the seed.

Unfortunately, an element of uncertainty attached to the evidence afforded by these experiments made under the superintendence of the Commission, which is very much to be regretted. A quantity of distilled water taken from the same bulk as that used for watering the experimental plants was saved for analysis. The examination of this water devolved on M. CLOEZ; who, unfortunately, was called away for some days, during the evaporation of the water with oxalic acid, with a view to the after-determination of any ammonia it might contain. M. PELIGOT determined the ammonia in the acid residue of the evaporation of this water, as well as in that of the water removed from the cases, after it had served in the experiments. The result was, that there was indicated such an excess of ammonia in the water before being used, over that in the residual water after removal from the larger case, as more than covered the increase in the Nitrogen of the plants over that in the seeds sown. M. CLOEZ found, however, that, in his absence, the evaporation of the water had been conducted by the side of ammoniacal emanations from other processes. But when new portions of the original water were evaporated with proper precautions, less ammonia was indicated in it than in the water at the close of the experiment; and then, also, a gain of Nitrogen by the plants in the larger apparatus was indicated.

At any rate, however, the result with the single pot, in the small apparatus, showed a considerable gain of Nitrogen, even supposing the first analysis of the supplied water to be correct.

* Compt. Rend. 1855.

From the result of the whole inquiry, the Commission announced the following con clusion:—

That the experiment made at the Muséum d'Histoire Naturelle by M. VILLE, *is consistent with the conclusions which he has drawn from his previous labours.*

8. M. G. VILLE's *experiments in which the plants were exposed to free air, and Nitrates or Ammonia salts were employed as manure**.

In 1855 and 1856, M. G. VILLE conducted a series of experiments with the double object, of investigating the action of nitrates upon vegetation, and of still further examining into the capability of plants to assimilate the free or uncombined Nitrogen of the atmosphere. The whole of the experiments now in question were made in free air, the plants being only shaded from rain; that is to say, without any enclosing apparatus, or artificial current of air and supply of carbonic acid. The soils consisted of calcined sand; ashes of plants such as those to be grown were added; and distilled water was used for watering. Colza and Wheat were the plants experimented upon. Lastly, the special conditions of the experiments were, that nitrate of potash in smaller or in larger quantity, or nitrate of potash and different ammonia salts, in equivalent quantities so far as their Nitrogen was concerned, were employed.

To the prosecution of this series of experiments, an exact method of estimating minute quantities of nitric acid was essential. M. VILLE succeeded in devising such a method, which was very favourably reported upon by M. PELOUZE, on behalf of a Commission composed of MM. BALARD, PELIGOT, and PELOUZE.

In 1855, two pots, and in 1856 one pot, of Colzas were grown, to each of which 0·5 gramme of nitrate of potash was supplied as manure. By examination of the soil, the point was ascertained when the whole of the nitrate had been drawn from it by the plants. The experiment was then stopped; and analysis showed that the total produce contained almost identically the amount of Nitrogen supplied in the seed and in the nitrate. The dry vegetable substance was, however, increased about 200-fold.

Again in 1855, two pots of Colzas were sown, to each of which 1 gramme instead of 0·5 gramme of nitrate was added; and in 1856 two more, with the same quantity. In each of these cases, the produce (which in dry matter was several hundred times that of the seed) contained considerably more nitrogen than had been supplied in the seed and in the nitrate. M. G. VILLE's conclusions were, that the plants had taken up the nitrate and assimilated its Nitrogen, and that when by the larger supply of nitrate the growth had been extended, the free Nitrogen of the atmosphere was also assimilated.

In 1855 an experiment was made with Wheat manured with 1·72 gramme of nitrate of potash. The plants were allowed to mature, and they gave 84 grains. There was more Nitrogen in the vegetable produce alone, than in the seed and nitrate, and very much more in the total products, taking into account the residual Nitrogen in the soil. In 1856, two pots of Wheat were sown, to each of which 1·765 gramme of nitrate were added. The plants of one pot were taken up at the time of flowering, and they contained

* Recherches Expérimentales sur la Végétation, 1857.

almost identically the same amount of Nitrogen as was provided in the seed and nitrate. Those in the other pot were allowed to go to seed, and 119 grains were formed. In this case, again, the Nitrogen in the produce was much more than had been supplied, and very much more when the residual Nitrogen in the soil and pot was taken into the calculation. Lastly, on this head, two pots of Wheat (also in 1856) were sown without nitrate, and two with 0·792 gramme of nitrate to each. There was a considerable gain of Nitrogen in each of the four cases. The actual amount of gain was greater in the cases where the nitrate was employed; but the proportion gained, to that supplied, was greater where no nitrate was used.

To show the comparative efficacy of Nitrogen supplied in different conditions of combination, the following experiments were made during the season of 1856.

Two pots of Colzas received, each 0·5 gramme of nitrate of potash; and two other pots of Colzas received each an amount of sal-ammoniac equivalent in Nitrogen to the 0·5 gramme of nitrate. The two experiments with Nitrate gave equal amounts of Nitrogen in the produce; and the two with sal-ammoniac, also equal amounts. But the two with nitrate gave more than 1½ time as much Nitrogen in the produce, as the two with sal-ammoniac. In two other experiments, double the quantity of nitrate and sal-ammoniac, respectively, was employed, and the growth was allowed to extend over a longer period. The amount of Nitrogen in the produce was, in both these cases, very much greater in proportion to the amount supplied, than in the preceding experiments where the smaller amounts of nitrate and sal-ammoniac were used. It was, moreover, more than three times as much where the nitrate, as where the sal-ammoniac was employed. There was, too, where the nitrate was used, a considerable amount of Nitrogen assimilated beyond that provided, in the combined form, in the seed and manure.

Experiments similar to the above were made with Wheat. Two pots, to each of which nitrate of potash was added, containing 0·110 gramme of Nitrogen, yielded, respectively, in produce, 0·218 and 0·224 gramme of Nitrogen. Two pots of Wheat, each manured with sal-ammoniac, containing also 0·110 gramme of Nitrogen, gave, respectively, in the produce, 0·161 and 0·124 gramme of Nitrogen. In the same way, nitrate of ammonia containing 0·110 gramme of Nitrogen gave 0·118 and 0·149 gramme, and phosphate of ammonia 0·116 and 0·150 gramme of Nitrogen in the matured Wheat plants.

In regard to the experiments of M. VILLE referred to in this Division (8), he remarks, that the point at which the artificially supplied Nitrogen becomes exhausted is indicated by a lightening of the colour of the leaves, and that it is then that the plants begin to assimilate the uncombined Nitrogen of the atmosphere. To secure this assimilation, he considers that it is not only necessary that the supply of combined Nitrogen, and the vigour of growth, should reach beyond a certain limit, but that the artificial supply itself should, on the other hand, not exceed a certain limit. Further, the gain of Nitrogen in the experiments conducted on the plan now under consideration was so great, that, bearing in mind previously obtained results wherein the limit of the effect of atmospheric ammonia had been ascertained, the influence of that source may, in the case of these new results, be entirely overlooked.

The fact that a given amount of Nitrogen in the form of combination of a nitrate was more efficacious than the same amount supplied in either of the ammoniacal salts experimented upon, was held to show that the nitrate was taken up by the plants as such, and was not previously transformed into ammonia.

M. VILLE's experiments, as a whole, thus indicated that plants can take up Nitrogen in three forms—namely, as nitric acid, as ammonia, and as free Nitrogen. He enumerates the following conclusions:—

1. By means of nitre we may prove, without the aid of an enclosing apparatus, that plants absorb and assimilate the gaseous Nitrogen of the atmosphere.
2. Nitre acts by its Nitrogen. It is absorbed in the state of nitre.
3. In relation to the amount of Nitrogen, nitre is more active than ammonia-salts.

9. M. G. VILLE's *collateral experiments to control or explain his results* *.

M. VILLE adduces evidence of yet another kind, in support of his view that plants assimilate the free Nitrogen of the air. Air was passed through an otherwise closed apparatus, in which was placed a vessel containing calcined sand, or calcined sand and decomposing organic matter. In no case was nitric acid formed. Nitrification, the result of the combination of the oxygen and nitrogen of the air within the porous soil, was not, therefore, the source of the Nitrogen gained by his experimental plants.

Experiments were made in which a given amount of organic matter (Lupins, Gelatine, &c.) was mixed with calcined sand, and exposed in an apparatus to a current of air, which carried the gaseous products into acid, to retain any ammonia that might be formed. The determination of the Nitrogen remaining in the matrix, and of the ammonia given off and absorbed by the acid, showed a loss of Nitrogen, which could only have passed away in the free gaseous form.

Other vessels of sand were prepared, to which similar known amounts of organic matter were added, and then seeds of Wheat were sown, the organic matter serving as manure. When the growth was stopped at a certain stage, almost exactly the same amount of Nitrogen was found in the Wheat plants and in the sand, &c., as was originally contained in the seeds sown and in the organic matter added. Assuming that the decomposition of the organic matter had taken the same course as in the other experiments—free Nitrogen being given off—it was obvious that a corresponding amount of free Nitrogen had been taken up by the plants. In other cases the growth of the Wheat was allowed to continue longer than in the experiments just alluded to; and then the total Nitrogen in the products not only equalled, but considerably exceeded, that in the seed sown and in the organic manure. In this instance, at least, it could not be said that the Nitrogen not received by the plant as ammonia had been taken up by it as nascent Nitrogen evolved in the decomposition.

* Recherches Expérimentales sur la Végétation, 1857.

The general conclusions from this part of the inquiry were as follow:—

1. Organic matters in decomposition lose a part of their Nitrogen as ammonia, and a part as Nitrogen gas.

2. Vegetation does not interfere with the progress of this decomposition.

3. Plants cultivated in a manured soil, give more Nitrogen in their produce than the manure yields as ammonia.

4. The excess of Nitrogen in the produce has been absorbed as free gaseous Nitrogen.

In regard to the explanation of the assimilation of free Nitrogen by plants, M. VILLE calls attention to the fact, that nascent hydrogen is said to give ammonia, and nascent oxygen nitric acid, with free Nitrogen; and he asks—Why should not the Nitrogen in the juices of the plant combine with the nascent carbon and oxygen in the leaves? He further refers to the supposition of M. DE LUCA, that the Nitrogen of the air combines with the nascent oxygen given off from the leaves of plants, and forms nitric acid. Again, the juice of some plants (mushrooms) has been observed to ozonize the oxygen of the air; is it not probable, then, that the Nitrogen dissolved in the juices will submit to the action of the ozonized oxygen with which it is mixed, when we bear in mind that the juices contain alkalies, and penetrate tissues the porosity of which exceeds that of spongy platinum, a body so apt to favour combinations?

Summary Statement of the results and conclusions of M. BOUSSINGAULT *and* M. G. VILLE.

M. BOUSSINGAULT, when, in his earlier investigations, he grew plants in free air, found only such indications of a gain of Nitrogen as, in his opinion, may be attributed to inaccuracies in the methods of experimenting and analysis at the early date, and to the combined influences of ammonia and organic corpuscles in the atmosphere; and when, more recently, he grew plants only shaded in such a manner as still to allow the free access of air, the gain of Nitrogen observed was not more than he considered might be due to the influences last mentioned. When he grew plants, either in confined and limited volumes of air, or in a current of air washed free from ammonia and organic corpuscles, the results did not show any appreciable gain of Nitrogen. Lastly, when he supplied either decomposing organic matter, or nitrate, to increase the activity of growth, he did not find such an amount of combined Nitrogen in his products, as to lead him to conclude that there had been any assimilation by the plants of free or uncombined Nitrogen. In these cases, indeed, he generally found a loss of combined Nitrogen during the experiment, supposed to be due to the evolution of free Nitrogen in the decomposition of the matters used as manure.

The results of M. G. VILLE, on the other hand, showed a very considerable gain of Nitrogen during growth, whether the plants were subjected to a current of unwashed air, or of ammonia-free air,—and also when the plants were grown in free air, and their activity of development increased by the use of nitrates, or other nitrogenous matters, as manure. This gain of Nitrogen he considers to be due to the assimilation of free or uncombined Nitrogen. It is remarkable, too, that the proportion of Nitrogen gained, to that supplied in the combined form, was observed to be the largest in some of the cases where no nitrogenous manure was employed, and where the total amount of combined Nitrogen within the reach of the plants was confined to a few milligrammes only, contained in the original young plants or seeds that were planted. In some such instances, the amount of combined Nitrogen found in the products was about forty times as much as was supplied. In other cases, the assimilation of free nitrogen only seemed to take place when the activity, and stage of growth, of the plants, had been forced beyond a certain point by the use of considerable amounts of nitrogenous manure.

Results and conclusions so astonishingly conflicting as those of M. BOUSSINGAULT and M. G. VILLE, have naturally incited others, either to investigate anew, or to seek, in the conditions provided in their experiments, for some explanation of the discordance. Before entering upon the consideration of our own experiments bearing upon the points in question, it will be desirable to add to the foregoing review a brief notice of the labours, or opinions, of these other experimenters or arbitrators.

C.—M. MÈNE'S EXPERIMENTS*.

In 1851, M. MÈNE made some experiments in reference to the assimilation of Nitrogen by plants. He seems to assume that BOUSSINGAULT had concluded from his experiments that the free Nitrogen of the atmosphere was appropriated by plants; and he refers to the experiments of M. G. VILLE as confirmatory of such a view. M. MÈNE made three sets of experiments in reference to this question.

1. He grew Wheat and Peas, respectively, in powdered glass as soil, allowing them contact with common air, and watering them with pure water. The Wheat increased in Nitrogen in amount equal to one-fourth of that contained in the seed sown; whilst its carbon, hydrogen, and oxygen were double those of the seed. The Pea-plants doubled the carbon, oxygen, and hydrogen of the seed sown, and their Nitrogen was threefold that of the seed.

2. Lentils, Peas, Haricots, Beans, Wheat, Rye, and Oats were grown in a sterile matrix under a bell-glass. They were respectively supplied with an atmosphere of known composition, and with acetate of ammonia in the soil. The plants increased in Nitrogen, and the ammonia in the soil diminished; but the free Nitrogen of the air was not perceptibly affected.

3. This series of experiments was in every way similar to the second, with the exception that the Nitrogen of the air was replaced by hydrogen. The plants flourished, and took up some of the acetate of ammonia.

M. MÈNE concludes that plants do not appropriate the free Nitrogen of the air.

D.—M. ROY'S VIEWS ON THE SUBJECT OF THE ASSIMILATION OF NITROGEN BY PLANTS†.

M. ROY gave a paper on this subject in 1854. His supposition was that carbonate of ammonia constituted the chief source of Nitrogen to plants. Leguminous plants, he

* Compt. Rend. xxxii.

† Ibid. xxxix.

considered, appropriated carbonate of ammonia from the atmosphere by their leaves. Graminaceous crops, on the other hand, he supposed, only took it up in solution by their spongioles. He further supposed that the free Nitrogen of the air was not appropriated by the leaves of plants, but that Nitrogen dissolved in water, and so taken up, by their roots, could be assimilated. He concluded that, in the case of M. BOUSSINGAULT's plants grown in limited air, there would be but little passage of solution of Nitrogen by their roots, and evaporation of water from their leaves, and that, hence, the necessary conditions did not exist for the assimilation of free Nitrogen. M. VILLE's rapid current of air would, on the other hand, cause a considerable amount of solution of Nitrogen to be drawn into the plants.

E.—THE EXPERIMENTS OF MM. CLOEZ AND GRATIOLET.

In 1850, MM. CLOEZ and GRATIOLET published the results of some experiments made with Water-plants. They found that, carbonic acid and air being both present, the plants gave off oxygen slowly, or very rapidly, according to the condition of the sunlight and the temperature. In water deprived of common air, but containing carbonic acid, the evolution of oxygen rapidly declined, Nitrogen was given off, and the plant contained less Nitrogen than a similar plant in water not deprived of its air. The evolution of Nitrogen diminished as the experiment proceeded. They considered that, in the vegetation of Water-plants, Nitrogen is given off from their nitrogenous constituents and that there must be restoration either from free or combined Nitrogen. And as their experiments showed that ammonia-salts were injurious to the plants, they concluded that they take up free Nitrogen dissolved in water.

In 1855 * M. CLOEZ published the results of some experimental inquiries on nitrification, with a view to the question of the source of the Nitrogen of plants. He made twenty experiments, passing washed air through as many different combinations of porous, earthy, and alkaline matters. The experiments continued from September 1854 to April 1855, when, in some cases, efflorescence was observed. He found nitrates to be formed in notable quantity in calcined brick, or pumice, impregnated with alkaline or earthy carbonates; also, in uncalcined brick similarly impregnated. In chalk, marl, a mixture of kaolin and precipitated carbonate of lime, &c., only traces of nitrate were formed.

M. CLOEZ concluded that nitrates would be formed when a current of air was passed over porous bodies, alkalies being present. He considered, therefore, that the porosity of the pots and brick fragments, the alkalinity of the ashes, the moisture, and the current of air, in M. VILLE's experiments with plants, provided the conditions for the formation of nitric acid. He asks, can such formation take place in limited air?

F.—THE EXPERIMENTS OF M. DE LUCA †.

M. DE LUCA found that, on passing moist ozonous air over potash and potassium, nitrate of potash was formed. He further found that the oxygen given off by plants

* Compt. Rend. xli. † Ibid. 1856.

in sunlight was in many cases ozonous. He aspirated a large quantity of air, in the neighbourhood of vegetation, through carded cotton, and then through sulphuric acid, to wash it. The washed air then passed over potassium, and through a dilute solution of pure potash, when nitrate of potash was formed. When, on the other hand, air in the midst of habitations was operated upon in a similar way, the formation of nitric acid was not observed. M. DE LUCA supposes the air surrounding vegetation, in sunlight, to be ozonous; that by its means the Nitrogen of the air may be converted into nitric acid; and that thus the Nitrogen of the air may be rendered available for assimilation by plants, under the influence of vegetation itself.

G.—THE EXPERIMENTS OF M. HARTING*.

In 1855, M. HARTING published some criticisms, and the results of some experiments, on the question of the assimilation of Nitrogen by plants. He considered that the Nitrogen of the air might contribute indirectly to vegetation. He attributed a formation of ammonia from the decomposing débris of seeds, &c., and the free Nitrogen of the air, in the case of M. VILLE's experiments; and also supposed that nitric acid might be formed by the oxidation of the atmospheric Nitrogen. The increase of Nitrogen in M. VILLE's plants, and of ammonia in the water of the enclosing apparatus, was taken as proof of such formation of ammonia.

M. HARTING made two sets of experiments, in one of which the plants grew in a limited volume of air, and in the other in a current of air washed free from ammonia—both arranged with a view to avoid the formation of ammonia. He employed enclosing-apparatus somewhat on the plan of M. BOUSSINGAULT and M. VILLE; but he used glass vases, instead of porous pots, for his plants. He grew Beans, Buckwheat, and Oats. After the seeds had germinated, and the plants had protruded a little above the surface of the artificial soil, he covered the latter with a mixture of wax and oil, to shut off the access of air. He further enclosed the stems of the plants in caoutchouc tubes; and inserted other caoutchouc tubes through the waxy coating, for the supply of water. Some of the plants were very vivacious at first; and in the case of the Beans, two began to flower; but then the leaves turned yellow, and the experiment was stopped. His apparatus consisted of tinned-iron pans, varnished, and surmounted by glass shades of 18 litres capacity. There was an aperture for the admission of carbonic acid, another for that of water, and so on.

The result was that the produced plants yielded no more dry matter than was contained in the seeds. M. HARTING considered, therefore, that the determination of the Nitrogen was superfluous. The growth evidently stopped when the supplies of the seeds were exhausted. M. HARTING's general conclusions on the subject were as follow:—

1. Plants absorb salts of ammonia, and nitrates, by their roots.

2. The Nitrogen of the air contributes to the formation of ammonia, and nitrates, in the soil.

3. It is not proved that Nitrogen serves directly for the nutrition of plants.

* Compt. Rend. xli. 1855.

H.—M. A. Petzholdt on the Source of the Nitrogen of Plants*.

In the years 1852 and 1853, M. H. M. Chlebodarow made some experiments on the subject of the assimilation of Nitrogen by plants, at Dorpat, under the direction of M. Petzholdt, who has reported the results of the inquiry.

M. Petzholdt assumes that if plants can appropriate the free Nitrogen of the air, they will not need ammonia; and that if they take Nitrogen from ammonia, the artificial supply of the latter will increase growth.

The experiments were made upon Barley. In 1852, an ignited yellow sand was taken as the soil. To one set of plants, no ammonia was supplied; to a second, carbonate of ammonia was provided in the soil; and to a third, carbonate of ammonia was supplied in the air. Both the crops with an artificial supply of ammonia gave three times as much produce as the crops without such supply. The Nitrogen in the produce was also very much greater, both in percentage, and in actual amount, where the ammonia was used.

In 1853, six sets of experiments were made, and as before, with Barley. The soils consisted of an artificial mixture of clay, sand, and felspar, decomposed by heating with lime. The first set of three pots was provided with this soil alone; the second had, in addition, 0·13 per cent. of bone-ash acted upon by sulphuric acid; and the third had 1·33 per cent., or ten times as much, of the same phosphatic manure. The three other sets were, respectively, so far like the three just described, but in addition ammonia was artificially supplied to the atmosphere in which the plants grew. The phosphatic manure, whether with or without the ammoniacal supply, much increased the produce of both corn and straw. The Nitrogen of the crops was also very much increased in actual amount (though diminished in percentage in the dry substance) by the aid of the phosphatic manure; and the actual amount of Nitrogen was still further increased by the addition of ammonia to the atmosphere of the plants; and the percentage of Nitrogen in the dry substance was also greater where the ammonia was supplied, than in the corresponding cases without it. The experiments without ammonia were made in free air. The Nitrogen in the produce was about seven times that of the seeds where no phosphates were employed; about twelve times that of the seed witn the smaller quantity of phosphate; and about twenty times that of the seed with the larger amount of phosphate.

M. Petzholdt considered it difficult to account for the fact of M. Boussingault getting little or no increase of Nitrogen when he grew plants in free air, which must have supplied some ammonia, even though rain and dew were excluded. He thinks the error must be on the side of M. Boussingault.

It is seen that the explanations or conclusions of these several arbitrators are nearly as conflicting as those of M. Boussingault and M. G. Ville themselves.

For ourselves we are free to confess that we are unable to discover, either in the

* Journ. für Prakt. Chem. Band lxv.

differences of plan adopted by M. BOUSSINGAULT and M. G. VILLE, so far as they have themselves described them, or in the results and explanations of other experimenters, any satisfactory solution of the difference of result arrived at. *À priori*, there are reasons for concluding, both from the chemical characters of Nitrogen itself, and from what we at present know of the chemistry of vegetation in other respects, that plants would not assimilate Nitrogen offered to them in the free state. On the other hand—to say nothing of the large total amount of combined Nitrogen actually existing—the statistics of Nitrogen-production show that there is an amount of Nitrogen periodically available for the vegetation of a given area of land, the source of a considerable proportion of which is as yet not satisfactorily explained. The question whether or not the assimilation of free Nitrogen by plants may account for all, or a part, of the otherwise unexplained fixation, is seen to be left in a dilemma almost inexplicable, by the conflicting character of the results that have been recorded relating to it. Yet, as has been already said, upon the decision finally come to in regard to this question, must materially depend the degree of importance to be attached to the investigation of the other actual or possible sources of Nitrogen to plants, which we have briefly noticed. Under these circumstances, it seemed desirable that any opinions we might offer or adopt on this subject should have the support of such evidence as might be afforded by renewed experiment. We proceed, then, to follow up our account of the Nitrogen-statistics of vegetable production, the consideration of the several possible sources of Nitrogen to plants, and the review of the results and opinions of others on some of the points at issue, by a statement of our own experimental evidence in regard to this important question.

PART SECOND.

EXPERIMENTAL RESULTS OBTAINED AT ROTHAMSTED DURING THE YEARS 1857, 1858, AND 1859.

Introductory observations.

In laying this part of the subject before the Fellows of the Royal Society, we shall follow the general order in which the questions involved were presented to ourselves in the investigation. In so doing it will be necessary:—

1. To consider all possible conditions to be fulfilled in order to effect the solution of the main question of the assimilation of free Nitrogen by plants, and to endeavour to eliminate all sources of error in our investigation.

2. To examine a number of collateral questions, which have a bearing upon the points at issue, and to endeavour so far to solve them as to reduce the general solution to that of a single question to be answered by a final set of experiments.

3. To give the results of the final experiments themselves, and to discuss their bearings upon the question which it is proposed to solve by them.

We shall dwell more fully upon the conditions involved in the experiments than upon the numerical results which they have afforded, since the value of these results is so wholly dependent on those conditions, that, if the latter are properly arranged and thoroughly considered, any conclusion with regard to the former will be sufficiently apparent from the numerical results themselves.

In studying the conditions, we shall be obliged to touch upon several collateral points, embracing some questions not necessarily involved in the investigation, and which, therefore, we have not attempted to treat with that fulness which, as distinct questions in vegetable Physiology, they merit. Yet, we think, it will appear that, in the degree in which we have followed them, their discussion is essential to complete the consideration of the main question of the investigation, and that, in relation to it, they possess an interest quite commensurate with the attention we have devoted to them.

These questions are embraced in the following:—

1. The preparation of the soil or matrix for the reception of the plant, and of the nutriment to be supplied to it.

2. The preparation of the nutriment to be supplied to the plant,—embracing that of mineral constituents (as in the ash), of certain solutions, and of water.

3. The conditions of the atmosphere to be supplied to the plant, together with the means of securing them,—involving a consideration of the circumstances affecting the composition of the atmosphere, and of the apparatus used to supply it.

4. The changes undergone by nitrogenous organic matter during its decomposition, affecting the quantity of combined Nitrogen present, in circumstances more or less analogous to those in which the plants were grown in our experiments upon the assimilation of Nitrogen.

5. The action of agents, as ozone, and the influence of other circumstances which may affect the quantity of combined Nitrogen present in connexion with the plant, and yet independent of the direct action of the vital (growing) process.

In considering these five questions, two important series of conditions must be fulfilled:—

1. Those that relate to the growth of the plant,—which must be so arranged as to include all that is necessary for healthy and vigorous growth, *excepting only*, in some instances, such conditions as may depend upon the presence of a supply of combined Nitrogen.

2. Those that relate to our means of measuring the quantity of combined Nitrogen present at different periods of growth,—it being essential that we should be able, with the means of investigation afforded in the present state of science, to ascertain the quantity of combined Nitrogen present with the plant at different periods of its growth, with sufficient exactness to detect any changes that may take place, so as to enable us to refer them to their proper source.

If we succeed in fulfilling all these conditions, we shall have at our command all the data requisite for the solution of the question whether plants assimilate free

Nitrogen. Our preliminary investigations will have enabled us to avoid, or to eliminate, all sources of error due to the incidental circumstances of the research; and the numerical results of a final series of experiments, showing the quantities of combined Nitrogen supplied, and those eventually found in connexion with the plant, will afford the necessary data for the solution desired.

In discussing the conditions involved in the experiments, and the researches undertaken to enable us to estimate the value of those conditions, we shall arrange the subject in such order as will most clearly bring out their bearings upon the main question, rather than according to the order as to time in which they were made. Several collateral experiments were made, to prove that our conditions of growth, provided in soil, atmosphere, and nutriment, were such as we had assumed them to be; for had they not been so, the object of the investigation could not be attained. The time required for the conduct of these collateral experiments, made it necessary that many of them should be performed simultaneously with the investigations the proper conditions of which they were designed to make known.

We shall first consider the arrangement of the main experiments, and the plan and results of the collateral inquiries with a view to show what the conditions of the former should be, and then show how far the conditions assumed for the first year's experiments, and those arranged in the second year, after the results of some of the collateral investigations were known, agree with the conditions indicated by the results of all the collateral investigations taken together.

SECTION I.—CONDITIONS REQUIRED, AND PLAN ADOPTED, IN EXPERIMENTS ON THE QUESTION OF THE ASSIMILATION OF FREE NITROGEN BY PLANTS.

A.—*Preparation of the Soil, or matrix, for the reception of the plant, and of the nutriment to be supplied to it.*

In considering the subject of the soil to be used, the remarks made above on the necessity of combining the conditions of healthy growth with the simplicity of constitution which would allow of a quantitative estimation of the results obtained, acquire a high degree of importance.

So complicated is the constitution of ordinary soils, and so intimately are the nitrogenous compounds existing within them associated with the other matters, that it is impossible either to estimate the Nitrogen with sufficient accuracy for our present purpose, or to extract it from the soil without entirely destroying the other conditions of vegetable growth. We are, moreover, so entirely ignorant of the character of the organic constituents of soils, of the state in which the principal part of the Nitrogen exists in them, of the changes to which it is subject during vegetable growth and decay, and, more especially, of its relations to vegetable growth, that an ordinary soil could not possibly be used for our purpose.

Our ignorance of the actual constitution of soils, as regards the state of the organic matter in them, and its relations to the inorganic substances, entirely precludes the possibility of our imitating, by artificial means, a natural soil, so as to include all its conditions excepting a supply of combined Nitrogen.

It is evident, therefore, that if all the conditions embraced in an ordinary soil were essential to vegetable growth, the solution of the question of the assimilation of free Nitrogen by plants would involve difficulties which our means of investigation in the present state of science could not overcome. But the experiments to which attention has been directed in the history of this subject, as well as others, the details of which we shall give further on, show that such is not the case. They show that many of the complicated conditions of an ordinary soil may be entirely dispensed with, so as to bring the examination of it within our means of investigation, and yet to retain all the conditions of healthy growth.

In the experiments of the first year, 1857, two kinds of soil, or matrix, were used.

One was prepared from an ordinary soil, so as more nearly to imitate the usual conditions of vegetable growth. The other was prepared from volcanic pumice, with the view to eliminate certain supposed sources of error which the prepared soil might introduce. It was found, however, in the experiments of 1857, that there was no necessity for this difference of matrix, and hence, in the experiments of 1858, only prepared soil was used.

The soil selected for the preparation of the matrix was a somewhat heavy one (clayey), resting upon chalk, and interspersed with flints. The large stones were removed by picking and sifting; and the clayey lumps were powdered to prevent them from baking into hard nodules during ignition. An attempt to ignite in ordinary clay crucibles was not successful, owing to the reduction of the peroxide of iron to the state of black oxide, and to the formation of sulphides from the reduction of the sulphates present, as indicated by the vapours of sulphurous acid emitted during the ignition, and by the evolution of sulphide of hydrogen on the addition of an acid to the mass after cooling.

The combustion proceeded satisfactorily in a large cast-iron muffle, through which a constant current of air could pass. The ignition was continued until a portion of the soil assumed, on cooling, the red colour due to peroxide of iron, and exhibited no trace of coaly matter. The mass thus prepared was taken from the muffle, and thrown into a large vessel filled with distilled water. The water was rendered highly alkaline by the quantity of caustic lime present. The fluid was decanted, and fresh portions of water added several times during eight or ten days, until all the soluble matter was removed. The residue was then dried, and retained for final ignition before being used. The ferruginous and aluminous character of this soil-matrix pointed to the danger there might be of its acting as a porous body, to promote the formation of nitrogenous compounds independently of vegetable growth, on the one hand, or to absorb and retain the ammonia given to the plant, or that which might be formed from the nitrogenous matter of the seed, on the other.

To ascertain the value of any influence exerted by the soil independently of the plant, in the manner just indicated, a pot of soil, prepared exactly as for an experiment with a plant, was submitted to the same conditions of air, temperature, moisture, &c., as the pots containing the experimental plants. The result was, that there was no accumulation of combined Nitrogen. The result with the matrix of pumice also showed, compared with that of the soil-matrix, that no error was to be feared from the influence of the latter in absorbing and retaining combined Nitrogen already in connexion with the plant.

For our purpose, pure volcanic pumice was used. It was powdered until the mass was quite fine and the largest pieces were about the size of peas. This powder was subjected to long washing in the same manner as the ignited soil. Lastly, it was dried ready for a final ignition before being used.

B.—*The Mineral Constituents added to the prepared Soil.*

In most cases the necessary Mineral Constituents were supplied in the form of the ash of the plant of the description to be grown. In a few instances, where this was not practicable, the ash of some other plant was selected. Weak solutions of sulphates and phosphates, as well as ash, were also sometimes used.

In some instances the ash was obtained by burning a quantity of the entire plant when in seed. In other cases, the seed and the rest of the plant being burnt separately, a mixture of the two ashes was made in such proportion as to represent the composition of the ash of the entire plant.

Thus, in the experiments of 1857, for Wheat a mixture of one part of the grain-ash and six parts of the straw-ash, for the Barley a mixture of one part of the grain-ash and three parts of the straw-ash, and for Beans a mixture of one part of the corn-ash and two parts of the straw-ash was used. In the experiments of 1858, the ash used for these crops was obtained by burning the entire plant. For Clover, the ash of Clover-hay was employed.

In some instances of Leguminous plants the ash was saturated with sulphuric acid, and then ignited, before being used.

Each ash was burnt in a large shallow platinum dish, heated in a current of air, in a cast-iron muffle. The burning was continued until all coaly matter had disappeared. The ash was then preserved, but was always submitted to a final ignition before being used. Examination failed to detect combined Nitrogen in any of the ashes so prepared.

In order that the roots of the plants should find an abundance of mineral matter at the most active period of growth, it was desirable that the matrix should contain as much of such matter as was consistent with healthy development. A consideration of the chemical constitution of soils suggested a proportion of 0·8 to 1·0 per cent. of ash; and this was the quantity added to the matrix for the experiments of 1857; but for those of 1858 only about half as much was employed.

C.—*The Distilled Water.*

The first two-fifths of the distillate from ordinary water was allowed to escape, and the next two-fifths were collected for further treatment. The water so obtained retained traces of ammonia. It was mixed with phosphoric acid, free from nitric acid and ammonia, in such quantity that the amount of acid present exceeded that of the ammonia several thousand times. It was then re-distilled from a copper vessel to which was attached a large Liebig's condenser.

Under these circumstances no ammonia could go over unless it were carried over mechanically, in which case it would be accompanied with several thousand times its own weight of phosphoric acid; and, as no distilled water was used that gave any evidence of the presence of this acid, the amount of ammonia in it, if any, must have been several thousand times less than that to which the term "traces" is applied.

The distilled water was so prepared only a few days prior to being required for use.

All parts of the apparatus, the presence of ammonia in which could possibly affect the result, were, after thorough washing both with ordinary and with common distilled water, finally well rinsed with this pure double-distilled water just before being used.

D.—*The Pots used to receive the Soil, Ash, Plant, &c.*

For the experiments of 1857 common flower-pots were used; their height, and diameter at the top, were each 6 inches, and their diameter at the bottom 3·2 inches; their weight was about 1 lb. Small common white glazed earthenware plates were used as the pans.

Subsequent observation suggested, for the experiments of 1858, the kind of pot, and pan beneath it, represented in Plate XII. figs. 1, 2 & 3.

The Pot, of which fig. 2, Plate XII., represents the elevation, was made of the same material as ordinary flower-pots. It was, however, made as light as possible, and was not baked so hard as the latter generally are. The height, and diameter at the top, were each 5 inches; and the diameter at the bottom was 4 inches. The bottom is perforated with about twenty holes of nearly one-fourth of an inch diameter, as is shown in figs. 1 & 2. There were also two rows of similar holes (A, B, fig. 2) round the sides at a distance of 0·5 to 1 inch from the bottom.

The Pan, represented with the pot placed in it in fig. 3, Plate XII., is made of hard-baked and well-glazed stone-ware. It is 1·5 inch deep and 5·2 inches in diameter at the bottom. At the top it is curved inwards (A, B, fig. 3), so as to adapt its upper rim to the sides of the pot.

These arrangements of pot and pan afford several advantages, for the purposes of the investigation, over those adopted in 1857. The surface for evaporation is less in proportion to the volume of soil. The facilities for the exit of roots, and for the access of air, are, on the other hand, greater. The pan affords room for an abundance of water, in which the roots develope luxuriantly*. Yet this water does not evaporate so freely as it otherwise would do, owing to the inward curve of the top of the pan, which also serves to protect the roots distributed through the water from the direct action of sunlight. All the conditions of growth are thus attained with a minimum of evaporation from all sources excepting through the plant itself; and a drier atmosphere is maintained. Consequently evaporation through the plant is favoured, and hence the conditions are provided for a constant supply to the plant of all the mineral and gaseous substances in solution in the fluid of the soil and pan.

E.—*Final preparation of the Soil, Ash, and Pot, for the Plant.*

The soil and ash, each prepared as described in the foregoing subsections, and the pot, also as described above, were simultaneously heated to redness; and the soil and ash, whilst red-hot, were mixed together in the red-hot pot, which was placed upon a red-hot brick over sulphuric acid. The pot and contents were then covered with a large glass shade, and left to cool.

The soil, as in its former preparation, was heated in a cast-iron muffle, from which it was removed with a small iron shovel adapted to the purpose, and heated to redness before being used.

Four or five pots were heated together, one inside the other, the top and bottom ones of which almost invariably broke, either on the application of the heat, or on removal from the fire; so that only about half of those operated upon were finally available for use.

From 2½ lbs. to 3 lbs. of ignited soil were put into each pot; but in the experiments of the second year, 1858, the lower part of the pot was first filled, to the depth of about 1 inch, with very coarsely broken-up red-hot flint. In 1857, about 14 grammes of ash, and in 1858 about 7 grammes only, were used for each pot. The greater portion of the ash was mixed with the lower layers of the soil; but some was distributed through the whole of it.

After cooling down sufficiently, the shade was removed, and about 500 cub. centims. of distilled water, prepared as described in subsection C, were added to the soil of each pot, this being as much as it would absorb. Then, after a lapse of ten to twenty hours, the seeds or plants were put in.

F.—*The Seeds and Plants taken for experiment.*

In all the experiments recorded, the plants were grown directly from *seed* sown in the soils prepared as above described.

In every case, seed of the best quality was taken, which was kindly presented to us for our purpose by the Messrs. THOMAS GIBBS and Co., of Half-Moon Street, Piccadilly,

* See Table, and general remarks at p. 524; also notes of root-development of Wheat No. 6 (1857), p. 553, Wheat No. 1 (1858), p. 560, and Wheat No. 9 (1858), p. 569.

Seedsmen to the Royal Agricultural Society of England, who bestowed much labour and attention upon the selection. From the quantity of each kind received, the largest and the smallest were picked out, as were also any that did not look quite healthy. Given numbers of the remainder were then weighed, and the average weight, per seed, was calculated. A few seeds, each weighing as nearly as possible the mean weight, were then selected for planting.

In order to estimate the quantity of Nitrogen in the seeds sown, in some cases a quantity of seeds equal in weight and number to those sown was submitted to analysis. But the difficulties of grinding, without loss, so small a quantity, and the consideration that one small quantity might differ more in composition from another such quantity, than either would from the average composition of a large number of well-selected seeds, led us generally to estimate the Nitrogen in the seeds sown from the percentage of it found in the mixture of a large number ground up together.

The seeds selected for growing were sown in the pots of soil prepared as already described, to the depth of about 1 inch below the surface. With large seeds, such as Beans, it was necessary that care should be taken so to deposit them that the radicle and plumule should each take its natural direction. If this precaution was neglected, the seed was liable to be raised out of the soil after sprouting, which involved the inconvenience of opening the apparatus in which the plant was enclosed, in order to re-bury the seed.

In some cases, as soon as the seeds were sown the pots were removed from over the sulphuric acid, and placed at once beneath the large glass shades which were to serve as the enclosing apparatus. In other instances, the pots were first placed under other shades, luted by mercury or sulphuric acid, and standing in the laboratory, and then, after a few days, they were removed to their final position.

G.—*The Atmosphere supplied to the Plants.*

As regards the essential conditions of growth, and the circumstances associated with it, which must be kept within the control of our means of investigation, the same remarks apply to the atmosphere, though with less force, as have already been made in reference to the soil (subsection A, p. 470).

It is true that the constitution of the atmosphere is less complicated, and that we are much better acquainted with it than we are with that of ordinary soils; yet the extreme mobility of the atmosphere renders the presence in it of exceedingly small quantities of substances calculated to influence vegetable growth much more dangerous in quantitative experiments on vegetation than would be their presence in the soil. Thus the presence of gaseous impurities, and of solids mechanically suspended, in the atmosphere cannot be overlooked. And hence, although it is not necessary to submit the natural atmosphere to such radical changes as those to which the natural soil must be subjected, some measures must be taken to exclude the sources of error to which allusion has just been made.

As in the case of the soil, so in that of the atmosphere, the only essential conditions to be attained are such as are required for healthy growth, and as will at the same time enable us to estimate the amount and the sources of the combined Nitrogen coming within the reach of the plant by its means.

In consequence of the mobility of the atmosphere above referred to, it was necessary to exclude the experimental plants from its free access. The quantity of ammonia in the air is, however, so very small, that, provided the atmosphere of the enclosing apparatus were allowed to remain unchanged throughout the period of an experiment, the amount of combined Nitrogen so coming within the reach of the plant might be altogether neglected. Nor, so far as regards the nitrogen and oxygen of the air, is there any necessity for change; but, owing to the peculiar circumstances of temperature and of moisture to which the air of the apparatus is subjected, conditions more closely allied to those of ordinary vegetation are attained by a frequent change of atmosphere. The large quantity of air which thus becomes involved in an experiment precluded the idea of neglecting the consideration of the combined Nitrogen which it contains. It devolved upon us, therefore, either to determine the total amount of combined Nitrogen in the air before and after it came in contact with the plant, or to free the air from combined Nitrogen before admission into the enclosing apparatus. The latter alternative was adopted as the most simple; and the manner in which the object was effected will appear from the following description of the apparatus employed.

II.—*The Apparatus used to enclose the Plants, and to supply them with Air, Water, Carbonic Acid, &c.*

Plate XIII. represents the entire apparatus as used for each separate experiment in 1857; and fig. 1, Plate XIV., that used, also for each separate experiment, in 1858, in which, as will be seen, several important modifications of the arrangement adopted in 1857 were made.

The same letters of reference apply to the two so far as the parts are alike; and where there has been any modification in the arrangement in 1858, as compared with that in 1857, the same letters represent the parts of the apparatus used for the same purpose in each, with the exception, that those which apply to the modification of the apparatus in 1858, are distinguished by a dash, thus ′.

A, Plate XIII. (and fig. 1, Plate XIV.), represents a large stone-ware Woulfe's bottle, 18 inches in diameter and 24 inches high.

B, C, and E are glass Woulfe's bottles of 30 ounces capacity.

F is a large glass shade, the dimensions of which were, in most of the experiments, diameter 9 inches, and height 40 inches; in other cases the dimensions were, diameter 16 inches, and height 28 inches.

a represents the cross section of a leaden pipe 1½ inch in diameter, which is in connexion with a reservoir of water, not shown. This pipe passes over all the vessels A (of which there is one included in the apparatus for each separate experiment) in a direction at right angles to the plan of the figure. It is connected with each vessel A by means of a tube *a b*, in which is fixed a stopcock, to open and shut the connexion between the water-supply tube *a* and the vessel A.

c d e, Plate XIII., is a leaden exit-tube for air. *c′ d′ e′*, fig. 1, Plate XIV., is the corresponding tube in the apparatus of 1858, which is enlarged at the point *c′* and downwards until it opens into the vessel A, thus allowing another, *q′ r′ s′*, to pass through it and down to the bottom of the vessel A, as indicated by the dotted line. This tube *q′ r′ s′* is a half-inch safety-tube, opening externally at *q′*, and in the apparatus of 1858 replaces the tube *q r s* shown in Plate XIII.

The bottles B and C are filled to the depth of 2½ inches with sulphuric acid of sp. gr. 1·85.

The tube D D is about 3 feet long and about 1 inch in diameter, and is filled with fragments of pumice saturated with sulphuric acid. At *f*, *f*, in this tube, are small indentations to prevent the sulphuric acid from draining against the corks.

The Woulfe's bottle E contains a saturated solution of ignited carbonate of soda.

g h is a bent and caoutchouc-jointed glass tube, connecting the interior of the Woulfe's bottle E with that of the large glass shade F.

i k, better indicated in fig. 2, Plate XIV., is the exit-tube for the air, connecting the interior of the shade F with an eight-bulbed apparatus M, containing sulphuric acid.

w w, Plate XIII., is a block of slate 12 inches square and 3½ inches thick, in which is a circular groove, half an inch wide and 2 inches deep, adapted to the diameter (9 inches) of the glass shade F, the bottom of which rests in it. The groove is filled with quicksilver, which shuts off the communication of the external air with the interior of the shade. It is widened and deepened at four equidistant points, to admit of glass tubes passing underneath the shade. Two of these tubes, *g h* and *n o*, are shown in Plate XIII., and *g h* also in fig. 1, Plate XIV., *n o* being there replaced by *n′ o′*. The other two are at right angles to these, and are best seen in the vertical section of the shade and lute, fig. 2, Plate XIV., lettered *u v* and *i k* respectively. The tube *u v* is for the supply of water to the plant; and the tube *i k* is for the exit of the air, from which it passes outwards through the sulphuric acid in the eight-bulb apparatus M. This vertical section of the shade and lute is at right angles to the view of them in fig. 1., Plate XIV.; and from it a judgment may be formed of that of the shade and lute of Plate XIII., as well as of the corresponding tubes to those last described, in the apparatus of 1857.

The tube *n o*, Plate XIII., passing from the outside, beneath the shade, and extending to the surface of the mercury in the groove within the shade, is for the purpose of withdrawing condensed water. In the apparatus for 1858, the arrangement for this object is rather different. Thus O, fig. 1 (and fig. 2), Plate XIV., is a bottle into which passes a tube *n′ o′*, opening into the bottom of the lute *w′ w′* by means of a hole at *n′*, seen better in figs. 4 & 5, Plate XII., which represent, respectively, the plan and the vertical section of the glazed stone-ware lute-vessel used in 1858. Another glass tube (t') passes to the bottom of the vessel O (figs. 1 & 2, Plate XIV.), for the purpose of withdrawing the condensed water which collects in it.

The plan of the stone-ware lute-vessel used in 1858 (fig. 4, Plate XII.) shows the groove for the mercury, the four widened and deepened points of it for the passage of the tubes under the shade (of which however three only were used), and the hole n' at the bottom, for the reception of the tube for carrying off the condensed water. This lute-vessel is made of hard-baked and well-glazed stone-ware, and is, in fact, simply a shallow dish with double concentric sides, the space between which latter forms the groove for the reception of the shade and of the mercury luting, and for the passage of the tubes. Figure 5, Plate XII., is a vertical section of the stone-ware lute-vessel, from A to B, fig. 4, through two of the widened and deepened portions of the groove, and through the hole n'. Figure 6, Plate XII., is also a vertical section of the lute-vessel, but from C to D, fig. 4.

The Woulfe's bottle T, fig. 1, Plate XIII., and T', fig. 1, Plate XIV., is for the supply of carbonic acid, and will be referred to, more fully, in the following subsection I.

I.—*Use of the Apparatus.*

If the stopcock below a (fig. 1, Plate XIII., and fig. 1, Plate XIV.) is opened, water flows into the vessel A from a large reservoir with which the leaden tube a is in connexion. As the pressure increases, the water rises in the safety tube $q\,r\,s$, or $q'\,r'\,s'$, above the level in the vessel A, and at the same time the air begins to escape by the tube $c\,d\,e$, or $c'\,d'\,e'$, to force its way through the sulphuric acid in the bottles B, C, then to traverse the tube D D, containing the pumice saturated with sulphuric acid, to bubble through the solution of carbonate of soda in E, and finally to enter the shade F by the bent and jointed tubes g, h; and from the shade it passes out through the tube $i\,k$ and the bulb-apparatus M containing sulphuric acid, into the external air.

The minimum pressure required to produce this passage of air, expressed in the height of a column of mercury which it would sustain, is equal to the sum of the products obtained by multiplying the height of each fluid through which the air has to pass by the sp. gr. of the same, divided by the sp. gr. of mercury, or

$$[(2{\cdot}5+2{\cdot}5+1{\cdot}0)\times1{\cdot}85+2{\cdot}5\times1{\cdot}2]\tfrac{1}{13{\cdot}6}=1{\cdot}037 \text{ inch},$$

in which 1·2 is the sp. gr. of the carbonate-of-soda solution.

The difference between the height of the water in the vessel A and in the safety-tube $q\,r\,s$, or $q'\,r'\,s'$, must always be equal to the weight of the mercury column obtained in the manner just indicated, multiplied by the sp. gr. of mercury.

If the difference between the height of the highest points of the tubes $q\,r\,s$ and $c\,d\,e$, fig. 1, Plate XIII. (that of the former being the higher), be less than the minimum height just referred to, then the water must flow out of A through the safety tube g, r, s before it can pass through the tube c, d, e, into the bottle B. In accordance with this consideration, the safety-tubes for the apparatus of 1857 were arranged as shown in Plate XIII. (g, r, s); but, owing to occasional leakage of the joints at the top of the vessel A, this principle could not be relied upon; and hence the arrangement shown in fig. 1, Plate XIV. was adopted in the experiments of 1858.

The height from the top of the vessel A to r' (fig. 1, Plate XIV.) was 12 inches, which is sufficient to allow the whole of the air to pass out of the vessel A, whilst the great height of d', of the tube c', d', e', entirely prevented the water from passing over into the bottle B,—an accident which unfortunately happened on a few occasions with the apparatus of 1857.

When the vessel A was full of water, it was drawn off by a cork-hole at the bottom, air being at the same time admitted by the tube x at the top of the vessel.

The minimum pressure upon the glass shade F would be

$$\frac{1\cdot0\times1\cdot85}{13\cdot6}=0\cdot136 \text{ inch,}$$

in which 1·0 is the difference between the height of the lowest and the highest level of the sulphuric acid in the bulb-apparatus M. Experiments showed, however, that owing to friction, &c., the maximum pressure on the inside of the glass shade would be raised to double the above estimated minimum.

The plants were supplied with water, as already said, through the tube $u\,v$, shown best in fig. 2, Plate XIV. At first fresh distilled water was supplied; but as soon as a sufficient quantity of condensed water had run through the tube $n'\,o'$ and collected in the bottle O, this was drawn off by means of the tube t' to water the plant when required. In the experiments of 1857, the condensed water was drawn off from time to time, from the surface of the slate and mercury, by means of the tube $n\,o$.

All the Woulfe's bottles were made as air-tight as possible by means of very good corks. Those of the bottles E, Plate XIII., and fig. 1, Plate XIV., and also those of O, fig. 1, Plate XIV., were, however, covered with a cement, composed of eight parts gutta percha, twelve parts common rosin, and one part Venice turpentine, well melted together. The glass tube $n'\,o'$ was also fixed into the lute-vessel $w\,w$, at n', with this cement.

In the experiments of 1857, tubes of unvulcanized caoutchouc, made by ourselves from the sheet, were used for the various joints indicated in the figures; but as these soon became unsound under the influence of the atmospheric changes to which they were exposed, tubes of vulcanized caoutchouc were substituted in 1858. The ends of the glass tubes o and u, Plate XIII., and of the tubes t' and u, fig. 1, Plate XIV., were fitted with pieces of caoutchouc tubing into which pieces of solid glass rod were fixed as stoppers.

In 1857, twelve such sets of apparatus, and in 1858 a larger number, were employed. The whole were arranged side by side, on stands of brickwork erected for the purpose, in the open air, and were protected from rain, or the too powerful rays of the sun, by a canvas awning which could be drawn down over them, or withdrawn, at pleasure.

In 1858, in addition to the sets of apparatus above described, two glazed cages, such as were used by M. G. VILLE in his experiments, and which he kindly sent over to us for the purpose, were employed.

J.—*The supply of Carbonic Acid to the Plants.*

Owing to the small proportion of carbonic acid in the atmosphere, and to the fact that a part of it would be absorbed in passing through the apparatus just described, it was necessary to give a supply of it to the plants artificially. It was obtained by the action of chlorhydric acid upon fragments of marble in the vessel T, Plate XIII., or T', fig. 1, Plate XIV.

In regulating the supply of carbonic acid, the points to be observed were, to keep the proportion in the enclosed atmosphere below that in which it would prove injurious to the plants, and at the same time to provide a sufficient quantity for the demands of vegetation at the most active periods of growth.

BOUSSINGAULT found* that the air surrounding a plant might, consistently with healthy growth, contain 8 per cent. of carbonic acid. This amount, then, on the one hand, and the very small quantity in the atmosphere which is sufficient for natural vegetation (about 0·04 per cent.), on the other hand, afford us limits between which a wide range is allowed for variation.

Calculation showed that a minimum quantity of 0·2 per cent. of carbonic acid in the air of the enclosing apparatus would supply 5 cubic inches of the gas within the shade at one time, corresponding to 0·0439 gramme of carbon—a quantity which, maintained daily throughout the sunlight, would be very much more than was required by the plants.

It is obvious, therefore, that a variation in the amount of carbonic acid in the atmosphere of the plants between 4·0 per cent. and 0·2 per cent. would be very safely within the limit suggested by the experiment of BOUSSINGAULT as the maximum, on the one hand, and that indicated by the above considerations as the minimum desirable in the experiment, on the other.

A question arises as to the influence which the *changes* in the proportion of carbonic acid in the air, between the assumed limits, may have upon the plant. In reference to this point, it may be mentioned that our own experiments upon the nature of the gas in plants (some of the results of which will be given further on) appear to show that the changes in the proportion of the carbonic acid in the air of the cells and intercellular passages, and in that in the fluids of the stem, are much greater, and more rapid than those which can take place in the atmosphere of our apparatus. In addition to this, may be stated the fact that plants derive much of their carbonic acid from aqueous solution absorbed by the roots; and most probably the remainder is absorbed by the fluids of the plant before influencing its growth. These absorptions can take place but

* Mémoires de Chimie Agricole et de Physiologie, 1854, p. 441.

slowly; so that somewhat rapid variations in the proportion of carbonic acid in the atmosphere surrounding the plant, will be accompanied by much less variation in the proportion of carbonic acid within the plant. The latter will, therefore, be a slightly varying mean between amounts corresponding to the foregoing extremes.

From the above considerations, it appeared probable that there would be no danger in so supplying carbonic acid to the atmosphere of the plants as that its proportion should reach its maximum in a short time, and then, by the passage of air, gradually fall again to the minimum. A few trials, adding different quantities of chlorhydric acid to the vessel T, Plate XIII. (or T', fig. 1, Plate XIV.), containing marble, enabled us to ascertain the proper quantity to add, to provide about 4 per cent. of carbonic acid in the shade F when air was not passing. Then passing air, it was found that the proportion of the gas was never reduced below that which we have above assumed as the proper minimum. In practice a little more chlorhydric acid than the amount so determined was used; and then the passage of the air was commenced simultaneously with the addition of the acid. Repeated analysis of the air in the enclosing apparatus showed that, operating in this way, our assumed limits for the maximum and minimum proportions, respectively, of carbonic acid were not passed.

The volume of the air passed through the apparatus daily, was that of the vessel A, Plate XIII. and fig. 1, Plate XIV., and was equal to about 2·5 times that of the enclosing shade F.

K.—*Advantages of the Apparatus above described.*

The advantages, for the purpose in question, of the plan of apparatus which has been described, over those of several of the forms that have been suggested or used by others, may be very briefly stated.

1. When once ready to receive the plant, the use of the apparatus is extremely simple and easy. It is only necessary to place the pot containing the soil, seed, &c., with its pan, in the stone-ware lute-vessel, to pour mercury into the groove, to arrange the several tubes, and to put on the shade. The plant is then entirely excluded from all external sources of combined Nitrogen; and, in case of its being necessary to open the vessel for any purpose, this can be done with great facility.

2. By means of the arrangement of the bottle O (fig. 1, Plate XIV.), the water which condenses within the shade is removed from the atmosphere of the plant as soon as it collects. The small pan in which the pot stands (fig. 3, Plate XII.), with its inward-turned sides, allows of a store of water being kept beneath the plant which is at the same time protected from free evaporation. The vessel O holds as much water as can be evaporated from the plant and soil during several days. The supply of water to the plant is exceedingly easy and simple, it being only necessary to remove that which has collected in the bottle O by means of the tube *t'*, and to pour it in at *u* (figs. 1 and 2, Plate XIV.). [In the arrangement for the experiments of 1857 the condensed water collected on the surface of the slate, until removed by means of the tube *n o*.]

3. A simple glass shade is liable to introduce fewer sources of error than a complicated metallic framework with panes of glass cemented into it. The shade is easier to clean before commencing the experiment, and it is less likely to retain, at the termination of it, any of the combined Nitrogen, either derived from the plant, or from that which has been supplied during growth. Lastly, the presence of oxidizable metallic surfaces, affording a possible quantity of nascent hydrogen which might form ammonia with the Nitrogen of the air, is avoided.

4. There is no organic matter present which can affect the result of the experiment. The only organic matter within the shade is that of a thin coating of the gutta-percha cement which has been described, by which the tube n' (fig. 1, Plate XIV.) is fixed into the hole n' (fig. 4, Plate XII.) at the bottom of the stone-ware lute. On analysis this cement was found to contain from 0·10 to 0·15 per cent. of Nitrogen. Hence, if the whole quantity of the cement in contact with the condensed water became decomposed, and yielded up its Nitrogen in such a manner as to become a product of the experiment, it would only so yield a few tenths of a milligramme of Nitrogen; but experiment proved that it did not suffer sensible decomposition when subjected, during a whole year, to exposure in the open air.

5. In the passage of the air through the apparatus, the excess of pressure was upon the inside, instead of, as in the experiments of others, upon the outside of the enclosing vessel. In experiments of the kind in question in which the apparatus is exposed to the open air, and so subjected to climatic vicissitudes during a considerable period of time, the ordinary means of securing tightness in the laboratory cannot be depended upon; and an apparatus proved to be tight at one time may, as the result of a variety of causes beyond our control, be subject to leakage at another. But a leakage from the inside of the apparatus outwards cannot affect the result of our experiment; whilst a leakage in the opposite direction might introduce combined Nitrogen from the external atmosphere. In the arrangement which has been described, the excess of pressure is always on the inside during the passage of the air; and when the air is not passing there cannot be any important amount in the opposite direction due to changes of temperature and barometric condition, for it can never exceed that required to drive the air inwards through the bulb-apparatus M (Plate XIII., and fig. 1, Plate XIV.), which is altogether insignificant.

6. That part of the apparatus which would be the most liable to leak, and which would be the most damaged by pressure, is subjected to the minimum amount of it. The entire pressure required to force the air through the apparatus, independently of that necessary to overcome friction, is

$$5\times 1{\cdot}85=9{\cdot}25 \text{ inches of water}$$

to pass through the sulphuric acid in the bottles B and C (Plate XIII., and fig. 1, Plate XIV.), and

$$2{\cdot}5\times 1{\cdot}2=3{\cdot}0 \text{ inches of water}$$

to pass through the solution of carbonate of soda in the bottle E, and

$$1\times1{\cdot}85=1{\cdot}85 \text{ inch of water}$$

to pass through the sulphuric acid in the bulb-apparatus M, equal a total of 14·10 inches water, or a minimum pressure of about 0·5 lb. per square inch. Direct experiment with a manometer showed, however, that the entire pressure, minus that due to the sulphuric acid in the bulb-apparatus M, might, owing to friction, &c., amount to 0·8 lb. per square inch. This would give a lateral pressure upon the sides of the glass shade of about 900 lbs., if the current of air were produced by aspiration instead of forcing—a condition which would be incompatible with the safety of the vessel. In the mode of experimenting adopted, however, the only pressure exerted upon the glass shade was the amount requisite to force the air through the bulb-apparatus M.

It remains to consider the influence upon the air of its contact (in the vessel A) with the water employed to force it through the apparatus. This can be of three kinds:—

1. The proportions of nitrogen and oxygen may be slightly affected by absorption, under the influence of the slightly increased pressure to which the air is subjected.

2. The air may lose its carbonic acid.

3. It may become more or less saturated with aqueous vapour.

The increase of pressure to which the air is subjected in the vessel A is so slight, and the time in which it is there in contact with the water is so short, that the total amount of oxygen and nitrogen absorbed by the water must be very small; and, since any change in the constitution of the total amount of air will be dependent on the ratio of the absorption coefficients of oxygen and nitrogen on the one hand, and on the ratio of the quantities of these gases in the air on the other, it will be very much less than in the actual amount of air absorbed; it will in fact be too small to be of any importance.

The whole of the carbonic acid of the air may be absorbed by the water; but as arrangements are made for the artifical supply of it, this is of no consequence.

The amount of water taken up by the air in the vessel A would at first sight appear to be of more importance. But the time during which the air is in contact with the water in the vessel A is very short, and probably too short for its saturation; it must lose most or all of its acquired water in passing through the sulphuric acid in the bottles B and C, and over the pumice saturated with sulphuric acid in the tube DD, whilst the redried air passes too rapidly through the carbonate of soda solution in the bottle E for re-saturation; and lastly, as the air in its previous course through the apparatus will be cooler than within the shade, it will not be so near its point of saturation in the latter as it may be before it reaches it.

L.—*Adaptation for healthy growth of the conditions of experiment adopted.*

We have thus far discussed the possible sources of error in an experiment on the question of the assmilation of Nitrogen by plants, so far as regards the soil, the inorganic nutriment, and the air, to be provided for the plant, and we have pointed out the means adopted to avoid them. From known considerations with regard to the requirements in the soil and inorganic nutriment on the one hand, and in the atmosphere of the plants on the other, and in all combined, we have concluded what are the proper conditions of vegetable growth. It remains, however, to appeal to the results of direct experiment, to show that our adopted conditions possess the value which we have assumed them to have.

A pot of good garden soil, capable of supporting luxuriant vegetation in the open air, was sown with Wheat, Barley, and Beans, and then placed under one of the experimental shades, and submitted to exactly the same atmospheric conditions as those provided in the experiments on the assimilation of Nitrogen. The result was, exceedingly luxuriant growth (see Records of growth in Appendix, Experiment No. 12, of "Plants grown in 1857," fig. 13, Plate XV.; and also Experiment No. 15, of "Plants grown in 1858." It was thus proved that the *aërial* conditions supplied in our experiments were adapted for healthy growth.

When pots of soil, prepared precisely as has been described above, were sown with seed and combined Nitrogen artificially supplied, vigorous growth was the result. Hence it was shown that the conditions of *soil* were properly selected.

Section II.—OTHER CONDITIONS OF EXPERIMENT, REQUIRING COLLATERAL INVESTIGATION.

There remain to be considered several conditions which might affect the result of a quantitative experiment on the assimilation of Nitrogen by plants, dependent upon the reciprocal action of the air and the soil, with or without the connexion of the plant.

The following conditions possibly affecting the result of such an experiment, due to the mutual action of the soil, air, and organic matter of the plant, require to be considered:—

1. The influence of ozone, either within the cells of the plant, or in connexion with it, in promoting the formation of nitrogenous compounds from free Nitrogen. The influence of ozone in promoting such formation within the soil, either directly, or in connexion with the organic matter of the plant.

2. The decomposition of nitrogenous organic matter, in relation to the question whether there be an evolution of free Nitrogen in the process.

3. The formation of nitrogenous compounds, through the mutual action of nascent hydrogen evolved by decomposing organic matter, and free Nitrogen.

A.—*General considerations in regard to the possible influence of Ozone on the supply of combined Nitrogen to growing plants.*

The consideration of Ozone in connexion with the plant suggests the possibility of its presence in two distinct ways. It may occur within the cells and intercellular passages of the plant, either in the gaseous state or in solution, or it may be simply around the plant, without existing within its structures.

With regard to the origin of Ozone in connexion with the plant, it may be a product of the action of the sun's rays, by virtue of which carbonic acid is decomposed, and oxygen evolved. Or, it may result from other causes, to which we shall refer presently.

In order to ascertain how far the presence of Ozone within the plant may have a bearing upon the point at issue, we have attempted to solve, by experiment, the following questions:—

1. Is there, during the growth of plants, Ozone within the cells or intercellular passages?

2. If Ozone be present within the structures of the plant, is it in circumstances in which it would be likely to oxidize free Nitrogen into any of its oxygen compounds?

3. Is Nitric acid present in the living cells of any plant of which it is not a natural product of growth?

In a number of experiments which we have made upon the gases obtained by exhausting plants placed in water freed from air by boiling, no Ozone was perceptible. Another series of experiments upon the oxygen evolved from plants immersed in water saturated with carbonic acid gave similar results.

In the latter series about 1 ounce of the green plant was placed in 500 cub. cents. of carbonated water, and the whole subjected to sunlight. The decomposition of carbonic acid commenced almost immediately, and the evolution of gas was rapid. In this way 100–200 cub. centims. of gas were obtained, which contained sufficient oxygen to inflame a glowing taper; yet no trace of Ozone was manifested on placing test-paper in the gas. That evolved from Wheat, Barley, Oats, Beans, and Clover behaved alike in this respect. Granting that these experiments may not be conclusive for all conditions of the decomposition of carbonic acid by plants, that under certain circumstances Ozone may exist within the vegetable cells and the passages between them, and that it is possible that some of the oxygen of the decomposed carbonic acid may at times appear as Ozone, still, it is difficult to see how it can exert any oxidizing influence upon the free Nitrogen within the plant, under the peculiar circumstances in which it must come in contact with it.

In order to study more fully the circumstances, and to examine, in some detail, the value of the oxidizing and reducing forces operating in the vegetable organism, in the different conditions to which it is subjected during growth, a number of experiments have been made upon plants, under a variety of conditions more or less analogous to those of ordinary growth. As the results of these investigations are too extended in their bearings for full consideration in the present Paper, and are, moreover, not yet sufficiently complete for publication, we shall give here only such of them as bear upon the point now in question.

It is obvious that the formation of Nitric acid, by the mutual action of Ozone and free Nitrogen within the plant, will be dependent upon the activity of the oxidizing power of the Ozone, and on the intensity of the reducing power of other substances in contact with the Nitrogen to be oxidized.

The investigations of SCHÖNBEIN and others appear to show that, under certain circumstances, nitric acid may be formed by the mutual action of Ozone and free Nitrogen. The question for our consideration here is, whether these circumstances are presented in the cells of plants, and in the passages between them, during growth? The subject of the relation of Ozone to organic matter is obviously too extensive for anything more than a passing consideration here; but we may refer to the well-known intense action of this peculiar body upon organic matter generally, by which carbonic acid is formed, and the Ozone destroyed. It is well known that Ozone is rapidly destroyed if kept in contact with phosphorus or any other reducing substance. If such conditions for the destruction of Ozone exist within the plant, the probability that it can there oxidate free Nitrogen, and so form nitrates, would appear to be exceedingly small. The actual conditions within the plant in regard to the points in question may be most efficiently studied by the examination of the gases they contain, under various circumstances. We proceed, therefore, to notice some of the results of such an examination.

B.—*Composition of the Gas in Plants.*

Experiments, Series 1.

Plants, or parts of plants, were put into a flask filled with water that had previously been well boiled to remove all air from it. A cork, through which a bent glass tube was passed, was then pressed into the flask, so that the tube was filled with the displaced water. The flask was then placed over a lamp, the water boiled, and the water and gas driven over collected over mercury, the boiling being continued until the water distilled over raised that first driven out with the gas to the boiling-point. The vapour thus produced expelled most of the water collected over the mercury. In this way the gas driven out from the plant at the boiling-point was obtained. The following Table (I.) shows the composition of the gas collected under these circumstances. It is seen that Nitrogen and Carbonic acid only were present.

TABLE I.—Showing the Percentage Composition of the Gas evolved from plants, in water, on continued boiling.

Date (1857).	Description of plant operated upon.			Per cent.		
	Plant.	Part of plant.	How manured, &c.	Nitrogen.	Oxygen.	Carbonic acid.
May 6.	Wheat.	Whole plant.	Mineral manure	45·47	0·0	54·53
May 2.	Wheat.	Whole plant.	Mineral manure	46·29	0·0	53·71
May 2.	Wheat.	Lower part.	Mineral manure	57·00	0·0	43·00
May 2.	Wheat.	Whole plant.	Mineral and Ammoniacal manure	39·14	0·0	60·86
May 2.	Wheat.	Upper part.	Mineral and Ammoniacal manure	37·53	0·0	62·47
May 6.	Bean.	Whole plant.	Mineral manure	62·79	0·0	37·21
May 6.	Bean.	Whole plant.	Mineral manure	63·80	0·0	36·20

Other experiments gave similar results, all tending to show that the reducing power of the vegetable cells, dependent on the character and conditions of the carbon compounds they contain, was sufficient, under the circumstances specified, to consume all the oxygen (or ozone) that might be present. But the high temperature at which the experiment was conducted must have tended very much to increase this action. In subsequent experiments a different plan of operation was adopted, not open to the same objection.

Experiments, Series 2.

In these experiments, as in all those subsequently referred to, the plants were put into a tall glass vessel (fig. 7, Plate XII.) 1·75 inch in diameter, and 14 inches in height. The mouth of this vessel is fitted with a long cork, previously well boiled in bees'-wax. Through the cork, two glass tubes, *a* and *b*, are inserted. The vessel being filled with water well boiled and then cooled without access of air, the plant is put in and well shaken to remove adherent air-bubbles. The cork, with its two tubes, is then forced in, taking care that both the tubes become filled with water and that no air remains in the vessel. As a further security for tightness, a piece of wide and thick caoutchouc tubing may be drawn over the neck of the vessel, projecting upwards a little above the cork, and then the cup thus formed partly filled with melted wax, forming a layer over the cork and its joints. A funnel is then attached to the tube *b*, by means of a caoutchouc tube which can be closed by a strong pinch-cock. Water being admitted through the funnel into the tube *b*, the tube *a* becomes filled, and it is then brought into connexion, by means of a glass tube and caoutchouc joint fitted with a pinch-cock, with a vessel filled with quicksilver. The connexion being opened, the quicksilver is allowed to flow from the vessel by means of a long tube of more than barometric length fitted into the lower part of it, thus forming a Torricellian vacuum in the mercury vessel. The gas from the plant passes over into this vacuum, and by a simple arrangement is collected in a eudiometer tube for examination.

The following Table shows the amount and composition of the gas obtained from different plants, in the shade, in the manner above described.

TABLE II.—Showing the amount and the composition of the Gas given off by plants, in the shade, into a Torricellian vacuum.

Date.	Description.		Total Gas collected, cub. cents.	Per cent.			
	Part of Plant.	How manured, &c.		Nitrogen.	Oxygen.	Carbonic acid.	Oxygen and Carbonic acid.
		Wheat; 1858.					
June 16.	Whole plant	Mineral manure	57·0	77·72	2·28	20·00	22·28
June 17.	Whole plant	Mineral manure	55·3	77·94	5·06	17·00	22·06
June 16.	Whole plant	Mineral and Ammoniacal manure	57·0	78·60	1·75	19·65	21·40
June 16.	Whole plant	Mineral and Ammoniacal manure	55·7	77·38	3·23	19·39	22·62
June 16.	Whole plant	Mineral and Ammoniacal manure	65·7	82·50	0·30	17·20	17·50
		Barley; 1857.					
June 24.	Whole plant	Unmanured	8·6	85·12	3·93	10·95	14·88
June 24.	Whole plant	Unmanured	20·9	81·48	1·97	16·55	18·52
		Beans; 1858.					
June 17.	Whole plants coming into Flower	Unmanured	54·3	79·74	5·16	15·10	20·26
June 17.	Whole plants coming into Flower	Unmanured	41·5	86·74	4·10	9·16	13·26
June 17.	Whole plants coming into Flower	Ammoniacal manure	52·5	80·38	4·38	15·24	19·62
June 17.	Whole plants coming into Flower	Ammoniacal manure	50·4	84·33	4·36	11·31	15·67
		Clover; 1857.					
Aug. 10.	Heads	Unmanured	47·7	85·61	6·00	8·39	14·39
Aug. 10.	Stems and Leaves	Unmanured	59·8	83·23	2·33	14·44	16·77
Aug. 11.	Heads	Unmanured	91·0	87·15	1·89	10·96	12·85
Aug. 11.	Stems and Leaves	Unmanured	42·3	78·32	1·31	20·37	21·68

These experiments also tend to show that the reducing-power of certain of the carbon compounds of the plant was sufficient to convert nearly all the oxygen (or ozone) present into carbonic acid, when in the shade.

The next point is to consider how far the conditions are favourable to the oxidation of Nitrogen in the vegetable organism, when the plant is subjected to the action of the direct rays of the sun.

Experiments, Series 3.

In these experiments, in which over 100 exhaustions were made, the operation was conducted precisely as in the case of the last experiments, with the exception that the plants were exposed during the whole process to the direct rays of the sun. The following Table exhibits a few of the results obtained, which are sufficient for our present purpose.

TABLE III.—Showing the amount and composition of the Gas given off into a Torricellian vacuum, by plants exposed to sunlight.

Date.	How manured, &c.	Total Gas collected, cub. cents.	Per cent.			
			Nitrogen.	Oxygen.	Carbonic acid.	Oxygen and Carbonic acid.
Wheat (whole plant), 1858.						
June 22.	Unmanured	44·4	73·65	21·17	5·18	26·35
June 23.	Unmanured	34·8	77·01	21·26	1·73	22·99
June 30.	Unmanured	44·1	72·79	20·86	6·35	27·21
June 22.	Mineral and Ammoniacal manure	54·5	73·76	21·29	4·95	26·24
June 23.	Mineral and Ammoniacal manure	42·1	78·15	15·44	6·41	21·85
June 25.	Mineral and Ammoniacal manure	37·2	78·76	19·09	2·15	21·24
Grass (whole plants), 1857.						
August 15.	Mineral and Ammoniacal manure: second crop	39·0	82·10	16·19	1·71	17·90
August 15.	Mineral and Ammoniacal manure: second crop	47·8	77·08	15·35	7·57	22·92
August 15.	Mineral and Ammoniacal manure: second crop	41·6	76·56	21·46	1·98	23·44
August 17.	Mineral and Ammoniacal manure: second crop	39·9	75·07	23·39	1·54	24·93
August 18.	Mineral and Ammoniacal manure: second crop	36·8	79·88	15·19	4·93	20·12
August 18.	Mineral and Ammoniacal manure: second crop	42·3	80·23	15·97	3·80	19·77
Beans, 1858.						
July 12.	Mineral manure; almost podding	44·3	71·11	18·28	10·61	28·89
July 12.	Farm-yard manure; almost podding	45·8	73·14	10·26	16·60	26·86
July 15.	Unmanured; almost podding	25·9	82·63	15·83	1·54	17·37
July 15.	Mineral and Ammoniacal manure; almost podding	30·9	70·55	20·71	8·74	29·45

The general accordance in the proportions of Nitrogen found throughout this Series, together with their general approximation to the amounts observed in Series 2 (Table II.), and the consequent similarity in range of the sums of the two remaining gases—carbonic acid and oxygen—point to the character of the change which has taken place, by virtue of which the proportion of carbonic acid is diminished, and that of oxygen increased. The variations in the amounts are, nevertheless, somewhat considerable; and we feel that it would be requisite to exercise considerable caution in attempting to refer them to any other than accidental circumstances beyond our control. There can be no doubt, however, that the carbonic acid, shown to exist in the plants in the shade, has yielded the oxygen evolved when in the sunlight. But the mutual relations of the two gases will be more clearly brought to view by a consideration of the results yet to be adduced.

Experiments, Series 4.

These experiments, as well as those of the succeeding Series, were arranged to show the influence of the time of action of the sunlight on the plant, upon the relative proportions of carbonic acid and oxygen.

In the Series of experiments now under consideration, duplicate quantities of the plant were operated upon at the same time. Both were prepared in the shade; an then the vessels containing them were each entirely excluded from the light, by means of a thick paper covering. In this condition each was attached to a Torricellian exhauster*. The paper was then removed from one of the vessels so as to expose it, with its contents, to the direct rays of the sun; the other vessel, with its enclosed plant, remaining covered. The exhaustion of both was then commenced immediately, and the action continued for half an hour.

The following Table shows the results obtained in this manner, in sunlight, and in the dark, respectively.

TABLE IV.—Showing the amount and composition of the gas evolved, during half an hour, into a Torricellian vacuum, by duplicate quantities of plant, both kept in the dark for some time before commencing the exhaustion, then one exposed to sunlight, and the other kept in the dark, during the process.

(1858.)

Date.	Description of Plant.	Conditions during Exhaustion.	Total Gas collected.	Per cent.			
				Nitrogen.	Oxygen.	Carbonic acid.	Oxygen and Carbonic acid.
			cub. cents.				
	Beans ...	In dark.........	25·7	66·93	2·33	30·74	**33·07**
		In sunlight ...	36·4	69·78	8·24	21·98	**30·22**
July 22.	Oats......	In dark.........	28·3	81·63	3·53	14·84	**18·37**
		In sunlight ...	25·9	70·27	13·13	16·60	**29·73**
July 23.	Oats......	In dark.........	26·4	73·11	8·33	18·56	**26·89**
		In sunlight ...	22·7	72·25	16·74	11·01	**27·75**
July 23.	Oats......	In dark.........	27·4	68·25	5·11	26·64	**31·75**
		In sunlight ...	29·2	67·47	19·86	12·67	**32·53**
July 23.	Oats......	In dark.........	31·4	77·39	6·69	15·92	**22·61**
		In sunlight ...	21·7	76·50	16·59	6·91	**23·50**

The amounts of carbonic acid and oxygen recorded in the Table, indicate very clearly the ready transformation of the one into the other—or, rather, the transformation of carbonic acid into a solid carbon compound, and free oxygen. In reference to the question we are considering, these results have a high importance, as showing the great reducing-force manifested under the influence of the sun's rays, by which the carbonic acid is so suddenly reduced.

* This term, for convenience, we apply to the apparatus which has been described at p. 487, by which the plant in the vessel, fig. 7, Plate XII., is exhausted.

Experiments, Series 5.

This set of experiments was arranged to show how far the reduction of the carbonic acid, with the evolution of oxygen, was due to the action of the sunlight, in conjunction with the fluids of the plant, at the moment of the passage of the gas through the walls of the cells.

If the decomposition of the carbonic acid resulted from a physico-chemical action, in the presence of sunlight, upon this gas only as it passed through the cell-walls, then there might be no oxygen liberated in the growing cell. If, on the contrary, it were decomposed before passing out of the cell, free oxygen would exist within the latter.

To settle this question, a set of experiments was made exactly similar to those the results of which are given in Table IV., with the exception, that now the time of the exhaustion, and of the action of the sunlight, was reduced to four or five minutes, and the quantity of plant operated upon was increased, so as to give sufficient gas for analysis during this short period. The following Table gives the results obtained.

TABLE V.—Showing the amount and composition of the Gas evolved into a Torricellian vacuum, during four or five minutes only, by duplicate quantities of plant, both kept in the dark for some time before commencing the exhaustion, then one still kept in the dark, and the other exposed to sunlight during the short period of the operation.

(1858.)

Date.	Description of Plant.	Conditions during Exhaustion.	Total Gas collected.	Per cent.			
				Nitrogen.	Oxygen.	Carbonic acid.	Oxygen and Carbonic acid.
			cub. cent.				
July 30.	Oats......	In dark.........	41·7	72·42	3·6	23·98	27·58
		In sunlight ...	42·5	72·23	4·71	23·06	27·77
July 30.	Oats......	In dark.........	55·7	71·46	3·23	25·31	28·54
		In sunlight ...	43·3	69·98	3·23	26·79	30·02
July 30.	Oats......	In dark.........	37·9	83·11	6·86	10·03	16·89
		In sunlight ...	38·5	77·14	9·09	13·77	22·86
July 31.	Oats......	In dark.........	34·4	78·49	7·27	14·24	21·51
		In sunlight ...	41·8	75·84	7·89	16·27	24·16

The above results show that the carbonic acid can pass through the cell-wall, in the presence of sunlight, without suffering decomposition. It would hence appear that the free oxygen which a plant yields after it has been for some time under the influence of the direct rays of the sun, existed as such in the cells before the exhaustion. The slight preponderance of oxygen observed in the gas exhausted in sunlight is doubtless due to its action upon the carbonic acid within the cell, during the short period of its operation upon it before it passes out; precisely analogous to the action when the plant is subjected to ordinary atmospheric pressure.

Experiments, Series 6.

In order to bring out more clearly the influence of sunlight before the exhaustion, a series of experiments were made, in which two vessels, containing the duplicate quantities of plant, were each kept covered with paper for some time, and then, from twenty to thirty minutes before commencing the exhaustion, the paper was removed from one of them, both being then exhausted,—the process continuing ten, fifteen, or twenty minutes. The following results were obtained.

TABLE VI.—Showing the amount and composition of the Gas evolved into a Torricellian vacuum, by duplicate quantities of plant, both kept in the dark for some time, and then one exposed to sunlight for about twenty minutes, when both were submitted to exhaustion.

Date.	Description of Plant.	Conditions during Exhaustion.	Total Gas collected.	Per cent.			
				Nitrogen.	Oxygen.	Carbonic acid.	Oxygen and Carbonic acid.
			cub. cents.				
July 31.	Oats......	In dark.........	24·0	77·08	3·75	19·17	22·92
		In sunlight ...	34·5	68·69	24·93	6·38	31·31
Aug. 2.	Oats......	In dark.........	18·6	68·28	10·21	21·51	31·72
		In sunlight ...	39·2	67·86	25·25	6·89	32·14
Aug. 2.	Oats......	In dark.........	30·7	76 87	8·14	14·99	23·13
		In sunlight ...	26·5	69·43	27·17	3·40	30·57
Aug. 2.	Oats......	In dark.........	17·0	79·41	7·65	12·94	20·59
		In sunlight ...	28·6	76·22	18·53	5·25	23·78
Aug. 3.	Oats......	In dark.........	29·8	81·88	6·38	11·74	18·12
		In sunlight ...	32·1	66·36	30·53	3·11	33·64
Aug. 3.	Oats......	In dark.........	11·6	65·52	6·90	27·58	34·48
		In sunlight ...	23·1	70·56	20·35	9·09	29·44
Aug. 3.	Oats......	In dark.........	17·0	80·00	5·88	14·12	20·00
		In sunlight ...	19·7	73·10	22·33	4·57	26·90

The comparison of the results in this Table with those in Table V., shows that the oxygen must have been liberated from the carbon, and been retained within the cells, until the instant of the exhaustion, as the gas was evolved from all parts of the leaf, and not from the surrounding water, as soon as the pressure was removed.

The conclusions to be drawn from the above several Series of experiments are not without an interesting bearing upon our present subject.

1. Carbonic acid, within growing vegetable cells, and intercellular passages, which are penetrated by the sun's rays, suffers decomposition with the evolution of oxygen, the latter remaining in the plant or being evolved from it. This takes place very rapidly after the penetration of the sun's rays.

2. Living vegetable cells, &c., which are in the dark, or are not penetrated by the direct rays of the sun, consume the oxygen they contained very rapidly after being placed in such circumstances, carbonic acid being formed.

3. There can hence be little or no oxygen in the living cells of plants during the night, or during cloudy days. The presence of oxygen in the cells of thick-leaved plants, or in the deeper layers of fruit, is also very problematical.

4. With every cloud that passes over the sun, the oxygen of the living cell will oscillate under the influence of the reducing-force of the carbon-matter, forming carbonic acid, on the one hand, and of the reducing-forces of the associated sun's rays, liberating pure oxygen and forming a carbon-compound containing less oxygen than carbonic acid, on the other.

5. The idea is suggested by the above considerations, that there may be in the outer cells, which are penetrated by the sun's rays, a reduction of carbonic acid, and a fixation of carbon, with the evolution of oxygen, at the same time that, in the deeper cells, the converse process of the oxidation of carbon and the formation of carbonic acid is taking place. If such be the case, the oxygen of the outer cells would, according to the laws in conformity with which the diffusion of gases and their passage through tissues are known to take place, be continually penetrating to the deeper cells, and there oxidizing their carbon-matter into carbonic acid; whilst the carbonic acid thus formed would pass in the opposite direction to be decomposed in the sunlight of the outer cells. As the process of cell-formation went forward, and the once outer cells became buried deeper by the still more recent ones above them, they would gradually pass from the state in which the sunlight was the greater reducing-agent, to that in which the carbon-matter of the cell became the greater—from the state in which there was a flow of carbonic acid to them and of oxygen from them, to that in which the reverse action took place. The effect of this action may be the formation of oxidized products—acids, or saccharine matter, &c.—in the deeper cells, whilst the great reducing-power of the sun's rays may form more highly carbonized substances in the outer cells, which in their turn become subject to oxidation when buried deeper. The physical and physiological phenomena of such interchanges are obviously worthy of a closer study; but the subject is too wide for any further development here.

6. The very great reducing-power operating in those parts of the plant where ozone is most likely, if at all, to be evolved, seems unfavourable to the idea of the oxidation of Nitrogen into nitric acid by its means—that is to say, under circumstances where the much more readily oxidizable substance, carbon, is not oxidized, but on the contrary its oxide, carbonic acid, is reduced; whilst, as has been seen, when beyond the influence of the direct rays of the sun, the cells seem to supply an abundance of the more easily oxidized carbon, in a condition of combination readily available for oxidation by free oxygen, or ozone, should it be present. The conclusion that free Nitrogen would not be likely to be oxidated into nitric acid within the structures of the plant, seems to be borne out by the well-known fact, that nitrates are as available a source of Nitrogen

to plants as ammonia; and hence, if we were to admit that Nitrogen can be oxidated into nitric acid in the plant, we must suppose, as in the case of carbon, that there are conditions under which the oxygen compound of Nitrogen is reduced within the organism, and that there are others in which the reverse action, namely, the oxidation of Nitrogen, can take place. In relation to this question, it may be mentioned that several specimens of green Wheat and Grass which had been liberally manured with nitrates were examined for nitric acid, but no trace of it was found in them.

7. To the foregoing six conclusions, another may be here added relating to this subject, though deduced from the results of experiments on the decomposition of organic matter, which will be referred to more fully presently (p. 509 *et seq.*). So great is the reducing power of certain carbon-compounds of vegetable substances, that when the vital (growing) process has ceased, and all the free oxygen in the cells has been consumed, in the formation of carbonic acid, water is decomposed, and hydrogen is evolved. This process does not, however, continue long, showing that the cell provides a certain amount of matter more easily oxidized than the remainder, or that the entire cell-matter, after becoming slightly oxidized, loses its energetic reducing-power. The former alternative is the more probable one.

The foregoing considerations with regard to the intensity of the reducing action of certain of the carbon-compounds in plants suggest the idea of a possible source of Ozone, very analogous to that by which it is ordinarily obtained by means of phosphorus. As is well known, the process consists in allowing oxygen to come into incomplete or only instantaneous contact with phosphorus. This substance having an intense avidity for oxygen, a part of the latter unites with it to form an oxygen-compound of phosphorus, when, if the contact be not too long, another part passes off in the state of Ozone. Certain carbon-compounds of the vegetable cell have also a great affinity for oxygen in the dark (p. 488); and the oscillations of the affinities, due to the degree of light (pages 489–492), and to the depth of the cell (p. 493), would afford conditions of molecular action somewhat similar to those under which Ozone is produced in the presence of phosphorus. According to this analogy the Ozone would be due to the action of the carbon-compounds of the cell on the common oxygen eliminated from carbonic acid by sunlight, and not to the direct action of the sunlight itself. The Ozone thus formed, if not instantly evolved from the plant, would be destroyed by the easily oxidizable carbon-compounds present. It is more probable, however, that the Ozone, stated by De Luca and others to be observable in the vicinity of vegetation, is due to the intense action of the oxygen of the air upon the minute quantities of volatile hydrocarbons emitted by the plants, and to which they owe their peculiar odours, than to any action going on within the cells. The rapidity of the oxidation in the air of the hydrocarbons, and the volatile principles of plants generally, goes to favour the view here suggested; so also does the fact, that Ozone has been observed most readily in the vicinity of such plants as are known to emit freely essential oils—as, for instance, those of the Labiate family.

Since it would appear that, under certain circumstances, Ozone is formed in the immediate vicinity of some plants, it remains to consider the possibility of its acting, in an indirect manner, as a source of combined Nitrogen to our experimental plants—that is, through the agency of the materials involved in the experiment—and thus compromising our result in regard to the question of the appropriation, by the plant itself, of free or uncombined Nitrogen. It might so act:—

1. By becoming absorbed by the water that condenses within the vessel enclosing the plant, and then oxidizing the free Nitrogen dissolved in the water.

2. By being absorbed by the soil—either directly from the air of the enclosing apparatus, or from the condensed water returned to the soil—and then, in connexion with it, as a moist, porous, and alkaline body, forming nitrates in the manner referred to by Pelouze and Fremy*, in their remarks upon the experiments of Cloez which we have shortly described at p. 465 of this paper.

3. By passing down in solution in water, or in the gaseous state, to the older and decomposing parts of the roots, and there forming nitric acid by the oxidation either of the free nitrogen contained in the older cells, or of that evolved in decomposition.

These questions have not been so fully investigated as, considered as independent subjects of inquiry and with reference to the results obtained by Schönbein and others, would be desirable. But so far as they can have a bearing upon the sources of error in our experiments upon the question of the assimilation of free Nitrogen by plants, they have received our careful consideration.

C.—*Experiments on the action of Ozonized air on decomposing Organic matter, and porous and alkaline substances.*

Experiments were made to ascertain the influence of Ozone upon organic matter, and certain porous and alkaline bodies, under various circumstances. The action of ordinary air upon sticks of phosphorus was had recourse to as the source of the Ozone. The arrangement was as follows:—Three large glass balloons (carboys), each of about 40 litres capacity, were connected together by glass tubes which passed through stone-ware stoppers fitted into their mouths, the joints being made tight with calcined gypsum cement. The bottom of each vessel was covered with water to the depth of about half an inch, so that, when pieces of phosphorus were put in, they were partly covered with the fluid. A tube, which could be opened or closed at pleasure, was fixed through each stopper for the supply of water, and fresh phosphorus, as needed. An Allen and Pepys gasometer, capable of holding about 2 cubic feet of air, was connected by a glass tube with the first of the series of vessels; and by its means, air could be forced in a continuous stream through the three vessels containing the phosphorus. On passing out of the last of them it was led through a wash-bottle, and then into a glass vessel, from which, by means of a number of glass tubes passing from it, it was distributed into bottles containing the substances to be submitted to the action

* Traité de Chimie Générale, tome sixième, p. 343 (1857).

of the Ozone. Thus, all the ozonized air passed the wash-bottle in its course from the balloons to the distributing apparatus.

The following substances were subjected to the action of the Ozone—each substance, or mixture, being enclosed in a glass bottle of about 1·5 litre capacity, fitted with an exit-tube in which were fragments of pumice saturated with sulphuric acid:—

(1) $\frac{3}{4}$ lb. of ignited soil, moistened with 100 cub. centims. water, this being just sufficient to make it slightly coherent.

(2) $\frac{3}{4}$ lb. of ignited soil, 300 cub. centims. water, 2·5 ounces boiled starch, and 2·5 ounces dry starch.

(3) $\frac{3}{4}$ lb. of ignited soil, 200 cub. cenitms. water, and 2·5 ounces saw-dust.

(4) 2·5 ounces saw-dust, and 100 cub. centims. water.

(5) $\frac{3}{4}$ lb. of ignited soil, 200 cub. centims. water, and 2·5 ounces bean-meal.

(6) $\frac{3}{4}$ lb. of ignited soil, 150 cub. centims. water, and 2·5 ounces bean-meal.

(7) 2·5 ounces bean-meal, and 50 cub. centims. water.

(8) 1 lb. garden-soil.

(9) $\frac{3}{4}$ lb. of slaked lime, and 2·5 ounces bean-meal, made slightly pasty with water.

(10) $\frac{3}{4}$ lb. of slaked lime, some starch, and saw-dust, made slightly pasty with water.

(11) 2·5 ounces of boiled starch, 2·5 ounces fresh starch, and 200 cub. centims. water.

All the bottles were placed before a window where the sun shone directly upon them for a considerable part of the day, as it did also for some hours daily upon the balloons.

Every day, about 9 o'clock in the morning, the cylinder of the gasometer was raised, and a slow current of air passed through the apparatus during about two hours. This process was generally repeated once or twice more during the day. The experiment commenced in April, and continued till the following autumn; that is, through all the warm weather of the summer, when a thermometer in the room frequently stood at 25° to 29° C. The amount of Ozone passing through the apparatus was so great, that the vulcanized caoutchouc which connected the tube from the last balloon with that passing into the wash-bottle was cut off with the passage of three or four gasometerfuls of air. The joint was then made by fixing a piece of larger glass tubing over the point of contact of the smaller connecting tubes, and closing the ends of the larger tube with corks well fitted upon the smaller ones.

Once every three or four days a small piece of phosphorus was dropped into each balloon. In this way the action was sufficiently maintained to produce a distinct odour of Ozone in the room whilst the air was passing.

During the first half of the period of the experiment, a wash-bottle filled with large lumps of pumice, and about half-full of a solution of caustic potash, was used; so that the ozonized air in bubbling rapidly through the solution continually threw it up, by which means the pumice was kept moistened with it.

A careful examination of this liquid, together with the washings of the pumice, failed to detect any nitric acid. About the 1st of July, the alkaline wash was replaced by a bottle containing only pure water. The latter also, at the termination of the experiment, failed to give evidence of even traces of nitric acid.

At the termination of the experiment, the contents of each of the eleven bottles were also examined. A portion was exhausted with water, and the extract concentrated by boiling, after the addition of permanganate of potash to destroy the organic matter. The excess of permanganic acid was removed by carbonate of lead, and the clear solution filtered off from the precipitate. Each solution so obtained was tested for nitric acid; but in no case, excepting that of the garden soil, was there any indication of its presence. An examination of the original garden soil showed that it contained nitric acid before being subjected to the action of the Ozone.

Owing to the negative character of the above results, it is not necessary to describe the apparatus, and the circumstances of the experiments, in any more detail, which would have been desirable had the results been of a positive kind.

We are, however, by no means prepared to infer, from the evidence just adduced, that under no circumstances in nature is it possible for Ozone to transform nitrogenous compounds of the ammonia class, or the nascent nitrogen evolved during decomposition, into oxides of Nitrogen. We would not say that it may not be possible for Ozone to form such compounds when in connexion with non-nitrogenous bodies or porous substances permeated with gaseous Nitrogen, or even in the atmosphere. Nor are we prepared to maintain that the nitric acid in soils is not in part due to some of these causes. These questions will require much further investigation before they can be satisfactorily settled. To some of them we shall refer again presently.

But we wish particularly to call attention to the fact that, in the experiments just referred to, there was a very much larger quantity of Ozone, acting upon organic matter, soil, &c., in a very wide range of circumstances, and for a much longer period of time, than was involved in our experiments on the question of the assimilation of free Nitrogen by plants. Yet there was no appreciable quantity of nitric acid formed. It may therefore be concluded that there will be no error introduced into the results of the experiments on the question of the assimilation of free Nitrogen by plants themselves, arising from the action of Ozone upon free Nitrogen under the circumstances of the experiments, and so providing to the plants an unaccounted supply of combined Nitrogen.

D.—*Evolution of free Nitrogen in the decomposition of Nitrogenous organic compounds.*

Two obvious methods of investigating the question, whether or not free Nitrogen is given off in the decomposition of nitrogenous organic matter, present themselves.

1. To allow the organic matter to decompose under circumstances in which any free Nitrogen that may be evolved can be collected and estimated.

2. To allow the organic matter to decompose under circumstances in which the total amount of the compounds of Nitrogen formed in the process can be estimated—the loss of Nitrogen then representing the free Nitrogen evolved.

A number of experiments according to the first of these methods has been made by REISET. He submitted nitrogenous animal and vegetable substances to decomposition under an enclosing vessel in ordinary air, into which he passed oxygen as that of the air was consumed. His result was, that the amount of Nitrogen in the air was gradually increased. He does not appear, however, to have completed the inquiries on this subject which he proposed to undertake.

The second method has been followed by M. G. VILLE. The conclusion he arrived at was, that in the decomposition of several nitrogenous vegetable substances, about one-third of their total Nitrogen was evolved in the free state.

The losses of Nitrogen which M. BOUSSINGAULT'S experiments on the question of the assimilation of free Nitrogen by plants indicated, when he used nitrogenous organic matter as manure, rendered it desirable to investigate the subject in its bearings upon the conditions provided in our own experiments on that question. The following plan was adopted:—

A given weight of nitrogenous organic matter, the percentage of Nitrogen in which had been previously determined, was mixed with burnt soil, or pumice, prepared as for the experiments on the assimilation of Nitrogen by plants (p. 471), and put into a bottle of about 360 cub. centims. capacity, as shown at B, fig. 8, Plate XII. A proper quantity of water was added; and then the bottle was closed with a cork, through which were tightly fitted two bent glass tubes, which passed externally in opposite directions. One of these tubes was connected with an eight-bulbed apparatus A, containing sulphuric acid, for the purpose of washing air drawn through it into the rest of the apparatus. The other tube, passing from B in the opposite direction, was connected with a similar eight-bulbed apparatus C, containing a solution of oxalic acid. From this again passed a tube extending, through a cork, to the bottom of a second bottle D (similar to B), which contained some sulphuric acid. Through the cork of the bottle D another tube E also passed, but it did not dip into the sulphuric acid. It is obvious that, on drawing the air from D by means of the tube E, a current of air would pass inwards through the sulphuric acid in A, into the bottle B, then through the oxalic acid in C, and so on. In this way, the air of the vessel B, containing the decomposing organic matter, could be renewed at pleasure by fresh air, washed free from ammonia. At the same time, any ammonia evolved from the decomposing organic matter was drawn into the eight-bulbed apparatus C, and there absorbed by the oxalic acid. At the termination of the experiment, the combined Nitrogen remaining in B, and that retained in the form of ammonia in the oxalic acid in C, were determined. The difference between the total amount of combined Nitrogen so found in the products and that originally contained in the organic substance submitted to decomposition, is taken to represent the amount of nitrogen given off, in the free state, during the process.

SERIES 1.—*Experiments on the decomposition of nitrogenous organic matter, made in* 1857.

Wheat-meal, Barley-meal, and Bean-meal were the nitrogenous organic substances submitted to decomposition. A quantity of each of these was mixed respectively with burnt soil and with pumice, making in all six separate experiments. About 100 grammes of soil, or about 60 grammes of pumice, were used—these quantities, together with the meal, filling the bottles B to the depth of about 2 inches. Sufficient water was added to bring the mixture into an agglutinated condition. The materials being so prepared, the apparatus was put together according to the arrangement above described. The six sets were then placed in a light room before a large window, so that, during the middle of the day, the sun shone directly upon them.

The experiments commenced on June 10, and terminated on October 8, 1857. Several litres of air were drawn through each apparatus daily, by applying the mouth to the tube E. After the first day the gas possessed a more or less disagreeable taste, and the odour of decomposing organic matter.

The following statement of the condition of the several mixtures, at the termination of the experiment, is condensed from the notes then made:—

1. *Wheat-meal and ignited Pumice.*—The meal slightly mouldy; the odour that of decomposing organic matter; quite moist, so that the particles of pumice adhered together.

2. *Wheat-meal and ignited Soil.*—A slight mouldy coating on the surface; odour like that of No. 1; the mass moist, but not sufficiently so for the particles of soil to agglutinate.

3. *Barley-meal and ignited Pumice.*—No mouldy coating on the surface; odour similar to that of the wheat but more intense, and sour, much like that of fermenting malt; the mass wet and clammy.

4. *Barley-meal and ignited Soil.*—No mouldy coating on the surface; odour like that of barley No. 3; sufficiently moist to agglutinate.

5. *Bean-meal and ignited Pumice.*—A little mould upon the surface, but not quite so much as with the wheat and soil (No. 2); odour very disagreeable and putrescent; the mass wet and clammy.

6. *Bean-meal and ignited Soil.* Very similar to the bean-meal and ignited pumice (No 5), but a little more wet and pasty.

In every case, carbonic acid was evolved on the addition of oxalic acid, preparatory to evaporating to dryness. The evolution was the greatest from the bean-meal with soil.

A known proportion, about one-half, of each dried mass, was burnt with soda-lime, and the Nitrogen capable of estimation in that way determined. The remainder was reserved for the determination of nitrates, provided any were present. On examination, however, no nitric acid was detected. To put the validity of the qualitative test for nitric acid beyond doubt, 0·001 gramme of nitric acid was added to the portion of substance which had been already exhausted to test for nitric acid, and had yielded a negative result. The mass was then re-exhausted with water, and the extract submitted to precisely the same process as before, when the presence of nitric acid was made manifest.

In the following Table are given the numerical results of the six experiments:—

TABLE VII.—Showing the Numerical results of experiments on the Decomposition of Nitrogenous organic matter, made in 1857.

	Substances submitted to experiment.				Nitrogen after Decomposition.		
	Description of Organic matter.	Description of Matrix.	Quantity of "Meal" taken.	Quantity of Nitrogen.	Total by Soda-lime.	Not recovered. Actual quantity.	Not recovered. Per cent.
			grammes.	grammes.	grammes.	grammes.	
1.	Wheat-meal...	Ignited pumice ...	2·0385	0·0370	0·0338	0·0032	8·51
2.	Wheat-meal...	Ignited soil	2·1282	0·0383	0·0335	0·0048	12·53
3.	Barley-meal...	Ignited pumice ...	2·2495	0·0380	0·0368	0·0012	3·16
4.	Barley-meal...	Ignited soil	2·0980	0·0355	0·0309	0·0046	12·96
5.	Bean-meal ...	Ignited pumice ...	2·0650	0·0803	0·0741	0·0062	7·72
6.	Bean-meal ...	Ignited soil	2·0800	0·0809	0·0823	(+0·0014)	+ (1·73)

The last two columns of this Table, which exhibit respectively the actual amount of Nitrogen not recoverable by the soda-lime process in the substance after decomposition, and the percentage proportion of this loss upon the Nitrogen submitted to experiment, are the most important to consider for our present purpose.

With one exception (the gain of Nitrogen in which is quite within the range of the error of analysis), all the experiments point to the fact, that a part of the Nitrogen of decomposing organic matter passes into a state in which it cannot be estimated by the soda-lime process. Neither did it exist as nitric acid. There appears, therefore, to be an evolution of free Nitrogen.

It is not a little remarkable, that although so large a proportion of the total Nitrogen present is lost, doubtless passing off as free Nitrogen, yet scarcely a trace of ammonia was given off from the mass; for the oxalic acid in the bulb-apparatus C was, in each case, separately rendered alkaline with caustic potash and distilled, the distillate being collected and examined quantitatively for ammonia, when, in only one case—that of the Bean-meal and Pumice—was there any ammonia indicated, and then only equal in amount to 0·0002 gramme Nitrogen. This was the case, notwithstanding that the Nitrogen in the mixtures amounted to from 0·03 to 0·08 per cent. of their entire quantity.

The questions here arise:—to what extent had the decomposition of the organic substance proceeded? what shall we accept as the measure of the amount of decomposition? what are the intermediate stages through which the substance has passed? what is the character of the organic compounds remaining in the mass? what is the nature of those that have been evolved? and what part does water play in the matter?

The subject of the character of the gradual changes which take place during the decomposition of mixtures of nitrogenous and non-nitrogenous substances, in variable proportions, in connexion with soil and water, involves points so highly complicated, that we cannot pretend satisfactorily to answer all the above questions.

We may, however, ascertain the character of some of the final products of the decomposition, and from a knowledge of these draw conclusions as to the changes of which they are the result under various circumstances.

SERIES II.—*Experiments on the Decomposition of nitrogenous Organic Matter, made in* 1858.

The following series of experiments was made with a view to embrace a wider range of conditions as to degree of moisture;—to observe the different stages of decomposition as manifested by the odour, &c.;—to include the circumstances of sprouting, early growth, and subsequent decay of the products of the vegetation;—and to afford material for a more elaborate inquiry into the character of the products of the decomposition.

The results given above, in Table VII., do not show any difference between soil and pumice as matrix that we can safely refer to other than incidental causes independent of the action of the matrix itself. Yet we continue the use of the two substances, in order to see if, with a larger percentage of organic matter, and a more complete decomposition, the pumice will retain the ammonia formed as well as the soil.

About 175 to 200 grammes of soil, or 120 to 150 grammes of pumice, were used as matrix in each experiment, and the other conditions were as follow:—

Wheat.	*a.*	171 seeds, weighing	8·0475 grammes,	50 c. c. water,	with ignited Soil.
	b.	171 seeds, weighing	8·0715 grammes,	100 c. c. water	with ignited Pumice.
	c.	Meal, weighing	9·8810 grammes,	40 c. c. water,	with ignited Soil.
Barley.	*a.*	163 seeds, weighing	8·0440 grammes,	50 c. c. water,	with ignited Soil.
	b.	163 seeds, weighing	8·1360 grammes,	100 c. c. water,	with ignited Pumice.
	c.	Meal, weighing	8·9670 grammes,	40 c. c. water,	with ignited Soil.
Bean.	*a.*	7 seeds, weighing	6·4700 grammes,	50 c. c. water,	with ignited Soil.
	b.	7 seeds, weighing	5·7830 grammes,	50 c. c. water,	with ignited Pumice.
	c.	Meal, weighing	6·1750 grammes,	40 c. c. water,	with ignited Soil.

Those of the mixtures to which about 50 cub. cent. of water were added, were about as moist as soils when in a good condition for vegetable growth. Those with 40 cub. cent. were much drier in appearance, there being no tendency to agglutination of the particles. Those with 100 cub. cent. were very wet, there being some free water above the solid matters.

The seeds sown with 50 cub. cent. water showed growth in a few days after being put in, and the vessels (B, fig. 8, Plate XII.) were soon filled with a mass of vegetation. Those sown with double this quantity, or 100 cub. cent. water, showed no indications of sprouting; and in a few days, the odour evolved from them showed that decomposition had set in. The mixtures of meal and soil, also, soon gave odours indicative of decomposition, though less foul than those from the whole seed and 100 cub. cent. water.

The following Notes, taken at different times during the experiments, will indicate the stages of growth, or decomposition, through which the several organic matters passed.

March 16.

Wheat (*a*)—*Seeds, in Soil with* 50 *cub. cent. water.*—Came up some days later than the corresponding Barley *a*; has not grown so rapidly; has kept green for a longer period; and is yet growing healthily, though much crowded in the small bottle. The air passing from the bottle has not the odour of decomposing organic matter. There is a slight mould on the soil due to a few seeds which did not grow.

Wheat (*b*)—*Seeds, in Pumice with* 100 *cub. cent. water.*—The Pumice in this case was covered with water to the depth of about one-fourth of an inch, and a few grains floated in the water. In a few days the air drawn through the bottle gave the odour and taste of decomposing organic matter. At the end of about a month the free water on the surface began to disappear rapidly, and in a short time it was all gone, leaving a grey mouldy coating of organic matter over the top of the pumice. This disappearance of water was too great to be due to simple evaporation in the air passed through the apparatus. It was doubtless consumed in the process of decomposition—a view which receives confirmation from our experiments on the nature of the gases evolved during decomposition.

Wheat (*c*)—*Meal, in Soil with* 40 *cub. cent. water.*—Gives little indication of decomposition by the air which passes from it. Compared with Wheat *b*, the difference in this respect is very marked.

Barley (*a*)—*Seeds, in Soil with* 50 *cub. cent. water*—Came up soon after being put in, grew rapidly, and in five weeks had grown to the top of the bottle, a height of about 5 inches. By the end of February the bottle was quite filled with green vegetable matter, and up to that time no odour of decomposition was distinguishable in the air which was passed through, but from that date the leaves became yellow, and decomposition has been manifested both by appearance and the taste of the air.

Barley (*b*)—*Seeds, in Pumice with* 100 *cub. cent. water.*—Progress almost exactly similar to that of the corresponding Wheat (*b*) described above.

Barley (*c*)—*Meal, in Soil with* 40 *cub. cent. water.*—Very like the corresponding Wheat (*c*) above.

Bean (*a*)—*Seeds, in Soil with* 50 *cub. cent. water.*—Came up a week after sowing. The sprouts pushed several seeds out of the soil, yet they have continued to grow up to the present time, lying upon the surface. At first there was a natural development of leaf and of roots; but soon the latter took a remarkable course, coming through the surface of the soil and extending through all parts of the bottle, mingling with the stems and leaves, and forming a densely crowded mass of vegetable matter. The rootlets from the main branches extending through the mass commenced their growth in all directions indiscriminately, but after growing about one-fourth of an inch they invariably turned downwards.

Bean (b)—Seeds, in Pumice with 50 *cub. cent. water.*—Identical in appearance with the last (Bean *a*), excepting a little further developed.

Bean (c)—Meal, in Soil with 40 *cub. cent. water.*—Almost exactly like the Wheat (*c*) and Barley (*c*) meals, described above.

In no one of the above nine cases was there any Ozone reaction to test-paper.

April 28.

Wheat (a)—Seeds, in Soil with 50 *cub. cent. water.*—Twelve to fifteen stems; leaves not unrolled, and scarcely any tendency to expansion. The vegetation not nearly so much crowded as in the case of the corresponding Barley (*a*); yet most of the shoots show signs of dying. A thin coat of fungoid growth covers the stems to the height of from 1 to 1·5 inch. The stems are from 2 to 2·5 inches high, those of the corresponding Barley being from 3 to 4 and 5 inches high. The air passed through the apparatus is not disagreeable either in taste or odour.

Wheat (b)—Seeds, in Pumice with 100 *cub. cent. water.*—The Pumice moist, but without visible water, and the surface covered with a grey mouldy coating. The air has had an unpleasant odour ever since March 16, and now it is exceedingly nauseating.

Wheat (c)—Meal, in Soil with 40 *cub. cent. water.*—The soil apparently dry, but slightly mouldy, and the air passed over is almost without odour.

Barley (a)—Seeds, in Soil with 50 *cub. cent. water.*—The bottle full of vegetable matter, all quite yellow at the top where it touches the cork, and yellowish lower down. The plants covered with a coating of greyish fungus. The odour and taste of the air slightly disagreeable. The soil looks quite dry.

Barley (b)—Seeds, in Pumice with 100 *cub. cent. water.*—The soil is moist and mouldy. The mould on the surface appears to be decreasing, and is now less abundant than in the case of the corresponding Wheat (*b*). The odour of the air is much less disagreeable; indeed there is scarcely any at all.

Barley (c)—Meal, in Soil with 40 *cub. cent. water.*—The soil mouldy and apparently dry. The air from the vessel tasteless, and inodorous.

Bean (a)—Seeds, in Soil with 50 *cub. cent. water.*—Continued to grow vigorously for a long time, filling the bottle with a confused mass of stems, leaves, and roots, which has commenced to decay rapidly during the last two weeks. The upper portions of the mass are now entirely dead and black; but nearer the soil the stems and leaves are green and long, whilst healthy roots are intermingled with them. The soil is also tolerably filled with roots. The odour of the air is not disagreeable.

Bean (*b*)—*Seeds, in Pumice with* 50 *cub. cent. water.*—Very much like the last (Bean *a* with soil), excepting that the development of roots is scarcely so great.

Bean (*c*)—*Meal, in Soil with* 40 *cub. cent. water.*—A little mouldy matter on the surface of the soil, which appears dry.

July 1.

Wheat (*a*)—*Seeds, in Soil with* 50 *cub. cent. water.*—Plants all dead; the entire contents of the bottle apparently quite dry. The air has a slight musty odour.

Wheat (*b*)—*Seeds, in Pumice with* 100 *cub. cent. water.*—Odour rather more marked than that of the last (Wheat *a*); a coating of organic matter on the surface of the pumice.

Wheat (*c*)—*Meal, in Soil with* 40 *cub. cent. water.*—Soil quite dry; covered with mould; odour of air slight.

Barley (*a*)—*Seeds, in Soil with* 50 *cub. cent. water.*—Plants quite dead and dry; air inodorous.

Barley (*b*)—*Seeds, in Pumice with* 100 *cub. cent. water.*—Soil dry and covered with mould. Air like that of Wheat *b*; more foul than that of any of the others.

Barley (*c*)—*Meal, in Soil with* 40 *cub. cent. water.*—Surface dry. The air has a slightly musty odour.

Bean (*a*)—*Seeds, in Soil with* 50 *cub. cent. water.*—Plants all dead, and much decomposed; forming a black mouldy mass of organic matter on the surface of the apparently dry soil. The air has no perceptible odour.

Bean (*b*)—*Seeds, in Pumice with* 50 *cub. cent. water.*—The same as the last (Bean *a*).

Bean (*c*)—*Meal, in Soil with* 40 *cub. cent. water.*—Soil dry; slightly mouldy; the air from over it inodorous.

In order to see the effect upon the organic matter of an increased amount of moisture, 100 cub. cent. of water were added to each of the nine bottles of decomposing matter, at this date (July 1).

August 28.

Final Report, and termination of the Experiment.

Wheat (*a*)—*Seeds, in Soil with* 50 *cub. cent. water.*—Very little odour, and that not unpleasant. On removal from the bottle, it was found that the organic matter was well decomposed, only very indefinite remains of stems and leaves being visible in the soil. On the addition of oxalic acid to the mass, to retain the ammonia during the evaporation to dryness, a copious evolution of carbonic acid took place, and the surface of the fluid was constantly covered with a brown froth during the process.

Wheat (*b*)—*Seeds, in Pumice with* 100 *cub. cent. water.*—The mass has a disgusting mouldy odour. The form of the grain is retained, but all the contents are gone, and the husk is filled with fluid. On evaporation with oxalic acid, there was evolution of carbonic acid, &c., as with the last; indeed it was the same with all those which follow.

Wheat (c)—Meal, in Soil with 40 *cub. cent. water.*—In this, as in all the other cases, owing to the water added on the 1st of July, the mass was covered to the depth of from ¼ to ½ an inch with fluid. In both the above cases with Wheat, the supernatant water was colourless, but in this it had a dirty, muddy, yellowish colour. The mass emitted a foul disagreeable odour, though not so intense as that of the corresponding Barley.

Barley (a)—Seeds, in Soil with 50 *cub. cent. water.*—The organic matter thoroughly decomposed; stems, roots, and leaves no longer distinguishable in the soil; other conditions about as those with the corresponding Wheat *a*.

Barley (b)—Seeds, in Pumice with 100 *cub. cent. water.*—The pumice covered with a black coating of organic matter; supernatant water clear. The odour of the air above the mixture exceedingly disgusting, resembling that of decaying excrements; traces of sulphide of hydrogen perceptible. The form of the seeds is preserved, but the shell contains only fluid.

Barley (c)—Meal, in Soil with 40 *cub. cent. water.*—Supernatant water yellowish; odour musty, but not very disagreeable. Decomposition so complete that traces of organic matter are hardly perceptible.

Bean (a)—Seed, in Soil with 50 *cub. cent. water.*—The organic matter well decomposed. Odour musty.

Bean (b)—Seeds, in Pumice with 50 *cub. cent. water.*—Plants well decomposed; only very indefinite skeletons of stems, leaves, and roots remaining. Odour musty, but not disagreeable.

Bean (c)—Meal, in Soil with 40 *cub. cent. water.*—Supernatant water slightly yellow. Odour musty, but not offensive.

The last description, dated August 28, refers to the state of the respective masses just before being dried for analysis. After drying, any slight remains of organic matter had become brittle; and the substance, in every case excepting where 100 cub. cent. water had been added at the commencement, presented the appearance of clean soil or pumice, without organic matter. In the excepted cases the shell of the grain was still visible. If we take into consideration the amount of growth in several of the cases on April 28, it will be seen how great must have been the subsequent decomposition so entirely to get rid of the organic matter.

It is worthy of remark, that, in a few instances, the sulphuric acid in the bottle D, fig. 8, Plate I., became coloured slightly brown, indicating the passage into it, through the oxalic acid, of some carbon-compound more complicated than carbonic acid. In the course of other parts of our investigation, we have observed phenomena indicative of a similar result; but as we have not followed up the subject, we leave it with only this remark as to the fact of what we have observed.

The following Tables (VIII. and IX.) show the numerical results of the investigation now under consideration :—

TABLE VIII.—Showing the conditions provided in Experiments on the Decomposition of Nitrogenous Organic Matter; and the amount and proportion of the original *Carbon* of the substance remaining after the decomposition, or given off during the process.

Substances involved in the Experiment.				Weight of Organic Matter.		Carbon in Organic Matter.			
Organic Matter.		Matrix.	Water.	Fresh.	Dry.	Before Decomposition.	After Decomposition.	Loss in Decomposition.	
Description.	Condition.							Actual quantity.	Per cent.
			cub. cent.	grammes.	grammes.	grammes.	grammes.	grammes.	
1. Wheat	a. 171 seeds	Ignited soil	50	8·0475	6·7438	3·1089	0·9274	2·1815	70·17
	b. 171 seeds	Ignited pumice ...	100	8·0715	6·7639	3·1182	0·9178	2·2001	70·56
	c. Meal	Ignited soil	40	9·8810	8·2803	3·8172	1·3199	2·4973	65·42
2. Barley	a. 163 seeds	Ignited soil	50	8·0440	6·7127	3·0523	0·9598	2·0925	68·55
	b. 163 seeds	Ignited pumice ...	100	8·1360	6·7895	3·0872	1·1952	1·8920	61·28
	c. Meal	Ignited soil	40	8·9671	7·4830	3·4025	1·0995	2·3030	67·68
3. Beans	a. 7 seeds	Ignited soil	50	5·7830	4·5830	2·2915	0·8511	1·4404	62·86
	b. 7 seeds	Ignited pumice ...	50	6·4700	5·1275	2·5637			
	c. Meal	Ignited soil	40	6·1750	4·8937	2·4468	0·9778	1·4690	60·04

TABLE IX.—Showing the conditions provided in Experiments on the Decomposition of Nitrogenous Organic Matter; the amount and proportion of the original *Nitrogen* remaining after the decomposition, or given off during the process; together with the amount *evolved* as *Ammonia*, or remaining in the products *as such*.

Substances involved in the Experiment.				Total Nitrogen in Organic Matter.				Nitrogen in the form of Ammonia.			
Organic Matter.		Matrix.	Water.	Before Decomposition.	After Decomposition.	Loss (or Gain).		Total quantity.	Per cent.	Absorbed by Oxalic acid during Decomposition.	
Description.	Condition.					Actual quantity.	Per cent.			Actual quantity.	Per cent.
			cub. cent.	grammes.	grammes.	grammes.		grammes.		grammes.	
1. Wheat	a. 171 seeds	Ignited soil ...	50	0·1392	0·1398	+0·0006	+ 0·43	0·0429	30·83	·00038	0·273
	b. 171 seeds	Ignited pumice	100	0·1396	0·1214	0·0182	13·08	0·0573	41·06	·00002	0·014
	c. Meal	Ignited soil ...	40	0·1709	0·1680	0·0029	1·74	0·0197	11·49	·00040	0·234
2. Barley	a. 163 seeds	Ignited soil ...	50	0·1247	0·0746	0·0501	40·20	0·0157	12·64	·00055	0·441
	b. 163 seeds	Ignited pumice	100	0·1261	0·1052	0·0209	16·62	0·0294	23·30	·00002	0·016
	c. Meal	Ignited soil ...	40	0·1390	0·1311	0·0079	5·66	0·0166	11·97	·00039	0·280
3. Beans...	a. 7 seeds ...	Ignited soil ...	50	0·2417	0·2107	0·0310	12·84	0·0140	57·01	·00341	1·424
	b. 7 seeds ...	Ignited pumice	50	0·2704	0·2380	0·0324	11·99	......	......	·00242	0·895
	c. Meal	Ignited soil ...	40	0·2581	0·2267	0·0314	12·16	0·1039	40·25	·00060	0·232

A comparison of the results in Tables VII. and IX. will show that they are confirmatory of each other as to their more general indications. Both series agree in the entire absence of any tangible relation between the varied circumstances of decomposition, and the products of that decomposition.

It is quite evident that, whilst in some instances there has been no evolution of Nitrogen, in others the amount of decomposition involving such evolution has been very great. Indeed, in some cases, the indication of the loss of Nitrogen in this way is so great that we could not have believed such a result possible had it not been attested by repeated analysis. But we have not been able to trace these differences to their ultimate causes.

The amount of decomposition, as indicated by the physical condition of the several substances at the termination of the experiment, as also by the proportion of carbon given off as shown in Table VIII., might lead to the conclusion that the process had gone about equally far, and attained about an equal completeness, in all the cases to which Tables VIII. and IX. refer. But here the equality of effect ceases. Thus, from 60 to 70 per cent. of the total carbon in the original organic matter has passed off; but the proportion of the original Nitrogen that is not recovered in the products varies, under the same circumstances, from 0 to 40 per cent. of it. The proportion of the Nitrogen of the original substance which was retained in the mass, or absorbed in the oxalic acid in the bulb-apparatus (C) in such form as to be given off as ammonia on distillation from a weak alkaline solution, and which probably existed, therefore, in the products as ammonia, ranged from 12 to 58 per cent. of the total quantity involved in the experiment. And, again, the proportion of the Nitrogen evolved from the mass as ammonia during the decomposition, and which was retained in the oxalic acid solution (C), varied from 0 to about 1·5 per cent. of the original or total Nitrogen.

If we attempt to trace a relation between the loss of carbon, the loss of nitrogen, the formation of ammonia, and the evolution of the small amounts of it during the decomposition, on the one hand, and the circumstances of matrix, moisture, growth, decay, &c., pointed out in the notes preceding the Tables, we fail to discover any connexion which we may with safety regard as exhibiting cause and consequence.

The most that we can venture to say is that, under a wide range of circumstances, a considerable loss of Nitrogen occurs in the decomposition of nitrogenous organic matter; that under particular, and apparently rather rare circumstances, this loss of Nitrogen does not occur; that the proportion of the Nitrogen taking, under the same circumstances, such form that it may be driven off as ammonia on the distillation of the products with a weak solution of alkali, varied from one-eighth to more than one-half of the total present; and that the amount of the Nitrogen evolved from the mass as ammonia during the process was quite inconsiderable.

These conclusions, though necessarily expressed in very general terms, have nevertheless a very important bearing on certain questions in practical agriculture. Whilst it would appear that there may be a very great loss of Nitrogen—a very important element in manure—under circumstances of decomposition of organic matter, closely allied to those to which, in practice, nitrogenous organic manures are subject, it is at the same time indicated that it is possible for such matters to pass through the process of decomposition without such loss. The importance of further investigation is hence suggested, to ascertain the causes of the difference of effect, in order, if possible, to control them. The results also point to the insignificance of the loss of Nitrogen in the form of ammonia, a supposed evil to which the attention of agricultural chemists has specially been directed in order to find means of preventing it, though nothing has as yet been done to avoid the loss, in apparently much larger quantity, of free Nitrogen. But as these questions are more appropriate for consideration in a purely agricultural paper, we shall not follow them further in this place.

Other investigations, to which we have to call attention, will throw some light upon the character of the molecular forces by which the decomposition of nitrogenous organic compounds is effected under such circumstances as we have been considering. These forces might be one or both of two kinds.

1. They might be of an oxidizing character, analogous to that of the action of chlorine upon ammonia by which free Nitrogen is evolved.

2. They might be of a reducing character, similar to that of a great number of substances upon the oxygen-compounds of Nitrogen, by which the oxygen of the latter is appropriated, and free Nitrogen given off.

3. These two actions may operate in succession the one to the other.

It is well known that an oxidizing action may be so intense as to deprive a nitrogenous organic compound of all its carbon and hydrogen, converting it into oxygen compounds, as is done by permanganic acid. The converse action of the transformation of oxygen-compounds of Nitrogen into ammonia is also very well known. An intermediate stage in either of these converse actions may give free Nitrogen.

There can be little doubt that the Nitrogen in the organic substances which we have submitted to decomposition existed in them in a condition more analogous to a hydrogen than to an oxygen compound of it. The able researches of HOFMANN into the nature of compounds formed upon the ammonia type, would lead us to suppose that the Nitrogen compounds upon which we have been operating are of the ammonia class. They are more difficult to oxidize into nitric acid than is ammonia; yet their transition into ammonia is so easy, that it is effected in almost all the chemical changes to which they are ordinarily subjected. And, since ammonias yield free Nitrogen under the influence of oxidizing forces, it may be inferred that it has been under the influence of such forces that Nitrogen has been set free in the cases recorded above. PELOUZE has remarked* that salts of nitric acid are converted into ammonia, in contact with decomposing organic matter. Experiments of our own have shown that, during the decomposition of organic matters in contact with nitrates, free Nitrogen is not evolved. The evolution of free Nitrogen in the experiments quoted above must, therefore, be referred to the action of oxidizing forces.

The experiments next referred to bear upon these points.

* Comptes Rendus, xliv. p. 118.

E.—*Experiments on the action of the oxidizing and reducing forces, as manifested in the decomposition of organic matters containing Nitrogen.*

Several qualitative experiments showed that when cereal grains and leguminous seeds were placed in water, over mercury, an evolution of gas took place, after about thirty-six to forty-eight hours. This went on rapidly for a week or two, after which all action appeared to cease, no more gas being evolved. The total quantity of gas evolved varied between 20 and 50 cub. cent. from 3 to 4 grammes of the seeds. An examination of the gas proved it to be almost entirely carbonic acid and hydrogen, the quantity of Nitrogen being very small.

To examine this action more thoroughly, about half a pound of a mixture of Wheat, Barley, and Beans was taken, put into a long narrow glass vessel (fig. 7, Plate XII.) of about 500 cub. cent. capacity, which was then filled with well-boiled water, and closed with a cork, through which two glass tubes (*a* and *b*) passed. The external ends of these tubes were fitted with caoutchouc tubing, for closing with pinch-cocks, or connexion with the Torricellian exhauster as described at p. 487. One of the tubes being so connected with the exhauster, it was allowed so to remain for several hours, in order to remove all the gaseous Nitrogen from the seeds. The vessel was then inverted in mercury, with one of the tubes (*b*) open under that fluid, and the whole placed in sunlight to favour the decomposition. This was done on the 28th of August, 1858. The seeds commenced swelling very soon, and on the 30th of August well-marked decomposition had set in.

On September 13th the vessel was about two-thirds full of gas, the displaced water having passed out through the quicksilver. Part of the seed was now above the water, in the gas, which commenced bubbling out through the tube (*b*). The arrangement was allowed so to remain until October 5, when 400 cub. cent. of gas were collected, of which the percentage composition was as follows:—

	Carbonic acid.	Hydrogen.	Nitrogen.
Experiment 1	64·87	34·83	0·30
Experiment 2	64·54	35·46	traces.

The quantity of the gas evolved points to the extent of the decomposition; the amount of carbonic acid and hydrogen shows how great must have been the reducing force exerted; and the small quantity of Nitrogen, which was probably due to accident, indicates that free Nitrogen was not a product of the action.

The vessel was again filled with boiled water, again connected for some time with the Torricellian exhauster, and again placed in its former position in the sunlight.

October 9.—A small bubble of gas collected in the top of the vessel.

November 3.—Only a few bubbles of gas at the top of the vessel.

November 17.—The vessel was removed into the laboratory and placed in a room, the temperature of which varied from a few degrees above the freezing-point to about 24° C.

December 1.—Very little gas evolved.

December 12.—The gas collected without exhaustion measured only 6·1 cub. cent., of which 4·6 were absorbed by potash, and the remainder proved to be combustible. Hence, up to this date, there has been no appreciable evolution of free Nitrogen. In order to see whether the organic matter present would reduce a nitrate, with the evolution of free Nitrogen, about 5 grammes of saltpetre were now put into the vessel, and it was replaced in the same room as before.

May 3, 1859.—Several times since December 12, 1858, when the nitrate of potash was put in, the vessel has been warmed up to 30° C.; but up to this date very little gas has been evolved.

May 25, 1859.—Still very little gas evolved; 4 cub. cent. only collected, one-fourth of which was carbonic acid, and the remainder was combustible. The vessel was now placed in the sunlight again, but up to the middle of June no further evolution of gas had taken place. The fluid still contained nitrate of potash. The vessel was then half filled with oxygen in order to see if this would cause a renewal of the decomposition. After ten days a portion of the gas was examined, when it was found that not one-fourth of the supplied oxygen had been consumed—a result which was quite unexpected. The total gas being removed, the vessel was again nearly filled with oxygen, driving out the greater part of the fluid, and leaving the partly decomposed seeds in an atmosphere of this gas. The apparatus so arranged was placed in the sunlight, and remained there during some very warm weather.

July 12, 1859.—The gas collected contained in 100 parts—

Carbonic acid.	Oxygen.	Nitrogen.
20	79	1

By accident a small quantity of air was admitted into the vessel, so that the analysis can only be taken to show how exceedingly slow was the oxidation of organic matter which had been treated as this had been.

On the removal of the matters from the vessel, the Beans were found to possess much of their original firmness and solidity. The other seeds, though they retained their form, were softer, and they had evidently undergone a more complete decomposition. They emitted very little odour, which was not unpleasant.

There can be no question as to the absence of any evolution of free Nitrogen during the long period that these three descriptions of seed were under experiment. A very small proportion of the combined Nitrogen present would, if set free, have been sufficient to fill the vessel with gas. But, as has been seen, only a few bubbles of gas were evolved during several months.

Several other experiments were made upon the products of the decomposition of organic matter, in the first stages of the process. In Table X., which follows, are given the amounts, and the composition, of the gas obtained from decomposing organic matter in a few out of a number of cases in which we have had occasion to observe them—including, for comparison, some of the results already referred to. The decomposition took place in water, in vessels similar to that used in the experiments last described (fig. 7, Plate XII.).

TABLE X.—Showing the products of the action of the reducing forces exercised in the decomposition of Nitrogenous organic matter, as exhibited by the composition of the gases evolved.

Description of Organic matter subjected to Decomposition.	Total Gas collected.	Composition of the Gas, Per Cent.		
		Carbonic acid.	Hydrogen.	Nitrogen.
	cub. cent.			
a. Wheat, Barley, and Bean seed ...	400	64·87	34·83	0·30
		64·54	35·46	traces.
b. Turnip plant; root with leaves ...	166·2	76·23	22·91	0·87
c. Turnip plant; root with leaves ...	162·2	68·83	23·93	7·24
d. Turnip plant; root with leaves ...	123·6	68·06	25·63	6·31
		67·52	25·43	7·05
e. Turnip plant; root with leaves ...	41·2	64·95	14·66	20·39

The first experiment (*a*) is that which has been considered above. In all the other cases about two ounces of young Turnip Plant, the root and leaves together, were operated upon. They were exposed in similar vessels to those used in the other experiments, from August 29 to October 5. At the termination of this period the structure of the plant was almost entirely destroyed; and there remained only a mass of decomposed matter deposited at the bottom of the vessels. The evolution of gas had entirely ceased.

The Turnip plant (*b*) was exhausted of its gas before exposure; and, as will be seen, there was, under these circumstances, a very small quantity of free Nitrogen found at the termination of the experiment.

All the other Turnip plants were submitted to decomposition without previous exhaustion; and hence the amount of Nitrogen eventually found. In the last experiment (*e*) there is a much larger percentage of Nitrogen than in the other cases. But the total quantity of gas was much less; and the comparison of this result with the others shows that there was an almost constant actual quantity of Nitrogen in the several cases, doubtless due to that existing within the plant at the commencement of the experiment. Hence it appears that, in the absence of free oxygen, no free Nitrogen is evolved from the nitrogenous compounds of the plant.

At all events the entire cessation of the evolution of gas after the decomposition has gone on for a few days, shows that the presence of free oxygen is essential to the evolution of Nitrogen, as it is conducive to that of carbonic acid. The loss of Nitrogen indicated in Tables VII. and IX. must be considered, therefore, to be the result of an oxidizing process.

We shall have to allude again to the results given in Table X. when we come to discuss the question of the formation of ammonia from the free Nitrogen of the air, and the nascent hydrogen evolved during the decomposition of organic matter.

In order to examine the character of the decomposition of organic matter in oxygen gas, an investigation was undertaken, which, owing to the difficulty of getting the requisite apparatus sufficiently air-tight, was not followed up to the extent which had been intended.

The plan proposed was, to place the organic matter in an atmosphere of pure oxygen, and to afford a constant supply of the gas as it became converted into carbonic acid, and was absorbed by a solution of caustic potash.

The results obtained go to show that, in the presence of free oxygen, Nitrogen gas is evolved. But as the investigation is as yet so incomplete, owing to the circumstance above alluded to, we prefer not to give the results until we can confirm them by a more extended series of experiments under more favourable conditions.

Taking together the results of all the experiments which have been made upon the decomposition of nitrogenous organic matters, they obviously point to a serious difficulty in the way of experiments made upon the question of the assimilation of free Nitrogen by plants. It is not possible to conduct any such experiments without exposing nitrogenous organic matter to conditions more or less analogous to those under which the loss of Nitrogen recorded in Tables VII. and IX. took place. For although, as BOUSSINGAULT has shown, there may be no loss of Nitrogen during germination, yet, during the entire period of the growth of a plant, certain portions of the vegetable substance may be subjected to conditions favourable to the decomposition of its nitrogenous compounds, and to the evolution of free Nitrogen.

As illustrative of how far these conditions are likely to be operative in the manner indicated, the following results, made with Wheat, Barley, and Oats respectively, are very instructive. Seeds of the three plants were sown, each in precisely the same kind and amount of soil, &c., as employed in the experiments on the assimilation question. The three pots were placed beneath a large glass shade, 16 inches in diameter, which fitted into the groove of a stone-ware lute-vessel, into which sulphuric acid was poured to exclude the access of external air. The whole stood on a table in the diffused light of the laboratory. The plants were at first supplied with distilled water; but with no carbonic acid beyond that which might be contained in the water. These conditions afforded all that was necessary for germination and growth, with little opportunity for the assimilation of free Nitrogen, even were this possible in the more favourable conditions of sunlight. Yet the conditions were more than ordinarily favourable to the decomposition of nitrogenous compounds, provided this would take place, under certain circumstances, during the growth of the plant. The succulent character of the stems and leaves so grown in the shade, would render the nitrogenous matters more liable to decomposition than in the case of the more firm and hardened stems of plants grown in sunlight.

Eight seeds of each plant were sown; and in a few days all came up, and grew very rapidly in height, without much tendency to development and expansion of leaf. The plants were all very much alike—tall, slender, delicate, and having the peculiar pale-green colour common to plants deprived of sufficient sunlight. In several other experiments it was found that plants which had proceeded for some t me in this delicate form of growth, immediately ceased this predominant upward tendency when removed into sunlight: then, after remaining stationary for a few days, during which time the extremities of the long delicate leaves lost their vitality, the plants commenced a new order of growth, producing many more leaves, which were much shorter and broader than the earlier ones; the stems also became thicker and more dense than before.

The seeds were put in on May 17 (1858); and on June 10 following, the plants had ceased to grow. Several of the long slender stems were too delicate to support themselves, and began to fall over. All the plants presented much the same appearance, each with a small sheath without any leaf at the base, and three leaves higher up—the two lateral ones being very long, from 8 to 12 inches, and the terminal ones, not unrolled, from 3 to 4 inches long from the axial of the next leaf below, the whole plant being from 7 to 11 or 12 inches high. On removing them from the soil, it was found that the roots were distributed very little through it. They consisted of short fibrils, with divaricated branchlets, extending principally around the seeds, and seldom more than 2 or 3 inches through the soil. The plants were so very much alike, that it was difficult to distinguish the different kinds. Fig. 9, Plate XII., is reduced from a sketch of one of these attenuated plants.

The following Table gives the quantitative particulars of the experiments.

TABLE XI.—Showing the effect of Germination, and Growth without direct Sun-light, or extraneous supply of Carbonic Acid or combined Nitrogen, upon the combined Nitrogen originally provided in the Seed.

Duration of experiment twenty-four days—from May 17 to June 10, 1858.

Particulars of the seed sown.					Dry vegetable matter produced.			Nitrogen.			
Description.	No.	Weight, fresh.	Weight, dry.	Nitrogen.	Stems.	Roots.	Total.	In stems and roots.	In soil and pot.	In total products.	Gain or loss.
		gramme.	gramme.	gramme.	gramme.	gramme.	gramme.	gramme.	gramme.	gramme.	gramme.
Wheat	8	0·4865	0·4077	0·00790	0·320	0·140	0·460	0·00697	0·0012	0·00817	+0·00027
Barley	8	0·3875	0·3234	0·00573	0·290	0·160	0·450	0·00570	traces	0·00570	−0·00003
Oats	8	0·3475	0·2900	0·00640	0·355	0·060	0·415	0·00640	traces	0·00640	+ traces

The weights given for the roots are a little too high, owing to their not having been washed entirely free from soil, the principal object being to ensure a correct result with regard to the Nitrogen which long washing might have endangered, or at least rendered less easy. There is, however, evidently a slight gain of dry matter, which, so far as its carbon is concerned, was doubtless due to carbonic acid in the distilled water, of which about 500 cub. cent. were added to each pot at the commencement of the experiment. None was added during the progress of the experiment; but the soil was moist when the plants were taken up.

The rapid growth of the plants, the short period of their contact with the soil, the very limited distribution of the roots, and the fact that no water was added during growth, which would tend to distribute any soluble or otherwise easily transportable matters, are conditions all consistent with the almost total absence of Nitrogen in the soil.

Lastly in regard to the results in the Table (XI.), the final column, showing the gain or loss of Nitrogen, affords us the means of judging how far the molecular actions by which free Nitrogen was given off in the cases of the experiments upon the decomposition of nitrogenous organic matter are likely to interfere with the results of our investigations on the question of assimilation of free Nitrogen by plants. It is seen that, in the experiments now under consideration, no free Nitrogen was given off during the process of germination and growth. At least, the assumption that free Nitrogen was given off implies the still more improbable one, that, under the circumstances detailed, assimilation of free Nitrogen has taken place; whilst the adoption of these two assumptions necessitates the yet more improbable one, that these two independent actions bear a most definite relation to each other—in fact, that the amount of free Nitrogen assimilated is exactly equal to that given off during decomposition.

It would appear, therefore, that we may rest satisfied that our results in regard to the question of assimilation will not be affected by a loss of free Nitrogen as the result of the decomposition of nitrogenous organic matter, so long as that matter is subjected to the ordinary process of germination, and exhaustion to supply materials for growth. Our results in regard to the products of decomposition of nitrogenous organic matter do, indeed, point to the danger of using nitrogenous organic manure in such experiments, and to the error that might occur from seeds decomposing in the soil instead of growing, or from the decomposition of dead leaves, of old roots, or of nitrogenous organic excretions; but they do not afford any evidence of what takes place within the range of the action of the living plant. And, judging from the amount of free Nitrogen evolved when, as in the experiments on decomposition, so large a proportion of the nitrogenous organic matter was decomposed, we may form some idea of the probable extent of such evolution when, as in experiments where vegetable growth is involved, and where the only nitrogenous organic matter supplied is that in the seed sown, but a small proportion of the total nitrogenous matter undergoes decomposition.

In relation to this question, it should be borne in mind that, in the cases where the large evolution of free Nitrogen took place, the organic substances were subjected to decomposition for a period of about six months, during which time they lost three-fourths of their carbon. In the experiments on the question of the assimilation of free Nitrogen, however, but a very small proportion of the total organic matter is subjected to decomposing actions apart from those associated with growth, and this for a comparatively short period of time, at the termination of which the organic form is retained, and therefore but little carbon is lost. It would appear, then, that we need not fear any serious error in our experiments in regard to the latter question, arising from the evolution of free Nitrogen in the decomposition of the nitrogenous organic matters involved. On the other hand, the facts adduced afford a probable explanation of any small loss of Nitrogen which may occur when seeds have not grown, or when leaves, or other dead matter, have suffered partial decomposition.

F.—*The mutual relations of Gaseous Nitrogen and the Nascent Hydrogen evolved during the decomposition of organic matter.*

The importance attached by MULDER, and others after him, to the action of nascent hydrogen, evolved in the decomposition of organic matter, upon gaseous Nitrogen, as a source of ammonia, is such as to require that we should refer to the subject here, in the course of the discussion of the conditions possibly affecting the supply of combined Nitrogen to our experimental plants. The results given in the last sub-section (pp. 509–511), leave no doubt of the evolution of hydrogen during the decomposition of organic matter. They suggest, therefore, the possibility that such an evolution may take place in any decomposition of organic matter involved in our experiments on the assimilation of free Nitrogen by plants, and hence prove a source of ammonia to them.

That nascent hydrogen may, under certain circumstances, combine with gaseous Nitrogen, has long been admitted. But the view so prominently put forth by MULDER*, and some others, that those circumstances occur in the evolution of nascent hydrogen accompanying the decomposition of organic matter, requires confirmation.

If only a very small part of the hydrogen evolved in the decomposition of organic matter were to form ammonia with the Nitrogen gas which must always be in most intimate contact with it, the amount of ammonia formed in this way would be enormous. Peat bogs, cesspools, and all stagnant water pregnant with organic matter, as well as many soils, would be constantly so accumulating ammonia. The extensive forests in different parts of the world, which have been annually depositing a coating of leaves upon the surface of the soil for thousands of years, must also have been a very fertile source of ammonia, as the leaves have gradually decayed under the influence of moisture and confined air beneath the succeeding layers. And when we contemplate the amount of decomposition that must have corresponded to the very exuberant growth of former geological periods, as manifested in the remains exhibited in our coal beds and limestones, we see a source of ammonia, if formed in the manner now under consideration, which would be incalculable.

The results given in the last subsection (E), upon the decomposition of nitrogenous organic matter, favour the view that the hydrogen evolved in such decomposition does not form ammonia with the Nitrogen of the air. The assumption that it did so, implies that the nascent hydrogen was capable of uniting with free gaseous Nitrogen (forming ammonia) under circumstances in which its affinities were not sufficiently powerful to prevent Nitrogen compounds very similar to ammonias (and which are easily transformed into them) from giving up Nitrogen in the free state. It implies also, that the nascent hydrogen can act upon ordinary Nitrogen, when it cannot do so upon this nascent Nitro-

* Chemistry of Vegetable and Animal Physiology, pp. 111–114, 149–152, &c.

gen of the decomposing nitrogenous body. Or, if it did act upon the latter in preference to the former, there would either be no free Nitrogen finally evolved, or, in case of Nitrogen being lost in the free state, it would be obvious that there had been less nascent Nitrogen converted into ammonia than had been liberated from its combinations, and hence that, as a resultant, there would be a *loss* and *not a gain* of combined Nitrogen due to the decomposition.

The fact that, in our experiments upon the gas evolved by vegetable matters in a state of decomposition, both free Nitrogen and free hydrogen were given off, bears strongly upon this question. The Nitrogen evolved has been in most intimate contact with the hydrogen given off. It has, indeed, been in the identical cells by the decomposition of the walls or contents of which the hydrogen was set free; yet both appear as gas.

From the above considerations it would appear that we need be under little apprehension of error in the results of our experiments on the question of the assimilation of free Nitrogen by plants, arising from an unaccounted supply of ammonia formed under the influence of nascent hydrogen, given off in any decomposition of the organic matter involved in the experiment.

Summary Statement of the Results of the foregoing consideration of the conditions required, or involved, in Experiments on the question of the assimilation of free Nitrogen by Plants.

Before entering upon the discussion of the results of our direct experiments upon the question whether or not plants assimilate free Nitrogen, it will be well, for the sake of perspicuity, to give a very brief enumeration of the results arrived at in the foregoing Sections I. and II. (Part II.), relating to the conditions of experiment required, and to the collateral investigations involved, in the inquiry. They may be stated as follow:—

1. Conditions of soil or matrix which are both adapted for healthy growth and are consistent with the other requirements of the investigation can be attained (Section I. Sub-sections A, p. 470, and L, p. 484).

2. The requirements of the experiment in regard to the selection of seeds or plants for growth, to the nutriment to be supplied in the soil, to the water, to the atmosphere, to the carbonic acid, and to other conditions involved, can be satisfactorily met (Section I. Sub-sections B–J, inclusive, pp. 472–481; and L, p. 484).

3. The conditions of experiment adopted have several advantages over some of those which have been suggested, or adopted, by others (Section I. Sub-section K, pp. 481–483).

4. The mutual actions of the soil, air, organic matter in the soil or in the plant, are not such as to be likely to affect the result of the experiment, by yielding to the plants a quantity of combined Nitrogen not taken into account. The influence of Ozone as a possible element in these actions would be less, in the circumstances of the experiments

on ssimilation, than in those of experiments the results of which showed no appreciable formation of compounds of Nitrogen (Section II. Sub-sections A–C, pp. 484–497).

5. The fact of the evolution of free Nitrogen during the decomposition of nitrogenous organic matter has been confirmed by experiment; but the circumstances of the decomposition in which the evolution of free Nitrogen was observed, when compared with those involved in an experiment on the question of assimilation, are not such as to lead to the conclusion that there would be a loss of Nitrogen from this source in experiments of the latter kind, unless in certain exceptional cases, in which it might be presupposed (Section II. Sub-section D, pp. 497–508).

6. The forces, by virtue of which free Nitrogen is eliminated from its compounds in organic matter, are of an oxidizing character; they are not exercised in the absence of oxygen. They are not likely to be operative in connexion with growing vegetable matter (Section II. Sub-section E, pp. 950, 951).

7. Although it is known that, under certain circumstances, nascent hydrogen may combine with free Nitrogen and form ammonia, it is questionable whether the nascent hydrogen eliminated during the decomposition of vegetable matter will be in the conditions to effect such a combination; nor are the circumstances of our experiments on the question of the assimilation of free Nitrogen by plants such as to lead to the supposition, that an error in the results can arise from the formation of any ammonia under the influence of the action supposed (Section II. Sub-section F, pp. 515, 516).

Section III.—CONDITIONS OF GROWTH UNDER WHICH ASSIMILATION OF FREE NITROGEN BY PLANTS IS MOST LIKELY TO TAKE PLACE; DIRECT EXPERIMENTS UPON THE QUESTION UNDER VARIOUS CIRCUMSTANCES OF GROWTH.

A.—*General consideration of conditions of growth.*

We have thus far discussed, in some detail, the arrangement adopted in our experiments on the question of the assimilation of free Nitrogen by plants, and the collateral points involved in the relation of gaseous Nitrogen to vegetation. In regard to the latter, we have dwelt particularly on those which relate to the sources of available Nitrogen to plants, and which, therefore, may tend to influence the quantitative results which we may obtain by the methods of experimenting followed. It remains to consider what are the circumstances under which it is most probable that free Nitrogen may be assimilated, provided the assimilation can take place at all.

The demonstration of the fact, that the process of cell-development could go on in the presence of free Nitrogen without the latter becoming incorporated into the cell wall, or into the contents of the cell, as a nitrogenous compound, would not carry with it the demonstration that free Nitrogen could, under no conditions of growth, undergo such change. Our aim should be, therefore, to seek the most probable circumstances for such change; and if we find that in them free Nitrogen is assimilated, we should then trace up the question through the circumstances in which such assimilation is less likely to take place.

If, on the contrary, we find that free Nitrogen is not assimilated under the circumstances which appear the most favourable for such an action, we may either generalize for other conditions from the negative results so obtained, or we may extend our experiments in order to widen the basis of our generalizations.

In the consideration of what are the cases in which the assimilation of free Nitrogen is most likely to take place, two important classes of conditions present themselves:—

1. Those which relate to the supply of combined Nitrogen at the disposal of the plant.

2. Those which relate to the activity of growth and stage of development of the plant.

These two questions, though logically distinct, are physiologically blended; for it may happen that a certain activity of growth, or certain stages of development, can only be attained by a given supply of combined Nitrogen beyond that contained in the seed.

If we examine these conditions a little more closely, we see that they give us the following possible cases for the assimilation of free Nitrogen by the plant:—

1. The plant may be able, in the process of cell-formation, to derive the whole of its Nitrogen from that presented to it in the free state.

2. It may be capable of assimilating a part of its Nitrogen from that presented to it in the free state, provided it be supplied with only a part of its required amount in some form of combination.

3. It may assimilate free Nitrogen in the presence of an excess of combined Nitrogen.

Again:—

1. It may be capable of assimilating free Nitrogen in the earlier stages of its development.

2. It may be so at the most active period of its growth.

3. It may when near the period of its maturity.

Combinations of these several circumstances present at least nine special cases, in one of which, if at all, an assimilation of free Nitrogen might take place without its doing so in any of the others. The question arises, how are we so to arrange our experiments as to include the greatest number of these cases, and those in which the assimilation of free Nitrogen is the most likely to occur?

The obviously most probable circumstances for the assimilation of free Nitrogen at any stage of development of the plant, are those in which it is brought to that stage in a healthy condition, and then deprived of all sources of combined Nitrogen. It is hardly to be supposed that an assimilation of free Nitrogen would take place if there were an excess of combined Nitrogen at the disposal of the plant; for, if we suppose that the molecular and vital forces are at the same time acting upon Nitrogen supplied by these two sources, in a manner tending to force that from both into the constitution of the living organism, it is only consistent with our established notions of force, that the form which yields with the greatest ease will yield first, and that, if its supplies be in sufficient quantity, it only will yield in an appreciable degree to the force applied.

If, on the other hand, the forces involved in vegetable growth, tending to form nitrogenous compounds, are capable of appropriating free Nitrogen only in the presence of a certain amount of assimilable combined Nitrogen, then the question of deciding upon the proper proportion of combined Nitrogen to effect the assimilation of that provided in the free state would seem, *à priori*, to present serious difficulty. For if the plant cannot assimilate free Nitrogen either in the presence of an excess of combined Nitrogen, or without the aid of a certain amount of it, it would, at first sight, appear that there might be some difficulty in so arranging an experiment as to hit the proper medium.

But within a certain range of conditions this supposed difficulty would not occur. If the assimilation of free Nitrogen be possible only as the result of the assimilating forces acting upon it in the presence, or with the aid, of a certain amount of combined Nitrogen, then, when the quantity of combined Nitrogen has become too small, the point must have been passed at which the maximum amount of free Nitrogen would be assimilated in relation to the then existing supply of combined Nitrogen. Hence, the analysis of a plant at the period at which its growth ceased in consequence of the falling short of the relative supply of Nitrogen in the combined form, would show whether or not an assimilation of free Nitrogen had taken place as the result of either of the conditions referred to in the last paragraph.

If, however, the plant cannot assimilate free Nitrogen under the conditions of the supply of combined Nitrogen just referred to, unless it has attained a certain vigour of growth, or reached a certain stage of its development, and the supply of combined Nitrogen has been insufficient to bring it to the supposed requisite point, then no assimilation of Nitrogen would take place, even though it might do so provided the proper stage of growth had been passed. To the cases here supposed we shall recur further on.

If the assimilation of free Nitrogen can take place at all periods of the growth of the plant, and in the absence of all sources of combined Nitrogen, the solution of our question becomes much more simple than in either of the cases above referred to.

In illustration of the fact that, within a certain range of other conditions, there can be no difficulty in securing in an experiment those involved in the presence of an excess, of a certain limited quantity, or of no combined Nitrogen, attention may be directed to the phenomena of vegetable growth when seeds are grown in a soil and atmosphere free from combined Nitrogen.

Under the circumstances supposed, all the conditions with regard simply to the relative quantity of combined Nitrogen are afforded. Thus, when the seed is first sown, it contains within itself an excess of combined Nitrogen, so far as the demands of the plant at the time are concerned. The rapidity with which the Nitrogen of the seed can be used, in the growing process, is seen in the results of the experiment in regard to the question of the decomposition of Nitrogenous matter during growth, as given in Table XI. (p. 513); and the extent to which it can carry the growth of the plant is illustrated in that experiment, as well as in others, to which we shall presently refer, relating to the question of assimilation itself. It is obvious that, during a part of the time at the end of which the plant has reached the limit of its supply of combined Nitrogen, it has had at its disposal an excess of combined Nitrogen for its immediate wants. It has then passed through a stage in which the particular relation of combined to free Nitrogen implied in another of our assumed conditions must have existed. It must finally have reached a point at which only free Nitrogen was presented to it.

If an analysis of the plant at the termination of the last-mentioned period showed no increase of Nitrogen, the result would afford conclusive evidence against the possibility of the assimilation of free Nitrogen under a wide range of conditions. If, on the contrary, a gain of Nitrogen were indicated, the question would still be open, to which of the several conditions to which the plant had been subjected it owed the increase found. But this question we need not discuss until we have recorded the results of our experiments on the point.

B.—*Direct experiments on the question of the assimilation of free Nitrogen by plants.*

We have thus far discussed the methods of experimenting to be adopted, the results of certain collateral inquiries, and the several conditions under which the assimilation of free Nitrogen by plants may be the more or the less likely to take place. We have thus endeavoured to eliminate all known sources of error, and to acquire the means of forming an estimate of the possible influence of certain unknown quantities, and so, as far as practicable, to reduce the solution of our question to that of a single point to be tested by direct experiment. It remains to consider the experimental evidence relating to this last and final point.

An investigation requiring several hundred analyses, and a series of observations made at intervals of a few days, through periods of several months, involves an amount of recorded detail much too voluminous for full publication. An abstract of the most important portions of the records will, however, be given for reference in the Appendix. A statement of the methods of analysis adopted, with illustrations of the limits of accuracy reached, together with a condensed summary of the details of growth of the plants, will there be given.

In the selection of the plants to submit to our adopted conditions of experiment, we have been guided by several considerations:—

1. To have such as would be adapted to the conditions of temperature, moisture, &c., to which they were to be subjected.

2. To have such as were of importance in an agricultural point of view.

3. To acquire the means of studying any difference, in reference to the point in question, between plants which belong respectively to the two great Natural Orders

the Graminaceæ and the Leguminosæ, which, in some points of view, appear to differ so widely in their demands upon combined Nitrogen provided within the soil.

4. To take such as had already been experimented upon, with such conflicting results, by M. BOUSSINGAULT and M. G. VILLE.

We shall first consider the results obtained with plants grown without any other supply of combined Nitrogen than that contained in the seed sown.

I.—*Experiments in which the plants had no other supply of combined Nitrogen than that contained in the seed sown.*

The following Table (XII.) gives, at one view, a summary of the numerical results obtained under this head; see also figs. 1–6, Plate XV., which are reduced from careful drawings taken of six out of the nine Graminaceæ experimented upon, and illustrate the character and extent of growth attained under the conditions in question.

After the full discussion in the foregoing pages of the circumstances under which the results recorded in the Table just given were obtained, but little need be said in pointing out their bearings upon the question at issue. The column showing the gain or loss in each experiment speaks for itself. In judging of the results of the experiments of 1857, the remarks made in discussing the results of Table XIV. (p. 532), with regard to the slates used as lute-vessels in that year, must be taken into consideration. The source of error referred to being obviated in the experiments of 1858, the results of 1857 acquire a greater value, as confirming those of the latter year, than, standing alone, they would possess.

The difference between the results obtained with soil and with pumice as matrix, in 1857, are not such as to lead us to attach any importance to them, or to attribute them in any way to the difference of matrix in question. The two experiments may therefore simply be considered as duplicates. Indeed, the character of the results in the one experiment with Wheat, and in the two with Barley, in 1857, was so similar, that the three experiments may be considered as triplicates.

Graminaceous Plants.

It will be observed that the largest gain of Nitrogen in the three experiments with Graminaceæ in 1857 was 0·0026 gramme. Keeping in view the probable source of error due to the use of slates in that year, and the difference of result in 1858 when slates were not employed, and, again, considering the fact that so small an amount of Nitrogen had to be determined in such a large amount of soil (0·003 gramme or less of Nitrogen in about 1500 grammes of soil), it seems indeed more than questionable whether the gain should not be attributed to the errors of experiment or analysis alluded to. In fact, we can but conclude that, under the circumstances of growth of the Graminaceous plants to which Table XII. relates, there has been no assimilation of free Nitrogen.

It should also be noticed that, even when a gain of Nitrogen in the total products is observed, there is, in no case, more Nitrogen in the plant itself than in the original

TABLE XII.—Showing the Numerical Results of Experiments to determine whether Plants supplied with no other combined Nitrogen than that contained in the original seed assimilate Free or uncombined Nitrogen.

General particulars of the Experiments.				Numerical particulars of the seeds sown.					Numerical results at the termination of the Experiments.					Summary.		
				Number.		Weights.			Dry weights of Plants produced.	Nitrogen.						
Year, &c.	Description of Plant.†	Description of soil or Matrix.	Period of Experiment.	Sown.	That grew.	Fresh.	Dry.	Nitrogen.		In total Plant.	In Soil.	In Pot.	In condensed water.	Nitrogen in seeds sown.	Nitrogen in total products.	Gain or loss of combined Nitrogen.
								Graminaceæ.								
						gramme.	gramme.	gramme.	gramme.	gramme.	gramme.	gramme.	gramme.	gramme.	gramme.	gramme.
1857 ...	Wheat (1) ...	Prepared soil ...	May 16—Oct. 3	6	5	0·3658	0·3065‡	0·0080	1·412	0·0072	traces	traces	......	0·0080	0·0072	—·0008
	Barley (2) ...	Prepared soil ...	May 20—Aug. 24	6	6	0·3230	0·2698	0·0056	0·810	0·0047	0·0024	0·0001	......	0·0056	0·0072	+·0016
	Barley (3) ...	Prepared pumice	May 20—Aug. 25	6	6	0·3233	0·2698	0·0056	0·925	0·0045	0·0030	0·0007	......	0·0056	0·0082	+·0026
1858 ...	Wheat (1) ...	Prepared soil ...	April 27—Oct. 25	8	8	0·4815	0·4035	0·0078	1·740	0·0056	0·0025		traces	0·0078	0·0081	+·0003
	Barley (2) ...	Prepared soil ...	April 27—Aug. 18	8	6	0·3860	0·3221	0·0057	0·560	0·0031	0·0027		traces	0·0057	0·0058	+·0001
	Oats (3)	Prepared soil ...	April 27—July 13	8	8	0·3425	0·2858	0·0063	1·148	0·0042	0·0011		0·0003	0·0063	0·0056	—·0007
1858, A.*	Wheat	Prepared soil ...	June 11—Nov. 6	8	7	0·4810	0·4031	0·0078	1·060	0·0041	0·0033		0·0004	0·0078	0·0078	0·000
	Barley	Prepared soil ...	June 11—Nov. 6	8	8	0·3840	0·3240	0·0057	0·710							
	Oats	Prepared soil ...	June 11—Nov. 6	8	7	0·3450	0·2879	0·0064	0·690	0·0038	0·0021		0·0004	0·0064	0·0063	—·0001
								Leguminosæ.								
1857	Bean (4)	Prepared soil ...	May 16—July 5	2	2	1·8907	1·4984	0·0796	7·028	0·0629	0·0146	0·0016	......	0·0796	0·0791	—·0005
1858 ...	Bean (5)	Prepared soil ...	June 11—Aug. 23	3	3	1·8700	1·4820	0·0750	4·875	0·0735	0·0016		0·0006	0·0750	0·0757	+·0007
	Pea (6)	Prepared soil ...	June 5—Aug. 24	3	3	0·6436	0·5405	0·0188	0·370	0·0102	0·0056		0·0009	0·0188	0·0167	—·0021
								Other Plants.								
1858	Buckwheat (7)	Prepared soil ...	Aug. 20—Oct. 28	24	13	1·0000	......	0·0200	0·450	0·0070	0·0108		0·0004	0·0200	0·0182	—·0018

* These experiments were conducted in the apparatus of M. G. VILLE.

† The numbers given in brackets are those under which the respective plants are described in the "Abstract of the Records of growth of the Plants," given in the Appendix, p. 548 *et seq.*

‡ The percentage of dry matter in the seed was not determined in this case; it is therefore assumed to be the same as in the wheat used in 1858, from which it would certainly not differ at all materially.

seed,—the gain appearing only when the Nitrogen in the soil and pot is taken into account. It will be remembered that the results of the experiments on the question whether there was an evolution of Nitrogen during germination and growth (Table XI., p. 513) showed how completely the plants could appropriate the Nitrogen of the seed from which they grew, leaving only traces of it in the soil. Again, the experiments on the decomposition of Nitrogenous organic matter (Tables VIII. and IX., p. 506) have shown how thorough was the decomposition coincident with the passage of any large percentage of the combined Nitrogen of the substance into the soluble state of ammonia. Taking together these facts, we have strong grounds for assuming that at least a part of the Nitrogen found in the soil, in the cases where there was a gain of it in the total products, has never been in actual connexion with the plant at all. Indeed, in view of the facts just referred to, any gain of Nitrogen in connexion with the plant, without there being a larger quantity of Nitrogen in the plant itself than that provided in the seed, would be very questionable evidence upon which to establish the fact of the assimilation of free Nitrogen.

But the results obtained with Graminaceæ in 1858, when all possible sources of error which the experience of the previous year had suggested had been eliminated, point, without exception, to the fact that, under the circumstances of growth to which the plants were subjected, no assimilation of free Nitrogen has taken place. The regular process of cell-formation has gone on; carbonic acid has been decomposed, and carbon and the elements of water have been transformed into cellulose; the plants have drawn the nitrogenous compounds from the older cells to perform the mysterious office of the formation of new cells (see Notes on growth, Appendix, pp. 559, 561); those parts have been developed which required the smallest amount of Nitrogen; and all the stages of growth have been passed through to the formation of glumes, pales, and awns for the seed. In fact, the plants have performed all the functions that it is possible for a plant to perform when deprived of a sufficient supply of combined Nitrogen. They have gone on thus increasing their organic constituents with one constant amount of combined Nitrogen, until the percentage of that element in the vegetable matter is far below the ordinary amount of it—that is, until the composition indicates that further development had ceased for want of a supply of available Nitrogen.

Throughout all these phases, water saturated with free Nitrogen has been passing through the plant; nitrogen dissolved in the fluid of the cells has constantly been in the most intimate contact with the contents of the cells and with the cell-walls. The newly forming cell, stunted in its development for want of assimilable Nitrogen, has nevertheless been surrounded by free Nitrogen. Its delicate membranes have been saturated with water, itself saturated with free Nitrogen; and such are the laws in accordance with which the absorption of gases, and the transmission of liquids through membranes take place, that the instant a part of the Nitrogen of the saturated fluid became assimilated, the equilibrium would be restored, by the penetration into the cell of other saturated liquid, and the re-saturation of that from which Nitrogen had been withdrawn. It would hardly be supposed that, under such circumstances, the process of cell-formation could go on without the assimilation of free Nitrogen, provided any forces were exerted in the cell the tendency of which was to fix free Nitrogen in the organism of the plant.

One fact, briefly alluded to above, we wish to call more special attention to, as affording strong evidence of the absence of the power on the part of these cereal plants to appropriate free Nitrogen—namely, the very large development of the root, requiring but little Nitrogen compared with that of other parts. It was observed, in the experiments of 1857, that several of the cereal plants developed a large proportion of root; but the danger of accident in analysis was such, that we hesitated to double the risk of losing the entire result by analysing the root and the portion of the plant above ground separately. They were, therefore, thoroughly mixed, and the mixture was carefully divided; so that, in case of accident, a duplicate was at our disposal, and in case of all going well, confirmatory evidence was obtained. So very marked, however, was the great development of root in the cereals of 1858, that, in several cases, it was analysed separately from the other parts of the plant. The remarkable result was obtained, that this great root-development was carried on (in two, at least, out of the three instances in question) with a consumption of an almost incredibly small amount of Nitrogen, as the figures given in the following Table will show:—

TABLE XIII.

Description of Plant. 1858.	Dry Matter in Produce (at 100° C.), grammes.			Nitrogen in Produce (grammes).			Per cent. of Total Dry Matter in Roots.	Per cent. of Total Nitrogen in Roots.
	In Stems, &c.	In Roots.	In Total Produce.	In Stems, &c.	In Roots.	In Total Produce.		
Wheat (1)	0·890	0·850	1·740	0·0039	0·0017	0·0056	48·85	30·36
Barley (2)	0·400	0·160	0·560	0·0027	0·0004	0·0031	28·57	12·90
Oats (3)	0·798	0·350	1·148	0·0040	0·0002	0·0042	30·49	4·76

The large proportion of root and its small proportion of Nitrogen, as here exhibited, are equally remarkable. Whether this great power of the plant to develop root be due to the fact that the process of cell-formation in the root requires less of the nitrogenous protoplasmic compound, or to the fact that, floating in water as these roots generally were, that fluid facilitated the withdrawal of the nitrogenous constituents resulting from the decomposition of protoplasma from the old cells, to form new protoplasma for the more active cells, is a question which, though foreign to our present subject, is of considerable interest in a physiological point of view. The fact that the roots from the base of the stem penetrated the soil, giving off very few branches into it, but immediately on reaching the water at the bottom of the pot exhibited such a remarkable development (see Notes on taking up the Wheat Plants, Appendix, p. 560), is in favour of the inference that the water afforded the necessary conditions for the character of growth referred to.

But, apart from the physiological points just referred to, as already said, this great development of a part of the plant requiring a minimum amount of Nitrogen affords strong evidence of its inability to assimilate free Nitrogen within the range of development possible when no combined Nitrogen is provided beyond that contained in the original seed. It exhibits the great tenacity of growth of the plant, and shows the activity of the vital force, long after the demands of the organism had begun to require more available Nitrogen than was at its disposal. When it is considered how great was the length of time during which the growing cells were exposed to the conditions in question, there would seem to be a combination of circumstances favourable to the exercise of any force tending to bring free Nitrogen into the constitution of the plant. But no such effect is manifested in the results.

The Graminaceæ referred to in the Table (XII.) under the Title of "1858, A.," and which were grown in the enclosing apparatus of M. G. VILLE, as already alluded to, give results quite similar in their bearings on the main question to those of 1857 and 1858 already discussed. Being sown later, however, and their period of growth being shorter, they did not manifest such an extraordinary development of root; nor was there so large an amount of vegetable matter produced. Unfortunately the barley grown in M. VILLE's Case without artificial supply of combined Nitrogen, was lost by the giving way of the tube in the combustion for the determination of Nitrogen. In its case, therefore, we can only give the amount of the dry matter of the plants produced. But, comparing this with that of the seed sown, and looking to the proportions of Nitrogen in the produce of barley in the other cases, there is no reason to believe that the result would have formed any exception to that indicated in the other experiments.

In concluding our remarks on the results with the Graminaceæ grown without any further supply of combined Nitrogen than that contained in the seed sown, we would beg to refer the reader to the foregoing consideration of the conditions possibly favourable to the assimilation of free Nitrogen (p. 517 *et seq.*).

It will be remembered that, in experimenting with Graminaceæ, including some of the same description as those experimented upon by ourselves, M. BOUSSINGAULT and M. G. VILLE obtained most unaccountably discordant results. It will be seen that our own results, from nine experiments with such plants, go to confirm those of M. BOUSSINGAULT. In fact, so far as our labours with these plants bear upon their experiments, they could not have given a more decided result.

For representations of some of the Graminaceæ grown without any supply of combined Nitrogen beyond that contained in the original seed, see figs. 1 to 6, Plate XV.

Leguminous Plants.

It still remains to consider the results of our experiments with Leguminous plants grown under similar conditions to those of the Graminaceous ones above discussed, and to see how far they serve to explain the known characteristics of such plants when grown in practical agriculture, to which attention has been directed in Part First of this Paper.

It will be remembered that, under equal circumstances of soil and season, Leguminous crops yield two, three, or more times as much Nitrogen per acre as Graminaceous ones. Yet, whilst the latter are very characteristically benefited by the use of direct nitrogenous manures, the former, yielding so much more Nitrogen, are not so. Again, the Graminaceous crop, requiring for full produce such direct supply of available Nitrogen within the soil, is very much increased, beyond what it would be if it succeeded a crop of the same description, when it follows a Leguminous crop, in which has been carried off so much Nitrogen.

Experiments such as those now specially under consideration can obviously bear upon a few only of the circumstances with which may be connected the causes of this difference between the Graminaceous and the Leguminous crops. Without, therefore, pretending adequately to discuss this wide subject, we will consider it only so far as our immediate facts appear to bear upon it; they seem to limit us to the consideration of the following cases:—

1. The difference may be due to the decomposition of nitrogenous compounds during the growth of the Graminaceous plants, and to the evolution of free Nitrogen.

2. The Leguminous plants may assimilate the free Nitrogen of the air, and thus, not only allow the resources of the soil to accumulate, but also leave within it an additional quantity, in roots and other vegetable débris, from that which has been assimilated, as above supposed.

3. It may be due to the operation of both these causes.

So far as the facts we have already considered go, the difference in question cannot be explained according to the first of the above suppositions; and others, to which we shall have presently to refer, will be seen to afford confirmatory evidence on the point.

With regard to the second supposed explanation, the results we have now to record of our experiments with Leguminous plants are not of themselves sufficient to settle every point which it involves. Reference to the Appendix will show that, in several cases, we failed to get healthy growth with Leguminous plants. A doubt might hence be raised, as to the value of those experiments in which we were successful under circumstances so nearly identical with those of our failures that it was not easy to account for the difference of result obtained. In those cases, however, in which we have succeeded in getting Leguminous plants to grow pretty healthily for a considerable length of time, the results, so far as they go, confirm those obtained with Graminaceæ, not showing in their case, any more than with the latter, an assimilation of free Nitrogen.

In 1857, we commenced several experiments with beans, but they grew well in only one of the shades. These, however (especially one plant out of the two in the same pot), progressed remarkably well for a period of 10 weeks, during which time the amount of carbon was increased five-fold, more than three-fourths of the total Nitrogen of the seed was appropriated, and the plants probably only ceased to grow when the remainder of the latter became so distributed in the soil as not to be available to them.

A reference to Table XII. will show the numerical results of this experiment with beans in 1857.

The beans and peas of 1858, the particulars of which are also given in Table XII., did not grow so satisfactorily as the beans of 1857, last noticed. Yet the beans of 1858 gave more than three times as much organic matter in the produce as was contained in the seed, and they appropriated even a much larger proportion of the Nitrogen of the seed than did those of 1857. The result with the peas was not so satisfactory, owing to the less healthy character and the more limited amount of their growth.

From the fact that these Leguminous plants did not go through a complete course of growth to the flowering process, it may be objected that hence they did not pass certain stages of growth in which they might possibly assimilate free Nitrogen. We shall refer to this objection again further on. At present we confine attention to the important fact, that active growth has taken place—that the process of cell-formation, with the accompanying one of the decomposition of carbonic acid and the fixation of carbon, has gone forward with a deficient supply of combined Nitrogen, and in the immediate presence of free Nitrogen, and yet none of it has been assimilated. The plants have in fact been subjected to a considerable range of the conditions which were considered, *à priori*, to be favourable to the assimilation of free Nitrogen; and yet this has not taken place.

It is a fact observed in agriculture, that manures rich in organic matter frequently favour the growth of Leguminous crops. We shall not here discuss the question whether these organic manures, as such, act simply as a source of carbonic acid, or of carbon compounds of a more complicated character. We would, however, call attention to the fact that, in the case of the experiments now under consideration, the vital forces were sufficiently energetic to perform the function of cell-development and multiplication, from carbonic acid as its source of carbon; yet these forces, capable of effecting this result, have been incapable of effecting the appropriation of free Nitrogen.

Buckwheat.

The evidence afforded by the numerical results in the Table XII. relating to this plant is not of so decisive a character as that with regard to the cereals, or even to the Leguminous plants; for the quantity of dry matter in the produced plants is less than that in the seed sown, whilst the Nitrogen in the plants is little more than one-third that of the seed. But when we come to compare the results of the experiments with Buckwheat grown with and without the supply of ammonia, it will be found that the physiological evidence of the dependence of vegetable growth upon a constant supply of combined Nitrogen is stronger in the case of these plants than in that of the cereals. The small proportion of the total Nitrogen of the seeds which the buckwheat seemed capable of appropriating might lead to the inference that, ceasing to grow with an abundance of combined Nitrogen apparently at its disposal, it had done so for some other reason than the want of available Nitrogen. But this question was set at rest by the fact that, on the addition of an amount of ammonia very small in its contents of

Nitrogen compared with the seed, to plants at the time in a precisely similar condition to those now under consideration, the increase in the rapidity of growth was most marked.

Most of the buckwheat seed sown came up; but about half of the plants lived for only a few days. The remainder, which survived, went through all the stages of development to flowering; but the entire amount of growth was on a very limited scale.

Reference to the last column of Table XII. will show that, under the conditions of growth above described, the buckwheat, like the plants already discussed, indicated no gain of Nitrogen. In fact there appeared to be a loss in the experiment of nearly 2 milligrammes of Nitrogen; and that the result should be to a small extent in this direction may, perhaps, be accounted for by the fact of some of the plants dying early, in consequence of which there may have been a slight evolution of free Nitrogen due to decomposition.

Bearing of the above results on the question of the evolution of free Nitrogen from the Nitrogenous Constituents of plants during growth.

We have thus far only considered the above results so far as they bear upon the question of the assimilation of free Nitrogen by plants. But from the constancy of the amount of combined Nitrogen maintained in relation to that supplied, throughout the experiments, they afford evidence of an important kind in regard to the converse question of whether plants give off free Nitrogen during growth. With no less force than they point to the absence of any assimilation of free Nitrogen, do these results show that, under the circumstances of growth involved, there has been no evolution of free Nitrogen from the nitrogenous compounds of the growing plant. At all events, the assumption that an evolution of free Nitrogen has taken place implies, as in the case of the experiments discussed at pp. 513, 514, the still more improbable one, that there has been an exactly compensating amount assimilated. But since the conditions of the experiments now under consideration were arranged with special reference to the question of assimilation, they necessarily do not embrace all the circumstances which, *à priori*, would be considered the most favourable for the evolution of free Nitrogen during growth.

Various experimenters, from the time of De Saussure until quite recently, have entertained the idea of the probability of the decomposition of nitrogenous compounds, and the concomitant evolution of free Nitrogen, during the growth of plants. We are ourselves engaged in following up the subject, by methods better qualified to settle the question than those adopted in regard to the question of assimilation of Nitrogen. We shall therefore not treat of this subject any further here, than to call attention to the incidental bearing upon it of the results now under consideration.

The fact that there has been no decomposition of nitrogenous compounds and loss of Nitrogen as the result of growth, in the particular conditions to which these experimental plants were subjected, affords little evidence that no such decomposition could take place under any other circumstances. When supplied with an insufficient quantity of nitrogenous matter, the vegetable organism might not decompose any of that matter; and yet, when an excess of combined Nitrogen was supplied, the decomposition might occur. The results we have given, therefore, afford evidence against the fact of such decomposition only within a very limited range of circumstances of growth. In discussing the results of the experiments the consideration of which we are now about to enter upon, we shall refer to this question again, in connexion with circumstances of growth which we should suppose would be more favourable to an evolution of free Nitrogen by the plant.

II.—*Experiments in which the plants had a known supply of combined Nitrogen beyond that contained in the Original seed.*

We have thus far considered the subject of the assimilation of free Nitrogen, by reference to the results of experiments upon plants grown without any supply of combined Nitrogen beyond that contained in the seed sown. We have found that, under these conditions, we have only been able to study the results of growth of a very limited character. The wheat, and barley, and oat plants, grown in 1858, did indeed progress so far as to produce glumes and pales for seed; but they did not afford the opportunity of studying the results of growth during the period of the formation and the ripening of seeds themselves.

It yet remains to consider, therefore, what may take place under circumstances of a more active and vigorous growth, and at a later stage of development of the plant. When considering the conditions apparently the most favourable for the assimilation of free Nitrogen by plants (p. 517 *et seq.*), we suggested the improbability of such an assimilation taking place in the presence of an abundant supply of combined Nitrogen. If the force of our remarks on this point be admitted, and it be still supposed that an assimilation of free Nitrogen is possible with vigorous growth, only attainable by means of a liberal supply of combined Nitrogen, we seem to be led to the following paradoxical conclusions:—

1. Healthy, active, and vigorous growth are favourable conditions for the assimilation of free Nitrogen by plants.

2. Healthy, active, and vigorous growth can only be attained by keeping within the reach of the plant an excess of combined Nitrogen.

3. Assimilation of free Nitrogen cannot take place in the presence of an excess of combined Nitrogen.

À priori conclusions with regard to the effect of molecular forces, and particularly of those which give rise to vital phenomena, are, however, very unsafe; and we have not been satisfied to rely upon such evidence only, in reference to the question under investigation, as could be afforded by experimenting with plants grown without an extraneous supply of combined Nitrogen. We have found that active and vigorous growth cannot be attained under the conditions provided, when no more combined Nitrogen than that contained in the seed sown is supplied. We have made a series of experiments, in which such growth was attained by means of a supply of combined Nitrogen beyond that contained in the seed. It remains to see whether, under these conditions of growth, the assimilation of free Nitrogen can take place, and thus the above paradox be obviated by the proof that the last of the three suppositions is incorrect.

It is true that we have pointed out the improbability of an assimilation of free Nitrogen in the presence of an excess of combined Nitrogen only so far as the vital process of the vegetable cell is concerned. In that intermediate process by which oxygen is taken up and carbonic acid formed in the cell, the results due to an excess of combined Nitrogen might be different.

Thus, the more active the growth, the greater must be the amount of newly-formed carbon-matter capable of consuming oxygen, when the plant is removed from the influence of sunlight into the dark. That is to say, the more vigorous the growth in the sunlight, the greater might be the reducing power of the plant in the dark. The greater the reducing power of the plant, the more nearly will the tendency of its molecular forces approximate to an evolution of hydrogen which, in the presence of free Nitrogen dissolved in the fluids of the cell, may tend to form ammoniacal compounds, to be, on the return of light, appropriated by the plant in the exercise of its growing functions. In connexion with this point, it may be here mentioned that in our investigation of the gases given off by plants under different circumstances, we have had an evolution of oxygen one day as a coincident of growth, and an evolution of hydrogen the next as the result of decomposition.

Our experiments in which the plants have been manured with limited amounts of combined Nitrogen will not only enable us to meet some of the questions above suggested, but they will also prove whether or not the conditions of soil, atmosphere, temperature, &c., to which our experimental plants have been subjected were consistent with active and vigorous growth.

The fact of the evolution of Nitrogen in the decomposition of nitrogenous organic matter, illustrated in Sub-section D, p. 497 *et seq.*, indicated the danger of using such matter as a source of supply of Nitrogen. We have therefore used solutions of sulphate of ammonia (see Appendix, p. 542), by means of which we have been enabled to supply the plants with known quantities of combined Nitrogen at pleasure, as the progress of growth seemed to require.

In the following Table (XIV.) are given the numerical results of the experiments on the question of the assimilation of free Nitrogen in which the plants were supplied with combined Nitrogen beyond that contained in the seed sown. See also figs. 7, 8, 9, 10, 11, and 12, Plate XV., showing the character and extent of growth of six Graminaceous plants with extraneous supply of combined Nitrogen, corresponding to the six above them without such supply.

TABLE XIV.—Showing the Numerical Results of Experiments to determine whether Plants supplied with known and limited quantities of combined Nitrogen beyond that contained in the original Seed assimilate free Nitrogen.

General particulars of the Experiments.				Numerical particulars of the seed sown, and of the combined Nitrogen added.							Numerical Results at the termination of the Experiment.					Summary.		
				Number of seeds		Weights of the seed sown		Nitrogen in seeds sown, and in manure.			Dry weights of Plants produced.	Nitrogen				Nitrogen in Seeds sown, and in Manure.	Nitrogen in Total Products.	Gain or Loss of Combined Nitrogen.
Year, &c.	Description of Plant.†	Description of soil or Matrix.	Period of Experiment.	Sown.	That grew.	Fresh.	Dry (at 100° C.).	In seeds.	In manure.	Total.		In total Plant.	In Soil.	In Pot.	In condensed water.			
Graminaceæ.																		
						grm.	grm.	grm.	grm.	grm.	grm.	grm.	grm.	grm.	grm.	grm.	grm.	grm.
1857	Wheat (6)	Prepared soil	May 16—Oct. 2	3	2	0·1830	0·1536‡	0·0040	0·0289	0·0329	6·835	0·0241	0·0133	0·0009	......	0·0329	0·0383	+0·0054
	Wheat (7)	Prepared pumice	May 16—Sept. 20	3	3	0·1838	0·1543‡	0·0040	0·0289	0·0329	3·822	0·0213	0·0102	0·0016	......	0·0329	0·0331	+0·0002
	Barley (8)	Prepared soil	May 20—Oct. 8	4	3	0·2160	0·1803	0·0037	0·0289	0·0326	3·034	0·0154	0·0171	0·0003	......	0·0326	0·0328	+0·0002
	Barley (9)	Prepared pumice	May 20—Sept. 24	4	4	0·2178	0·1818	0·0037	0·0231	0·0268	4·401	0·0145	0·0171	0·0021	......	0·0268	0·0337	+0·0069
1858	Wheat (9)	Prepared soil	April 27—Oct. 26	4	4	0·243	0·204	0·0040	0·0508	0·0548	7·31	0·0398	0·0138		traces	0·0548	0·0536	−0·0012
	Barley (10)	Prepared soil	April 27—Oct. 26	4	2	0·190	0·158	0·0028	0·0468	0·0496	5·47	0·0349	0·0113		0·0002	0·0496	0·0464	−0·0032
	Oats (11)	Prepared soil	April 27—July 30	4	3	0·174	0·145	0·0032	0·0280	0·0312	1·204	0·0125	0·0040		0·0051	0·0312	0·0216	−0·0096
1858, A.*	Wheat	Prepared soil	June 29—Dec. 9	4	4	0·246	0·206	0·0040	0·0228	0·0268	3·82	0·0181	0·0092		0·0001	0·0268	0·0274	+0·0006
	Barley	Prepared soil	June 29—Dec. 9	4	3	0·194	0·162	0·0029	0·0228	0·0257	2·98	0·0160	0·0081		0·0001	0·0257	0·0242	−0·0015
	Oats	Prepared soil	June 29—Dec. 9	4	2	0·173	0·144	0·0032	0·0228	0·0260	1·28	0·0146	0·0051		0·0001	0·0260	0·0198	−0·0062
Leguminosæ.																		
1858	Pea (13)	Prepared soil	April 27—Aug. 24	3	3	0·642	0·539	0·0187	0·0040	0·0227	1·01	0·0114	0·0086		0·0011	0·0227	0·0211	−0·0016
	Clover (14)	Prepared soil	June 6—Oct. 26	...	...	0·5015	......	0·0284	0·0428	0·0712	4·20	0·0313	0·0339		0·0013	0·0712	0·0665	−0·0047
1858, A.*	Bean	Prepared soil	June 29—Dec. 9	3	3	1·380	1·094	0·0523	0·0188	0·0711	4·30	0·0401	0·0253		0·0001	0·0711	0·0655	−0·0056
Other Plants.																		
1858	Buckwheat (16)	Prepared soil	Aug. 20—Nov. 22	42	24	1·0000	0·850	0·0200	0·0402	0·0308	1·97	0·0183	0·0101		0·0008	0·0308	0·0292	−0·0016

* These experiments were conducted in the apparatus of M. G. VILLE.

† The numbers given in brackets are those under which the respective plants are described in the "Abstract of the Records of growth of the Plants" given in the Appendix, p. 548 *et seq.*

‡ The percentage of dry matter in the seed was not determined in these two cases; it is therefore assumed to be the same as in the wheat used in 1858, from which it would certainly not differ at all materially.

As in the case of the experiments already considered, so again with those to which the Table just given relates, it is seen, by reference to the last column, that there was a slight gain of Nitrogen in the experiments of 1857, but, almost without exception, a loss rather than a gain in those of 1858. Considering that there was a possible source of gain in 1857 in connexion with the slates used in that year (as explained below), and with the results of 1858 showing generally a loss rather than a gain when slates were not employed, we can interpret the whole in but one way.

In order to bring out fully the evidence afforded by these results of experiments in which the plants were supplied with more or less of combined Nitrogen during the progress of growth, we must consider them in three separate aspects:—

1. As regards the actual gain or loss of Nitrogen, as indicated by the figures given in the last column of the Table (XIV.).

2. As presented in the physiological evidence afforded during growth.

3. As exhibited on comparison with the experiments in which the plants had no other supply of combined Nitrogen than that of the original seed.

1. *The Numerical Results of Table XIV.*

Much that has been said with respect to the plants grown without extraneous supply of combined Nitrogen applies with equal force to those now under consideration; and, so far as the evidence relating to the latter is of a different character, owing to the amount of combined Nitrogen at the disposal of the plants, it still is no more indicative of an assimilation of free Nitrogen than was that obtained with the plants grown without any artificial supply of combined Nitrogen.

In illustration of the probability that the slates used as lute-vessels were a source of Nitrogen to the plants grown in 1857, some of the observations made during growth should be adverted to. It is seen that the barley grown in pumice (1857) gives the largest gain of Nitrogen; and it was observed that, soon after watering with the fluid drawn off from the surface of the slate, the pumice became covered with a slight coating of green matter. And nearly all the slates were found at the end of the experiment to have a slight coating of similar character beneath the pans in which the pots which contained the plants stood; whilst, in the experiments of 1858, when glazed earthenware lute-vessels were employed, no such phenomenon was observed.

The slight loss of Nitrogen exhibited in the experiments of 1858 is easily accounted for on a consideration of the conditions involved. With regard to the peas, clover, and beans, the physiological circumstances of growth detailed in the Appendix, taken in connexion with the evidence that has been adduced as to the loss of Nitrogen during the decomposition of nitrogenous organic matter, must be supposed to explain the loss in their case, as in some of the experiments in which no extraneous supply of combined Nitrogen was employed.

The loss of Nitrogen indicated in the cases of the wheat, barley, oats, and buckwheat (1858) would not be so easily explained, had not the Nitrogen in the drain-water remaining at the end of the experiment been determined. Our object in doing this was twofold:—

1. To ascertain whether the luting at the bottom of the shade had allowed rain-water to pass, thus affording a source of combined Nitrogen to the plants.

2. To see if the plants growing in soil to which combined Nitrogen was added, had evolved any ammonia.

It was, of course, not possible to accomplish both these purposes. But the fact that ammonia was found in the condensed water only in the cases where there was a *loss* in the total quantity of combined Nitrogen would lead to the inference that both the presence of ammonia in this water, and the loss of combined Nitrogen in the experiment, were due to the same cause.

The condensed water showing the amount of combined Nitrogen recorded in the Table (XIV.) was that which had been evaporated and condensed during the last four weeks of growth (1858); and during this period the high temperature, and the advanced stage of the plants, were favourable to the evaporation of ammoniacal water. A considerable part would condense on the interior of the shade, owing to its comparatively low temperature; but a certain quantity of that which was in the state of vapour during the passage of the air through the apparatus would be borne forward into the sulphuric acid in the bulb-apparatus M, and thus occasion a loss in the amount of combined Nitrogen determined in connexion with the plants. The reason why the loss is greater with the oats (as it is in both experiments) than with the other cereals is not perfectly clear; but the circumstances of growth seemed to afford some explanation of the fact. In one case, at least, they ripened at a much warmer period of the season, and they became much drier in stem and leaf, and were therefore more liable to evolve ammonia. On these points, the circumstances of growth detailed in the Appendix should be consulted.

In considering the column of gain or loss of Nitrogen, it is very desirable to take into account the total quantity of Nitrogen at the disposal of the plant, in the different series of experiments. It is also important to consider the amount of growth in the experiments made under the different conditions. The following Tables (XV. and XVI.) bring out the character of the results in these respects more clearly than they can be gathered from Tables XII. and XIV. Table XV. shows, for the plants grown without supply of combined Nitrogen beyond that contained in the seed, and Table XVI. for those grown with such supply, the dry matter, and the Nitrogen, per seed sown,—the dry matter, and the Nitrogen, in the total produce of each seed that grew,—and the per cent. of the total Nitrogen at the disposal of the plant which it appropriated. Finally, the last two columns of Table XVI. show the amounts of dry matter, and of Nitrogen, in the produce grown with the extraneous supply of combined Nitrogen, in relation to those in the produce grown without such supply.

TABLE XV.

General particulars of the Experiments.			Number of Seeds.		Dry Matter.			Nitrogen.			
Year, &c.	Description of Plants.	Description of Soil or Matrix.	Sown.	That grew.	Per seed sown.	In the Produce, per seed that grew.	In Produce, that in seed taken as 1.	Per seed sown.	In the Produce, per seed that grew.	In Produce, that in seed taken as 100.	Per cent. in Dry Produce.
Gramineæ.											
					grm.	grm.		grm.	grm.		
1857 ...	Wheat ...	Prepared soil	6	5	0·0511	0·2824	......	0·00133	0·00144	108·3†	0·51
	Barley ...	Prepared soil	6	6	0·0449	0·1350	3·01	0·00093	0·00078	83·9	0·58
	Barley ...	Prepared pumice .	6	6	0·0449	0·1542	3·43	0·00093	0·00075	80·6	0·48
1858 ...	Wheat ...	Prepared soil	8	8	0·0504	0·2175	4·31	0·00098	0·00070	71·4	0·32
	Barley ...	Prepared soil	8	6	0·0403	0·0933	2·31	0·00071	0·00052	73·2	0·54
	Oats	Prepared soil	8	8	0·0357	0·1435	4·02	0·00080	0·000525	65·6	0·36
1858, A.*	Wheat ...	Prepared soil	8	7	0·0504	0·15143	3·00	0·00098	0·00058	59·2	0·38
	Barley ...	Prepared soil	8	8	0·0401	0·0888					
	Oats	Prepared soil	8	7	0·0360	0·09857	2·74	0·00080	0·00054	67·5	0·55
Leguminosæ.											
1857	Bean	Prepared soil	2	2	0·7492	3·514	4·69	0·03980	0·03145	79·0	0·89
1858 ...	Bean	Prepared soil	8	3	0·4940	1·6250	3·29	0·02500	0·0245	98·0	1·51
	Pea	Prepared soil	3	3	0·1802	0·3233	1·79	0·00630	0·0034	54·0	1·05
Other Plants.											
1858	Buckwheat	Prepared soil	24	13	......	0·03461	......	0·00083	0·00054	65·1	1·56

TABLE XVI.

General particulars of the Experiments.			Number of Seeds.		Dry Matter.			Nitrogen.				Relation of Produce per seed with Ammonia, to that without it taken as 1.	
Year, &c.	Description of Plants.	Description of Soil or Matrix.	Sown.	That grew.	Per seed sown.	In Produce, per seed that grew.	In Produce, that in seed taken as 1.	Per seed sown.	In the Produce, per seed that grew.	In Produce, that in seed and manure taken as 100.	Per cent. in Dry Produce.	Dry Matter.	Nitrogen.
Gramineæ.													
					grm.	grm.		grm.	grm.				
1857 ...	Wheat ...	Prepared soil	3	2	0·0512	3·4175	66·75	0·00133	0·01205	73·2	0·35	12·10	8·36
	Wheat ...	Prepared pumice .	3	3	0·0514	1·2740	24·79	0·00133	0·00710	64·7	0·55	4·51	4·93
	Barley ...	Prepared soil	4	3	0·0451	1·0113	22·42	0·00092	0·00513	47·2	0·51	7·49	6·58
	Barley ...	Prepared pumice .	4	4	0·0455	1·1002	24·18	0·00092	0·00362	54·1	0·33	7·13	4·85
1858 ...	Wheat ...	Prepared soil	4	4	0·0510	1·8275	35·83	0·00103	0·00935	72·8	0·54	8·40	14·21
	Barley ...	Prepared soil	4	2	0·0395	2·7350	69·24	0·00070	0·01745	70·5	0·64	29·31	34·21
	Oats	Prepared soil	4	3	0·0362	0·4013	11·08	0·00080	0·00416	45·9	1·04	2·80	7·92
1858, A.*	Wheat ...	Prepared soil	4	4	0·0515	0·9550	18·54	0·00100	0·00452	67·5	0·47	6·31	7·79
	Barley ...	Prepared soil	4	3	0·0405	0·9933	24·52	0·00072	0·00533	62·2	0·54		
	Oats	Prepared soil	4	2	0·0360	0·6400	17·78	0·00080	0·00730	56·1	1·14	6·49	13·52
Leguminosæ.													
1858 ...	Pea	Prepared soil	3	3	0·1797	0·3366	1·87	0·00623	0·00380	50·2	1·13		
	Clover ...	Prepared soil	...	...	......	......	......	....	....	44·0			
1858, A.*	Bean	Prepared soil	3	3	0·3646	1·4338	3·93	0·01743	0·01337	56·4	0·93		
Other Plants.													
1858	Buckwheat	Prepared soil	42	24	0·0202	0·0821	4·06	0·00047	0·00076	57·6	0·92	2·37	1·41

* These experiments were conducted in the apparatus of M. G. VILLE.

† There is here evidence that a part of the Nitrogen of the seed that did not grow was appropriated by the plants growing from the other seeds.

There are several obvious inferences to be drawn from the figures in these Tables. To some we shall refer further on, in the proper order of the discussion. We here simply call attention to the very great increase of growth when an extraneous supply of combined Nitrogen was provided, as exhibited in the last two columns of Table XVI.

2. *Consideration of the Physiological Evidence as bearing upon the question of the assimilation of free Nitrogen.*

However directly the quantitative details given in the Tables may bear upon the question at issue, it is very important to consider them in connexion with the physiological details of the experiments. In order to estimate the value of the evidence afforded in this particular, the indications manifested from the earliest period of growth should be noticed.

Reference to the Notes of the progress of the plants, given in the Appendix, will show that all the plants when they first came up looked green and vigorous, indicative of their being at that period in circumstances embracing all the conditions essential to healthy growth. As already pointed out, they at that time were probably supplied with an excess of combined Nitrogen in relation to their immediate wants. After some days, varying with the nature of the plants, they began to lose their deep-green colour, and to assume a lighter-green, or pale-yellow tint, indicative of a want of combined Nitrogen. We have already pointed out how favourable, probably, would be the conditions here afforded for the assimilation of free Nitrogen, when the plant was passing from the state in which it had an excess to that in which it had a deficiency of combined Nitrogen for the demands of growth. The vigorous development of the plants grown in garden soil, but under the same conditions as to atmosphere, &c. as the other experimental plants, indicates that the conditions of atmosphere provided in the experiments were not at fault (see Appendix, Experiments Nos. 12, 1857, and 15, 1858; also fig. 13, Plate XV.). In order to test whether the sum of all the conditions, excepting those connected with a sufficient supply of combined Nitrogen, were appropriate for vigorous growth, we have only to provide some combined Nitrogen when the plants show the declining vigour just described; and if this be all they require, they will resume their healthy green colour. Or if we add the combined Nitrogen before the plants arrive at the period in question, it will prevent them assuming the pale-green or yellow colour. We have had recourse to both of these expedients; and each, so far as the Cereals, buckwheat, and clover are concerned, has yielded a result indicating that all the conditions of the experiments, excepting those connected with a sufficient supply of combined Nitrogen, were adapted for healthy growth.

The plants to which ammonia was given in 1857, were allowed to suffer more before they received it than those of 1858; yet in thirty-six hours after the addition of combined Nitrogen to the soil, in amount not exceeding $1\frac{1}{2}$ milligramme of the element to each plant, they began to manifest an improved appearance. In two or three days the improvement was quite marked; but at the termination of periods varying from nine to eighteen days, the plants seemed to have consumed all the combined Nitrogen supplied to them—or rather all of it that had not become inaccessible to them in the soil. They then began to manifest the same indications of defective supply as before. Plants so circumstanced must therefore, at a more advanced stage of growth than before they had been supplied with ammonia, have passed from a point at which they had an excess of combined Nitrogen, to that in which they had an insufficiency. They must hence, again, have been subjected to those conditions which we have assumed to be probably very favourable to the assimilation of free Nitrogen.

Reference to the details of growth given in the Appendix will show that several times during the progress of the plants the above phenomena were manifested. A new increment of combined Nitrogen caused a new increment of growth, a greener colour, and a more vigorous appearance generally. This was soon followed by the recurrence of the pale colour. In some instances, more ammonia was not supplied until the plants seemed almost past recovery: in a few cases they were quite so. The addition of ammonia now (excepting in the few cases just referred to) produced a revivification, to be followed in a short time by the indications of some want, and so on.

A considerable range of conditions of growth was thus provided. Just after each addition of combined Nitrogen the plants must have been supplied with an excess of this element in an available form. The evidence of this was afforded in the obviously increased means of consumption, evinced in the formation of new shoots from the base of the plants, or from their nodes. But these new shoots were too vigorous to allow the plants to go on long without suffering for want of a new supply of combined Nitrogen. In passing to this point, the newly-formed and vigorously-growing portion of the vegetable matter would be in the condition we have assumed to be the most favourable for assimilating free Nitrogen. Instead of doing this, however, it soon began to suffer, and continued to do so until a new supply of combined Nitrogen was added, when new vigour succeeded, to be followed again shortly by a cessation of growth. This cycle of conditions, repeated several times during the growth of the same plant, and the experiment similarly conducted with a number of pots of plants of different kinds, with like results in all the cases, affords a wide range of circumstances such as we have assumed to be favourable to the assimilation of free Nitrogen; but such an assimilation has not taken place.

Without the physiological details, it might not have been clear that the plant had not an excess of combined Nitrogen at its disposal during the greater period of its growth after the addition of the artificial supplies of it, since a considerable proportion of that added remained in the soil at the termination of the experiments, as Tables XIV. and XVI. show. But it is not difficult to imagine that a few milligrammes of ammonia intermingled with 1500 or 1600 grammes of soil (and pot), might become distributed over such an extent of surface, and be so completely absorbed, as that a considerable proportion should remain inaccessible to the plant. The physiological evidence leaves no doubt this was the case.

The Graminaceous plants of the experiments of 1858 were supplied with a considerable quantity of combined Nitrogen at an earlier period of growth than those of 1857 (see Tables showing the dates of addition, Appendix, pp. 542, 543), and they were not allowed to exhibit such marked signs of decline of vigour before receiving their fresh supplies. There is, however, no marked distinction in the proportion of the total supply appropriated by the plants, and left in the soil, respectively, in the two cases.

The Graminaceæ under the title of "1858, A" (those grown in M. G. VILLE's case) were treated similarly to the others of 1858, excepting that the combined Nitrogen was given to them at an earlier period of their growth, and they were not allowed to suffer at any time for want of it. We shall notice the difference in result presently.

In addition to the evidence of the physiological phenomena as bearing upon the amount of growth due to the supply of ammonia, attention should be called to the remarkable character of growth which was manifested. The evidence afforded on this head, is of interest in considering the question of the character of the conditions most favourable to the assimilation of free Nitrogen; and it also brings to view some remarkable features in vegetable physiology.

It will be seen, by reference to the Notes in the Appendix, that, shortly after the addition of ammonia for the first time to the Graminaceæ (1857 and 1858), the plants began to throw out new shoots at the base of the principal stem. It would thus appear that the plant, being supplied at the commencement of its growth with only the limited quantity of combined Nitrogen contained in its seed, had developed a stem commensurate with that quantity. But when new quantities of combined Nitrogen were placed at the disposal of the plant, forces were thus called into activity which were greater than could operate through the medium of the original stem. Some of the new shoots have come forth close to the surface of the soil, some at the first, and some at the second nodes. The character of growth in this respect can be best studied by reference to the drawings of the plants given in Plate XV.

Another and no less remarkable feature was the formation of roots at the second and third nodes above the ground in the case of most of the Graminaceous plants to which ammonia-salt was added as manure (see Plate XV.). These roots came out around the node, and extended downwards—several of them reaching the soil from heights varying from $\frac{1}{2}$ to $1\frac{1}{2}$, or even 2 inches, and penetrating it to the bottom of the pot. The most marked instance of this kind of growth was that of the barley represented in fig. 11, Plate XV., and in more detail, with special reference to the points now under consideration, in fig. 16, Plate XV. As will be seen in the figures, roots and new stems come from the same node, making the latter a veritable starting-point, or new axis of growth, like the seed in the first instance. The original stems, below these nodes, did not increase much in size beyond what they had attained before the addition of ammonia; but the stems above the nodes became much larger than the portions below them, as also did those of the new shoots.

Finally, so long as the conditions of growth of the plants were such that an additional supply of combined Nitrogen would cause increased development, so long must the physiological conditions have been such as to require available Nitrogen, and they must therefore have been more or less favourable to the assimilation of free Nitrogen, provided such assimilation were possible. Hence, the fact that this did not take place under the circumstances which have been described, seems to show that, at least in the case of these Graminaceæ, it is not possible.

Some of the remarks which we have made with regard to the influence of a supply of combined Nitrogen upon the growth of the Graminaceæ, apply also, in a greater or less degree, to the other plants experimented upon. We shall not comment here in detail upon the value of each experiment, but simply call attention to the columns of gain or loss of Nitrogen, in the Tables, and to the notes in the Appendix indicating the circumstances of growth of the plants.

With regard to the Leguminosæ experimented upon, it is to be observed that the development was by no means so satisfactory as in the case of the Graminaceæ. Hence the evidence which the results relating to them afford against the fact of assimilation of free Nitrogen must be admitted to apply to a more limited range of conditions of growth, and, therefore, to be less conclusive against the possibility of such assimilation. Still, so far as they go, the results with these plants, and also those with buckwheat, tend to confirm those obtained under the more favourable circumstances of growth with the cereals. It will be remembered, however, that M. BOUSSINGAULT experimented with a great many Leguminous plants, and generally succeeded in getting much more healthy growth than we were able to do in the cases to which the figures in the Tables refer. Yet in no case did he find any such gain of Nitrogen as to lead him to the conclusion that these plants, any more than the Graminaceæ, assimilated free or uncombined Nitrogen. Our own experiments with Leguminous plants are, however, not yet concluded; so that we hope to supply some additional evidence on this subject, on a future occasion.

Relations of the Plants grown with a supply of ammonia to those grown without it.

We have already called attention to the fact that the physiological phenomena exhibited in the progress of the plants grown under the two different conditions as regards the supply of combined Nitrogen at their disposal, afford satisfactory evidence that the conditions provided in soil and atmosphere were all that were requisite in experiments for the solution of the question at issue with regard to the Cereals. The great development of these plants when ammonia was supplied (which was in fact almost in proportion to the amount supplied), the cessation of growth with the limit of the supply, together with the contrast between the growth with the aid of the ammonia and that without it, all afford evidence in one direction in regard to the question at issue, so far as these plants are concerned.

In Table XIV., relating to the plants to which ammonia was supplied, an experiment with clover is recorded. Reference to the remarks in the Appendix, p. 573, will show that we failed to get any growth with clover without the addition of ammonia. Hence, excepting so far as this fact is itself a point for remark, no contrast can be drawn between the growth of this plant with and without an extraneous supply of combined Nitrogen.

From what has already been said, it will be easily understood that the contrast between the beans and peas grown with and without the addition of ammonia is not very satisfactory. These plants proved to be so sensitive, under the conditions provided in the experiments, that it was obvious that, in many cases, they suffered from other causes than a want of combined Nitrogen, which we were not able to control. In but one experiment with such plants, that with the bean "1858, A." (Table XIV.), was the influence of a supply of combined Nitrogen so marked as to indicate that the plants were previously suffering for want of such supply. It will be seen, by reference to the Table, that, in the case here referred to, the seeds sown contained 0·0523 gramme of Nitrogen, and that 0·0188 gramme was added in the form of ammonia-salt—making in all 0·0711 gramme of combined Nitrogen involved in the experiment. Of this the plants appropriated 0·0401 gramme—about one-fifth less, therefore, than was supplied in the seeds alone. Yet, although the numerical results, taken by themselves, thus afford but little evidence of the effect of the 0·0188 gramme of Nitrogen added in the form of ammonia, the increased vigour of growth on the addition did afford such evidence. In contrast with this single result, however, attention may be called to the results with the beans grown without any other supply of combined Nitrogen than that contained in the seed sown. The bean plants so grown in 1857, appropriated nearly four-fifths of the Nitrogen of their seed; and those grown in a similar way in 1858, appropriated a considerably larger proportion of the combined Nitrogen so provided to them.

From a review of the whole of the results considered in this Section, it appears, then, that in the case of the Graminaceous plants experimented upon the growth was the most healthy, and such as provided a wide range of conditions for the assimilation of free Nitrogen, provided this were at all possible. The growth of the Leguminous plants was not so healthy, and did not, therefore, provide such a wide range of conditions for the possible assimilation of free Nitrogen. Nor was the growth of other plants so satisfactory as that of the Graminaceous ones. In all, the growth was more or less increased by the supply of combined Nitrogen beyond that contained in the seed. The effect of such supply was the most marked with the Graminaceous plants—the increase in the produce of dry vegetable substance due to extraneous supply of combined Nitrogen being, in their case, eight, twelve, and even nearly thirty-fold, according to the amount of Nitrogen so provided. Yet, with nineteen experiments with Graminaceous plants, six with Leguminous ones, and some with plants of other descriptions—with such great variation in the amount and character of growth in the several cases—and with such great variation in the amount of combined Nitrogen involved in the experiments, in no case have the results been such as to lead to the conclusion that there was an assimilation of free, or uncombined, Nitrogen.

The results of the whole inquiry may be very briefly enumerated as follow:—

The yield of Nitrogen in the vegetation over a given area of land, within a given time, especially in the case of Leguminous crops, is not satisfactorily explained by reference to the hitherto quantitatively determined periodical supplies of *combined* Nitrogen.

Numerous experiments have been made by M. BOUSSINGAULT, from which he concludes that free or uncombined Nitrogen is not a direct source of the Nitrogen of vegetation. M. G. VILLE, on the other hand, concludes, from his results, that free Nitrogen may be a source of a considerable proportion of the Nitrogen of growing plants. The views, or explanations, of other experimenters, on this disputed point, are various, and inconclusive.

It was found that the conditions of growth adopted in our own experiments, on the question of the assimilation of free Nitrogen by plants, were consistent with the healthy development of various Graminaceous plants, but not so much so for that of the Leguminous plants experimented upon.

From the results of various investigations, as well as from other considerations, we think it may be concluded that, under the circumstances of our experiments on the question of the assimilation of free Nitrogen by plants, there would not be any supply to them of an unaccounted quantity of combined Nitrogen, due either to the formation of oxygen-compounds of it under the influence of ozone, or to that of ammonia under the influence of nascent hydrogen.

We have found that free Nitrogen is given off in the decomposition of nitrogenous organic matter, under certain circumstances. But, considering the circumstances of such evolution, and those to which the nitrogenous organic matter necessarily involved in experiments on the question of the assimilation of free Nitrogen by plants is subjected, it may, we think, be concluded that there would be no loss of combined Nitrogen from this cause in such an experiment, excepting in certain cases, when it might be presupposed.

Our experimental evidence, so far as it goes, does not favour the supposition that there would be any loss of combined Nitrogen in our experiments on the question of assimilation, due to the evolution of free Nitrogen from the nitrogenous constituents of the plants during growth.

In numerous experiments with Graminaceous plants, grown both with and without a supply of combined Nitrogen beyond that contained in the seed sown, in which there was great variation in the amount of combined nitrogen involved, and a wide range in the conditions, character, and amount of growth, we have in no case found any evidence of an assimilation of free or uncombined Nitrogen.

In our experiments with Leguminous plants the growth was less satisfactory; and the range of conditions possibly favourable for the assimilation of free Nitrogen was, therefore, more limited. But the results recorded with these plants, so far as they go, do not indicate any assimilation of free Nitrogen. Since, however, in practice, Leguminous crops assimilate, from some source, so very much more Nitrogen than Gramінaceous ones, under ostensibly equal circumstances of supply of combined Nitrogen, it is desirable that the evidence of further experiments with these plants, under conditions of more healthy growth, should be obtained.

Results obtained with some other plants are in the same sense as those obtained with Graminaceæ and Leguminosæ, in regard to the question of the assimilation of free Nitrogen.

In view of the evidence afforded of the non-assimilation of free Nitrogen by plants under the wide range of circumstances provided in the experiments, it is desirable that the several actual or possible sources of *combined* Nitrogen to plants should be more fully investigated, both qualitatively and quantitatively.

If it be established that the processes of vegetation do not bring free Nitrogen into combination, it still remains not very obvious to what actions a large proportion of the existing combined Nitrogen may be attributed.

Appendix.

Received subsequently to the reading of the paper.

A.—*Preparation of solutions for manuring the Plants, dates of application, and quantities applied.*

Sulphate-of-Ammonia solution.—Ordinary ammonia-water was distilled from a flask, the vapour condensed in a receiver containing pure distilled water, and the strength of the solution determined by the volumetric method, by means of dilute sulphuric acid of known strength, the preparation of which is described further on, at p. 545. A given volume of the ammoniacal liquid thus prepared was neutralized by pure dilute sulphuric acid, of which the quantity added was determined by measurement, and the strength of the solution calculated accordingly. It was intended that each cubic centimetre should supply about one-tenth of a milligramme of combined nitrogen. The exact strength of the sulphate-of-ammonia solutions used in the course of the experiments was as under:—

Table I.

When used.	Volume of the pipette measure employed.	Combined nitrogen in a pipette measure of the solution.
	septems*.	gramme.
In the experiments of 1857	111·2	0·00578
In the experiments of 1858, to August 10 inclusive	100·0	0·004
In the experiments of 1858, after August 10	100·0	0·00359

Tables II. and III. show the dates of the application of the above solutions to the different plants, and the amounts of nitrogen so supplied.

Table II.—Showing the supply of combined Nitrogen, as Sulphate-of-Ammonia solution, to plants grown in 1857.

Dates.	Nitrogen supplied.			
	Wheat, in prepared soil.	Wheat, in prepared pumice.	Barley, in prepared soil.	Barley, in prepared pumice.
	gramme.	gramme.	gramme.	gramme.
June 10	·00578	·00578	·00578	·00578
July 4	·00578	·00578	·00578	·00578
July 11	·00578	·00578	·00578	·00578
July 22	·00578	·00578	·00578	·00578
July 29	·00578	·00578	·00578	
Total	·02890	·02890	·02890	·02312

* A septem measure is that of 7 grains ($=\frac{1}{1000}$ of a pound avoirdupois) of water; that is, rather less than half a cubic centimetre, which is equal to 15·43235 grains (or 1 gramme) of water.

TABLE III.—Showing the supply of combined Nitrogen, as Sulphate-of-Ammonia solution, to plants grown in 1858.

Dates.	Nitrogen supplied.									
	Wheat.	Barley.	Oats.	Wheat *.	Barley *.	Oats *.	Pea.	Clover.	Bean *.	Buck-wheat.
	grm.	grm.	grm.	grm.	grm.	grm.	grm.	grm.	grm.	grm.
May 22	·0040	·0040	·0040							
June 7	·0040	·0040	·0040	......	......	......	·0040	·0040		
June 21	·0040	·0040	·0040							
June 26	·0040	·0040	·0040	......	......	......	......	·0040		
July 3	·0040	·0040	·0040	......	......	......	......	·0040		
July 12	·0040	·0040	·0040	......	......	......	......	·0040		
July 14	·0040	·0040	·0040	·0040	·0040	·0040	......	·0040	·0040	
July 19	·0040	·0040	......	·0040	·0040	·0040	......	·0040	·0040	
July 28	......	·0040	......	·0040	·0040	·0040	......	·0040		
July 29	·0040									
August 10	·0040	......	......	......	......	......	......	·0040		
August 17	·0036	·0036	......	·0036	·0036	·0036	......	·0036	·0036	
August 24	......	·0036								
August 26	·0036									
September 7	·0036	·0036	......	·0036	·0036	·0036	......	·0036	·0036	·0036
October 5	......	......	......	......	......	......	......	·0036		·0036
October 24	......	......	......	·0036	·0036	·0036	......	......	·0036	·0036
Total	·0508	·0468	·0280	·0228	·0228	·0228	·0040	·0428	·0188	·0108

Phosphate-of-Soda solution.—The strength of a dilute solution of phosphoric acid was determined by means of a titrated alkali-solution (for the preparation of which see page 545); and it was then neutralized by carbonate of soda. Each pipette measure of this solution given to the plants supplied about ·01 gramme phosphate of soda. It was only employed in the experiments of 1858. In the records of growth of the plants, it is stated whenever they were manured with this solution.

Sulphuric-Acid solution.—The strength of some very dilute pure sulphuric acid was determined in the same manner as was that of the phosphoric acid, as stated above. It was then so far reduced, that the pipette measure by which it was applied to the plants contained exactly as much SO_3 as the pipette of sulphate-of-ammonia solution then in use, namely, ·0114 gramme SO_3, corresponding to ·004 gramme N. For the application of this solution see the records of growth of the plants.

The value of each of the above solutions was determined by analysis, to ensure that it was such as was supposed.

B.—*Taking up the Plants, preparation for analysis, methods of analysis, &c.*

At the termination of growth the glass shade was washed outside, quicksilver was poured into the groove to displace from it the condensed water not removable by the arrangement of apparatus of 1857, or already collected in the drain-water bottle adopted in that of 1858, as the case might be, and the shade was then removed. The

* These plants were grown in M. G. VILLE's case.

previously covered portions of the slate or stone-ware lute were then washed with pure distilled water, and the wash-water was added to the condensed or drain-water. In the experiments of 1858 this fluid was analysed separately, but in those of 1857 it was mixed and dried down with the soil.

The pot, with the soil and plants, was removed to a clean table covered with white paper, the plants measured in all their parts and then cut off at the surface of the soil; the roots were removed, slightly washed from soil, and observed. The plants were then put into a small wide-mouthed bottle, generally stem and root together, but sometimes they were put into separate bottles. In the experiments of 1857 the contents of the bottles were dried in a water-bath, with a current of air, previously washed through sulphuric acid, passing through the bottle and thence through a solution of a known quantity of pure oxalic acid. But it was found that no appreciable amount of ammonia was thus accumulated. Hence, in 1858, a little oxalic acid (in solution) was added to the vegetable matter, and the whole dried in the water-bath without the above precaution.

When dry, the vegetable matter was cut small by means of a pair of clean long scissors, reaching to the bottom of the bottle. In this way the substance was reduced to a considerable degree of fineness, and it was still further ground up in the mortar when mixed with soda-lime for analysis. When duplicate analyses were to be made, the matter was carefully divided so as to ensure equal proportions of stem, fine leafy matter, &c., in each half. Hence, if both analyses were successfully conducted, the results were mutually confirmatory; or if one portion were lost, the other still represented a proportionate amount of the whole material.

The *soil* was removed from the pot to a porcelain dish, and a sufficient amount of a solution of oxalic acid added to keep it acid. The mixture was then heated on a sand-bath (stirring constantly) until most of the water was expelled, more fully dried in a water-bath, and then preserved in well-corked bottles for analysis. The pots were pounded up; those of 1857 being preserved and analysed separately, and those of 1858 mixed with the soil before it was dried with oxalic acid. The pieces of flint at the bottom of the pot were also pounded and mixed with the soil.

For analysis, 150 to 200 grammes of the soil, pot, or mixture, were mixed with about half the volume of soda-lime, the whole put into a large combustion-tube, some soda-lime put in advance of the mixture, and then asbestos, as usual. The combustions were made in charcoal furnaces, and the ammonia collected in titrated sulphuric acid, of which the strength, and the amounts employed, are described at pp. 545, 546. When very small quantities of nitrogen were involved, the ammonia from two or three tubes of substance was sometimes collected in the same quantity of acid, so as to diminish the error of titration. It was found, however, to be better to use very small quantities of acid, and to estimate the product of each combustion separately; for, by the former method, if any accident occurred in the second or third combustion, it involved the loss of the determination of the products previously collected.

Preparation of the titrated solutions.

A weighed quantity of pure, dry carbonate of soda was dissolved in water, and to the solution water added to a given volume. As a preliminary step, the strength of some dilute sulphuric acid was tested against a given volume of the carbonate-of-soda solution; and from the data thus obtained, by further dilution a large quantity of acid was made of about the strength desired. The exact value of this acid was then ascertained by repeated trials with the standard carbonate-of-soda solution. To accomplish this, a given volume of the soda-solution was put into a beaker, a little litmus added, and the mixture heated over a spirit-lamp. The acid to be tested was then allowed to flow from a burette until a wine-red colour (indicating that the carbonate is converted into sulphate and bicarbonate with carbonic acid in solution) was produced. On boiling, the blue colour is restored; acid is added until red; the boiling is repeated, till the blue returns; acid again added, and so on, until the solution remains red on the addition of the last drop. The point at which the permanent change takes place in the first trial being known, the experiment is easily repeated so as to ensure great accuracy.

Thus, 50 septems of a solution of carbonate of soda, of which 1000 septems contained 6·652 grammes of the salt, required, for neutralization as above, the following number of septems of the dilute acid, in six different trials—

58·3, 58·2, 58·3, 58·3, 58·2, 58·2; mean 58·25.

Hence—

$$\frac{6·652}{1000}\times\frac{50}{58·25}\times\frac{\text{N}}{\text{NaO, CO}_2}=\frac{6·652}{1000}\times\frac{50}{58·25}\times\frac{14}{52·98}=0·001508 \text{ gramme N.}$$

The mean of six experiments with a solution of carbonate of soda of another strength gave in the same way 0·0015008 gramme N; and we adopted the mean, or 0·001504 gramme, as the amount corresponding to one septem of the titrated acid.

It remained to prepare an alkaline solution to test against this standard acid. At first a solution of sugar-lime was employed; but this being found to be liable to constant change, due doubtless to fermentation, a solution of caustic soda was had recourse to. This solution was prepared of such dilution that the extreme error possible in reading off a unit of volume on the burette should be much less than would be admissible as the maximum error of analysis. The burette was of small enough diameter to allow of one-tenth of a septem being read off on it; and the alkali-solution was so dilute that it required about three septems of it to neutralize one septem of the titrated acid. Hence one septem of the alkali-solution corresponded to only about one-half of a milligramme of nitrogen, and the probable error of reading would therefore amount to only about one-twentieth of a milligramme.

In the case of the sugar-lime solution, it was found necessary to test its strength against that of the acid every day that it was employed. But the soda-solution, if properly prepared, and well preserved, remained for months unchanged; so that, when its value was once established against that of the standard acid, it could be expressed by a number of four or five digits, which, multiplied by the number of septems of alkali representing the product in an analysis, gave the actual quantity, in grammes, of the nitrogen to be estimated.

Amount, and measurement, of the titrated acid used in Nitrogen determinations.

It was desirable that at least three times as much acid should be used as would be neutralized by the ammonia formed. The acid being more concentrated than the alkali, it required a more exact method of measurement than was afforded by the burette used for the latter. Pipettes, of which the diameter at the point of reading off is comparatively small, and which hence admit of a higher degree of accuracy, were therefore employed. In the construction of those to be used, care was taken to maintain the same relation of the diameter of the neck at the point of reading to the entire volume in instruments of different sizes—a condition seldom observed by makers of pipettes. When the quantity of nitrogen involved in an analysis was very small—as in the case of the soils and pots in the experiments without nitrogenous manure—only about six septems of the titrated acid, measured in a small pipette with a very narrow neck, were used. The exact volume of the pipette-ful of acid was not a matter of any consequence. It was only essential to ascertain its exact value expressed in septems of the titrated alkali-solution. When the amount of nitrogen involved was larger, and more under control—as for example when grains were to be analysed—care was taken to operate on such a quantity of nitrogenous material that the number of septems of the alkali representing its nitrogen should be sufficiently large to render the constant errors of titrating, reading, &c., inappreciable. This end was attained when the substance experimented upon contained 5 to 8 milligrammes, or more, of nitrogen.

Combustion-tubes, bulbs, &c.

The combustion-tubes used in the determinations of nitrogen in the soils, pots, &c., were about 3 feet long and about 1 inch in diameter. The bulb-apparatus was capable of holding two-and-a-half to three times as much fluid as that usually employed; but the central and lowest bulb, and particularly its tubular connexions with the other bulbs, were very small, so that a small quantity of liquid could close the passage. This arrangement was necessary owing to the small quantity of acid frequently used, and the large amount of water driven off in the combustion from the large quantities of soil and soda-lime. For the combustion of the experimentally grown plants smaller tubes were employed; and for seeds, &c., ordinary combustion-tubing was used.

The Soda-lime.

Before use, the soda-lime was ignited with 2 per cent. of pure sugar, in order to ensure its freedom from ammonia-yielding matter. It was then slaked with pure distilled water, dried, and kept in well-corked bottles.

Accuracy of the method for the determination of nitrogen by combustion with soda-lime, &c.

In order to ascertain the accuracy of the method before relying upon it for the purposes of the investigation, a few preliminary experiments were made upon the determination of small and known quantities of nitrogen, mixed with large quantities of soil, which had been previously freed from combined nitrogen as in the preparation of the soils for the plant-experiments. The nitrogenous substance taken for the purpose was the powdered crystals of purified quadroxalate of ammonia, $\left\{ \begin{matrix} NH_3 \\ H \end{matrix} \right\} O, (C_2 O_3)_4 + 7 HO$. The results were as follow—

Experiment 1.—50 grammes of the prepared soil were mixed with quadroxalate containing by calculation 0·0024 gramme nitrogen; and on burning with soda-lime, and determining as above described, 0·0027 gramme nitrogen was found.

Experiment 2.—100 grammes of the soil mixed with quadroxalate equal, by calculation, to 0·0035 gramme nitrogen, gave on combustion 0·0037 gramme nitrogen.

The error of analysis was, therefore, three-tenths of a milligramme of nitrogen with the 50 grammes, and two-tenths with the 100 grammes of soil. These results were obtained at the commencement of the inquiry, with comparatively large quantities of titrated acid, and therefore before experience had suggested the precautions to be adopted to reduce the errors of determination to the minimum. They may hence be taken as examples of the maximum errors of analysis, but they are less than would affect the bearing of the results in the investigation on the question of assimilation.

Testing for Nitric acid.

The indigo test, as recently refined by BOUSSINGAULT*, and the protosulphate-of-iron test, were both employed. When nitric acid was sought for and not found, if practicable the negative result was always confirmed by the addition to some of the substance under examination of a quantity of nitric acid (in the form of nitrate) less than could affect any conclusions to be drawn from the fact of its presence or absence in the substance in question. In all the cases of such addition the re-examination showed the presence of nitric acid.

The method of BOUSSINGAULT was much more delicate than the protosulphate-of-iron test; but, on the other hand, the latter was much less liable to give deceptive indications, dependent on other circumstances than the presence of nitric acid. In using the protosulphate test, the aqueous extract of the substance under examination was evaporated to a small volume with excess of fixed alkali, then transferred to a test-tube, and further evaporated till only a few drops remained. A considerable excess of concentrated sulphuric acid was then added, and on the surface of the liquid a concentrated solution of protosulphate of iron was carefully poured without agitation, by means of a small pipette with a mouth of almost capillary fineness. The characteristic brown tinge indicated the presence of nitric acid.

* Ann. de Chim. et de Phys., vol. xlviii. (1856) p. 153 *et seq.*

C.—Abstract of the Records of Growth of the Plants.

I.—Plants grown in 1857*.

The following list indicates the original arrangement of the experiments in 1857: but, as the records will show, beans sown and resown under shades Nos. 5, 10, and 11 died before they had attained any material amount of growth; and hence the products in these cases were not submitted to analysis.

Series 1. With no other combined nitrogen than that contained in the seed:—

1. Wheat; in prepared soil.
2. Barley; in prepared soil.
3. Barley; in prepared pumice.
4. Beans; in prepared soil.
5. Beans; in prepared pumice.

Series 2. With a supply of known quantities of combined nitrogen beyond that contained in the seed:—

6. Wheat; in prepared soil.
7. Wheat; in prepared pumice.
8. Barley; in prepared soil.
9. Barley; in prepared pumice.
10. Beans; in prepared soil.
11. Beans; in prepared pumice.

And also—

12. Wheat, Barley, and Beans, together; in rich garden soil.

Records of Sowing, and Early Stages of Growth, of all the Plants collectively.

May 12.—The weighed seeds of wheat (Nos. 1, 6, & 7), of barley (Nos. 2, 3, 8, & 9), and of beans (Nos. 4, 5, 10, & 11) were respectively put into small bottles, a few septems of pure distilled water added to soak them, and then corked up.

May 16.—The wheats (Nos. 1, 6, & 7), and the beans (Nos. 4, 5, 10, & 11), were sown, and the pots removed to their places on the stand, and covered with the shades; seeds all swelled; some sprouting.

May 20.—The barleys (Nos. 2, 3, 8, & 9), freshly weighed seeds (the soaked ones being abandoned), were set, and the pots removed to their position under the shades.

May 27.—Nearly all show shoots above the surface, all of which look green and healthy.

June 2.—Wheat and barley plants two or three leaves each, healthy, but pale green. No. 4 beans (soil) healthy and vigorous. No. 5 beans (pumice) one plant up, with three leaves speckled with black spots; the other plant blackened and apparently dead. Beans No. 10 (soil) and No. 11 (pumice) slightly speckled with black spots.

June 3.—Commenced the daily passage of washed air over the plants, in quantity

* The figures (Plate XV.) of the plants grown in 1857 are reduced from drawings taken, for the most part, about the middle of August.

equal to about 2½ times the volume of the shade. Carbonic acid also daily supplied, in amount as described at pp. 480, 481.

June 6.—Graminaceous plants (Nos. 1, 2, 3, 6, 7, 8, & 9) all healthy, though with a tendency to turn yellow at the tips of the leaves. Of the Leguminous plants, Nos. 5, 10, and 11 give indications of dying.

June 8.—Some of the wheat and barley plants turning yellow. Beans Nos. 5, 10, and 11 obviously dying; probably injured by the causticity of the ash added to the soil, as No. 4 beans, the seeds and roots of which happen to be washed when water is supplied, are healthy and vigorous.

Records for each Experiment given separately.

No. 1.—*Wheat* (1857); *six seeds; prepared soil; without nitrogenous manure.*

(See Plate XV. fig. 1.)

June 9.—Five plants up; one quite small, the others 2 to 4 inches high, with two leaves developed and a third appearing; yellowish at the tips of some of the leaves.

June 15.—Five healthy plants, each with three fully developed leaves; tips of the lower leaves slightly yellow.

June 24.—Plants 5 inches high; lower leaves dead and dry, upper pale green; with some of the tips yellow, but general appearance of the upper leaves healthy.

July 4.—Plants 6 to 7 inches high; 5 leaves on each; upper ones pale green, lower ones yellow.

[Note.—Drops of water condense rapidly on the tips of the leaves of all the Cereals, but not of the Leguminous plants; they also form and run down the inner surface of all the shades, casting focal rays apparently injurious to the plants when not shaded from direct sunlight.]

July 11.—Same number of leaves; very little further growth; lower leaves more dried up.

July 22.—Very little improvement.

July 29.—Very little growth, though upper leaves continue green; but little tendency to form stem.

[Note.—Shade opened a few seconds to substitute a tube for one accidentally broken.]

August 10.—Green colour maintained, but no apparent increase in size.

August 24.—Five plants, 6 to 9 inches high, with eight or nine leaves each, all dried up but the two upper ones, which are green and healthy, one expanded, the other folded in the axis of growth. The healthy appearance of the upper leaves has been maintained several weeks, with otherwise almost total cessation of growth.

October 3.—*Plants taken up*:—

The plants have been almost stationary since the last report; termination of the ascending axis keeps green; no indication of heading. (See Plate XV. fig. 1.)

Soil moist, soft, and spongy.

Roots not distributed generally throughout the soil; a few isolated ramifications extended to the lower part of the pot; but the great mass remained near the base of the stem. Total quantity of root very small compared with that of wheat No. 6 manured with ammonia-salts. For general character of root-development, see Plate XV. fig. 15.

For method of further treatment see pp. 543, 544.

No. 2.—*Barley* (1857); *six seeds; prepared soil; without nitrogenous manure.*
(See Plate XV. fig. 2.)

June 9.—Six plants; 2 to 3 inches high, with two fully developed leaves; tips of some of the leaves slightly yellow.

June 15.—Three plants with three leaves, and three with two leaves each; tips of lower leaves slightly yellow, but general appearance healthy.

June 24.—Plants 4 to 6 inches high, with three or four leaves each; much the same condition as wheat No. 1 at this date.

July 4.—6 to 7 inches high, with four or five leaves; paler than wheat No. 1; looking sickly. Drops of water on tips of leaves and inner surface of shade: see Note thereon to wheat No. 1, same date.

July 11.—Lower leaves drying up; upper ones growing a little, apparently at expense of the lower. Stems of these and the other barley plants reddish, and have been so since the formation of true stems with nodes. The barleys form stem more readily than the wheats, which are more leafy.

July 22.—Not much improvement.

July 29.—Only two small leaves at the top green; the amount green at one time does not increase; lower leaves dry up as new ones form.

August 10.—Very little change, except that one stem shows slight indications of heading.

August 24.—*Plants taken up*:—

Six plants, 5 to 17 inches high, with six to nine leaves on each plant. Two indicate slight tendency to heading, the sheath being swollen; but growth obviously ceased, the two upper leaves having at last lost colour and dried up. On opening, one head showed a rachis 2 inches long. The plant was very dry, so no fresh weight taken.

Prepared and analysed as described at pp. 543, 544.

No. 3.—*Barley* (1857); *six seeds; prepared pumice; without nitrogenous manure.*
(See Plate XV. fig. 3.)

June 9.—Six plants, 2½ to 4 inches high; more developed, but more slender than the barleys in soil (Nos. 2 & 8). Leaves turning yellow at the tips.

June 15.—Six plants, 6 inches high, each with three fully developed leaves; tips of lower leaves dried up; middle leaves have yellow tips; upper ones pale green but healthy. Plants appear to have almost done growing.

June 24.—Height about the same; three or four leaves each plant; lowest dried up, next drying, and upper ones green.

July 4.—Plants 6 to 7 inches high; five or six leaves each; upper leaves only pale green.

[Drops of water collect as described in reference to No. 1 Wheat at this date.]

July 11.—Plants 6 to 8 inches high; five or six leaves each; upper ones green and growing a little as the lower ones dry up; general aspect stationary.

July 22.—Very little growth.

July 29.—Plants 8 to 10 inches high, very slender, like mere threads; all lower leaves dried up; upper ones 1 to 2 inches long and pale yellow. The six plants show twenty nodes. Slight tendency to form very small heads.

August 10.—Plants quite dried up.

August 25.—*Plants taken up*:—

Six very slender plants, mere filaments, 8 to 20 inches long; with four to six nodes, and six to eight leaves each. Stems zigzag at the nodes; leaves dried up and brown. The top sheath of five of the plants indicates an excessively small head with zigzag rachis, at the upper part of which is a well-defined husk but no seed; the lower parts have beards and small rudimentary husks.

Preparation and analysis as described at pp. 543, 544.

No. 4.—*Beans* (1857); *two seeds; prepared soil; without nitrogenous manure.*

June 9.—Two plants up; one 6 inches high, four leaves with two leaflets each and two large stipules; the other smaller; both healthy and vigorous.

June 15.—One plant 7½ inches high, with five leaves, each with two or three leaflets and two stipules; the other 3½ inches high, with four leaves and corresponding stipules. Tips of some of the lower leaves slightly speckled, but the upper ones green, and both plants healthy and vigorous.

June 24.—One plant 15 inches high, with seven leaves, each with two or three leaflets and two stipules; lower leaves yellow, with dark specks at the edge, upper leaves and stem light green; the other plant 9 inches high, four or five leaves with two to three leaflets, &c., each; lower leaves as on the other plant, but upper ones greener. Plants appear to have nearly done growing.

July 4.—One plant 19 inches high; five leaves fallen off within two days, three upper ones remain, these green, appear to live on nutriment drawn from the lower ones. The other plant 12 inches high, seven leaves, and a small sprout just at the surface of the soil; lower leaves dead, upper ones nearly done growing.

July 5.—*Plants taken up* *:—

Preparation and analysis as described at pp. 543, 544.

* After removal of the beans, a barley plant from the field was potted with its own soil which was comparatively dry, and placed under the shade without being watered, in order to see whether water was given off and condensed within the glass as freely as in the case of the experimental plants. It was so; and hence it was concluded that the experimental soils were not too wet.

No. 5.—*Beans* (1857); *two seeds; prepared pumice; without nitrogenous manure.*

June 9.—One plant 1½ inch high, blackened, and dying; the other smaller and already dead.

As will be seen by the records (p. 557), Beans Nos. 10 & 11 showed equally unhealthy growth; all were therefore removed and re-planted. It was obvious that the failure was too early to be due to want of available nitrogen; especially, as No. 4 Beans with a similar amount of nitrogen lived. The result was considered to be due to the causticity of the ash, as beans set in ash-free soil and pumice flourished much longer, and in the case of No. 4 the seeds happened to be so placed as to be washed when water was applied.

It was found on examination that all showed signs of recommencement of growth; new roots and stems were forming. The seeds, &c. were removed; a little sulphuric acid added to the soil (or pumice) to neutralize the ash, and it was then ignited as originally, put into fresh red-hot pots, and cooled and moistened over sulphuric acid. Before putting in fresh seeds, holes were made for them in the soil, and water poured in to remove soluble matter from the neighbourhood of the young rootlets. The experiments were then continued as before.

Report of No. 5 Beans continued.

June 24.—One plant just up.

July 1.—An accident occurred to this experiment. A fresh pot of soil, prepared precisely as above, was planted with beans that had been set in small glass tubes ready for any contingency, and the experiment continued.

July 4.—One plant, leaves just opening.

July 11.—Still only one plant up, and it looks very unhealthy.

July 22.—One plant, obviously dying.

July 29.—Dead.

No. 6.—*Wheat* (1857); *three seeds; prepared soil; with nitrogenous manure.*

(See Plate XV. fig. 7.)

June 9.—Two plants up; one 2½, the other 4½ inches high; three leaves each. Tips of leaves slightly yellower than those of Wheat No. 1.

June 10.—A pipette-ful of the solution of sulphate of ammonia (=·00578 gramme N.) added to the soil.

June 15.—Two plants; green and vigorous; marked improvement since the addition of ammonia-salt; the leaves wider and of a deeper green. Three leaves each plant.

June 24.—Two plants; 7 inches high; four or five leaves each; lower ones dried up, upper ones deeper green than Wheats No. 1.

July 4.—Two plants; 9 inches high; six leaves each; lower ones yellow, upper ones broad, long, and of a healthy deep green; but the vigour due to the first addition of ammonia appears to have ceased. Second pipette-ful of ammonia-solution (same quantity) added.

July 11.—Two plants, 10 inches high; seven leaves each; upper ones deep green, broad, and vigorous. Third pipette-ful of the ammonia-solution added.

July 22.—Growth vigorous; shooting out at the base of the stems. Fourth pipette-ful of the ammonia-solution added.

July 29.—Much greater tendency to form leaf than stem. One plant with four, and the other with two subdivisions. 12 to 16 inches high, the height greatly due to the length of the leaves. Not a single node clear of the sheath of the one below it; thus essentially different from the barleys, which have great tendency to form nodes and stem. Fifth pipette-ful of the ammonia-solution added.

August 10.—Green and flourishing.

August 24.—Plants 17 to 20 inches high; ten to twelve leaves on each; upper ones long, broad, and green; lower ones dried up. But little tendency to form stem; leaves larger than on plants in the field; some 12 inches long and ½ inch wide; no nodes clear: the leaves spring out so close together as to appear almost opposite. Five stems from the two seeds.

October 2.—*Plants taken up*:—

One seed has given three strong and one small stem; another one stem; the third did not grow. Leaves very numerous and close together, giving several thicknesses of sheath around the stem, and hiding all the nodes; lower leaves dried up; upper leaves and central axis of growth green. Condition nearly stationary for the last two or three weeks. Average height of plants about 18 inches.

Soil quite moist throughout; also soft, and spongy, rather more so than the pumice soils; a little water remained in the plate below the pot.

Roots much, but very irregularly distributed—a large bunch around the base of the stem; small, long, isolated roots extended to the bottom and up the sides of the pot; quite a mass of ramified roots over the bottom, and somewhat up the sides of the pot; and a greater mass in the dish under the pot, forming a circular web the size of the bottom of the pot. A crack in the bottom of the pot was penetrated with roots throughout, showing, perhaps, that more openings than the one hole at the bottom might be advantageous. For representation of the root-development, see Plate XV. fig. 14.

Preparation and analysis as described at pp. 543, 544.

No. 7.—*Wheat* (1857); *three seeds; prepared pumice; with nitrogenous manure.*

June 9.—Three plants up, 3 to 4 inches high; each with three leaves completely formed, of which the tips are slightly yellower than those of Nos. 1 and 6, but no appearance of diseased condition in any of the wheats.

June 10.—A pipette-ful of the ammonia-solution (=·00578 gramme N.) added to the soil.

June 15.—Plants 5 to 6 inches high, with four leaves each; the tips of the lower ones yellow; the newer and upper leaves green, healthy, and vigorous; marked improvement since adding the ammonia-solution on June 10, the effect of which was manifest within two days after the addition.

June 24.—Plants 5 to 7 inches high, with four leaves each; lower leaves dried up, but upper ones green and vigorous; obviously improving; forming stem with nodes.

July 4.—Plants 7 to 8 inches high, with five to seven leaves each; the newer ones broad, well developed, and of a deep green colour; upon the whole vigorous. Second pipette-ful of the ammonia-solution added.

[Drops of water accumulate as described in reference to No. 1 of this date.]

July 11.—Plants 8 to 9 inches high, with six or seven leaves each; lower ones pale yellow, upper ones green and vigorous. One of the stems sending out a shoot at its base. Third pipette-ful of ammonia-solution added.

July 22.—Growing very well; tillering very much. Fourth pipette-ful of the ammonia-solution added.

July 29.—Plants 12 to 16 inches high; one with six shoots 4 to 8 inches long; one with one shoot 3 inches long; and the other with two shoots just forming; shoots, and upper leaves, green. The ammonia seems to induce multiplication of shoots instead of upward growth; no nodes clear of the sheath. Fifth pipette-ful of the ammonia-solution added.

August 10.—Green and flourishing.

August 24.—Very similar to Wheat No. 6 at this date.

September 20.—*Plants taken up*:—

The lower leaves begin to lose colour considerably, no increase of growth apparent for some days, nor any tendency to form seed; hence, the season being far advanced, the plants taken up.

Great development of root; the plate under the pot covered with a dense network ramified from a few fibres extended to the bottom of the pot; a similar network at the bottom and partially up the sides within the pot; comparatively little in the centre of the soil.

Preparation and analysis as described at pp. 543, 544.

No. 8.—*Barley* (1857); *four seeds; prepared soil; with nitrogenous manure.*
(See Plate XV. fig. 8.)

June 9.—Three plants up; two $1\frac{1}{2}$ inch and one $3\frac{1}{2}$ inches high; colour pale.

June 10.—A pipette-ful of ammonia-solution (=·00578 gramme N.) added to the soil.

June 15.—Three plants; about $4\frac{1}{2}$ inches high; each with two leaves and another forming. Improved by the ammonia added June 10, but not so much as the Wheat No. 6.

June 19–20.—During thenight the shade was cracked, from the bottom in the quicksilver, 9 inches upwards. The pot with its contents was removed and put under a shade over sulphuric acid. After four days it was returned to its place, and covered with the shade of Experiment No. 12 (with plants in garden soil), the latter being replaced by the damaged shade after the crack had been mended with strips of bladder cemented with albumen and lime-water. All the circumstances of this accident were carefully considered, and it was concluded that no appreciable error could arise from it.

June 24.—Three plants, 3 to 5 inches high; three or four leaves each; lower ones dried up, upper ones pale green; plants slender, but improved since the addition of the ammonia-solution.

July 4.—Plants 6 to 7 inches high; five leaves each; the most delicate and slender of the plants that have had ammonia-solution; upper leaves darker green than those without ammonia; lower leaves yellow. Second pipette-ful of ammonia-solution added.

[The same remarks apply here, as were made to No. 1 at this date, in reference to condensation of drops of water.]

July 11.—Plants 7 to 9 inches high; six or seven leaves each; stem reddish; upper leaves healthy and deep green. Third pipette-ful of ammonia-solution added.

July 22.—Growing vigorously. Fourth pipette-ful of ammonia-solution added.

July 29.—Four plants, 16 to 20 inches high. Since the last two additions of ammonia-solution, two of the plants have sent out at the base two new shoots, 6 to 8 inches high; one, two new shoots 2 to 4 inches high; and the other, one shoot. All these shoots are deep green and growing vigorously. A great tendency to develope new foliage; and though some of the stems were just beginning to swell, indicative of heading, and one showed a beard, yet this growth was arrested, and the energies of the plant directed to the new growths at the base. In all, seventeen nodes clear of the sheaths. Fifth pipette-ful of the ammonia-solution added.

August 10.—Since the last three additions of ammonia the old stems ceased to develope, but some of the new ones are on the point of heading.

August 24.—Eight plants from the three seeds. One seed has given one plant 24 inches high, with seven nodes clear, and nine leaves, of which the seven lower ones are dried up; the plant terminated by a well-formed head. Another seed has four stems, 16 to 20 inches high; one dried up just as it was heading; the three others green and healthy, and two just commencing to head; each stem four to six nodes, and six to ten leaves. The third seed has three stems 12 to 24 inches high, each with three to five nodes and five to ten leaves; one stem dried up.

October 8.—*Plants taken up*:—

Eight stems from three seeds, as under:—

(*a*) Seed with one stem; 18 to 20 inches high; seven nodes. This was the first plant that headed; all ripe and dry; six glumes, containing only rudimentary or undeveloped seeds.

(*b*) Seed with three stems. One 17 inches high; head ripe, and rather decaying. Another 25 inches high; grown several inches, and formed head, since August 24; head green, with five soft milky unripe grains. The third stem green at top, and upper sheath swollen with the head.

(c) Seed with four stems:—(1) 22 to 23 inches high, with green head and six unripe grains; leaves dry and ripe; (2) stem 15 inches high, dried up, head-sheath formed; (3) 19 inches high; yellowish-green head, with nine glumes, and undeveloped seeds; (4) about 15 inches high; rather green, sheath swollen, and beard appearing.

During the last three weeks some heads came out more, and indications of others developed; otherwise not much change. From the low temperature and lateness of the season, it was thought the plants would not mature further.

Preparation and analysis as described at pp. 543, 544.

No. 9.—*Barley* (1857); *four seeds; prepared pumice; with nitrogenous manure.* (See Plate XV. fig. 9.)

June 9.—Four plants; one quite small; the others 3 to 4 inches high. These more grown than the Barley plants Nos. 2, 3 & 8; but the leaves, particularly the lower ones, yellower at the ends.

June 10.—A pipette-ful of ammonia-solution (=·00578 gramme N.) added to the soil.

June 15.—Four plants; 5 to 6 inches high; four leaves each; lower ones losing vitality. Lower leaves were too far gone, but a most marked improvement in the upper ones since the ammonia-salt was added; it was manifest in two to three days after the addition.

June 24.—Four plants; height 6 to 8 inches; improved very much by the addition of the ammonia-solution.

July 4.—Plants 8 to 13 inches high; six or seven leaves each; stems very slender, but show well-formed nodes. Second pipette-ful of ammonia-solution added.

[Drops of water accumulate as described in reference to No. 1 of this date.]

July 11.—Plants 9 to 14 inches high; seven or eight leaves each; upper ones deep green; lower ones yellow; stems red. Third pipette-ful of ammonia-solution added.

July 22.—Growing very well; showing indications of heading. Fourth pipette-ful of ammonia-solution added.

July 29.—The four plants all out in head; about 30 inches high; each stem six nodes; two of the plants have shoots 5 inches high. The ammonia seems to tend more to new growth than to the development of the old.

August 10.—Heads well developed.

August 24.—The plants appear to be ripening; heads turning brown; but one new stem is still green and growing.

September 24.—*Plants taken up*:—

Seven plants; five 2 to 2½ feet high, one green; one 1½ foot high, green head; one 14 inches high, green. Six with heads, four ripe and two green; the shortest plant with green leaves and without head. Heads 1½ inch long; glumes all along the rachis, but only some with grains.

Roots by no means so abundant as those of Wheat with ammonia-salt; only a few fibres extended through the hole at the bottom, or to the sides of the pot.

Preparation and analysis as described at pp. 543, 544.

No. 10.—*Beans* (1857); *two seeds; prepared soil; intended to have nitrogenous manure.*

June 9.—Only one plant up; 2 inches high; turning black and obviously dying.

For particulars of taking up, setting fresh seeds and recommencement of the experiment, see remarks made on June 9 to Bean No. 5, p. 552.

June 15.—Not yet up.

June 24.—Two plants just appearing.

July 4.—Two plants well up and growing; leaves just opening.

July 11.—Two plants; 6 to 8 inches high; leaves deep green.

July 22.—Green, healthy, and vigorous.

July 29.—Nearly as at last date, but somewhat declining.

August 10.—Obviously dying.

August 24.—Dead.

The season too far advanced to repeat this experiment.

No. 11.—*Beans* (1857); *two seeds; prepared pumice; intended to have nitrogenous manure.*

June 9.—One up; slender; black spots on the leaves; obviously unhealthy. Taken up, and the experiment recommenced; for particulars of resetting, &c., see remarks to Bean No. 5 of this date, p. 552.

June 15.—Not yet up.

June 24.—Two plants just up.

July 11.—Apparently not going to grow.

July 22.—Dead; the season too far advanced to repeat this experiment.

No. 12.—*Wheat, Barley, and Beans* (1857); *Wheat and Barley three seeds each, Beans two seeds; in rich Garden soil.* (See Plate XV. fig. 13.)

May 18.—Seeds of wheat, barley, and beans, all sown together in a single pot of good garden soil, and placed under a shade (No. 12), to be supplied with washed air, &c., just as in the other experiments. The seeds germinated well.

May 28–29.—During the night, owing to a leakage of water from the reservoir into the vessel A (see description at p. 476 *et seq.*, and Plate XIII.), it passed over into the sulphuric acid and carbonate of soda wash-bottles, and the mixed liquid passed into the shade to the depth of some inches, and destroyed the experiment.

May 30.—Plants from seeds which had been set at the same date as the foregoing, were transplanted into a fresh pot of garden soil, which was placed under the shade, and the experiment recommenced. The wheat and barley plants were about 5 inches, and the beans about 4 inches high.

June 15.—Healthy, and growing vigorously.

June 24.—Three wheats, three barleys, and two beans. Wheat 14 inches, barley

13 inches, and beans 11 inches high. Wheat and barley much branched at the base, giving fourteen stems from the six seeds; all a deep green colour. Beans deep green, and growing well, excepting that one has a few black specks on the lower leaves. So much growth that the plants are considerably crowded in the shade.

July 4.—Much crowded. Graminaceæ 20 inches, Leguminosæ 15 inches high. The former growing as well as in the open air. The latter appear to suffer from crowding; their lower leaves dying.

July 12.—The Graminaceæ growing very healthily; Leguminosæ apparently not so.

July 22.—The Graminaceæ growing vigorously; Leguminosæ revived, and also growing vigorously at the top. During the last few days they have been protected from the direct sun by a sheet of paper tied round the shade.

July 29.—Four barleys in head; wheat not so advanced, but nearly as high; the beans had again suffered, but one is recovering. Too much crowded.

August 10.—About as at last date.

August 24.—About as at last date; barley slowly ripening.

The object of the experiment being attained, which was to determine whether the conditions of atmosphere were suited to healthy growth, provided the soil supplied sufficient nutriment, no further records of growth were made.

II. Plants grown in 1858*.

As in the experiments of 1857, so in those of 1858, the plants grown may be divided into two Series, as under:—

Series 1. With no other combined Nitrogen than that contained in the seed sown.

Series 2. With a supply of known quantities of combined Nitrogen beyond that contained in the seed.

The notes of growth of the plants grown without any extraneous supply of combined nitrogen are given first, and then those of the plants grown with such supply. As before, in several experiments instituted with Leguminous plants they died before attaining a sufficient amount of growth to render it of any use to analyse the products. The records of their progress, such as it was, are, nevertheless, shortly given.

No. 1.—*Wheat* (1858); *eight seeds; prepared soil; without nitrogenous manure.* (See Plate XV. fig. 4.)

April 27.—Seeds set, and the pot placed under a shade over sulphuric acid.

May 7.—All the plants up; the pot removed to its shade on the stand.

May 20.—Eight plants; all of a healthy green colour; seven 4 inches high, one just above the soil.

* The figures (Plate XV.) of the plants grown in 1858 are reduced from drawings taken, in most cases, not many days before the plants were taken up.

May 22.—A pipette-ful of the sulphuric-acid solution added.

May 29.—Eight plants, 4 to 6 inches high; each with four leaves, the two lower yellow, the two upper green and healthy. A drop of water appears on the tip of the upper leaves in the morning, but it disappears before midday, as the air is passed through the shade. A pipette-ful of the phosphate-solution added.

June 7.—A pipette-ful of the phosphate-solution, and a pipette-ful of the sulphuric-acid solution added.

June 19.—Plants 5 to 7 inches high; two lowest leaves on each dried up; upper ones yellowish green.

June 26.—Eight plants, 6 to 7 inches high; six leaves each, three lower ones dried up, next two pale green, only upper central one green and healthy. Apparently at limit of growth without more combined nitrogen; very much as last year without nitrogenous manure.

July 3.—A pipette-ful of the phosphate-solution, and a pipette-ful of the sulphuric-acid solution added.

July 14.—Plants 6 to 8 inches high, with six or seven leaves each; only the two upper ones yellowish green; apparent stagnation of growth.

July 29.—Much as last; two upper leaves seem to sustain life at the expense of the rest.

August 17.—After long inactivity several plants show tendency to grow in *stem*. In this, somewhat more like the barley than wheat of last year. Some disposition to heading.

September 7.—Still developing stem; nodes and internodes distinctly marked. Plant (*a*) 13 inches high, ten leaves, three nodes bare, slightly swelled at top as if heading; new stem-leaves, only 2 to 3 inches long. Plants (*b* and *c*) 9½ inches high, nine leaves, two or three bare nodes; slight indication of heading. Plants (*d*, *e*, and *f*) 7½ inches high, two bare nodes; stems shorter, leaves eight or nine, a little longer than above. Plant (*g*) two branches; the first short, and dried up; a new one formed from its base, green, but only 4½ inches high, with four green leaves. Plant (*h*), dried up stem with three long leaves; but a new green shoot with two leaves, though little growth. General remark:—all lower and first-formed leaves dried up, the next yellowish, and only the two upper ones green. Drops of water collect at the tips, and axils, of the green leaves. The later growth obviously at the expense of the earlier.

October 5.—Little change, except riper. Plant (*a*) 14 inches high, eleven leaves, nearly all dried up, four bare nodes, a head with indications of seeding: (*b*) 10½ inches high, eleven leaves, all ripe but the uppermost, three bare nodes, and indication of heading: (*c*) 9½ inches high, nine leaves, three nodes: (*d* and *e*) 8½ inches high, eleven leaves each: (*f* and *g*) 4 to 7 inches high, dead stems with eight to ten leaves each, but green shoots at the base: (*h*) 7 inches high and seven leaves, dead ripe.

October 24.—Weather much warmer again lately, and slight renewal of growth; drops of water again appear on the green top leaves. The chief growth is further development of the rudimentary head; a definite rachis formed, with joints and rudimentary husks, but no indication of seed.

October 25.—*Plants taken up*:—

Soil quite wet, loose, and open, to the bottom; roots pass through the pot at nearly all the bottom holes, and at some of the side ones; long roots distributed among the flints; very few roots come to the sides of the pot (see Plate XV. fig. 17).

Plant 1. Dead ripe, 7 inches high, seven long leaves, one dead shoot; roots long, apparently going to the bottom, very little distributed.

Plant 2. Seven inches high; two stems; one with six leaves, dead ripe; the other with three leaves, one still slightly green; no nodes visible; each, a moderate amount of root.

Plant 3. Eight inches high; ten leaves, lower long and dead, two upper green; no nodes visible. Many roots at the base, some extending downwards. Roots of this and all the plants have short forked branches, $\frac{1}{4}$ to $\frac{1}{2}$ inch long, blunt and thick, and generally forked at the end; strikingly different from the roots among the loose flints at the bottom, and those under the pot.

Plant 4. Height $10\frac{1}{2}$ inches; thirteen leaves; six visible nodes; slight swelling at the head. Fewer roots branched and distributed in the soil near the base of the stem; most go to the bottom, or even under the pot, thus taking nutriment from the water in the dish rather than from the soil;—perhaps associated with this the superior growth over plants 1, 2, and 3.

Plant 5. Very similar to No. 4.

Plant 6. Very similar to Nos. 4 and 5; but the head rather more developed, and visible through the transparent sheath, and the roots with rather more the character of pot or *soil* roots.

Plant 7. Eleven inches high; twelve leaves; five nodes visible; head with chaff without grain, and beard $\frac{3}{4}$ inch long; rachis 1 inch long. Roots but little branched, going down and developed more at the bottom and in the dish than in the soil.

Plant 8. The largest and most developed plant. Fourteen inches high; twelve leaves; lower ones long and crowded, upper ones shorter and further apart (as in all); four nodes; head with rachis $1\frac{1}{4}$ inch long, with glumes and pales. Roots very similar to No. 7, forming under the pot a thick matted mass, running round the dish, some of which, when untangled, are 3 to 4 feet long; white, transparent, and with many small thread-like branches; the whole somewhat resembling a mass of white thread.

Preparation and analysis as described at pp. 543, 544.

No. 2.—*Barley* (1858); *eight seeds*; *prepared soil*; *without nitrogenous manure.* (See Plate XV. fig. 5.)

April 27.—Seeds set, and the pot placed under a shade over sulphuric acid.

May 7.—Pot removed to its shade on the stand.

May 20.—Five plants 4 inches high, and one 1 inch. Were at first quite green and healthy, but the last few days turning yellowish green.

May 22.—A pipette-ful of the sulphuric-acid solution added.

May 29.—Five plants 4 to 5 inches high, with three or four leaves each; lower ones yellow and dried up; upper pale yellowish green. A sixth plant, smaller. A pipette-ful of the phosphate-solution added.

June 7.—A pipette-ful of the phosphate-solution, and a pipette-ful of the sulphuric-acid solution added.

June 19.—One plant dead; two about 4 inches high with shoots at the base; other two about 8 inches high.

June 26.—Plant (*a*) dead; cause not obvious. Plant (*b*) 10 inches high; as last year, forming stem well. Plant (*c*) 8 inches high. Plant (*d*) a main stem which is dead, and a new shoot which is green (each 3 to 4 inches high). Plant (*e*) a good deal like (*d*).

July 3.—A pipette-ful of the phosphate-solution, and a pipette-ful of the sulphuric-acid solution added.

July 14.—Plant (*b*) 9 to 10 inches high; six dried up, and two green leaves; swelling apparently for heading. Plant (*c*) about 7 inches high; seven dried up and two green leaves. Plant (*d*) two stems 4 to 6 inches high; six dried up and two green leaves. Plant (*e*) two stems 4 to 6 inches high, with five dead and two green leaves.

The upper leaves quite short (1–1½ inch long), and apparently live at the expense of the lower.

July 29.—Plant (*a*) dead; six leaves, becoming brown-yellow; a black mildew has attacked the leaves and stem; and a white gossamer-like fungus has attached itself in places to the stem and leaves. Leaves 3½ to 4 inches long; the upper thread-like and drooping. Plant (*b*) the most flourishing; 14 inches high; but very spindly; six nodes, which, with portions of the adjoining culm, especially the upper part, are dark purplish; eight leaves; lower ones yellow, and the lowest two, which are in contact with plant (*a*), affected with the mildew; all but the uppermost leaf 2 to 2½ inches long; the upper one 1½ inch long, pale green, and quite erect, apparently the last effort of the plant, no new leaves forming. Plant (*c*), divided just beneath the soil into three shoots; two apparently suckers from the other, each 3 inches high, and dead. The main plant 6 inches high; has seven leaves; the four lower dead, and the three upper, making up half the plant, pale green; the uppermost only ½ an inch long, in the fold of the second. Only one node visible; the culm, where seen, is purplish. The white fungus occurs, but no mildew. Plant (*d*) much like the main plant (*c*); evidence of early effort to put out shoots at the base. Twelve leaves; ten lower ones dead; two upper ones living; all 2 to 2½ inches long. Plant (*e*) the second in size. Eleven inches high; ten leaves; eight lower ones dead, two upper ones living; all erect but the lowest two; each 2 to 3 inches long.

August 18.—*Plants taken up*:—

Evidently done growing; four stems swelled for head; all leaves except the uppermost dried up. Roots not much distributed; general characters much like those of barley without nitrogenous manure last year (1857). Soil moist, loose, and open.

Preparation and analysis as described at pp. 543, 544.

No. 3.—*Oats* (1858); *eight seeds; prepared soil; without nitrogenous manure.*
(See Plate XV. fig. 6.)

April 27.—Seeds set, and the pot placed under a shade over sulphuric acid.

May 7.—The pot removed to its shade on the stand.

May 22.—A pipette-ful of the sulphuric-acid solution added.

May 29.—Eight plants, 4 to 6 inches high; four or five leaves each; lower ones yellow, upper ones green and growing. These Oats growing rather better than either No. 1 Wheat, or No. 2 Barley. A pipette-ful of the phosphate-solution added.

June 7.—A pipette-ful of the phosphate-solution, and a pipette-ful of the sulphuric-acid solution added.

June 19.—Eight plants, 6 to 9 inches high; five or six leaves each, lower yellow and dead, upper green. Tips of some of the leaves injured by action of direct sun-rays.

[General note.—White paper had been tied over all the shades to screen from the direct rays of the sun; but in this case not quite high enough.]

June 26.—Eight plants; five 10 to 11 inches high, and in head; three 8 to 9 inches high; no appearance of heading, and two of them a green shoot at the base. Six or seven leaves on each plant. The rachis of the seeding plants long and crooked, with one or two seeds at top, without signs of seed below. All the plants apparently at termination of growth; remain only to see how far they will ripen.

July 3.—A pipette-ful of the phosphate-solution, and a pipette-ful of the sulphuric-acid solution added.

July 13.—*Plants taken up*:—

Eight plants, quite dead ripe for some days, having had a hot sun.

Plant (1) 13$\frac{1}{2}$ inches high; five leaves; rachis 1$\frac{1}{4}$ inch long, with one seed. Plant (2) 11$\frac{1}{2}$ inches high; five leaves; rachis 1$\frac{1}{2}$ inch. Plant (3) 12$\frac{1}{4}$ inches high; five leaves; rachis 1$\frac{1}{2}$ inch long, with two seeds. Plant (4) 12$\frac{1}{2}$ inches high; with shoot appearing at base; rachis 1$\frac{1}{2}$ inch long, with two seeds. Plant (5) 11$\frac{1}{2}$ inches high; five leaves; with shoot appearing at base. Plant (6) 9 inches high; five leaves; and shoot at the base, 4 inches long. Plant (7) 10 inches high; five leaves; and shoot at the base 4 inches long. Plant (8) 10$\frac{1}{2}$ inches high; five leaves; rachis 1$\frac{1}{2}$ inch long, two seeds. Roots only extended about 2 inches deep in the pot. Soil wet and soft; the lower part firm, but not hard.

Preparation and analysis as described at pp. 543, 544.

No. 4.—*Beans* (1858); *three seeds; prepared soil; without nitrogenous manure.*

April 27.—Seeds set, and the pot placed under a shade over sulphuric acid.

May 20.—Pot removed to its shade on the stand. Three plants up, 2$\frac{1}{2}$ inches high; three leaves on each; dark green and healthy.

May 22.—A pipette-ful of the sulphuric-acid solution added.

May 29.—Plants 3 to 4 inches high; one looks to be dying; the others have specks on their leaves. A pipette-ful of the phosphate-solution added.

June 7.—A pipette-ful of the phosphate-solution, and a pipette-ful of the sulphuric-acid solution added to the soil.

June 19.—One plant dead; another looking unhealthy; the third 4 to 5 inches high, with five leaves, growing pretty well.

June 26.—Two plants dead; the other growing, 7 to 8 inches high, with nine leaves, each with two stipules.

July 3.—A pipette-ful of the phosphate-solution, and a pipette-ful of the sulphuric-acid solution added.

July 14.—The third or only surviving plant has ten leaves, but looks unhealthy.

July 29.—The two dead plants fallen, moulded, and dried up. The other blackened and mouldy at the base of the stem, and thence to the top yellow; three top leaves partly yellow, but the remainder black.

August 17.—All three entirely dead. Pot removed, but products not analysed, as there had not been sufficient healthy growth. It is difficult to account for this failure; but it is possibly due to the very hot weather.

No. 5.—*Beans* (1858); *three seeds; prepared soil; without (but intended to have) nitrogenous manure.*

June 11.—Seeds set in prepared soil, with ash that had been neutralized with sulphuric acid, and gently re-ignited; and the pot placed over sulphuric acid and covered with a glass shade.

June 21.—The pot removed to its place on the stand.

June 26.—Three plants up; green and healthy; four leaves, each with two leaflets, and two stipules. Plants delicate, but healthy green colour; one shows air-roots.

July 3.—A pipette-ful of the phosphate-solution, and a pipette-ful of the sulphuric-acid solution added.

July 14.—Three plants, healthy and vigorous; 8 to 12 inches high; eight leaves on each; a few black specks on some of the leaves, otherwise healthy. The weather has been comparatively cool since planting till now; but now hotter with bright sun. A few air-roots at the base of the stems.

July 29.—Three plants; 8, 8½, and 12 inches high. Plant (*a*) lost all its leaves, except rudimentary ones at the top. A shoot 2 inches long with four small leaves about an inch from the base, more growing than the parent plant; another shoot appearing about an inch above. Plant (*b*) very unhealthy; lost all leaves but six small and partly black ones at the top; a vigorous shoot 5 inches long, springing an inch from the base, seems to exhaust its strength; another small shoot 1 inch long, about 2 inches higher up. Plant (*c*), most of the leaves dropped; but several of the petioles remain, and are green; some small withering leaves at the top; two shoots starting near the base.

August 17.—Three plants; the main stem of each lost nearly all the leaves. Each plant has living shoots with several leaves each near the base.

August 23.—*Plants taken up*:—

There has been scarcely perceptible growth for two or three weeks; leaves nearly all off. Soil moist. Roots extend only a little way, and consist of a thick mat around the base, much divided; none reached the flint; the upper ones dead, the lower living; less root than last year.

Preparation and analysis as described at pp. 543, 544.

No. 6.—*Pea* (1858); *three seeds; prepared soil; without nitrogenous manure.*

June 5.—Three peas previously set died. Three more set to-day in prepared soil, with ash that had been neutralized with sulphuric acid, and gently re-ignited; and the pot placed over sulphuric acid and covered with a glass shade.

June 7.—A pipette-ful of the phosphate-solution, and a pipette-ful of the sulphuric-acid solution added.

June 19.—Pot removed to its place on the stand.

June 26.—Three plants, 6 to 7 inches high, with four leaves each; not growing well.

July 3.—A pipette-ful of the phosphate-solution, and a pipette-ful of the sulphuric-acid solution added.

July 14.—Three plants; doubtful whether they will live.

July 29.—Three plants; two 6 inches, and one 7 inches high; apparently dead some days, yellow, and a few spots of mould.

August 24.—*Plants taken up*:—

All dead for some time past; probably owing to the heat. Products submitted to analysis, but the results can only be of confirmatory value.

No. 7.—*Buckwheat* (1858); *seed*, 1 *gramme; prepared soil; without nitrogenous manure.*

August 20.—Seed sown, and the pot placed over sulphuric acid, and covered with a glass shade.

August 24.—Removed to its shade on the stand. Several plants up.

September 7.—Growing well.

October 5.—Sixteen plants, 2 to 4 inches high, four to six leaves each.

October 24.—Eighteen plants, 3 to 4 inches high, with four to six leaves each; leaves $\frac{1}{3}$ to $\frac{2}{3}$ inch wide, but have begun to look yellow and curl up; some plants dead. The plants appear to have attained their maximum growth without nitrogenous manure.

October 28.—*Plants taken up*:—

Eighteen plants with four to six leaves each, including the seminal opposite ones; 2 to 3 inches high; obviously done growing; only five or six with green leaves remaining. Roots only 2 to 3 inches long, slim, delicate, and very little distributed. Soil quite loose, porous, and friable.

Preparation and analysis as described at pp. 543, 544.

No. 8 (1858).—Plants grown without Nitrogenous Manure in M. G. Ville's Case*.

M. Ville kindly forwarded porous pots, and glazed white pans to set them in, such

* The experiments conducted in M. G. Ville's cases were commenced later in the season than those with the shades, as we waited some time in the hope that M. Ville might be able to come over and superintend the arrangement himself.

as he used in his experiments; but as too many were broken in transit to use these entirely, it was decided to use pots and pans the same as for our other experiments in 1858. The soil, ash, &c., were also prepared in the same way as for the other experiments of 1858—the ash, however, being saturated with sulphuric acid and re-ignited before being used, as in a few only of the other cases; for description, see pp. 470–472.

Pot 1—Wheat; eight seeds.
Pot 2—Barley; eight seeds.
Pot 3—Oats; eight seeds.
Pot 4—Beans; three seeds.

June 11.—Wheat, Barley, and Oats; seeds set, and the pots placed over sulphuric acid, and covered with a shade.

June 12.—The three pots removed to M. VILLE'S Case.

June 19.—Wheat, Barley, and Oats all up, and looking green and healthy.

June 25.—Cereals all about the same size, with three leaves each; wheat quite pale; barley and oats green at the top, and lower leaves dead.

The Case was opened, and the pot of three beans put in.

July 1.—Wheat pale and blanched; barley and oats, lower leaves dead, upper ones green and growing.

July 3.—All the Cereals getting quite pale; beans healthy.

July 14.—Bean, three plants up; two cotyledons and two leaves on each, healthy. Wheat, seven plants; 4 to 6 inches high; four leaves on each, upper green, lower dead. Oats, seven plants; very like the wheat; but little more disposition to form stem. Barley, eight plants; much like the oats.

August 2.—Beans, 4 inches high; lower leaves dead, and show a white mould; small stems putting out languidly. Barley, eight plants; 4 to 5 inches high; lower leaves yellow and dead; upper blades green; stems appear mouldy. Oats, seven plants about 5 inches high; lower leaves dead and mouldy; upper part of stem green, and slightly swelled as if going to head. Wheat, very much like the barley.

August 17.—Cereals appear to have nearly done growing; beans dying.

September 7.—Beans dead. Wheat green at the tops, but dead below; 4 to 6 inches high; about ten leaves each. Oats nearly dead. Barley nearly dead.

October 24.—Wheat still green at the top; oats and barley dead. Beans dead (not analysed).

November 6.—*Plants taken up.* Notes as under:—

Wheat. Seven plants; 4 to 5 inches high; no nodes visible; little tendency to form stem; lower leaves dead; top leaf green, and on some the next greenish yellow. Soil moist. Very little root.

Oats. Seven plants, 4 to 6 inches high; about six leaves each; generally four nodes visible; most forming head. Roots but little distributed; very little below 1½ inch; fewer and more slender than those of the wheat. All the plants dead or ripe, but not decomposed; the stems firm and elastic.

Barley. Eight plants, 4 to 6½ inches high; two to four nodes visible in all; six or seven leaves on each; most have a leaf-like heading stretching upwards; lower leaves generally very long, 4 or 5 inches. Roots very little distributed; perhaps a little deeper than the oats; but few deeper than 1½ to 2 inches. Soil dry, loose, and porous; flints quite open.

Wheat, Oats, and Barley prepared and analysed as described at pp. 543, 544.

Plants grown in 1858, *with a supply of combined Nitrogen beyond that contained in the seed sown.*

No. 9.—*Wheat* (1858); *four seeds; prepared soil; with nitrogenous manure.* (See Plate XV. fig. 10.)

April 27. Seeds set, and the pot placed over sulphuric acid, and covered with a glass shade.

May 20.—Four plants up; healthy, green, and growing; about 4 inches high; very similar to Wheats No. 1 of this date.

May 22.—A pipette-ful of the sulphate-of-ammonia solution (=0·004 gramme N.) added to the soil.

May 29.—Four plants, from 4 to 6 inches high. Greener and fresher since the addition of the ammonia-solution; new shoots appearing; only the lowest leaf on each yellow. A pipette-ful of the phosphate-solution added.

June 7.—Second pipette-ful of the sulphate-of-ammonia solution added; and a pipette-ful of the phosphate-solution.

June 19.—Four plants; one with four shoots or stems, and two others with two stems each; in all nine stems or plants; 5 to 7 inches high; leaves more healthy, green and vigorous.

June 21.—Third pipette-ful of ammonia-solution added. Plants had begun to show the want of available nitrogen.

June 26.—Fourth pipette-ful of the ammonia-solution added. As intimated May 29, the ammonia tends much to new shoots from the base. The four seeds have given—No. 1, one stem, with seven leaves: No. 2, two stems, each with six leaves: No. 3, three stems, each with five or six leaves: No. 4, four stems, with four, five, or six leaves each: in all ten stems. The two lowest leaves dead, the others green and vigorous. More vegetable matter from these four seeds, with ammonia, than from the eight (No. 1 Wheat) without it. Plants 8 to 11 inches high, and improve with each addition of ammonia.

July 1.—The shade slightly cracked at the bottom during the night, but still sufficiently air-tight for changes of temperature to affect the level of the sulphuric acid in the bulb-apparatus. Shade replaced by a small one temporarily. An immaterial amount of condensed water lost. Many roots found to be distributed through the bottom of the pot, and growing in the dish beneath it.

July 3.—Fifth pipette-ful of ammonia-solution added. [It is intended that none of the plants shall suffer so much for want of combined nitrogen, as in 1857.] Also a pipette-ful of the phosphate-solution added.

July 12.—Sixth pipette-ful of ammonia-solution added.

July 14.—Seventh pipette-ful of ammonia-solution added. Details of growth from the four seeds as follow:—

No. 1, one stem only, 8 to 10 inches high; three upper leaves green and vigorous, four lower yellow. No. 2, three stems: (*a*) 3 to 4 inches high, two yellow and two green leaves; (*b*) 4 to 6 inches high, two yellow and two green leaves; (*c*) 12 to 14 inches high, three yellow and three green leaves. No. 3, three stems: (*a*) 4 to 6 inches high, two yellow and two green leaves; (*b*) 8 to 10 inches high, two yellow and three green leaves; (*c*) 13 to 15 inches high, two yellow and three green leaves. No. 4, four stems, 8 to 10 inches high, three yellow and three green leaves each.

The "yellow" leaves are small ones at the base, developed before ammonia was added, and are dead. The ammonia strikingly developes the new shoots, and their leaves are much larger. As last year, much more tendency to form leaf than run to stem. The height given above includes that of the erect leaves extending above the ascending axis.

July 19.—Eighth pipette-ful of ammonia-solution added.

July 29.—Ninth pipette-ful of ammonia-solution added. The following details will show how dependent is the development upon the proximity to the mouth of the tube by which the ammonia-solution is applied.

No. 1 (furthest from the tube), one stem strong and vigorous at the base, and 13 inches high. No. 2 (third from the tube), three stems; one 12 to 13 inches high, the others smaller. No. 3 (second from the tube), five stems; three 12 to 13 inches high, and two new ones 1 to 2 inches high. No. 4 (nearest the tube), seven stems; four 8 to 13 inches high, and three new ones 1 to 3 inches high.

All upper leaves green and vigorous, most of the lower yellow and dead; some of the shoots entirely green.

August 10.—Tenth pipette-ful of ammonia-solution added.

August 17.—Eleventh pipette-ful of ammonia-solution added (a new solution, the pipette-ful $=0{\cdot}00359$ gramme N.).

Recently, much more disposition to form stem; several plants from 18 to 30 inches high; nodes clear of the sheaths. Comparing with the Wheat without ammonia, which also tends more to stem of late, it appears that the amount of growth is due to the supply of combined nitrogen, and its character (stemmy) more to the season.

August 26.—Twelfth pipette-ful of ammonia-solution added.

September 7.—Thirteenth pipette-ful of ammonia-solution (the last application; in all, 0·0508 gramme N.) added. Growth from each seed as under:—

No. 1 (furthest from the ammonia-solution tube), one stem 23 inches high; twelve leaves; two nodes clear; slight indication of heading.

No. 2 (third from the tube), one main stem growing, and two shoots dead; main stem 23 inches high; three upper leaves green, six lower ones yellowish; not heading yet.

No. 3 (second from the tube), three stems; two like "No. 2"; the third 12 to 14 inches high; little tendency to form stem, but long leaves from the axis.

No. 4 (nearest the tube, some of the roots washed when the solution, or water, is added), two stems and five small shoots:—(*a*) highest leaf touches the top of the shade, and 3 inches of it lie against the wet glass, by which it is injured; ten leaves; three bare nodes; (*b*) 23 inches high; nine leaves, three upper green, others yellowish; nodes not clear of the sheath; not heading yet; (*c*) three small stems from the base, 6 to 8 inches high, ceased to grow, and apparently dying; (*d*) two small rudimentary shoots; ceased to grow, and dying.

Main stems—lower leaves yellow or dead; those starting a few inches from the soil numerous, and 12 to 16 inches long; those higher up, 4 to 6 inches long, green, and healthy; apparently incapable of supporting all the shoots started.

October 5.—Plants principally increasing in height of stem; three touch the top of the shade; upper leaves green. Shaded from the direct sun to prevent injury from the little aqueous lenses formed on the interior of the shade; yet sun apparently wanted for ripening.

October 24.—Shade entirely full of vegetable matter, some stems touching the top, and leaves touching on all sides. Season for growth about over; plants seemed stationary during some recent cold weather, but, the last few days being warmer, they have revived again. [This remark applies to all the Cereals.]

October 26.—*Plants taken up*; produce from each seed as under:—

No. 1 (furthest from the ammonia-solution tube), a mass of tufted leaves at the base; five leaves higher up below any visible node, formed before the plants began to run up stem (it was the same with the other plants, and with the leafy growth last year); higher up five more leaves, four visible nodes, and a head; total height 30 inches; rachis 1½ inch; three barren joints, and six with unripe seeds.

No. 2 (third from the tube), two dead shoots at the base, with several leaves each; twelve leaves higher up on the main stem, lower ones 6 to 9 inches long, upper ones shorter; four nodes visible; total height 28 inches; rachis 1½ inch long, three barren joints, and six with glumes and pales, but still green.

No. 3 (second from the tube), three stems: (*a*) 6 inches high; ten long narrow leaves; stem dead. (*b*) 24 inches high; fourteen leaves below the first node, and three higher up; two nodes visible; plant still growing and vigorous. (*c*) Height 31 inches; twelve leaves below the first node, and three above it; swelled at the top with a head not yet out.

No. 4 (nearest the tube), seven plants—five being small shoots 2 to 8 inches high, and two main stems. As mentioned in respect to No. 1, and applicable pretty generally to the Cereals with ammonia, a dense matted mass of leaves below the first node near the base, 8, 12, and 15 inches long, with thick sheaths forming a dense coat at the base of the stem. These plants are individually as follow:—(*a*) 28 inches high; three nodes; rachis two inches long, with five barren joints, and seven with glumes and pales, and seeds forming, green. (*b*) 35 inches high; four visible nodes; rachis 2½ inches long, with five barren joints and seven with glumes and pales, and shrivelled seeds turning yellow.

The soil wet, soft, and loose, and not filling up the interstices among the flints.

The roots tolerably distributed throughout the whole pot, though not extending much to the sides, but passing through all the holes at the bottom, and some at the sides, of the pot, and forming a dense matted mass underneath it in the pan. Those of the plants nearest to the watering and manuring tube have sent by far the most roots downwards into the pan,—those furthest from it having their roots proportionally much more confined in the soil near the base of the plant, where they are much matted, with divaricate branches and short branchlets—these characters being more nearly those of the Cereals grown without nitrogenous manure.

Preparation and analysis as described at pp. 543, 544.

No. 10.—*Barley* (1858); *four seeds; prepared soil; with nitrogenous manure.* (See Plate XV. fig. 11.)

April 27.—Seeds set, and the pot placed over sulphuric acid, and covered with a glass shade.

May 7.—The pot removed to its shade on the stand.

May 20.—Two plants up.

May 22.—A pipette-ful of the sulphate-of-ammonia solution (=0·004 gramme N.) added to the soil.

May 29.—Two plants; 4 to 6 inches high; five leaves on each, the lowest dead, the others green; improved since the addition of ammonia, more active growth and colour deeper green. A pipette-ful of the phosphate-solution added.

June 7.—Second pipette-ful of the sulphate-of-ammonia solution added; also a pipette-ful of the phosphate-solution.

June 19.—Two plants; 10 to 12 inches high, forming stem well; each plant seven leaves; one stem has a small shoot forming at its base.

June 21.—Third pipette-ful of the sulphate-of-ammonia solution added.

June 26.—Fourth pipette-ful of the sulphate-of-ammonia solution added. Two plants; 16 to 18 inches high, healthy and vigorous; eight leaves each; also each a vigorously growing shoot 4 to 5 inches long.

July 3.—Fifth pipette-ful of the sulphate-of-ammonia solution added; also a pipette-ful of the phosphate-solution.

July 12.—Sixth pipette-ful of the sulphate-of-ammonia solution added.

July 14.—Seventh pipette-ful of the sulphate-of-ammonia solution added. Two plants, namely,—

No. 1. (*a*) Main stem, 26 inches high; lower leaves ripe or dead, and yellow, upper ones green and growing; beard just appearing at the head. (*b*) Shoot, 18 inches high; three ripe or dead leaves, and three green.

No. 2. (*a*) Main stem, 28 inches high; lower leaves ripe or dead, four upper ones green; air-roots developing. (*b*) Shoot, 12 to 14 inches high; one dead, and four green leaves. (*c*) Shoot, 4 to 6 inches high; one dead, and three green leaves.

July 19.—Eighth pipette-ful of the sulphate-of-ammonia solution added.

July 28.—Ninth pipette-ful of the sulphate-of-ammonia solution added.

July 29.—Only two of the seeds germinated; plants as follow:—

No. 1. (*a*) Main stem, out of the ground single, and then gives off (*b*) and (*c*); is 22 inches high; lower leaves dead, and lowest shows a fungous growth; six air-roots (two still growing) from first joint or point of separation; five nodes, each giving a leaf, only the top one green; head bursting forth. (*b*) 28 inches high; five nodes, with leaves, upper two only growing; stem slim below and thicker higher up; awns of head appearing. (*c*) 5 inches high; two leaves; fresh and green.

No. 2. More vigorous than No. 1, and livelier colour; leaves the ground single; half an inch up divides, and also gives off roots which go into the soil; three-quarters of an inch higher a second shoot, and more roots given off; one reaches the soil, two growing downwards, and several withered; lowest leaves dead and show fungous growth, particularly where they lie on the soil.

August 17.—Tenth pipette-ful of the ammonia-solution added (new solution =0·00359 N). Plants growing vigorously under the influence of the ammonia; nearly at the top of the shade; several heads appearing.

August 24.—Eleventh pipette-ful of the ammonia-solution added.

September 7.—Twelfth pipette-ful of the ammonia-solution added.

October 5.—Plants ripening; seven stems with heads; lower leaves of each dead or ripe, and two or three upper ones of each green. Some new shoots appearing at the base.

October 24.—Three heads green, the others ripe.

October 26.—*Plants taken up*:—

Only two seeds grew, and gave plants as follow:—

No. 1. Stem divided a little above the surface of the soil, giving plant (*a*), and an inch higher up divides again, giving (*b*) and (*c*); below the first point of separation the stem scarcely thicker than a pin, hard and solid. (*a*) 34 inches high; six visible nodes; stem below the lowest very thin and hard, but larger, soft and succulent higher up; head 3 inches long, having sixteen joints, with glumes and pales, and awns 4 to 6 inches long; two ripe plump seeds, and others shrivelled up. (*b*) 28 inches high; five nodes; below the lowest stem hard, firm, dry, and almost solid, and but little thicker than a pin; stem higher up larger, but still quite delicate; head 1½ inch long, with three joints barren, and seven with glumes, pales, and long awns, but no seed. (*c*) 30 inches high; five nodes; lower part of stem not quite so thick as (*a*) and (*b*); head ripe; rachis 2½ inches long, with two joints barren, and thirteen with glumes, pales, and awns; also some shrivelled seeds.

No. 2. Stem to 1½ inch above the soil little thicker than a pin, quite solid, and firm; then a thick and bunchy node and six stems. Stem (*a*) 18 inches high to rachis; four nodes; four leaves; crooked rachis 1¼ inch long, with three joints barren, and seven with glumes, pales, and awns. (*b*) 21 inches high to head; rachis 2½ inches long, with three joints barren, and thirteen with glumes, pales, and long awns; four nodes; five leaves. (*c*) green; 2½ inches high, and still growing. (*d*), (*e*), and (*f*) about 25 inches high to rachis; each with four or five nodes; rachis 1½ inch long, with three or four joints barren, and nine or ten with glumes, pales, and some green seeds.

The Root-development of these Barley plants was very extraordinary. Plant No. 1 has about ten roots coming from the first node or point of separation, extending deep into the soil, and some even through the bottom of the pot; roots also come out from the next joint above, on each of the separate stems, but these do not reach the soil. Plant No. 2, from the first joint, whence spring the six stems, throws out more than a dozen small roots, five of which reach the soil and ramify in it, some of the ramifications going down into the pan. The roots starting within the soil not so much matted near the base of the stem as those of the Wheat; a good many go down and ramify amongst the flints, or go through into the pan; they are finer, and not so much blunted and divaricated as the Wheat roots. For illustration of the curious root-development of the barley plant, see Plates XV. fig. 16.

Soil dry, loose, and porous.

Preparation and analysis as described at pp. 543, 544.

No. 11.—*Oats* (1858); *four seeds; prepared soil; with nitrogenous manure.*
(See Plate XV. fig. 12.)

April 27.—Seeds set, and pot placed over sulphuric acid, and covered with a glass shade.

May 7.—The pot removed to its place on the stand.

May 20.—Three plants up; 4 to 4½ inches high; two leaves each; green and healthy.

May 22.—A pipette-ful of the sulphate-of-ammonia solution added (=0·004 grm. N.).

May 29.—Three plants; 5 to 7 inches high; four or five leaves each; two lowest dead, three uppermost green and growing. These plants have increased the most of any since the addition of ammonia. A pipette-ful of the phosphate-solution added.

June 7.—Second pipette-ful of the sulphate-of-ammonia solution added; also a pipette-ful of the phosphate-solution.

June 19.—Three plants; 10 to 14 inches high; six leaves each; apparently somewhat injured by hot sun the last few days.

June 21.—Third pipette-ful of the sulphate-of-ammonia solution added.

June 26.—Fourth pipette-ful of the sulphate-of-ammonia solution added. Three plants, 12 to 14 inches high. No. 1, head developed and obviously seeds forming; one shoot 1 inch, and one 4 inches long from the base. No. 2, head forming; two shoots from the base 4 to 5 inches long. No. 3, much like No. 2. Growth of main stems apparently checked and that of shoots increased by some recent hot weather; in all, six shoots; green, healthy, and promising further growth.

July 3.—Fifth pipette-ful of the sulphate-of-ammonia solution, also a pipette-ful of the phosphate-solution added.

July 12.—Sixth pipette-ful of the sulphate-of-ammonia solution added.

July 14.—Seventh pipette-ful of the sulphate-of-ammonia solution added. Plants as follow:—

No. 1. Two stems; one ripe, with two or three seeds; six leaves, lowest dead ripe, and five green. The other stem 12 to 14 inches high; green; forming head.

No. 2. Three stems, from 12 to 15 inches high. One stem swelled at the top with a head, but not maturing; checked early, apparently from want of available nitrogen, after which the ammonia added developed the two shoots, whose stems are green, with one dead and four green leaves, and heads forming.

No. 3. Two stems; one 8 to 10 inches high, dead or ripe; the other 14 to 15 inches high, green and healthy.

July 30.—*The plants taken up*:—

The experiment stopped rather prematurely, the shade getting slightly cracked. The plants had manifested three orders of growth, as follow:—

(1) The first growth, which was forming head when a fresh supply of ammonia gave rise to shoots at the base. (2) The above shoots gave three headed stems: one with three full and two imperfect seeds; one with two full and one imperfect seed; and one with one full and two imperfect seeds. (3) New shoots from the base on the further addition of ammonia; green and healthy at the close, but promising to go to seed.

The roots were very little more distributed than those of the Oats without nitrogenous manure in No. 3 shade, and only extended about half the depth of the pot. The soil was wet and soft.

Preparation and analysis as described at pp. 543, 544.

No. 12.—*Beans* (1858); *three seeds; prepared soil; with nitrogenous manure.*

April 27.—Seeds set, and the pot placed over sulphuric acid, and covered with a glass shade.

May 20.—Pot removed to its shade on the stand. Three plants up; 2½ inches high; three leaves on each, colour dark green; healthy.

May 22.—A pipette-ful of the sulphuric-acid solution added.

May 29.—Three plants; one dead, one much specked, the third improving. A pipette-ful of the phosphate-solution added.

June 7.—A pipette-ful of the sulphate-of-ammonia solution added; also a pipette-ful of the phosphate-solution.

June 19.—All apparently dying; leaves much specked with black.

June 21.—Plants all obviously past recovery; removed but not analysed.

No. 13.—*Peas* (1858); *three seeds; prepared soil; with nitrogenous manure.*

April 27.—Seeds set, and the pot placed over sulphuric acid, and covered with a glass shade.

May 20.—Pot removed to its shade on the stand. Three plants up, growing exceedingly well; 3, 2½, and 1 inch high; three, two, and two leaves, respectively.

May 22.—A pipette-ful of the sulphuric acid solution added.

May 29.—One plant dead; another sickly; the third has given off shoots 3 to 4 inches high, which appear healthy. A pipette-ful of the phosphate-solution added.

June 7.—A pipette-ful of the sulphate-of-ammonia solution (=0·004 gramme N.) added; also a pipette-ful of the phosphate-solution.

June 19.—Two plants dead; the third has two green shoots, 3 and 5 inches high, but delicate.

June 26.—The two shoots growing languidly; seven leaves each; also some leaflets.

July 3.—A pipette-ful of the phosphate-solution added.

July 14.—Main shoot 12 to 13 inches high; four lower leaves dead, four upper green; two shoots at the base dead, and one green and thriving.

July 29.—The two dead plants entirely prostrate, and near one a pale-green moss formed on the surface of the soil. The third plant has three dead branches, and one about 6 inches high with green leaves at the top.

August 17.—All the plants dead.

August 24.—Plants taken up, and submitted to analysis, although the growth so unsatisfactory. Of course, of themselves, the results can have little weight in reference to the question at issue.

No. 14.—*Clover* (1858); 226 *seeds*; *prepared soil*; *with nitrogenous manure.*

Two pots of Clover had been sown at the same time as the other plants, one to be without, and the other with nitrogenous manure. They came up well, but very soon died; and on June 6 two more pots were sown in the same manner as before, excepting that the ash was neutralized with sulphuric acid, and re-ignited before being mixed with the soil; both also had a pipette-ful of the phosphate-solution, and the one that was to have nitrogenous manure a pipette-ful of the ammonia-solution, at the time of sowing the seed. The one sown without the ammonia-solution failed so soon that the experiment was abandoned early; the other (with the ammonia) forms the subject of the following record.

June 6.—Seeds set as above, in soil with neutralized ash, and both phosphate and sulphate-of-ammonia solution added*.

June 19.—A good deal up; actively and healthily growing.

June 21.—Second pipette-ful of the sulphate-of-ammonia solution added*.

June 26.—Third pipette-ful of the sulphate-of-ammonia solution added. Plants quite green and healthy.

July 3.—Fourth pipette-ful of the sulphate-of-ammonia solution added; also a pipette-ful of the phosphate-solution.

July 12.—Fifth pipette-ful of the sulphate-of-ammonia solution added.

July 14.—Sixth pipette-ful of the sulphate-of-ammonia solution added. Surface of

* It is not quite certain that the ammonia-solution was added at this date; and in the Table of the results (XIV. p. 531) it is assumed that it was not.

the soil covered with plants, growing well; 3 to 4 inches high, with two or three trifoliate leaves each.

July 19.—Seventh pipette-ful of the sulphate-of-ammonia solution added.

July 28.—Eighth pipette-ful of the sulphate-of-ammonia solution added.

July 29.—The plants growing, but not vigorously; some black and dead, and some withering leaves; some petioles more than 4 inches long.

August 10.—Ninth pipette-ful of the sulphate-of-ammonia solution added.

August 17.—Tenth pipette-ful of the sulphate-of-ammonia solution added (new solution =0·00359 gramme N.). Green and growing well; twenty to twenty-five stems 4 to 6 inches high; a good many roots above ground.

September 7.—Eleventh pipette-ful of the sulphate-of-ammonia solution added. Large strong roots visible; numerous leaves from the base; not much development of stem: length of petioles 3 to 5 inches.

October 5.—Twelfth pipette-ful of the sulphate-of-ammonia solution added. Not growing much, yet not dying; stems becoming bushy.

October 24.—Many of the lower petioles and leaves dead, and some a little mouldy; from the base of the dead petioles generally spring a number of green leaves, and petioles 2 to 4 inches long bearing green leaves, which look healthy, but almost stationary from day to day.

October 26.—*Plants taken up*:—

Twenty-one plants; much as at last date.

Roots somewhat matted at the base, and throughout the surface of the soil; extending 2 to 3 inches through the soil, and some to the inner sides of the pot; none among the flints, or in the pan under the pot.

Soil rather wet, loose, and porous.

Preparation and analysis as described at pp. 543, 544.

No. 15 (1858).—*Wheat, Barley, Oats, Beans, Peas, and Clover, in a pot of Garden soil.*

May 20.—Some of the plants just coming up.

May 29.—Wheat, Barley, and Oats, 6 to 8 inches high; Beans 4 to 6 inches high, with some specks on the leaves; Clover up and growing. The condensed water yellowish, and gives a yellowish-green deposit.

June 19.—The pot full of green herbage. Wheat, Barley, Oats, and Beans, all healthy and growing well; Peas 3 to 4 inches high; Clover 2 to 3 inches, with three leaflets.

June 26.—Wheat and Barley touch the top of the shade, and the plants crowded; Clover 3 to 4 inches high.

July 14.—Shade full of growing matter. Wheat and Barley just heading.

August 2.—The Oat heading, with two grains; Wheat growing, but the ends of some of the leaves dying. The two Beans quite black and dead. Several kinds of weed come up; two in bloom.

August 17.—Shade full of vegetable matter. Wheat, Barley, Oats, and weeds growing; but Leguminous plants dead.

September 7.—A good deal of growth yet.

October 5.—A good deal of grass and weeds growing. Cereals ripening.

October 24.—Shade full; experiment stopped. Wheat not quite ripe. Barley and Oats dead ripe; Beans and Peas all dead; a little Clover still living; some grass, and other weeds, green, and some seeded. The whole soil filled with roots, many distributed through the flints, and a large quantity growing in the pan under the pot.

No. 16.—*Buckwheat* (1858); *forty-two seeds* (1 *gramme*); *prepared soil; with nitrogenous manure.*

August 20.—Seed sown, and the pot placed over sulphuric acid, and covered with a glass shade.

August 24.—Pot removed to its shade on the stand. Several plants up.

September 7.—A pipette-ful of the sulphate-of-ammonia solution added (=0·00359 gramme N.). Plants growing well.

October 5.—Second pipette-ful of the sulphate-of-ammonia solution added. Much more vigorous than the Buckwheat without ammonia (No. 7); about twenty plants; 5 to 7 inches high; four to six leaves on each.

October 24.—Third pipette-ful of the sulphate-of-ammonia solution added. Growing well; 5 to 7 inches high; six plants in bloom. Comparing with No. 7, the influence of ammonia here is very marked, as shown in size, vigour, and maturation.

November 22.—*Plants taken up*:—

Twenty-four plants; 4 to 7 inches high; five to seven leaves on each; six stems have flowered; bloom gone off and rudimentary seed formed; would probably have grown more but for frost.

Roots less in proportion to upward growth than with Buckwheat without ammonia; none deeper in the soil than 1½ to 2 inches; slim, delicate, and but little distributed.

Soil loose and porous.

Preparation and analysis as described at pp. 543, 544.

No. 17 (1858).—PLANTS GROWN WITH NITROGENOUS MANURE IN M. G. VILLE'S CASE.

The same descriptions of pot, pan, soil, ash, &c., were used for these experiments as for the others, as explained at page 565. Plants as under:—

Wheat, four seeds; Barley, four seeds; Oats, four seeds; Beans, three seeds.

June 29.—Seeds set, and the pots placed over sulphuric acid, and covered with a glass shade.

July 5.—Pots removed to M. VILLE's Case.

July 14.—A pipette-ful of the sulphate-of-ammonia solution given to each pot (=0·004 gramme N.). Wheat, four plants just appearing; Barley, three plants 1½ inch high; Oats, two plants just appearing; Beans, one plant 4 inches high, two others just appearing.

July 19.—Second pipette-ful of the sulphate-of-ammonia solution to each pot.

July 28.—Third pipette-ful of the sulphate-of-ammonia solution to each pot of Cereals.

August 2.—Wheat, four plants; 7 inches high; extremities of some of the leaves dying. Barley, three plants; two 9 inches, and one 7 inches high; two lower leaves of each yellow, remainder green. Oats, two plants; 10 inches high; the lower leaf of each dead, and the tips of some of the others turning yellow. Beans, two plants up; one 8, and the other 6 inches high.

August 17.—Fourth pipette-ful of the sulphate-of-ammonia solution added (new solution, =0·00359 gramme N.). All the plants growing luxuriantly. Wheat, about 14 inches high; Barley and Oats, 8 to 12 inches high; Beans, 9 and 12 inches high.

September 7.—Fifth pipette-ful of the sulphate-of-ammonia solution added.

Wheat, four plants; (*a*) 14 inches high with ten leaves; (*b*) 13 inches high with nine leaves; (*c*) 15 inches high with ten leaves; (*d*) 11 inches high with ten leaves.

Barley, three plants; (*a*) 23 inches high with eleven leaves; (*b*) 14 inches high with ten leaves; (*c*) 25 inches high with eleven leaves.

Oats, two plants; (*a*) 26 inches high with seven leaves; (*b*) 29 inches high, nine leaves.

Beans, two plants; main stems dead, but new shoots growing.

October 5.—Wheat, four healthy and vigorous plants; (*a*) 14 inches high; two green and eight dead leaves; (*b*) 14 inches high; two green and seven dead leaves; (*c*) 15 inches high; two green and eight dead leaves; (*d*) 14 inches high; three green and eight dead leaves.

Barley, three plants; two healthy and vigorous, and one less so; (*a*) 24 inches high; three green and eight dead leaves; (*b*) 18 inches high; three green and seven dead leaves; (*c*) 28 inches high; three green and eight dead leaves.

Oats, two healthy and vigorous plants, in ear; (*a*) 30 inches high; two green and five dead leaves; (*b*) 30 inches high; two green and seven dead leaves.

Beans, two plants; (*a*) 9 inches high with three branches; (*b*) 14 inches high with three branches.

October 24.—Wheat, four plants, erect and firm; much as on October 5, but larger; no nodes visible; but little tendency to form stem. Barley, much as on October 5. Oats, much as on October 5. Beans, apparently ceased to grow.

Sixth pipette-ful of the sulphate-of-ammonia solution added. Wheat, four plants, 14 to 18 inches high; stems stout and erect, but without visible nodes; very leafy. Barley, four plants, just coming to ear. Oats, two plants, main stems touching the top of the Case; (*a*) has a shoot 22 inches long springing from the first node 2 inches from the soil, and coming into head; (*b*) has three small shoots, one ½ inch and one 1½ inch long, springing from the base, and one 3 inches long from the first node. Beans, slightly revived since the last report.

Notes on taking up the Plants.

Wheat taken up December 9.—The four plants all about the same size; strong, healthy, and vigorous; ten to twelve long dead leaves each, 8, 10, or 12 inches long, closely compacted one above another at their base, and two or three green flourishing leaves each at the top. Roots very thick and matted at the base, extending immediately around in all directions, with short rootlets covered with divaricated branches, filling the upper layers of soil; not many extend more than 2½ inches down, very few go through the bottom of the pot into the pan, and none ramify there. Soil loose, porous, and moist; and some water in the pan.

Barley taken up December 9.—Three plants; (*a*) 29 inches high, with a small shoot (second growth) 1 inch long, from the base; fifteen leaves, two top ones green and growing; swelled at the top with a head forming; (*b*) 20 inches high; thirteen leaves, upper ones green and growing; and indications of head forming; (*c*) much like (*a*) in height, leaves, and shoot; a short air-root from the first node. Roots the same character in all; branched, considerably matted at the base, finely divided with numerous little divaricate branchlets; only a few extend down into the pan, and they do not ramify in it. Soil loose, open, porous, and moist; some water in the pan.

Oats taken up December 9.—Two plants:—(*a*) with two stems; one 32 inches high, eleven imperfect seeds, and seven leaves; the other 26 inches high, coming from the second node 2 inches up the main stem, with twelve seeds; six or eight air-roots 1 to 2 inches long, coming from the base node; a shoot an inch long from the lowest node, and another lower down at the base. (*b*) A main stem with two long branched ones; main stem 32 inches long, with five leaves and ten undeveloped seeds without solid nucleus; one branched stem, from the third node, 3 inches up the main stem, 14 inches long, with three leaves, still green and growing; the other branch from the base of the main stem 10 inches long, green and growing; some air-roots 1 to 2 inches long come from the base of the largest branch, also several from the next node below, one or two of which extend to the soil and ramify in it. There is also another small branch 2 to 3 inches long coming from the base of the plant and still green and growing. Roots much alike in both; considerably matted at the base, little distributed, extending 3 or 4 inches in the upper parts of the soil, with many small divaricate branches; no roots in the pan. Soil loose, porous, and moist; and some water in the pan.

Beans taken up December 9.—Two plants, with eight or ten leaves each; one 9 inches, the other 14 inches high; both dead. The roots of both very much branched at the base of the stem, but not extending deep into the pot, none going down to the flints.

The Wheat, Barley, Oats, and Beans, prepared and analysed as described at pp. 543, 544.

Fig. 1. Plan of Pot.

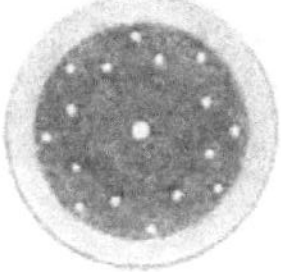

Fig. 2. Elevation of Pot

Fig. 3. Elevation of Pot & Pan

Fig. 4. Plan of Stoneware Lute

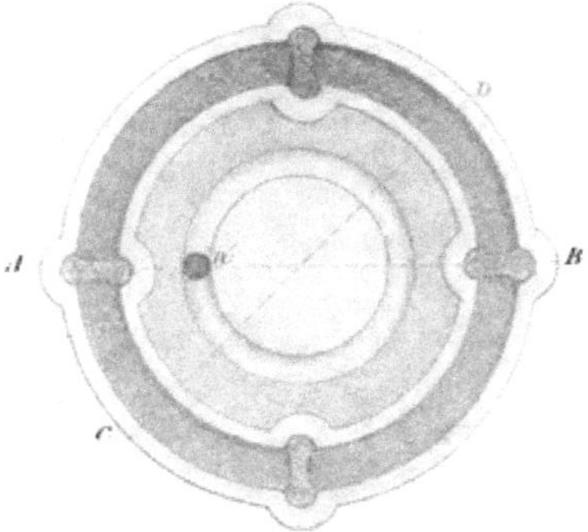

Section of Stoneware Lute Fig. 5.

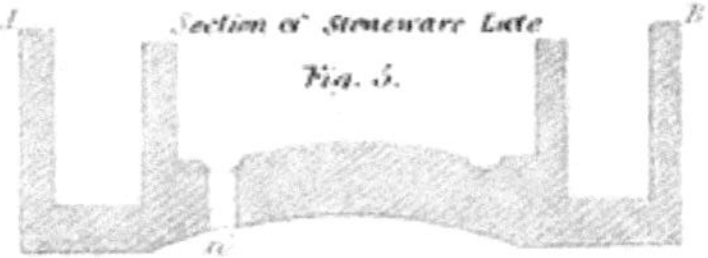

Section of Stoneware Lute Fig. 6.

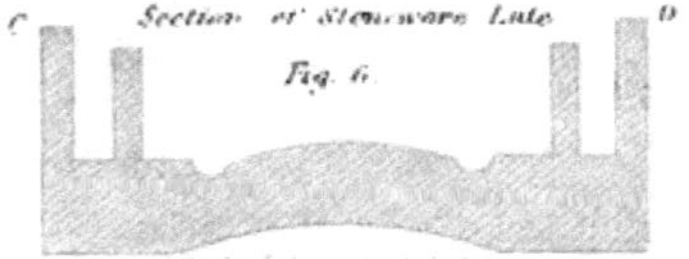

Scale ½ Inch to 1 Inch

Fig. 7

Fig. 8

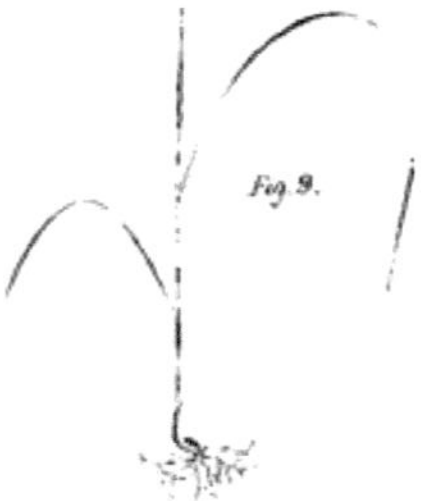

Fig. 9.

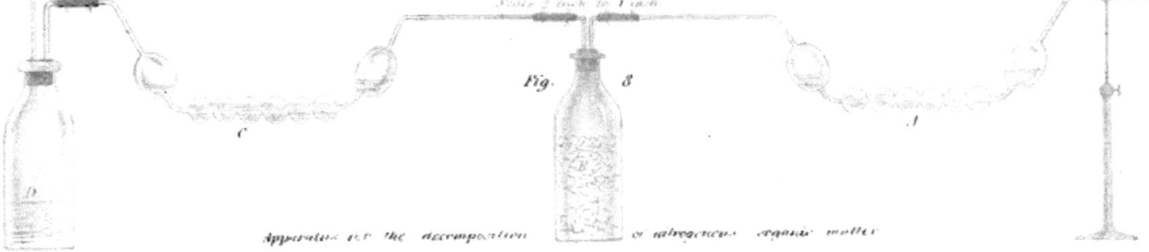

Apparatus for the decomposition of nitrogenous organic matter

APPARATUS USED IN 1857,

in Experiments on the question whether Plants assimilate Free Nitrogen

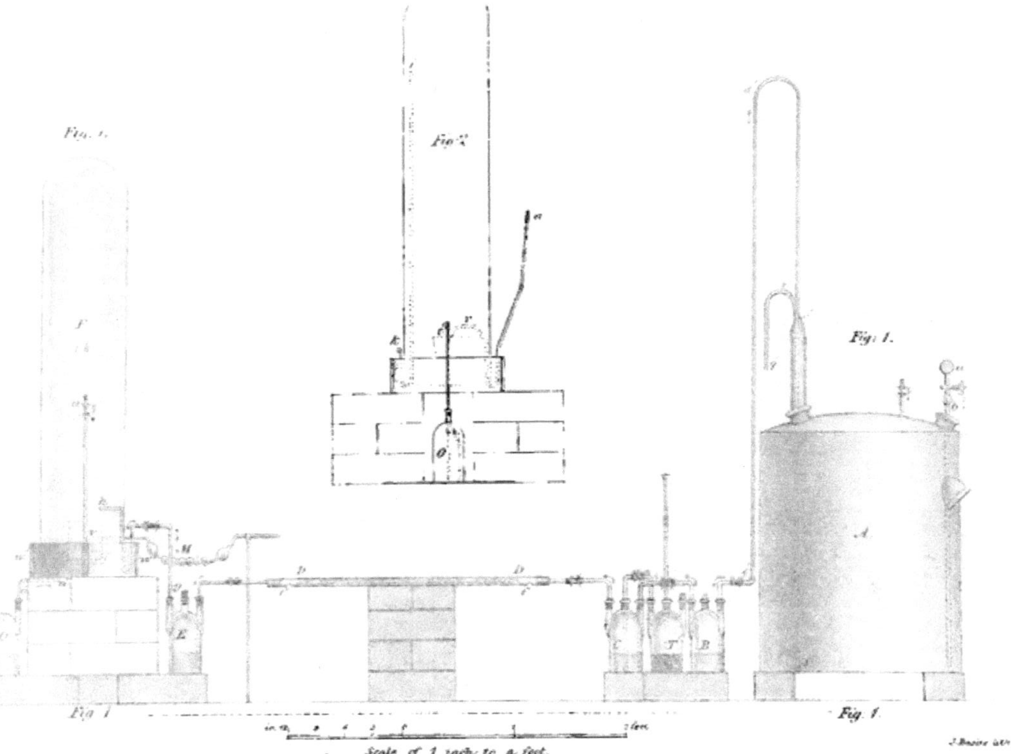

Apparatus used in 1858, in Experiments on the Question whether Plants assimilate Free Nitrogen.

GRAMINACEOUS PLANTS

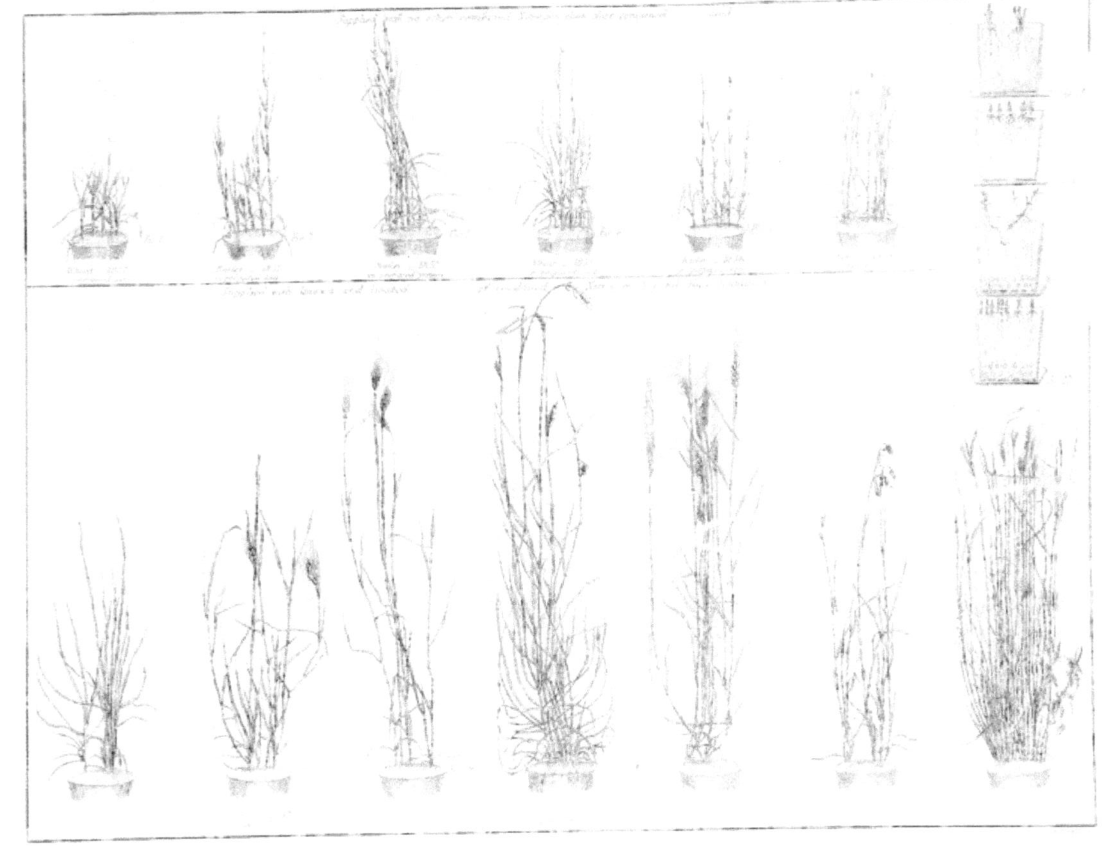

MEMORANDA

OF THE

PLAN AND RESULTS

OF THE

ROTHAMSTED FIELD EXPERIMENTS.

MAY, 1866.

Experiments with different Manures on PERMANENT MEADOW LAND.

THE PARK.

The Land has probably been laid down with Grass for some centuries. No fresh seed has been artificially sown within the last 30 years certainly, nor is there record of having been sown since the Grass was first laid down. The experiments commenced in 1856, at which time the character of the herbage appeared uniform over all Plots. Excepting as explained in the Table, and in the foot-notes, the same description of Manure has been applied to the same Plots year after year.

(Area under experiment, about 6½ acres.)

1 acre	= (about)	0·40 Hectare	or 1·59 Prussian Morgen.
1 lb. (pound avoir.)	= (about)	0·45 Kilogrammes	or 0·91 Zollverein Pfund.
1 cwt. (hundredweight)	= (about)	51·0 Kilogrammes	or 1·02 Centner.
1 ton	= (about)	1016·0 Kilogrammes	or 20·33 Centner.
1 lb. per acre	= (about)	1·12 Kilogramme per Hectare	or 0·57 Zollv. Pfd. per Pr. Morgen.
1 cwt. per acre	= (about)	125.5 Kilogrammes per Hectare	or 0·64 Centner per Pr. Morgen.

Plots.	Manures, per acre; eleventh season—1866.	Produce per Acre, weighed as Hay. Average per Annum; 10 Years 1856–1865.	Produce per Acre, weighed as Hay. Tenth Season 1865
		Cwts.	Cwt
1	200 lbs. Ammonia-salts (1) [also 14 tons Farmyard Manure per acre per annum, for 8 years, 1856–1863]	49½ } (7)	32
2	Unmanured, 1864 and since [14 tons Farmyard Manure per acre per annum, for 8 years, 1856–1863]	43 } (7)	25
3	Unmanured, continuously	22½	11
4a	Superphosphate of Lime (2)	24½ } (8)	11
4b	ditto ; and 400 lbs. "Ammonia-salts"	39½ } (8)	26
5	400 lbs. "Ammonia-salts"	30½	15
(3) 6	400 lbs. ditto	31½	16
7	Sulphates of Potass, Soda, and Magnesia (4); and "Superphosphate of Lime"	34	22
(3) 8	Sulphates of Soda and Magnesia (5) ; ditto	33¾	17
9	Sulphates of Potass, Soda, and Magnesia (4); ditto ; and 400 lbs. "Ammonia-salts"	53½	34
(3) 10	Sulphates of Soda and Magnesia (5) ; ditto ; 400 lbs. "Ammonia-salts"	32¾	32
11	Sulphates of Potass, Soda, and Magnesia (4); ditto ; 800 lbs. (6) "Ammonia-salts"	61¾	52
11a	Sulphates of Potass, Soda, and Magnesia (4); ditto ; 800 lbs. (6) "Ammonia-salts; and 200 lbs. each, Silicate of Soda and Silicate of Lime	66¼ (9)	55
12	Unmanured, continuously	25	17
13	Sulphates of Potass, Soda, and Magnesia (4); "Superphosphate of Lime" ; 400 lbs. "Ammonia-salts;" and 2000 lbs. Cut Wheat-straw	54½	41
14	Sulphates of Potass, Soda, and Magnesia (4); "Superphosphate of Lime" ; and 550 lbs. Nitrate of Soda	53 } (10)	47
15	none ; none ; 550 lbs. ditto	36 } (10)	28
16	Sulphates of Potass, Soda, and Magnesia (4); "Superphosphate of Lime" ; and 275 lbs. ditto	45½ } (10)	36
17	none ; none ; 275 lbs. ditto	34½ } (10)	26
18	Mixture supplying the quantity of Potass, Soda, Lime, Magnesia, Phosphoric Acid, Silica, and Nitrogen contained in 1 ton of hay (commencing in 1865)	...	2[illegible]

(1) Equal parts Sulphate and Muriate of Ammonia of Commerce.
(2) 200 lbs. Bone-ash, 150 lbs. Sulphuric Acid (Sp. gr. 1·7).
(3) Plots 6, 8, and 10, had, besides the Manures specified, 2000 lbs. Sawdust per acre per annum for 7 years, 1856–1862, but without effect.
(4) 300 lbs. Sulphate of Potass, 100 lbs. Sulphate of Soda (200 lbs. 1856–1863), and 100 lbs. Sulphate of Magnesia.
(5) 250 lbs. Sulphate of Soda (500 lbs. in 1862 and 1863), and 100 lbs. Sulphate of Magnesia (Sulphate of Potass also as on Plots 7, &c., 1856–1861).
(6) 800 lbs. in 1856-7-8; only 400 lbs. in 1859-60-61; and 800 lbs. since

Experiments on the Growth of **BARLEY** year after year on the same Land, without Manure, and with different kinds of Manure.

HOOS FIELD.

Previous Cropping—1847, Swedish Turnips, with Dung and Superphosphate of Lime, the Roots carted off; 1848, Barley; 1849, Clover; 1850, Wheat; 1851, Barley manured with Ammonia-salts.

First Experimental Barley Crop in 1852. Barley every year since; and, with one or two exceptions, the same Manures on the same Plots each year.

(Area under experiment, about 4½ acres.)

1 acre .. .. .. = (about)	0·40 Hectare	or 1·59 Prussian Morgen.
1 bushel .. .. .. = (about)	0·36 Hectolitre	or 0·66 Prussian Scheffel.
1 lb. (pound avoir.) .. = (about)	0·45 Kilogramme	or 0·91 Zollverein Pfund.
1 cwt. (hundredweight) = (about)	51·0 Kilogrammes	or 1·02 Centner.
1 bushel per acre .. = (about)	0·9 Hectolitre per Hectare	or 0·42 Pr. Scheffel per Pr. Morgen.
1 lb. per acre .. .. = (about)	1·12 Kilogramme per Hectare	or 0·57 Zollv. Pfd. per Pr. Morgen.
1 cwt. per acre .. = (about)	125·5 Kilogrammes per Hectare	or 0·64 Centner per Pr. Morgen.

Plots.	Manures, per acre; fifteenth Season—1866.	Produce per Acre. Average per Annum, over 14 Years, 1852–1865. Dressed Corn. Quantity.	Weight per Bushel.	Total Straw.	Fourteenth Season, 186[illegible]. Dressed Corn. Quantity.	Weight per Bushel.	Total Straw.
		Bushels.	lbs.	cwts.	Bushels.	lbs.	cwts.
1 O.	Unmanured continuously	21¾	52	12¼	18	54	8
2 O.	Superphosphate of Lime (1)	27¾	52¾	14¼	22½	53¾	9
3 O.	Mixed Alkalies (2)	24¼	52¼	13¼	22	54½	9½
4 O.	Ditto; and "Superphosphate of Lime"	30¼	53	15¼	24½	54	10
6 {1	Unmanured continuously	24½	52½	13¾	21	53¾	8¼
6 {2	Ashes (burnt soil, turf, and weeds)	23¾	52½	12¾	19¼	53¾	8¾
7	Farm-yard dung (14 tons every year)	48¼	53½	28¼	52¾	54½	25½
1 A.	200 lbs. Ammonia-salts (3)	34½	51¾	19¼	29¾	53¾	13
2 A.	200 lbs. ditto; and "Superphosphate of Lime"	48¼	52¾	28¼	48½	52¾	21¾
3 A.	200 lbs. ditto; none; and "Mixed Alkalies"	36½	52¼	21¼	33¼	54¾	16
4 A.	200 lbs. ditto; "Superphosphate of Lime"; and ditto	47¾	53½	¼	46½	53½	22½
1 AA.	200 lbs. (4) ditto	39½	51½	23¼	33¾	53½	16
2 AA.	200 lbs. (4) ditto; and "Superphosphate of Lime"	50¼	52¼	31½	47½	52¼	23
3 AA.	200 lbs. (4) ditto; none; and "Mixed Alkalies"	39¾	51¾	25¼	34¼	54¾	17
4 AA.	200 lbs. (4) ditto; "Superphosphate of Lime"; and ditto	51	52¼	34	49	53¼	24¾
1 AAS.	200 lbs. (4) ditto; none; none; and 200 lbs. each, Silicate of Soda and Silicate of Lime (5)	39½	55¼	24¼	35	54½	22¼
2 AAS.	200 lbs. (4) ditto; and "Superphosphate of Lime"; none; ditto	51	54¾	28½	47½	52¼	23¼
3 AAS.	200 lbs. (4) ditto; none; "Mixed Alkalies"; ditto	45½	56	25¼	41	54¾	20½
4 AAS.	200 lbs. (4) ditto; "Superphosphate of Lime"; ditto; ditto	54¾	55	33¼	50½	53	25½
1 C.	1000 lbs. (6) Rape-cake	46¾	52¾	28¼	45	53¾	21¾
2 C.	1000 lbs. (6) ditto; and "Superphosphate of Lime"	48¼	52¾	30	46¼	53¼	22
3 C.	1000 lbs. (6) ditto; none; and "Mixed Alkalies"	44¾	52¾	28¼	48¾	53¾	22
4 C.	1000 lbs. (6) ditto; "Superphosphate of Lime"; and ditto	48¼	52½	30¾	48¼	53½	22
1 N. (7)	275 lbs. Nitrate of Soda	38¾ (11)	52½ (11)	23¾ (11)	37	54	18½
2 N. (8)	275 lbs. (8) ditto	43 (11)	52 (11)	27¼ (11)	39¾	53¾	21½
5 O.	200 lbs. (9) Sulphate of Potass; and "Superphosphate of Lime" (10)	24¼ (12)	52¾ (12)	13¼ (12)	23	54½	10¾
5 A.	200 lbs. (9) ditto; ditto; and 200 lbs. "Ammonia-salts"	45¾ (12)	52¾ (12)	29¼ (12)	48½	54¼	24¾
M.	100 lbs. each, Sulph. Soda and Sulph. Magnesia; and ditto	23¼ (13)	52¾ (13)	12¾ (13)	19¾	54½	9½

(1) 200 lbs. Bone-ash, **150** lbs. Sulphuric acid (sp. gr. 1·7). (2) 200 lbs. Sulphate of Potass, 100 lbs. Sulphate of Soda, and 100 lbs. Magnesia (for the first six years, 300 lbs., 200 lbs., and **100 lbs., respectively).**

(3) Equal parts Sulphate and Muriate of Ammonia of Commerce. (4) 400 lbs. per annum for the first six years, and 200 lbs. only each year since.

(5) The application of Silicates did not commence until 1864, so that the average produce given applies to two years only (1864 and 1865). These Silicated plots (**"AAS") comprise, respectively, one half of the original "AA" plots**, and, as will be seen, they continue to be, in other respects, manured in the same way as the remaining halves.

(6) 2000 lbs. per annum for the first six years, and 1000 lbs. only, each year since. (7) 300 lbs. Sulphate of Potass, 200 lbs. Bone-ash, and 150 lbs. Sulphuric acid (sp. gr. 1·7), without Nitrate of Soda, the first year (1852); Nitrate alone each year since. (8) 550 lbs. Nitrate of Soda for 1853-4-5-6, and 7; and 275 lbs. only each year since. (9) 300 lbs. per annum for the first six years, and 200 lbs. each year since.

(10) Ammonia-salts also the first year, but not since. (11) Average of 13 years only. (12) Average of 13 years only. (13) Average of 11 years only.

EXPERIMENTS ON THE GROWTH OF **WHEAT** YEAR AFTER YEAR ON THE SAME LAND; WITHOUT MANURE, AND WITH DIFFERENT KINDS OF MANURE.

BROADBALK FIELD.

Previous Cropping—1839, Turnips, with Farmyard Manure; 1840, Barley; 1841, Peas; 1842, Wheat; 1843, Oats; the last four Crops Unmanured.

First Experimental Wheat Crop in 1844. Wheat every year since; and, with some exceptions, nearly the same description of Manure on the same Plots each year—especially during the last 14 years.

(Area under experiment, about 13 acres.)

1 acre = (about) 0·40 Hectare	or 1·59 Prussian Morgen.
1 bushel = (about) 0·36 Hectolitre	or 0·66 Prussian Scheffel.
1 lb. (pound avoir.) = (about) 0·45 Kilogramme	or 0·91 Zollverein Pfund.
1 cwt. (hundredweight) = (about) 51·0 Kilogrammes	or 1·02 Centner.
1 bushel per acre = (about) 0·9 Hectolitre per Hectare	or 0·42 Pr. Scheffel per Pr. Morgen.
1 lb. per acre = (about) 1·12 Kilogramme per Hectare	or 0·57 Zollv. Pfd. per Pr. Morgen.
1 cwt. per acre = (about) 125·5 Kilogrammes per Hectare	or 0·64 Centner per Pr. Morgen.

Plots.	Manures, per acre; twenty-third season—1866.	Produce per Acre. Average per Annum, over 14 Years, 1852–1865. Dressed Corn. Quantity.	Weight per Bushel.	Total Straw.	Twenty-second Season, 1865. Dressed Corn. Quantity.	Weight per Bushel.	Total Straw.
		Bushels.	lbs.	cwts.	Bushels.	lbs.	cwts.
0	Superphosphate of Lime (three times as much as on No. 5 and succeeding Plots)	18	58	15⅝	15¼	59	10¼
1	Mixed Alkalies (twice as much as on No. 5 and succeeding Plots)	16	57¾	15	12¼	59	9½
2	Farm-yard dung (14 tons every year)	35⅞	59⅞	34	37¼	61¼	27⅞
3	Unmanured continuously	15⅛	57½	14½	13⅜	60¼	9¼
4	Unmanured for Crop of 1852, and since (previously Superphosphate and Ammonia-salts)	16⅞	57⅝	14⅝	14¼	60¼	10¼
5 (a and b)	Mixed Alkalies[1] ; and Superphosphate of Lime[2]	18	58½	16¼	14¾	61	10⅛
6 (a and b)	ditto ; ditto ; and 200 lbs. Ammonia-salts[3]	28⅛	59	26⅛	25	61	18
7 (a and b)	ditto ; ditto ; and 400 lbs. ditto	37½	59	37⅞	40¾	61¼	32⅞
8 (a and b)	ditto ; ditto ; and 600 lbs. ditto	39½	58¼	42½	43⅝	61⅛	41
9 a	ditto ; ditto ; and 550 lbs. Nitrate of Soda	36½	57⅞	40⅞	41	61	41⅞
9 b	none ; none ; 550 lbs. ditto	29¾	56¼	28⅛	29⅛	59½	28
10 a	none since 1844 ; none since 1844 ; 400 lbs. "Ammonia-salts"	23⅝	56⅜	23⅛	25⅛	59¼	21⅛
10 b	none (except 1844, '48 and '50) ; none (except 1844, '48, & '50) ; 400 lbs. ditto	27⅞	57⅛	27⅛	30⅛	59⅞	24
11 (a and b)	none ; "Superphosphate of Lime" ; and 400 lbs. ditto	30	56⅞	28⅞	27⅛	57⅛	22⅛
12 (a and b)	366½ lbs.[4] Sulphate of Soda ; ditto ; and 400 lbs. ditto	35⅞	58⅞	35	34⅛	60	27⅞
13 (a and b)	200 lbs.[4] Sulphate of Potass ; ditto ; and 400 lbs. ditto	35⅛	59	35⅛	37	61	30⅞
14 (a and b)	280 lbs.[4] Sulphate of Magnesia ; ditto ; and 400 lbs. ditto	35⅛	58⅞	35⅛	36⅛	60⅛	28¼
15 a	"Mixed Alkalies" ; ditto[5] ; and 400 lbs. ditto	33⅞	59	33⅛	35⅛	60⅞	28
15 b	ditto ; ditto[6] ; 300 lbs. ditto ; and 500 lbs. Rape-cake	35⅛	59⅛	35⅛	36⅛	61⅛	30⅛
16 (a and b)	none ; none ; none	39	58⅛	45	32⅛	61⅞	25⅞
17 (a and b)	none ; none ; 400 lbs. "Ammonia-Salts"	32⅛(7)	59 (7)	33 (7)	17 (9)	60⅞ (9)	13⅛ (9)
18 (a and b)	"Mixed Alkalies" ; "Superphosphate of Lime" ; none	18⅞(8)	58⅛(8)	17 (8)	31⅛(10)	60⅞(10)	25⅛ (10)
19	none ; ditto[5] ; 300 lbs. "Ammonia-salts"; and 500 lbs. Rape-cake	32⅛	58⅛	31	32⅞	58⅞	26⅞
20	Unmanured continuously	15⅛	57⅞	14⅞	13⅞	60⅛	11⅞
21	"Mixed Alkalies" ; "Superphosphate of Lime" ; and 100 lbs. Muriate Ammonia	22	58⅛	20⅛	18⅛	58	19
22	ditto ; ditto ; and 100 lbs. Sulphate Ammonia	21⅞	58⅛	20	19⅞	58¼	13⅞

EXPERIMENTS ON THE GROWTH OF LEGUMINOUS CROPS.

I.—Beans, Peas, and Tares.

Experiments on the growth of Leguminous corn-crops, with different descriptions of manure, were commenced in 1847, about 9 acres being devoted to the purpose.

Experiments with Beans were continued for thirteen consecutive seasons, to 1859 inclusive; but, during the later years, the crop fell off very much, and the land became very foul.

In 1860 the land was fallowed.

In 1861 a crop of wheat, without manure, was taken.

In 1862 beans were again sown, but with some variation in the manuring.

In 1863 the land was fallowed.

In 1864, and since, beans have been grown with much the same manures on the same plots as in 1862.

The general result of the experiments with Beans was, that mineral constituents added as manure (more particularly potass, and, to some extent, phosphoric acid also), increased the crop very much during the early years; and, to a certain extent, afterwards, whenever the season was favourable for the crop. Ammonia-salts, on the other hand, produced very little effect; notwithstanding that a Leguminous crop contains two, three, or more times as much nitrogen as a Graminaceous one grown under parallel circumstances. Nitrate of soda, however, has produced very striking effects. But Leguminous crops grown too frequently on the same land seem to be peculiarly subject to disease, which no combination of manuring that we have hitherto tried seems to obviate.

Experiments with Peas were soon abandoned, owing to the difficulty of keeping the land free from weeds; and an alternation of Beans and Wheat was substituted; the beans being manured much as in the experiments with the same crop above described.

In alternating Wheat with Beans, the remarkable result has been obtained, that nearly as much wheat, and nearly as much nitrogen, were yielded in 8 crops of wheat in alternation with the highly nitrogenous beans, as in 16 crops of wheat grown consecutively without manure, and also nearly as much as were obtained in another field in 8 crops alternated with bare fallow.

Experiments with Tares were also soon abandoned, for the same reason; beans being at first substituted, with some variation in the description of the manures employed; but of late this experiment has likewise been abandoned.

II.—Red Clover (*Trifolium pratense*).

Experiments on the growth of Clover, with different descriptions of manure, were commenced in 1849, and, with the occasional interposition of a corn-crop, or fallow, have been continued up to the present time. As with beans, the result was, that mineral constituents applied as manures (particularly potass, and, more or less, phosphoric acid also), considerably increased the early crops; whereas ammoniacal-salts had little or no effect. But since the first few years, all attempts to grow Clover year after year on this land have failed to give anything like a fair crop, or a plant that would stand the usual time on the ground; notwithstanding that fresh seed has been sown again and again. In one year, a portion of the land was trenched two feet deep; one-third of the manure being applied at a depth of 16 inches, one-third at a depth of 8 inches, and the remainder on the surface.

The general result of the experiments is, that neither ammoniacal-salts, nor nitrate of soda, nor organic matter rich in carbon as well as other constituents, nor mineral manures, nor a complex mixture, has availed to restore the clover-yielding capabilities of the land.

It is, however, worthy of remark that, in 1854, Red Clover was sown in a kitchen-garden only a few hundred yards distant from the experimental field, on soil which has been under ordinary garden cultivation for, probably, two or three centuries, and it has every year since shown very luxuriant growth; and, after re-sowing twice during the period (in 1860 and 1865), there is, at the present time, little or no indication of failure.

EXPERIMENTS ON THE GROWTH OF ROOT-CROPS.

EXPERIMENTS with TURNIPS were commenced in 1843. Eight acres, divided into numerous plots, were set apart for the purpose; and the crop was grown for ten consecutive years on the same land ("Norfolk Whites" 1843-1848 and "Swedes" 1849-1852); on some plots without manure, and on others with different descriptions of manure. Barley was then grown for three consecutive seasons (1853-1855) without manure, in order to test the comparative corn-growing condition of the different plots, and also to equalize their condition, as far as possible, by the exhaustion of some of the most active and immediately available constituents supplied by the previous manuring. A new series of experiments with Swedes was then arranged, having regard to the character of the manures previously applied on the different plots, and to the results previously obtained. This second series was commenced in 1856, and is still in progress.

It is impossible adequately to state the bearing of the results in a few words, but the following are some of the most characteristic indications:—

1. Without manure of any kind, the pro was reduced in a few years to a few cwts. p the diminutive plants (both root and leaf) con unusually high percentage of nitrogen.

2. Of "mineral" constituents, phosphoric form of superphosphate of lime) was by effective manure; but, when this manure is the immediately available nitrogen of the s exhausted.

3. Really large crops of turnips can only when the soil supplies a liberal amount bonaceous and nitrogenous matter (as well constituents); and when they are already ava the soil, or are supplied in the form of farm rape-cake, Peruvian guano, ammonia-salts, &c. of growth, and the amount of the crop, are gre by the use of superphosphate of lime applie seed.

AGDELL FIELD.

These Experiments were commenced in 1848; so that the present crop (1866) is the 19th experimental one, or the third crop of the Fifth Course.
One-third of the land has been continuously unmanured; one-third manured with Superphosphate of Lime alone once every four years, that is, for the turnip-crop commencing each course; and one-third manured (also for the turnip-crop only) with a complex manure, as described in the foot-note, No. 2.
In the Second, Third, and Fourth Courses, instead of clover, half of each plot was sown with beans, and the other half left fallow.
From half of each of the three plots the whole turnip-crop (roots and leaves) was removed; and on the other half the roots were eaten on the land by sheep, and the uneaten leaves were spread and ploughed in. In the case of all the other crops, the total produce was removed from the land.
The abstract of results given below relates to the portions of each plot from which the turnip-crops were entirely removed; and on which, in the later courses, beans (not fallow) replaced the clover.

(Area under experiment, about 2½ acres.)

1 lb. (pound avoir.) per acre .. = (about) 1·12 Kilogrammes per Hectare, or 0·37 Zollverein Pfund. per Prussian Morgen.
1 cwt. (hundredweight) per acre = (about) 125·5 Kilogrammes per Hectare, or 0·64 Centner per Pr. Morgen.

Years.	Description of Crop.	Produce per Acre.								
		Plot 1. Unmanured continuously.			Plot 2. Superphosphate of Lime (1), alone, for the Turnip Crops only.			Plot 3. Complex Manure (2), for the Turnip Crops only.		
		Corn (or roots).	Straw (or Leaf).	Total Produce.	Corn (or Roots).	Straw (or Leaf).	Total Produce.	Corn (or Roots).	Straw (or Leaf).	Total Produce.
					1st Course, 1848–51.					
1848	Swedish Turnips	175¼ cwts.	19¾ cwts.	195 cwts.	292 cwts.	35 cwts.	327 cwts.	394¾ cwts.	46¾ cwts.	441 cwts.
1849	Barley	1706 lbs.	2088 lbs.	3794 lbs.	1705 lbs.	1870 lbs.	3575 lbs.	2673 lbs.	2983 lbs.	5656 lbs.
1850	Clover (weighed green) ..	.. ..	.. ..	194¾ cwts.	.. ..	.. ..	199¾ cwts.	.. ..	.. ..	219½ cwts.
1851	Wheat	1958 lbs.	3431 lbs.	5389 lbs.	1882 lbs.	3371 lbs.	5253 lbs.	1948 lbs.	3552 lbs.	5500 lbs.
					2nd Course, 1852–55.					
1852	Swedish Turnips	26 cwts.	4½ cwts.	30½ cwts.	223¾ cwts.	20¾ cwts.	243¼ cwts.	396½ cwts.	36½ cwts.	433 cwts.
1853	Barley	2035 lbs.	2430 lbs.	4465 lbs.	1687 lbs.	1873 lbs.	3560 lbs.	2269 lbs.	2604 lbs.	4873 lbs.
1854	Beans	390 lbs.	1055 lbs.	1445 lbs.	431 lbs.	1103 lbs.	1534 lbs.	710 lbs.	1355 lbs.	2065 lbs.
1855	Wheat	2240 lbs.	3619 lbs.	5859 lbs.	2264 lbs.	3525 lbs.	5789 lbs.	2429 lbs.	3942 lbs.	6371 lbs.
					3rd Course, 1856–59.					
1856	Swedish Turnips	32 cwts.	2½ cwts.	34½ cwts.	136 cwts.	7¾ cwts.	142¼ cwts.	333¾ cwts.	12¼ cwts.	346½ cwts.
1857	Barley	2737 lbs.	2600 lbs.	5337 lbs.	1601 lbs.	1475 lbs.	3076 lbs.	2733 lbs.	2435 lbs.	5168 lbs.
1858	Beans	415 lbs.	1100 lbs.	1515 lbs.	450 lbs.	1155 lbs.	1605 lbs.	837 lbs.	1520 lbs.	2357 lbs.
1859	Wheat	2252 lbs.	4030 lbs.	6262 lbs.	2190 lbs.	3930 lbs.	6120 lbs.	2544 lbs.	4610 lbs.	7154 lbs.
					4th Course, 1860–63.					
1860	Swedish Turnips	1 cwt.	(6½ lbs.)	1 cwt.	29½ cwts.	1½ cwts.	30¾ cwts.	67¼ cwts.	3½ cwts.	90¾ cwts.
1861	Barley	2196 lbs.	2522 lbs.	4718 lbs.	1775 lbs.	2000 lbs.	3775 lbs.	3451 lbs.	3940 lbs.	7391 lbs.
1862	Beans	1821 lbs.	1840 lbs.	3661 lbs.	1890 lbs.	2150 lbs.	4040 lbs.	2710 lbs.	3280 lbs.	5990 lbs.
1863	Wheat	2583 lbs.	3467 lbs.	6350 lbs.	2229 lbs.	3390 lbs.	5619 lbs.	2929 lbs.	4697 lbs.	7626 lbs.
					5th Course, 1864–67.					
1864	Swedish Turnips	8¾ cwts.	3¾ cwts.	9½ cwts.	68 cwts.	4¾ cwts.	72¾ cwts.	176¼ cwts.	8¾ cwts.	185 cwts.
1865	Barley	2028 lbs.	2154 lbs.	4182 lbs.	1779 lbs.	1615 lbs.	3394 lbs.	2553 lbs.	2595 lbs.	5148 lbs.
1866	Beans	lbs.	lbs.	lbs.	lbs.	lbs.	lbs.	lbs.	lbs.	lbs.
1867	Wheat	lbs.	lbs.	lbs.	lbs.	lbs.	lbs.	lbs.	lbs.	lbs.

(1) First Course—100 lbs. Bone-ash, and 100 lbs. Sulphuric Acid (sp. gr. 1·7); Second Course—160 lbs. Bone-ash, 120 lbs. Sulphuric Acid; Third, Fourth and Fifth Courses—200 lbs. Bone-ash, and 150 lbs. Sulphuric Acid *per acre*.

(2) First Course—100 lbs. Pearl-ash, 100 lbs. Bone-ash, 100 lbs. Sulphuric Acid, 100 lbs. Sulphate of Ammonia, 100 lbs. Muriate of Ammonia, and 1000 lbs. Rape-cake; Second Course—300 lbs. Sulphate of Potass, 100 lbs. Sulphate of Soda, 100 lbs. Sulphate of Magnesia, 160 lbs. Bone-ash, 120 lbs. Sulphuric Acid, 100 lbs. Sulphate of Ammonia, 100 lbs. Muriate of Ammonia, and 2000 lbs. Rape-cake; Third, Fourth and Fifth Courses—300 lbs. Sulphate of Potass, 200 lbs., Sulphate of Soda, 100 lbs. Sulphate of Magnesia, 200 lbs. Bone-ash, 150 lbs. Sulphuric Acid, 100 lbs. Sulphate of Ammonia, 100 lbs. Muriate of Ammonia, and 2000 lbs. Rape-cake, *per acre*.

LONDON:
PRINTED BY W. CLOWES AND SONS, STAMFORD STREET,
AND CHARING CROSS.

RESEARCHES

ON THE

VOLATILE HYDROCARBONS.

(TWO MEMOIRS.)

BY C. M. WARREN.

[From the Memoirs of the American Academy, New Series, Vol. IX.]

CAMBRIDGE:
WELCH, BIGELOW, AND COMPANY,
PRINTERS TO THE UNIVERSITY.
1865.

VII.

Researches on the Volatile Hydrocarbons.

By C. M. WARREN.

Communicated October 11th, 1864.

Introductory Remarks. — While engaged, a few years since, in attempting to separate some of the constituents of coal-tar naphtha by the common process of fractional distillation, I was forced to the conviction that that process could not be safely relied upon for anything like a complete and accurate analysis of such a complex mixture of liquids; and that, at best, the products thus obtained could not be regarded as anything better than remote approximations to pure substances; leaving reason to fear that there might still be other bodies present, in lesser quantities perhaps, which had escaped detection.

An examination of the results of previous researches on tars, petroleums, etc., served in general to confirm the impressions induced by my own less extended experiments; and to increase, rather than lessen, the doubts already existing in my mind as to the trustworthiness of the results which had hitherto been published concerning the neutral constituents of such mixtures. Influenced by these considerations, and by the belief that, if I could succeed in finding a process capable of effecting a more complete separation of the constituents of such mixtures, it might probably lead to the discovery of new bodies, lying between those which had already been described, — I was led to undertake the researches, the results of which I am about to record. Even if this chief purpose should fail, I was convinced that the expenditure of labor in isolating those bodies in a state of greater purity, would be amply compensated by the much needed confirmation, or perhaps correction, of the results previously published, in addition to the valuable incidental evidence of the absence of other bodies which would thus be furnished. The results which I have obtained in the pursuit of this object are abundantly sufficient to show that I did not undervalue the work of my predecessors, nor over-estimate the importance of the work before me.

The success which attended my efforts in search of a better process of separation has already been described in detail, in a memoir "On Fractional Condensation," etc. (Memoirs of the American Academy, 1864.)

This new process was first applied, more especially for the purpose of testing its efficiency, in the separation of benzole from coal-tar naphtha. This mixture was selected for the test on account of the property which benzole possesses, in contradistinction from its associates, of being crystallizable at a low temperature, thus affording an additional test of the purity of the product which might be obtained by the process of fractioning. Somewhat to my surprise I found that, after only the fifth series of fractionings, I had obtained benzole so nearly pure that the whole of it would distil from a tubulated retort between 80° and 81° C.; and that when congealed, which was effected by placing the containing bottle in pounded ice, not a drop of liquid could be poured from the mass of crystals. From this result, — which, at the least, indicated a near approximation to purity, — taken in connection with other favorable indications, I felt confident that I had accomplished my first object, and had found a process that could, in all probability, be successfully applied in the study of the petroleums, which up to that time (1861) had baffled every attempt to resolve them into their proximate constituents.

Being naturally anxious to apply the new process in this seemingly more promising field of inquiry, I at once suspended, for the time being, my operations on coal-tar naphtha, and commenced simultaneously the investigation of Pennsylvanian petroleum, and of the oils distilled from Albert coal (from Hillsboro, New Brunswick) in the process of manufacturing illuminating oil. These two substances, neither of which had ever been made the subject of special scientific investigation, were selected as being fair representative types, on the one hand of the native liquid petroleums, and on the other of the artificial coal oils. The comparative study of these two substances seemed to promise additional interest on account of the close analogies which they present, especially when this circumstance is considered in connection with the fact of their great diversity of origin. This is the limit which at that time was assigned for these researches; my intention being, so soon as the separations and analyses should be completed, and the boiling-points and some of the other more important physical characteristics determined, briefly to publish the results, together with the process of fractioning, — preliminary to a complete memoir at a more advanced stage of the work. Before this work had been accomplished, however, it became evident that the bodies contained in these mixtures could not be studied so satisfactorily by themselves as in comparison with other series of hydrocarbons, especially with reference to certain important questions of more general interest; for example, the question in regard to the increment of boiling-point corresponding to the addition of $C_2 H_2$ in homologous series. It was therefore deemed advisable to extend the inquiry so as to include the naphthas from coal- and wood-tars, and the oil of cumin. And there are still other mixtures of hydrocarbons, that have been made the subjects of previous research, which must yet be brought into the work, in order to clear up, in a satisfactory manner, the confusion and obscurity that seem to exist in our publications regarding some questions relating to the different series of this class of bodies.

This digression from my original plan, having caused much additional labor, has necessarily delayed publication longer than was desirable, until now the results of more than three years of work have accumulated. In this connection I may remark, so far as regards petroleum, that I had nearly completed the fractional separations — except of the bodies of high boiling-point — so long ago as June, 1862, having been for a long time occupied with this work before the appearance, in that month, of the first memoir of Pelouze and Cahours on the same subject. At that time my work was considerably in advance of theirs, and their results differed widely from mine in some important particulars; yet after the publication of their memoir I felt reconciled to a continuance of the delay which had been caused by the change of plan above mentioned, considering it due to these chemists that they should have time to complete the publication of the results of their investigations before I should publish mine. Similar remarks might be made respecting the first publication of Schorlemmer, which appeared soon after, on the products of distillation of cannel coal; this substance being so closely analogous to the Albert coal (upon the products of which I had at that time been long engaged) as to induce the belief that, under the same circumstances, either would afford the same products.

I.

On the Volatile Hydrocarbons from Coal-tar Naphtha, Oil of Cumin, and Cuminic Acid.

PART I.

HYDROCARBONS FROM COAL-TAR NAPHTHA.

In presenting the results of a re-examination of a series of substances upon which so much labor had already been bestowed, and upon the nature and properties of which so little doubt has seemed to exist, it may confer an interest on the subject to state briefly some of the more important results and conclusions that previous investigators have arrived at in the study of these substances.

The discovery by Faraday,* in 1825, of benzole ("bicarburetted hydrogen") in the oil compressed from oil-gas, rendered it highly probable, and indeed led this distinguished philosopher to suspect, that this substance might be found in coal-tar naphtha. His search for it, however, proved unsuccessful, it having been first detected by Hofmann in 1845.† This chemist, however, did not attempt to isolate this body, and the bare fact of its presence appears to be all that was definitely known of the composition of coal-tar naphtha prior to 1849, in which year Mansfield‡ published his elaborate and valuable research, being the first effort at a proximate analysis of this mixture which appears to have been attended with any considerable measure of success. Although a fatal accident, while engaged in his experiments, prevented Mansfield from completing the investigation which he had so well begun, yet the work that he had already published in an unfinished state must always be regarded as having contributed much towards a clear and definite knowledge of the nature of the neutral pyrogenous oils contained in coal-tar naphtha. Indeed, it may be said that little has since been added to our knowledge on this subject. Notwithstanding the incompleteness of his separations of the hydrocarbons, the extent to which he had carried them, with the limited means employed, is truly remarkable, and could not have been accomplished without an expenditure of labor, and a degree of patient endurance, which only those who have experienced the tediousness of such operations can appreciate.

Mansfield claimed to show that the light coal-tar naphtha is composed of a mixture of four distinct hydrocarbons, boiling within the range of 80° to 175°, C.; and probably having the general formula $C_n H_{n-6}$. The first of these, which he found to boil constant at 80°, was proved to be identical with benzole, $C_{12} H_6$. The second, boiling at about 113°, was determined, from certain reactions, to be identical with toluole, $C_{14} H_8$. The special study of this body was deferred, however, with the remark that it had not yet been isolated in a state of sufficient purity to claim an analysis. The third body, boiling at about 140° to 145°, was said to present all the characteristics of cumole, $C_{18} H_{12}$; but this view was not founded on a careful study and comparison of the chemical or physical properties of these bodies, but was merely an expression of opinion in advance of anticipated results. Of the fourth body, boiling at about 170° to 175°, Mansfield remarks that it bears so strong a resemblance, in odor and other properties, to cymole, $C_{20} H_{14}$, as to induce the belief that this substance is

* Philosophical Transactions of the Royal Society, 1825, CXV. 465.

† Annalen der Chemie und Pharmacie, 1845, LV. 200.

‡ Quarterly Journal of the Chemical Society, 1849, I. 244.

identical with the hydrocarbon existing in oil of cumin. It thus appears that of the four bodies which Mansfield detected in coal-tar naphtha, benzole is the only one which he had studied in any detail. Indeed he distinctly states that the others had not yet been isolated in such a state of purity as to entitle them to analysis. And yet his conjectures as to the identity of these bodies, thrown out by way of preliminary notice of results which were acknowledged to be incomplete and inaccurate, have nevertheless been extensively quoted, and generally received as established facts. In addition to the bodies already mentioned, Mansfield also detected the presence of a body more volatile than benzole, having an alliaceous odor, which he found to boil between 60° and 70°. Ritthausen* made a re-examination of the light coal-tar naphtha, in order to obtain the hydrocarbons in a state of greater purity, and to prove the correctness of Mansfield's view of the composition of this naphtha. In regard to the results which he obtained, he says they fully confirm those of Mansfield. Of the body which Mansfield designated as probably identical with cymole, and of the oil more volatile than benzole, Ritthausen obtained quantities too small to admit of investigation. In regard to the latter, however, he remarks,† that to Mansfield's account he can add, that "its nitro-product quite resembles that of benzole, and hence that at all events it belongs to the series $C_n H_{n-6}$, and perhaps has the formula $C_{10} H_4$."‡ It is to be regretted that Ritthausen also omitted to analyze and determine the vapor density of any one of these substances, he having added, therefore, nothing more than a confirmation of the results of Mansfield. He gives the boiling-point of benzole at 80°, of toluole at 109°, and of the so-called cumole at 139 – 140°, which will be found to agree very nearly with my own determinations. Church,§ in the following year, published a paper on the "Determination of Boiling-points" in the "Ben-

* Journal für praktische Chemie, 1854, LXI. 74.

† "Ich kann den Angaben von Mansfield aber das letztere nur das hinzufügen, das seine Nitroproducte denen des Benzols, etc. ganz ähnlich sind, daher es jedenfalls der Reihe $C_n H_{n-6}$ angehört und vielleicht die Formel $C_{10} H_4$ besitzt."

‡ On a future occasion I shall show that Ritthausen was in error in placing this body in the benzole series, and indeed in considering it as a hydrocarbon at all. He was evidently deceived by operating on a mixture containing benzole. Furthermore, as Mansfield suggested might be possible, that part of the naphtha more volatile than benzole is by no means composed of a single substance. Having had a large quantity of this volatile material at my command, I have been able to obtain the separate constituents apparently in a state of great purity. Of the two bodies separated, one of them boils constant at about 40°, and the other near 0°. Both are compounds containing sulphur, and therefore will more properly form the subject of a separate paper.

§ Philosophical Magazine, 1855, 4th Series, IX. 256.

zole Series." I cannot better present his results than by quoting the following table : —

	Formula.	Boiling-point.	Difference.
Benzole,	$C_{12} H_6 = C_6 3 (C_2 H_2)$	80°.8	
			22°.9
Toluole,	$C_{14} H_8 = C_6 4 (C_2 H_2)$	103°.7	
			22°.5
Xylole,	$C_{16} H_{10} = C_6 5 (C_2 H_2)$	126°.2	
			22°.2
Cumole,	$C_{18} H_{12} = C_6 6 (C_2 H_2)$	148°.4	
			22°.3
Cymole,	$C_{20} H_{14} = C_6 7 (C_2 H_2)$	170°.7	

Church states that he obtained all of these bodies from coal-naphtha, and also that he obtained benzole from benzoic acid, toluole from toluylic acid, xylole from wood-spirit, cumole from cuminic acid, and cymole from oil of cumin; and that he has found the corresponding bodies from these different sources to be identical. It will be observed that Church claims to have found in coal-tar a body boiling at 126°.2, which he calls *xylole*, thus supplying from this source a fifth member of the benzole series; whereas Mansfield and Ritthausen found only four bodies within the range of temperature indicated by the table. It will also be observed that his determination of the boiling-point of toluole is much lower, and that of cumole much higher, than the corresponding determinations of Mansfield and Ritthausen; thus giving room for a middle member between them, and preserving a remarkable uniformity of difference — viz. 22° and a fraction — between the boiling-points of any two contiguous members of the series, for the addition of $C_2 H_2$.

That the earlier investigators had found in coal-tar naphtha only the two lower members ($C_{12} H_6$ and $C_{14} H_8$) and the two upper members ($C_{18} H_{12}$ and $C_{20} H_{14}$), indicating the absence of the middle member ($C_{16} H_{10}$) of the benzole series, was always to me an anomaly which I could not reconcile with any plausible theory in regard to the formation of these bodies; and I was led, therefore, to question whether this body had not been overlooked in making the separations. The alleged discovery of this body in coal-naphtha by Church, together with the beautiful uniformity of the boiling-point difference throughout the series which he presented, and the apparent care with which the whole research had been conducted, led me to regard his results as being more reliable than those which had previously been published. I remained under this conviction until I had discovered the boiling-point difference of 30° in other series of hydrocarbons,* which led me to doubt the accuracy of Church's determinations of boiling-points, and to consider those of Mansfield and Ritthausen as probably more correct.

In the first paragraph of his paper, Church remarks that, "although doubts still

* See the following Memoir on this subject.

remain as to the relations of these bodies to one another, yet their composition has been ascertained with certainty." It does not appear, however, that an analysis or vapor density of any one of the members of this series, as obtained from coal-tar, except benzole, had ever been published. As already indicated by the title of his paper, it appears to have been the design of Church to treat only of the boiling-points of these bodies; yet finding that his preparations of toluole — prepared both from coal-naphtha and toluylic acid — gave a boiling-point differing considerably from observations previously published, he took occasion to make analyses of his preparations of this substance, which he regards as "perfectly satisfactory"; and adds that "the details and numerical results of these analyses, and of many others which the present inquiry necessitated, the limits and special object of the present paper do not admit of my giving here." As he undertook to correct the work of his predecessors, to do which fairly would seem to require the publication of these "details and numerical results," their omission is to be regretted, the more since he found space and purpose for matter apparently less relevant to his special subject. I am prompted to these remarks from having been led to undertake the tedious task of making a re-examination of coal-tar naphtha mainly on account of the disagreement between Church's determinations, which I have found to be mostly incorrect, and those which had been previously published.

In addition to the bodies mentioned in the foregoing table, Church alludes to the discovery of two other bodies, boiling respectively at 97° and 112°. Subsequently, in a "Note on Parabenzole, a new Hydrocarbon from Coal-Naphtha,"* he publishes the details of an investigation of the former of these two bodies, which he finally found to boil "*perfectly constant at* 97°.5," and to be isomeric with benzole.

I think I shall be able to show in the following pages, —

1. That coal-tar naphtha contains only four hydrocarbons within the range of 80° to 170°, as taught by Mansfield, and confirmed by Ritthausen.

2. That the benzole series within that range of temperature is limited to four members, and therefore does not contain five, as has been generally supposed.

3. That these four members have the boiling-points 80°, 110°, 140°, and 170° respectively; and consequently that the boiling-point difference in this series, for an elementary difference of C_2H_2, is 30°, instead of 22° and a fraction, as alleged by Church.

4. That the body obtained from coal-tar naphtha, boiling at 140°, is not identical with cumole from cuminic acid, as assumed by Mansfield, nor even isomeric with it;

* Philosophical Magazine, 1857, 4th Series, XIII. 415.

but that it has the formula which has been assigned to xylole, containing $C_2 H_2$ less than that of cumole.

5. That the body obtained from coal-tar naphtha, boiling at 170°, is quite a different body from cymole obtained from oil of cumin, — with which it has been considered identical, as assumed by Mansfield, — these bodies differing from each other by $C_2 H_2$.

6. That cumole from cuminic acid, and cymole from oil of cumin, do not even belong to the benzole series.

7. That the Parabenzole of Church was in all probability only a mixture of benzole and toluole.

Of the Quality of Naphtha employed in this Investigation. — As I have taken occasion to question the existence in coal-tar naphtha of two of the substances which it has been said to contain, — viz. cymole, $C_{20} H_{14}$, and parabenzole, $C_{12} H_6$, — it is a matter of some importance that I should clearly state the kind or quality of the naphtha employed. The tar from which this naphtha was obtained was a mixture of the tar furnished by the following companies, viz. the New York and the Manhattan Gas-Light Companies, of New York; Brooklyn Gas-Light Company, of Brooklyn, N. Y.; Albany Gas-Light Company, of Albany, N. Y.; and the Gas-Light Companies of Newark and Jersey City, in New Jersey. It was mostly made from Cannel and Newcastle caking coals, which were imported from Liverpool, and mixed in the proportions of one third to five eighths Cannel, to two thirds to three eighths Newcastle. In some of the works a portion of the caking coal was from mines in Pennsylvania. The tar from these different gas-works, as regularly received at the naphtha manufactory, was poured into a large tank provided for this purpose. The stills were uniformly charged with tar directly from this tank; so that there can be no doubt that the naphtha employed was made from a mixture of the tar supplied by the six different companies above enumerated. Most of the gas-works referred to are large, the annual production of tar amounting in the aggregate to upwards of 50,000 barrels. It does not appear, therefore, that the absence of the bodies in question from the naphtha which I have employed, can be attributed to any peculiarity of the tar. The naphtha was prepared in a manufactory in New York over which I had at that time personal control, and was purified under my own direction. The process of purification did not differ essentially from that in common use in England, the reagents employed being oil of vitriol and alkali. One hundred barrels of the purified naphtha were subjected, under my personal superintendence, to repeated fractional distillation from an iron still. The chief object in operating on so large a quantity, was to insure the detection of any constituent which might be present in small proportion. The process of fractioning was continued on this large scale until the separations had so far progressed, that at certain temperatures a full barrel of distillate would come off from the ten-barrel still employed, without a variation of more than one or two degrees of the thermometer. Finally a sample gallon was taken from each of the barrels composing the last series of products, and these samples were set aside for this investigation, which was afterwards conducted in the laboratory.

Of the Results of Fractional Condensation. — Such of the samples above mentioned as promised to yield the different constituents of the naphtha in the largest proportion, were subjected to repeated series of fractionings by my process of "Fractional Condensation."* As full details of this process have already been given in the memoir referred to, it will be needless to repeat them here. It will suffice to say that the fractioning in this case was conducted in all respects as there described, and continued until the whole of the naphtha taken, boiling between 80° and 170°, had accumulated at the four points already indicated, viz. at 80°, 110°, 140°, and 170°; or so nearly the whole that the intermediate quantities had become too small to admit of being further operated upon. Having therefore so thoroughly exhausted the intermediate fractions, I can have no hesitation in asserting that no other body than those alluded to was present in the naphtha, — at least, in appreciable quantity, — hence, that the parabenzole of Church was probably only a mixture of benzole and toluole. I may here remark that each of the sample-gallons employed, when subjected to my process of fractioning, was found to contain, in variable proportion, all of the constituents of the naphtha.

Of some of the Properties of the Bodies obtained by Fractioning.

1. Benzole.

Specific gravity, 0.8957 at 0°, and 0.882 at 15°.5.†

Determination of Boiling-point. — This experiment was conducted in a tubulated retort, operating on 150–200 *c. c.* of the benzole, containing some pieces of sodium. The benzole employed had previously been repeatedly boiled with sodium, until the latter

* Memoirs of the American Academy, 1864.

† It would appear that the specific gravities of liquids are usually determined at the temperature of the air. The result of this is that the determinations made by different observers are not comparable with one another. That these specific gravities are not uniformly taken at 0° C. — the temperature which, on account of greater convenience, etc. is generally acknowledged to be preferable — is probably due to the fact that the more

ceased to have any action. The thermometer bulb extended into the liquid * nearly to the bottom of the retort. A second thermometer was attached, by means of flexible bands, to the side of the one in the retort; the bulb being placed, during ebullition, at a point midway between the centre of the cork (—5°) and the upper end of the mercurial column, viz. at 35°. A paper screen, closely fitting the thermometer spindle, was placed across at the top of the cork. With the retort neck slightly inclined upward, and cooled to prevent the escape of vapor, ebullition was continued for considerable time, until the mercury in the thermometer ceased to rise. The lamp being removed for the moment, the neck of the retort was then turned downward, and quickly inserted in a Liebig's condenser. On replacing the lamp, distillation commenced almost immediately at 79°.

Observations. —

Temperature.		Time.		Temper. by Side Thermom.
°		h. m.		
79.0	at	2.40		
			5 minutes.	
79.2	"	2.45		22°.
			15 "	
79.4	"	3.00		24°.
			12 "	
79.5	"	3.12		25°.
			20 "	
79.6	"	3.32		26°.
			18 "	
79.6	"	3.50		26°.

common specific gravity bottle is not suited to this purpose. Indeed, with a volatile body that bottle cannot serve for an accurate determination at any temperature. A reform in this regard being highly desirable, I would call attention to a specific gravity bottle which I obtained a few years ago from Fastré, in Paris, which is admirably adapted for taking specific gravities, even of volatile liquids, at a low temperature. The accompanying figure represents this bottle of one half its natural size. Who was the author of this particular form I am not informed, although it may have been already noticed in some publication. A bottle analogous to this is figured by Schiel ("Einleitung in das Studium der organischen Chemie," page 76); but his bottle has an oval bottom, which makes it less convenient. The particular advantage of this bottle over the more common one, which advantage Schiel omits to notice, consists in this: that the space or chamber above the line on the capillary neck is large enough to allow for the expansion of the liquid consequent upon the elevation of temperature from 0° to that of the surrounding air; and that the ground stopper fits so closely that no perceptible loss from evaporation can take place during the time occupied by an experiment.

In order to furnish determinations of the specific gravities of the bodies to be treated of in these researches, which shall be comparable with corresponding determinations by other observers, I shall generally record one or more special determinations made for this purpose.

* For critical remarks on the question of propriety of placing the thermometer bulb in the liquid, etc.; and for further details of the method of taking boiling-points, especially at low temperatures, see the accompanying Memoir, "On the Influence of C_2H_2 on the Boiling-points in Homologous Series of Hydrocarbons," etc.

Distillation therefore occupied one hour and ten minutes, during which time the thermometer rose only 0°.6, being fifty minutes in rising 0°.2 from 79°.4 to 79°.6, at which temperature it had distilled nearly to dryness. Height of the barometer during the experiment reduced to 0° = 761.9$^{mm.}$ Taking 79°.4, this being the average of the last five observations, and applying the corrections for the upper column of mercury, and for atmospheric pressure, according to the directions given by Kopp,* we find the corrected boiling-point of benzole to be 80°.1.

Analysis. — 0.2339 gramme of benzole gave, by my process† of combustion in a stream of oxygen gas, 0.7903 of carbonic acid, and 0.1683 of water.

		Calculated.		Found.
Carbon,	C_{12}	72	92.31	92.15
Hydrogen,	H_6	6	7.69	7.99
		78	100.00	100.14

Determination of Vapor Density. —

Temperature of balance,	15°
Temperature of oil bath,	171°
Height of barometer,	764.1$^{mm.}$ at 9°
Increment of balloon,	0.2447
Capacity of balloon,	265 *c. c.*

Density of vapor found,	2.688
Theory $C_{12}H_6$ = 4 volumes,	2.698

2. Toluole.

Specific gravity, 0.8824 at 0°, and 0.872 at 15°.

Determination of Boiling-point. — The preparation employed for this determination had also been repeatedly boiled with sodium until the latter ceased to have any action upon it. Operating in this case also upon a pretty large quantity, the distillation occupied about an hour. The experiment was conducted as detailed under the head of Benzole. Distillation commenced at 110°.6; two minutes later the temperature had fallen to 110.4, at which point it remained absolutely constant during the lapse of forty-eight minutes. Five minutes later the temperature had risen again to 110°.6;

* Poggendorff's Annalen, 1847, LXXII. 38.

† Proceedings of the American Academy, 1864, p. 251.

and five minutes later to 110°.8, at which point, having distilled nearly to dryness, the operation was suspended. The corrections for pressure (— 0°.16) and for the upper column of mercury — which, with the thermometer used in this experiment, was only 7° in length, — gives 110°.3 as the corrected boiling-point of toluole. Church* remarks that toluole, when distilled in the ordinary manner, is liable to become oxidized, and its boiling-point thereby raised, in consequence of the upper part of the retort becoming heated above the boiling-point of toluole. He found that toluole which, by ordinary distillation, had come over between 108° and 109°, would distil eight tenths between 103° and 104°, after repeated purification with sodium. I would therefore state that my preparation of toluole was never subjected to a temperature above its boiling-point; and that I have never noticed any reduction of the boiling-point of this body by purification with sodium.

Analysis. — 0.1628 gramme of toluole gave, by combustion in a stream of oxygen gas, 0.5447 of carbonic acid, and 0.1315 of water.

		Calculated.		Found.
Carbon,	C_{14}	84	91.3	91.20
Hydrogen,	H_8	8	8.7	8.97
		92	100.0	100.17

Determination of Vapor Density. —

Temperature of balance,	17°
Temperature of oil bath,	209°
Height of barometer,	760.1$^{mm.}$ at 15°
Increment of balloon,	0.287
Capacity of balloon,	249.5 *c. c.*
Density of vapor found,	3.2196
Theory $C_{14}H_8$ = 4 volumes,	3.1822

3. Xylole. (*Cumole of Mansfield and Ritthausen.*)

Specific gravity, 0.878 at 0°, and 0.866 at 15°.5.

Determination of Boiling-point. — This determination was made in all respects like that of benzole, the xylole employed having been also subjected to the same treatment. The quantity operated upon was, however, smaller, and the experiment con-

* Philosophical Magazine, 1855 (4), IX. 256.

ducted more rapidly. Distillation began at 138°.6, and terminated at 139°, having distilled almost to dryness. The time occupied was seventeen minutes. Taking the average of these observations, viz. 138°.4, and applying the customary corrections, we find 139°.8 to be the corrected boiling-point of xylole.

Analysis. — 0.1333 gramme of xylole gave, by combustion in a stream of oxygen gas, 0.4413 of carbonic acid, and 0.1185 of water.

		Calculated.		Found.
Carbon,	C_{16}	96	90.57	90.29
Hydrogen,	H_{10}	10	9.43	9.87
		106	100.00	100.16

Determination of Vapor Density. —

Temperature of balance,	16°.5
Temperature of oil bath,	207°.5
Height of barometer,	760mm. at 14°
Increment of balloon,	0.3528
Capacity of balloon,	223 c. c.
Density of vapor found,	3.7517
Theory $C_{16}H_{10}$,	3.6665

These results show clearly that this body has the formula $C_{16}H_{10}$, and that it is doubtless the third member of the benzole series.* Although xylole, first discovered by Cahours in the oil separated from wood-spirit, has had a much lower boiling-point assigned to it, I have retained that name for this body, since the results which I have obtained in the study of the light oil from wood-tar indicate that when the corresponding body from this source is in a state of equal purity, its boiling-point will agree with the above determination. I may here mention that in my researches on the light oil from wood-tar, I have obtained a body at about 140°, but nothing between that and 110° (these temperatures are not corrected), although special pains were taken to work up the intermediate fractions. So that I am in a position to justify

* As this memoir is passing through the press, the receipt of my journals for September calls attention to late publications of Hugo Müller, Béchamp, and Naquet concerning this hydrocarbon. Müller concludes that it is xylole, a result which agrees with my own. (Annalen der Chemie und Pharmacie, 1864, CXXXI. 321.) Béchamp, on the contrary, erroneously regards it as being a *new* hydrocarbon, not belonging to the benzole series. (Bulletin de la Société Chimique, Paris, 1864, 204.) Naquet also calls it a *new* hydrocarbon, and gives it the formula $C_{16}H_{12}$. (Bulletin de la Société Chimique, Paris, 1864, 205.)

the assertion that no other body was present in appreciable quantity between the temperatures mentioned.

That this body from coal-tar naphtha, boiling at 140°, is not identical with cumole from cuminic acid, will be made apparent on comparison of the results above stated, with those which will be given when treating of cumole.

4. Isocumole. (*Cymole of Mansfield.*)

Specific gravity, 0.8643 at 0°, and 0.853 at 15°.

Determination of Boiling-point. — This was conducted with the usual precautions, and under conditions similar to those detailed above. The distillation, as in the foregoing determinations, was continued nearly to dryness, and occupied twenty-five minutes. Before distillation was commenced, the temperature of the boiling liquid was found to be 166°.5, and at the close of distillation 167°. Applying the customary corrections to the average of these observations, viz. 166°.75, we obtain for the corrected boiling-point 169°.8.

Analysis. — 0.1944 gramme of the substance gave, by combustion in a stream of oxygen, 0.6366 of carbonic acid, and 0.1896 of water.

		Calculated.		Found.
Carbon,	C_{18}	108	90.00	89.31
Hydrogen,	H_{12}	12	10.00	10.84
		120	100.00	100.15

Determination of Vapor Density. —

Temperature of balance,	13°.5
Temperature of oil bath,	241°.0
Height of barometer,	769.5mm. at 9°
Increment of balloon,	0.4206
Capacity of balloon,	239 *c. c.*

Density of vapor found, ... 4.3019

Theory $C_{18}H_{12}$, ... 4.151

Hence it appears that the calculated density on the formula $C_{18}H_{12}$ is 0.151 *less* than that found by experiment. The calculated density on the formula $C_{20}H_{14}$, which has previously been assigned to this body, — although, as above stated, without an analysis or determination of vapor density, — is 4.645; which is 0.302 *greater* than that found by experiment. It will be observed that the difference between the density found and that calculated on the formula $C_{20}H_{14}$ is not only more than twice as large as the corresponding difference calculated on the formula $C_{18}H_{12}$, but that the error is reversed; being with $C_{20}H_{14}$ a *deficiency*, while with $C_{18}H_{12}$ it is an *excess*. This circumstance has to my mind a good deal of significance, as it goes strongly to show that the lower formula is the true one. For of the many vapor densities of hydrocarbons which I have determined, I have but rarely met with an instance in which the density found was not greater than the theoretical density. And I have usually observed that the excess of the experimental over the theoretical density is larger in proportion as the boiling-point of the body is higher, a fact which needs explanation. Wurtz* observed a similar difference between the determined and calculated vapor densities of bodies of the formulæ C_nH_n and C_nH_{n+2}, which he accounted for on the ground that his preparations contained an admixture of bodies less volatile, the vapors of which would remain in the balloon, and increase the density. But I cannot accept this explanation for the substances here treated of, since they invariably distil without residue within a range of one degree of temperature. I would rather rely upon the supposition that the high temperature employed causes partial decomposition of the substance, which would be the more liable to occur the higher the boiling-point of the body. I do not, however, offer this as an explanation, but merely make the suggestion.

PART II.

HYDROCARBONS FROM OIL OF CUMIN AND CUMINIC ACID.

The oil of cumin employed in this research was furnished by Messrs. Reed and Cutler, wholesale importers of drugs, etc. of Boston. The package bore the label of Eduard Büttner, manufacturer, of Leipzig, and purported to be a genuine preparation, answering in all of its obvious physical properties — odor, color, etc. — the description given of this oil by Gerhardt and Cahours† in their original memoir on this substance, who, it appears, also employed a commercial preparation. Its behavior in distillation left no doubt of its being a genuine article; and this was afterwards confirmed by treatment of the cuminole with fused potash, for the production of cuminic acid, its comportment with this reagent being in all respects identical with that described by Gerhardt and Cahours. Subjected to repeated series of fractionings by my process of

* Bulletin de la Société Chimique de Paris, 1863, 309.

† Annales de Chimie et de Physique, 1841, 3e Série, I. 60.

fractional condensation already referred to, it gave, in addition to cymole and the residue of cuminole, a body boiling at about 155°, which so closely resembles oil of turpentine in odor, etc. as to be hardly distinguishable from the latter substance. The presence of this body may account for the very low boiling-point which Gerhardt and Cahours assigned to cymole, viz. 165°. The boiling-point of cymole was subsequently found by Gerhardt* to be 175°, but my own determination places it still lower by about 5°. It is evident, therefore, from a comparison of their own determinations, that the oil of cumin which they originally operated upon contained an oil boiling below cymole; and hence the finding of such an oil in that which I employed need not raise a doubt as to its being genuine. This lighter body is present in so small quantity as hardly to admit of its being detected, or at least identified, by the old process of fractioning; and its detection and isolation by the new process is but another illustration of the superior excellence of this method.

1. Of the Body resembling Oil of Turpentine.

Specific gravity, 0.8772 at 0°, and 0.8657 at 15°.

Determination of Boiling-point. — The quantity of material at command was too small to admit of attaining so high a degree of purity for this body as was desirable. The product obtained, however, distilled almost to dryness between 153°.4 and 155°.5. Taking the average of these observations, and applying the usual corrections, we obtain 155°.8 for the boiling-point of this body.

Analysis. — 0.2575 gramme of the substance gave, by combustion with oxide of copper, 0.8283 of carbonic acid, and 0.2766 of water.

		Calculated.		Found.
Carbon,	C_{20}	120	88.24	87.73
Hydrogen,	H_{16}	16	11.76	11.94
		136	100.00	99.67

Determination of Vapor Density. —

Temperature of balance,	16°
Temperature of oil bath,	211°
Height of barometer,	758°.4mm. at 14°
Increment of balloon,	0.4939
Capacity of balloon,	221 *c. c.*

* Annales de Chimie et de Physique, 1845, 3e Série, IV. p. 111.

Density of vapor found,	4.7281
Theory $C_{20}H_{16}$ = 4 volumes,	4.7028
Excess found,	.0253

The calculated density on the formula $C_{20}H_{14}$ is 4.635; which, compared with the density found, would increase the excess to 0.093. Although the determination agrees more nearly, indeed almost exactly, with the calculated density on the formula $C_{20}H_{16}$, the calculation on the formula $C_{20}H_{14}$ does not show a greater variation from the density found, than we have observed to be quite frequent with hydrocarbons of so high boiling-point; so that it may be questionable which of these formulæ is the true one. I cannot regard the determination of a vapor density as reliable for fixing the formula nearer than to within two equivalents of hydrogen. In the absence of opposing evidence, it will be wiser, however, to take the formula which agrees best with the results of experiment; at least until it shall be shown that the discrepancy between the calculated and observed vapor densities of bodies of high boiling-point, which appears to be so frequent, is nearly constant, or variable by some fixed law by which the amount of the error, in any given case, may be pretty nearly estimated. I shall therefore regard this body as having the formula $C_{20}H_{16}$, which is also better supported by the results of analysis. On account of its source, and close resemblance to oil of turpentine, I think of no better appellation for this body than cumo-oil of turpentine; thus adding another to the long list of isomers of the former substance, the chemical relations of which stand in so much need of being further studied.

2. Cumole.

This body was first obtained by Gerhardt and Cahours,* by the dry distillation of a mixture of six parts of crystallized cuminic acid, and twenty-four parts of caustic baryta. Abel † obtained the same result by substituting caustic lime for the baryta. His product, however, was found to boil 4° above that of Gerhardt and Cahours. My preparation was also made by the use of lime. Although the results of my experiments confirm the conclusions arrived at by Gerhardt and Cahours as to the composition of this body, yet the numerical results differ considerably from theirs. I have also observed some new facts regarding the formation of this body. They have described the reaction between the baryta and cuminic acid as being much more simple than my experiments seem to indicate. On this point they re-

* Annales de Chimie et de Physique, 1845, 3e Série, IV. 87.

† Annalen der Chemie und Pharmacie, 1847, LXIV. 312.

mark: "The formation of cumene is easily explained. In effect, the cuminic acid being represented by $C_{40} H_{24} O_4$, it appears that $C_4 O_4$, that is to say, 2 equivalents of carbonic acid, are retained by the baryta, while $C_{36} H_{24}$ are set free." *

$$C_{10} H_{12} O_2 = C O_2 + C_9 H_{12}.$$

In another place (p. 88) they remark, that "by suitably managing the heat, and employing no more than 6 gr. of cuminic acid at a time, no other products are ever obtained than those which we mention." † My experiments show that this reaction is by no means so simple as thus described. The crude product obtained from the mixture of lime and cuminic acid, when subjected to a simple distillation from a tubulated retort, was found to distil between 155° and 250°, leaving a residue at the latter temperature which became semi-fluid on cooling. The distillate thus obtained gave, by my process of fractional condensation, an oil boiling at 151°.1, and a residue at 170°. It is not improbable that the latter may prove to be mostly cymole, $C_{20} H_{14}$; but the quantity was too small to admit of pursuing this inquiry with the probability of deciding the question. There is evidence, however, that the product obtained by Gerhardt and Cahours was not simply pure cumole, as they described it, but a mixture of different bodies, which would necessitate a more complicated reaction than that which they assigned. Gerhardt and Cahours found the boiling-point of their cumole to be constant at 144°. Four years later, Gerhardt, ‡ having occasion to make a very accurate determination of the boiling-point of this body, in connection with his research to find a law governing the boiling-points of the hydrocarbons, found its boiling-point to be 9° higher, viz. 153°, which is but 2° higher than my own determination. The disagreement between their determinations, it being so considerable, may be more reasonably accounted for on the supposition that they operated, in the first instance, upon a mixture of different bodies; and yet I cannot see how they could have obtained the product boiling below 150°. Additional evidence on this point will be found in the discrepancy which appears between their determination of the vapor density, and that calculated upon theory.

The specific gravity of my preparation of cumole was found to be 0.8792 at 0°, and 0.8675 at 15°.

* "La formation du cumène s'explique aisément. En effet, l'acide cuminique etant représenté par $C_{40} H_{24} O_4$, on voit que $C_4 O_4$, c'est-a-dire 2 equivalents d'acide carbonique sont retenus par la baryte, tandis que $C_{36} H_{24}$ sont dégage." — Annales de Chimie et de Physique, 1841, 3ᵉ Série, I. 89.

† "En dirigeant la chaleur convenablement, et en n'employant pas plus de 6gr. d'acide cuminique à la fois, on n'obtient jamais d'autre produits que ceux que nous venons de nommer."

‡ Annales de Chimie et de Physique, 1845 (3), XIV. 107.

Determination of Boiling-point. — The quantity of material being quite small, this determination was made in a large test tube, with the usual precautions. It had not a perfectly constant boiling-point, the distillation ranging from 148°.4 to 151°.6. Applying the proper corrections to the mean of these observations, gives, for the boiling-point of cumole, 151°.1, which is doubtless a little too high from the impracticability of making a complete separation with the small quantity of material employed. If the boiling-point difference between cumole and cymole, for the difference of $C_2 H_2$ in their elementary formulæ, is 30°, as there is every reason to believe, then the boiling-point of cumole should be 150°, as I have found the boiling-point of cymole to be but a fraction under 180°.

Analysis. — 0.1700 gramme of cumole gave, by combustion with oxide of copper, 0.563 of carbonic acid, and 0.1557 of water.

		Calculated.		Found.
Carbon,	C_{18}	108	90.00	90.35
Hydrogen,	H_{12}	12	10.00	10.18
		120	100.00	100.53

Determination of Vapor Density. —

Temperature of balance,	17°
Temperature of oil bath,	203°
Height of barometer,	760.1^{mm} at 15°
Increment of balloon,	0.4428
Capacity of balloon,	232 *c. c.*

Density of vapor found,	4.2003
Theory $C_{18} H_{12}$ = 4 volumes,	4.151

This determination, as well as the results of analysis, confirms, therefore, the formula which Gerhardt and Cahours had assigned to this body. I had anticipated a different result from this, inasmuch as the hydrocarbon from coal-tar naphtha, which I have called *iso-cumole*, boiling at 170°, or nearly 20° higher than cumole from cuminic acid, — had been found, as I have shown above, to have the formula $C_{18} H_{12}$. I am forced to the conclusion, therefore, that these two bodies are isomeric, and belong to different series. A preliminary examination of their behavior with reagents indicates that their chemical properties are also different. These will be treated of on a future occasion, in Part III.

3. Cymole.

Notwithstanding that this body is so much more volatile than the cuminole with which it is associated in the oil of cumin, — there being a difference of 40° between their boiling-points, — Gerhardt and Cahours found it necessary to resort to chemical means, viz. treatment with fused potash, in order to isolate it. Being desirous of testing the efficiency of my process in effecting the separation, the preparation employed in this investigation was obtained by fractional condensation, this process having been found as effective in this as in other cases. This will appear by a comparison of the results obtained in the study of this body before and after treatment with concentrated sulphuric acid, which is also effective to remove cuminole.

Specific Gravity. —

At 0°, before treatment with HO SO_3,	0.8697
At 0°, after " " "	0.8724
At 14°, before " " "	0.8592

Determination of Boiling-point before Treatment with Sulphuric Acid. — The preparation was found to distil to dryness between 175°.8 and 177°. The temperature remained absolutely constant at 176° during the lapse of ten minutes, and occupied fifteen minutes in rising from 176° to 176°.5. Taking the mean of the former numbers, viz. 176°.4, and applying the proper corrections for pressure, etc., we obtain 179°.5 for the boiling-point of cymole.

After Treatment with Sulphuric Acid. — The preparation distilled to dryness between 176° and 177°, the temperature remaining thirteen minutes constant at 176°.3, indicating that no essential change in the boiling-point had been produced by the acid treatment. It was nevertheless evident that some impurity was being removed by the acid, as the first portions of the latter became dark-colored and thickened on being agitated with the oil. Successive portions of acid were therefore employed, until it ceased to produce any marked effect.

Analysis before Treatment with Sulphuric Acid. — 0.1589 gramme of cymole gave, by combustion in a stream of oxygen gas, 0.5200 of carbonic acid, and 0.1532 of water.

		Calculated.		Found.
Carbon,	C_{20}	120	89.55	89.25
Hydrogen,	H_{14}	14	10.45	10.71
		134	100.00	99.96

After Treatment with Sulphuric Acid, and Distillation in Vacuo. — 0.1623 gramme of cymole, by combustion in a stream of oxygen gas, gave 0.5324 of carbonic acid, and 0.1561 of water.

		Calculated.		Found.
Carbon,	C_{20}	120	89.55	89.46
Hydrogen,	H_{14}	14	10.45	10.68
		134	100.00	100.14

The removal of impurity by treatment with sulphuric acid had therefore hardly a sensible effect on the results of analysis.

Determination of Vapor Density before Treatment with Sulphuric Acid. —

Temperature of balance,	11°
Temperature of oil bath,	259°
Height of barometer,	740.6$^{mm.}$ at 5°
Increment of balloon,	0.4446
Capacity of balloon,	239 *c. c.*
Density of vapor found,	4.742
Theory $C_{20} H_{14}$ = 4 volumes,	4.6351

After Treatment with Sulphuric Acid. —

Temperature of balance,	25°.5
Temperature of oil bath,	255°
Height of barometer,	760$^{mm.}$ at 26°
Increment of balloon,	0.4647
Capacity of balloon,	252 *c. c.*
Density of vapor found,	4.7536
Ditto before treatment with HO SO_3,	4.742
Difference,	.0116

The results of the two determinations are therefore almost identical.

A comparison of the above results with those obtained in the study of isocumole, the body from coal-tar naphtha boiling at 170°, will show that the two bodies are far from being the same substance, as Mansfield assumed, and that they have a constitutional difference of $C_2 H_2$, and therefore doubtless belong to different series.

NOTE. — I had hoped to be able to present on this occasion the results of the study of some of the more important reactions of the hydrocarbons treated of in the preceding pages, — at least, of those in regard to which I have differed from my predecessors; but as this work is yet incomplete, and as I am at present occupied with the study of other substances of more immediate interest, I will defer this branch of the subject for future consideration, in Part III. I may here remark, however, that the behavior of these bodies with reagents is such as to strengthen the conclusions already expressed in regard to them.

II.

On the Influence of $C_2 H_2$ *upon the Boiling-points in Homologous Series of Hydrocarbons, and in some Series of their Derivatives; with Critical Observations on Methods of taking Boiling-points.*

It is well known that we are indebted to H. Kopp* for the discovery of certain definite relations existing between the chemical constitution and some of the physical properties of homologous liquid bodies. Of these, one of the most important is that of a uniform difference between the boiling-points of the contiguous members of an homologous series, corresponding to the uniform difference in their elementary constitution. Kopp has shown by numerous examples, that, as a general rule, in those series which are characterized by a common elementary difference of $C_2 H_2$ between the members, in the order of the series, the corresponding difference of boiling-point is about 19° C.; hence, that the difference between the boiling-points of any two members of such a series is x.19° for a difference of $x\, C_2 H_2$ in the elementary formulæ. In the earlier observations on this subject, this relation between the boiling-points and formulæ was found so nearly constant in the different series examined, that any deviations from this apparent general law were referred, not unreasonably, to assumed inaccuracies in the determination of the boiling-points of the bodies compared. But the more recent and extended generalizations of Kopp† have led him to point out several exceptional series, in which the boiling-point difference is greater, and others in which it is less, than 19° for an elementary difference of $C_2 H_2$. That there are such exceptional series is confirmed in a very decisive manner by my own observations, as I shall proceed to show. My determinations make the boiling-point differences in some cases so much larger than those of other observers as to leave no room for doubt on this point; especially if the comparative value of these determinations be duly estimated with reference to the more reliable character to which the preparations are entitled, on account of the more efficient means which I have employed for separating the liquids. Since Kopp first called the attention of chemists to this subject, different theories have from time to time been advanced by Schröder, Löwig, Gerhardt, and others, and supported by laborious research and observation. It will be interesting to examine some of these theories in the light

* Annalen der Chemie und Pharmacie, 1842, XLI. 79, 169; 1845, LV. 177, etc.

† Annalen der Chemie und Pharmacie, 1855, XCVI. 2.

of the new facts which I am about to present. Schröder,* not satisfied with Kopp's explanation of the discrepancies between the observed and theoretical boiling-points, on the ground of errors of determination of the former, argues that the influence of $C_2 H_2$ on boiling-points is variable in different series according to the peculiar nature of the $C_2 H_2$ in each case. He regards organic compounds for the most part made up of radicals, which he calls "components," of which he makes seven. Three of these are composed of carbon and hydrogen, viz.: —

Formyl = $(C_4 H_2)$ — ("$C_4 H_4$") — which is supposed to raise the boiling-point of a substance 52° C.

Methylen = $(C_2 H_2)^n$ — "$(C_2 H_4)^n$" — which is supposed to raise the boiling-point of a body 21°.

Elayl = $(C_2 H_2)^n$ — "$(C_2 H_4)^n$" — which is supposed to raise the boiling-point 17°. Subsequently (Pogg. Ann., 64, 101) the latter number was changed by Schröder to 16°.

A fourth component was made up of a double atom of hydrogen, (H_2) — "(H_4)" —, which was supposed to lower the boiling-point 3°; but this also was afterwards changed to 10° (Pogg. Ann., 64, 372). (The other three components, having no direct bearing on the hydrocarbons, are omitted.) By means of these components Schröder (Pogg. Ann., 62, 188) proposed to calculate the boiling-points of different substances in the following manner. Having estimated the sum of the influence of the different components of a body, the number 70 was in all cases to be deducted. Subsequently Schröder† was led to substitute, in these calculations, the influence of the separate elements for that of the components. Each double atom of carbon (C_2) was estimated to raise the boiling-point of a compound 31°; and each double atom of hydrogen (H_2) to lower it 10°. As in the former case, the number 70 was to be deducted from the sum of the influences of the different elements contained in the compound, to give the true boiling-point. Example: calculation of the boiling-point of benzole, $C_{12} H_6$; $C_{12} = 6\ C_2$; $31° \times 6 = 186°$; $H_6 = 3\ H_2$; $-10° \times 3 = -30°$; $186° - 30° - 70° = 86°$ = the calculated boiling-point of benzole by this method; which agrees exactly with the latest determination at the date of Schröder's memoir.

Löwig ‡ estimates the influence of the elementary atoms on the boiling-point differently from Schröder; and obtains numbers such that, to find the boiling-point of a compound it is only required to add together the numbers corresponding to the

* Poggendorff's Annalen, 1844, LXII. 184, 337.

† Poggendorff's Annalen, 1845, LXIV. 367; 1846, LXVII. 45.

‡ Poggendorff's Annalen, 1845, LXIV. 250.

elementary atoms which it contains, without deducting from this sum a constant number, as by Schröder's method. According to Löwig's theory, one atom of carbon (C) raises the boiling-point 38°.4, and one atom of hydrogen (H) lowers it 29°.2; these numbers being for carbon nearly two and one half times, and for hydrogen nearly three times as great, as those of Schröder. Gerhardt,* in a special paper "On the Boiling-point of the Hydrocarbons," observes that "The boiling-point of the hydrocarbons appears to obey a very simple law, according to which it is raised or depressed a certain number of degrees, corresponding to the number of equivalents of carbon or hydrogen contained in its equivalent."† From a comparison of the boiling-points and formulæ of several well-known hydrocarbons, the determinations of which were repeated with special care for this purpose, Gerhardt finds that the addition of C_2 to the molecule of an hydrocarbon raises its boiling-point 35°.5, and that the addition of H_2 lowers it 15°. The boiling-point of a body is calculated from these numbers by comparing its formula with oil of turpentine, $C_{20}H_{16}$, as a standard, the boiling-point of which is taken at 160° C. Example: cumole (from cuminic acid) has the formula $C_{18}H_{12}$; hence it contains C_2 less than oil of turpentine; therefore 35°.5 must be deducted from 160° (the boiling-point of oil of turpentine), which leaves 124°.5; but as the cumole contains 2 H_2 less than oil of turpentine, $15° \times 2 = 30°$ is to be added to the above remainder; thus $124°.5 + 30° = 154°.5$, the calculated boiling-point of cumole. Gerhardt's direct determination was 153°, which very nearly coincides with his theory.

It would be foreign from my purpose on the present occasion to consider these different hypotheses, or even the empirical law of Kopp, beyond their special relation to the boiling-points of the hydrocarbons, and such other series, derivatives from the hydrocarbons, as have been made the subjects of my own experiments. Anything more than this would be merely speculative. The want of more accurate determinations of boiling-points as essential to safe and reliable deductions and generalizations on this question, has frequently been observed. The need of this will be made strikingly apparent by comparison of my results with those of previous observers. Indeed, if my determinations may be taken as a criterion, — which, considering the nature of the materials operated upon, might not be quite fair, — the inaccuracies of the boiling-points which have hitherto been published are probably so numerous, and

* Annales de Chimie et de Physique, 1845, 3e Série, XIV. 107.

† "Il paraît que le point d'ébullition des hydrogène carbonés est soumis à une loi fort simple, d'après laquelle il s'élèverait ou s'abaisserait d'un certain nombre de degrés suivant le nombre des équivalents de carbone ou d'hydrogène renfermés dans leur équivalent."

in many cases so considerable, as to make it appear almost useless to attempt further generalizations upon those unreliable data. It may be hoped, however, that the superior means which my process furnishes for separating mixtures of liquids, will lead to the accumulation of reliable facts of sufficient number and variety for a profitable review of this question in its different bearings, which, from its importance, it clearly merits.

The frequent inaccuracy of the determinations of boiling-points, upon which Kopp has justly laid so much stress, may, I think, be more reasonably attributed, at least in a majority of cases, to a want of purity in the substances themselves, rather than to a neglect of the precautions and corrections which he recommends to be observed in such determinations; although errors as great as those mentioned by Kopp* may doubtless occur, and in the particular instances which he had in mind may have occurred from the cause which he assigned for them. It should be borne in mind, however, that these errors, in the case of an impure substance, may be compensating errors; or, on the other hand, they may go to increase that which would arise from impurity.

That the conditions under which my results have been obtained may be clearly understood, and hence the value of these results fairly estimated, in comparison with those of others, I shall endeavor, as I proceed with these researches, to specify, in sufficient detail, the processes which I have employed. Having, in the memoir previously referred to, described the process by which the hydrocarbons were separated, the special object of this paper only requires, in this regard, that I should add a description of the method employed in determining the boiling-points of these bodies, which has already been partially given in the foregoing memoir, when treating of the boiling-point of benzole.

Of the Method of determining Boiling-points. — I use for this purpose a small tubulated glass retort, and usually operate on about 150 *c. c.* of the liquid. The thermometer extends into the liquid, even nearly to the bottom of the retort, taking care that the bulb shall not come in contact with the glass, but remain free in the liquid. To prevent abnormal elevation of temperature from adhesion to the glass, — which I have observed in some instances, when operating on impure hydrocarbons, to amount to several degrees, — I introduce pieces of sodium, instead of platinum, as it seems to serve at least as well for this purpose, and at the same time tends to preserve the purity of the material. Sodium has also this advantage over platinum for hydrocar-

* "Bestimmung des Siedepunkts." Poggendorff's Annalen, 1847, LXXII. 38.

bons, viz. that it does not lose its virtue by use, so long as any of it remains; platinum, on the contrary, being liable, especially if the liquid is not quite pure, to become after a while slightly coated, and its efficiency thus impaired.*

Except for low temperatures, the retort rests on a piece of wire gauze laid over the ring of an iron lamp-stand, and is heated with a small gas-flame. When operating on liquids of low boiling-point, I have observed the liability of the thermometer to be considerably affected by the ascending current of hot air striking the sides of the retort above the level of the liquid, thus causing an elevation of several degrees of temperature. To prevent this, I proceed as follows. For low temperatures, and yet above the common temperature, I place upon the gauze on which the retort is to stand, a screen of felt or thick woollen paper, which has been provided with a hole in the centre about two inches in diameter. This screen extends several inches from the sides of the retort, and has been found effectual for the purpose.

For temperatures below the common temperature, the retort is set in a water-bath containing ice-water, the temperature of the bath being gradually raised by means of a small gas-flame.

As is customary, in order to ascertain the temperature by which to calculate the correction for the upper column of mercury, a thermometer is attached, by means of elastic bands, to the side of the thermometer in the retort; the bulb being placed, during ebullition, midway between the centre of the cork and the upper extremity of the mercurial column. And, as usual, a paper screen, closely fitting the thermometer, is placed across at the top of the cork to shield the upper column of mercury from the direct influence of the ascending heat.

I have observed that it often requires considerable time — variable according to its length and the thickness of the glass spindle — for that part of the thermometer above the retort to acquire the highest temperature which the boiling liquid can communicate to it. During this time the thermometer evidently is not in a fit state for an observation. While this gradual change in the condition of the thermometer is taking place, it is desirable, for obvious reasons, that no vapors should escape from the retort. I therefore proceed as follows. The retort, the neck of which has previously been wrapped with a wet cloth, is placed in such a position that the neck

* For common use in fractioning, when not desirable to use sodium, I have found pieces of coke to be more effectual and much more durable than platinum. Not unlikely it would be found equally preferable to platinum for general use in taking the boiling-points of liquids in which sodium could not be employed. It is certain that nothing could operate better than coke for the nitro-compounds and alkaloids derived from benzole and its homologues.

shall slightly incline towards the body of the retort. If necessary, some pieces of ice, which will adhere firmly to the cloth, may be laid along the neck to insure complete condensation of the vapors during ebullition. While the retort is in this position, ebullition is continued for considerable time, until it ceases to have any effect on the height of the mercury in the thermometer. The lamp being now removed for the moment, the neck of the retort is turned down, and quickly connected with a Liebig condenser. The lamp being now replaced, the distillation is commenced. So soon as the mercury in the thermometer shall have become constant, which will now occupy but a few seconds, the temperatures by the retort thermometer and the side thermometer are carefully noted, and also the time at which these observations are made. During the distillation, which is continued nearly to dryness, the readings of the thermometers and of the watch are noted at regular intervals, or so often as any appreciable variation of the retort thermometer shall have taken place. The average of the several observations, or of those corresponding to the longer intervals of time, applying the corrections for atmospheric pressure and for the upper column of mercury, according to Kopp,* is taken for the true boiling-point. I have generally obtained the hydrocarbons so pure that the whole quantity operated upon would distil within the range of 1° of temperature, and not unfrequently within 0°.5. In a few cases, however, when the quantity of material at command would not permit of the attainment of so high a degree of purity, the distillation would range over two or three degrees; in such cases I have generally taken the average of the temperatures corresponding to the longest interval of time, as probably representing more nearly the true boiling-point of the body. In stating my results, however, I shall give the limits of temperature within which the distillation was effected. The thermometers employed in the determinations were the best that I could obtain from Fastrè of Paris; for the temperatures below 100° the instrument used was calibrated, and the scale divided into fifths of a degree. The determinations above 100° were all made with one thermometer.

The method just described differs in some respects from that of Kopp. He objects to the practice of taking boiling-points with the thermometer bulb immersed in the liquid,† on the ground that the thermometer in this condition hardly ever indicates a

* Poggendorff's Annalen, 1847, LXXII. 38.

† "Lässt man die Kugel des Thermometers in die siedende Flüssigkeit tauchen, so zeigt fast nie das Instrument eine constante Temperatur, sondern das Ende des Quecksilberfadens ist in stetter hüpfender oder zittender Bewegung; der auf diese Art gefundene Siedepunkt kann nur mehrere Grade höher liegen, als der, welcher gefunden wird, wenn sich die Kugel des Thermometers in dem Dampf der siedenden Flüssigkeit befindet."

constant temperature, the end of the mercurial column being in a state of motion. He states that a boiling-point taken in this manner may lie several degrees above that found with the thermometer bulb in the vapor. As bearing on this point, I propose, a little farther on, to give the results of a few experiments and observations, which, with others of similar character, have induced me to depart from the now more common custom of taking boiling-points with the thermometer bulb in the vapor.

Under normal conditions, the temperature of the boiling liquid and that of the vapor evolved should be the same. The only disturbing influence which appears to have been specially dwelt upon as likely to alter these conditions in the taking of boiling-points, is the liability of some liquids to adhere to the surface of the glass in such a manner as to produce abnormal elevation of temperature, generally attended with irregular ebullition, and consequent fluctuation of the thermometer. To remedy this it is usual to introduce pieces of platinum; iron filings, coal, etc., have also been employed. As above remarked, pieces of coke — or, when admissible, sodium — are found to be more surely effectual with hydrocarbons than platinum. Indeed, during more than three years of experience and careful observation upon a large number of hydrocarbons, I have not yet met with a single instance in which irregular ebullition and its consequent disturbing influence upon the boiling-point might not be completely prevented by these means. Although I cannot, of course, go so far as to say that equally satisfactory results would be obtained with other liquids by the use of coke, it is nevertheless my belief that in a majority of instances such would be the case.

I have dwelt upon this point for the reason that the objections to the custom of taking boiling-points with the bulb in the vapor, appear to be even greater than those which Kopp has raised against the opposite course of placing the bulb in the liquid, as I shall proceed to show. It therefore becomes a matter of some importance that the objections to one or the other custom should be removed; and I think it will be found easier to overcome the objections to placing the bulb in the liquid, as I have done in the case of many hydrocarbons, even if coke shall not be found equally efficient with most other liquids.

My experience has shown that, when irregular ebullition is effectually prevented, the temperature of the vapor from a boiling liquid is more liable to lead to an erroneous determination of the boiling-point, than the temperature of the liquid itself. The reasons for this are, first, that the vapor is liable to become superheated by the hot air from the flame coming in contact with the sides of the retort above the surface of the liquid; second, that, with the bulb in the vapor, the thermometer is more liable to sudden depression from currents of cool air passing over the retort.

If the bulb be in the vapor, the occurrence of either of these disturbing influences would then affect the principal mass of the mercury in the thermometer; while, on the contrary, if the bulb were in the liquid, only the small quantity of mercury in the stem of the thermometer would be subjected to these influences; the liquid then serving as a regulator, and reducing the error from these sources to a minimum. Fluctuations from currents of cold air are comparatively slight, and more easily prevented than those from overheating the vapor. The latter is the more likely to occur the lower the boiling-point of the liquid, or when the quantity of liquid in the retort is small. I have, however, observed from this cause an elevation of 3°–4° in distilling a body boiling as high as 98° C., without an unnecessarily large flame. But the liquid in this instance was pretty low in the retort.

In the case of liquids boiling below the common temperature, it seems indispensable that the bulb of the thermometer should be placed in the liquid. As evidence of this I will here state the results of observations made while occupied in fractioning some exceedingly volatile products from American petroleum.

Experiment 1. — The liquid operated upon boiled at so low a temperature that the distillation was effected by the heat of the surrounding atmosphere. The distillation was conducted in a flask, and the bulb of the thermometer placed in the vapor. The flask was attached to my condensing apparatus, including the "refrigerator, B, Fig. 2."* The temperature of the condensing-worm contained in the "elevated bath, *aa*, Fig. 2,"* and also that of the "first receiver, *k*, Fig. 2,"* was 11°.5. The temperature of the "cold bath, *ii*, Fig. 2,"* was 11°. The condenser in "the refrigerator, B," and the "second receiver," were cooled in a mixture of ice and salt. With the liquid boiling steadily from several points on the bottom of the flask, and the condensed product from the distillation running well from the refrigerator into the "second receiver," not a drop was condensed in any of the apparatus intervening between the flask and the "second receiver," although this part of the apparatus was cooled, as already stated, to about 11°. The temperature of the vapor in the flask at this time was 18°.5, or only 2°.5 below the temperature of the laboratory. These observations show that the liquid was boiling at a temperature considerably below that indicated by the thermometer in the vapor. Additional evidence of this was furnished by the fact that, during the distillation, the exterior of the flask, from the bottom to about one quarter of an inch above the surface of the liquid, was thickly covered with water condensed from the atmosphere, resembling heavy dew; while above, the sides of the

* See Memoir "On Process of Fractional Condensation," Memoirs of the American Academy, 1864.

flask were perfectly dry. It was these observations which first directed my attention to the fact that the temperature of the vapor could not in all cases be depended upon for the true boiling-point of a liquid, and naturally led me to make other experiments with special reference to this question.

Experiment 2. — The conditions of this experiment were somewhat different from those of the first. The liquid operated upon was the extremely volatile product collected in the "second receiver" of Experiment 1. The flask employed was smaller, and provided with two thermometers; the bulb of one of these was placed in the liquid, and that of the other in the vapor. The flask stood in a water-bath containing ice-water; this bath was also provided with a thermometer. The temperature of the ice-water bath was very gradually raised by means of a small flame from a Bunsen's burner. Temperature of the laboratory, 20° C. Observations during the distillation: —

	1.	Temperature of the water-bath,	10°
		" " boiling liquid,	8°
		" " vapor,	18°.5
	2.	Temperature of the water-bath,	12°
		" " boiling liquid,	9°
		" " vapor,	18°
15 minutes later.	3.	Temperature of the water-bath,	18°
		" " boiling liquid,	10°
		" " vapor,	14°
10 minutes later.	4.	Temperature of the water-bath,	20°
		" " boiling liquid,	12°
		" " vapor,	19°
20 minutes later.	5.	Temperature of the water-bath,	23°
		" " boiling liquid,	15°
		" " vapor,	19°

Experiment 3. — The subject of this experiment was a liquid which I had separated from the most volatile product of the re-distillation, on a manufacturing scale, of the crude benzole obtained in the distillation of coal-tar. The apparatus employed was essentially the same as that used in Experiment 1, with the addition of the extra thermometers, as in Experiment 2. The condensing-worm in the "elevated bath," and that in the "cold bath," and also the "first receiver," were all cooled in pounded ice. The condenser in the "refrigerator," and also the "second receiver," were both cooled in a mixture of ice and salt. The retort, which stood in a small copper bath containing pounded ice, was charged with about 250 *c. c.* of the liquid, which had been previously cooled in a mixture of ice and salt. Temperature of the laboratory, 16° C. Observations during the distillation : —

	1.	Temperature of the retort-bath,	0°
		" " boiling liquid,	0°.6
		" " vapor,	13°.5
45 minutes later.*	2.	Temperature of the retort-bath,	0°
		" " boiling liquid,	1°.3
		" " vapor,	12°.2
15 minutes later.	3.	Temperature of the retort-bath,	6°
		" " boiling liquid,	1°.8
		" " vapor,	12°.6
30 minutes later.	4.	Temperature of the retort-bath,	11°
		" " boiling liquid,	3°.8
		" " vapor,	12°.4
30 minutes later.	5.	Temperature of the retort-bath,	14°.5
		" " boiling liquid,	7°.3
		" " vapor,	13°.8

The apparent inconsistency that the temperature of the boiling liquid should be above that of the heating medium, — viz. an ice-bath — which continued during the first forty-five minutes of the experiment, is to be explained by the fact that there was a long column of mercury, above the surface of the liquid, which was subjected to the heating influence of the vapor. I would further remark that the gradual elevation of the boiling-point, as indicated by the thermometer in the liquid, is also only apparent, and is due to the gradual uncovering of the bulb as the liquid was distilled off. At the close of the experiment only about one fifth of the bulb, which unfortunately was a long one, was under the surface of the liquid. That this is the true explanation is evinced by the fact that during the experiment not a drop of liquid was observed to fall back into the retort from the "elevated condenser," although this was a tube ten feet in length, and cooled to the temperature of 0°.

I will now proceed to give my determinations of the boiling-points of various hydrocarbons, and of some of their derivatives, and then pass directly to consider the bearing of these results on the question concerning the increment of boiling-point for

* From this point the temperature of the retort-bath was gradually raised by means of a small gas-flame.

the addition of $C_2 H_2$ in homologous series.* The data for these considerations may be more conveniently arranged in tabular form, exhibiting at once, in serial order, the formulæ, boiling-points, elementary difference, and the corresponding difference of boiling-point.

1. *Of the Hydrocarbons obtained from Pennsylvania Petroleum.*

1ST SERIES.

Formula.	Boiling-point.	Elementary Difference.	Difference of boiling-point found.	Range of Temperature within which the substance would all distil.†
	°		°	°
$C_8 H_{10}$	6.0 (?)			
$C_{10} H_{12}$	30.2	$C_2 H_2$	30.2	1.5
$C_{12} H_{14}$	61.3	$C_2 H_2$	31.1	0.8
$C_{14} H_{16}$	90.4	$C_2 H_2$	29.1	1.0
$C_{16} H_{18}$	119.5	$C_2 H_2$	29.1	1.0
$C_{18} H_{20}$	150.8	$C_2 H_2$	31.3	0.8
			150.8 ÷ 5 = 30°.16	

Average increment of boiling-point for the addition of $C_2 H_2$ = 30°.16.

* In considering this question I shall include the boiling-points of the substances which I have separated from Pennsylvania petroleum, and the oil distilled from Albert coal; reserving for a subsequent memoir all other facts which have been derived from the study of these bodies.

† The ranges of temperature given in this and in the corresponding columns of the following tables, are for the purpose of showing the impossibility of there having been any essential error in the determinations of the boiling-points; as is evinced by the fact, in each case, that the whole product was found to distil without residue within such narrow limits. With so small a range of temperature, it is evident that it would make no practical difference whether either extreme or the mean of the observations be taken for the boiling-point.

The fact that these substances distil without residue within so short a range of temperature, is also of much value as proof of the existence of the two parallel series in petroleum and in coal-oil, with boiling-points so near together; [as shown by comparison of the boiling-points of the first with the second series from petroleum; and also of the two corresponding series from Albert coal-oil]; especially if this is considered in connection with the fact, so far as my experience goes, that the quantities of material in one series are generally about equal to those in the other.

That no erroneous conception may be formed as to the degree of purity of the substances treated of in this and in the following tables, from a mere inspection of the *ranges* of temperature here given; and in order that the almost absolute constancy of the boiling-points, in most cases, may not be overlooked, I would refer to the preceding memoir for further details concerning the boiling-points of such of these bodies as are therein treated of. For example, it will be found under the head "Determination of boiling-point" of benzole, that in the distillation it required 50 minutes for the temperature to rise 0°.2; while in one of the following tables it will be seen that the *range* of temperature within which the benzole distilled to dryness was found to be 0°.8. Likewise, by reference to the "Determination of boiling-point" of toluole it will be observed that it was found to boil absolutely constant 48 minutes; while the *range* of temperature given in the table referred to is 0°.7. In such cases as these, the slight rise of temperature which takes place just before going to dryness, is doubtless to be attributed to superheating of the vapor, in consequence of there being so small

2D SERIES.*

Formula. (?)	Boiling-point.	Elementary difference.	Difference of boiling-point found.	Range of Temperature within which the substance would all distil.
	°		°	°
$C_{8}H_{10}$	8 .9			
$C_{10}H_{12}$	37.0	$C_{2}H_{2}$	29.0	0.4
$C_{12}H_{14}$	68.5	$C_{2}H_{2}$	31.5	0.6
$C_{14}H_{16}$	98.1	$C_{2}H_{2}$	29.6	1.2
$C_{16}H_{18}$	127.6	$C_{2}H_{2}$	29.5	1.5
			119.6 ÷ 4 = 29°.9	

Average increment of boiling-point for the addition of $C_{2}H_{2}$ = 29°.9.

3D SERIES. (*Not completed.*)

Formula.	Boiling-point.	Elementary difference.	Difference of boiling-point found.	Range of Temperature within which the substance would all distil.
	°		°	°
$C_{22}H_{20}$	174.9			1.7
$C_{24}H_{22}$	195.8	$C_{2}H_{2}$	20.9	1.5
$C_{26}H_{24}$	216.2	$C_{2}H_{2}$	20.3	2.2
			41.2 ÷ 2 = 20°.6	

Average increment of boiling-point for the addition of $C_{2}H_{2}$ = 20°.6.

2. *Of the Hydrocarbons obtained from Albert Coal.*

1ST SERIES. (*Not completed.*)

Formula.	Boiling-point.	Elementary difference.	Difference of boiling-point found.	Range of Temperature within which the substance would all distil.
	°		°	°
$C_{10}H_{12}$				
$C_{12}H_{14}$	59.9	$C_{2}H_{2}$		1.5
$C_{14}H_{16}$	90.6	$C_{2}H_{2}$	30.7	0.5
$C_{16}H_{18}$	119.7	$C_{2}H_{2}$	29.1	0.5
			59.8 ÷ 2 = 29°.9	

The average boiling-point difference, in this series, for the addition of $C_{2}H_{2}$ is, therefore, 29°.9.

a quantity of liquid in the retort. Similar instances of absolute constancy of boiling-point as those just cited, might be given from among the products in either series from petroleum and Albert coal; which the *ranges* of temperature given in these tables do not indicate.

* I am somewhat in doubt whether the bodies composing this series and the 2d Series from Albert coal have the formula $C_{n}H_{n+2}$ as here represented, there being some indication that they contain less of hydrogen. For the purpose for which they are now presented, it is immaterial which formula is employed, as the common elementary difference and the boiling-point differences would remain the same; the solution of this question is therefore deferred for a subsequent memoir.

2D SERIES. (*Not completed.*)*

Formula. (?)	Boiling-point.	Elementary difference.	Difference of boiling-point found.	Range of Temperature within which the substance would all distil.
	°		°	°
$C_{10} H_{12}$				
$C_{12} H_{14}$	68.0	$C_2 H_2$		1.0
$C_{14} H_{16}$	98.5	$C_2 H_2$	30.5	0.6
$C_{16} H_{18}$	125.1	$C_2 H_2$	26.6	
			$57.1 \div 2 = 28°.6$	
Average boiling-point difference = 28°.6.				

3. *Of Hydrocarbons obtained from Coal-tar Naphtha.*

Name of Substance.	Formula.	Boiling-point.	Elementary difference.	Difference of boiling-point found.	Range of Temperature within which the substance would all distil.
		°		°	°
Benzole,	$C_{12} H_6$	80.0			0.3
Toluole,	$C_{14} H_8$	110.3	$C_2 H_2$	30.3	0.7
Xylole,	$C_{16} H_{10}$	139.8	$C_2 H_2$	29.5	0.4
Isocumole,	$C_{18} H_{12}$	169.9	$C_2 H_2$	30.1	1.0
				89.9	
Average increment of boiling-point for the addition of $C_2 H_2 = 89.9 \div 3 = 29°.97$.					

4. *Of Cumole from Cuminic Acid, and Cymole from Oil of Cumin.*

Name of Substance.	Formula.	Boiling point.	Elementary difference.	Difference of boiling-point found.	Range of Temperature within which the substance would all distil.
		°		°	°
Cumole,	$C_{18} H_{12}$	151.1			3.6
Cymole,	$C_{20} H_{14}$	179.6	$C_2 H_2$	28.5	1.2

With only a single exception, the results presented in the above tables point clearly to 30° as the common increment for the addition of $C_2 H_2$ in homologous series of hydrocarbons. Indeed, leaving out of the calculation the third series from petroleum (having the general formula C_nH_n), — which must remain anomalous, — and also the products from oil of cumin, the average of all the other boiling-point differences is 29°.75. The few individual variations from the number 30°, rarely exceeding a single degree, may reasonably be attributed to errors of the thermometer (especially in case of temperatures above 100°), or in some instances to a want of purity of one of the compared substances; which latter cause I doubt not is the case with the body from petroleum boiling at 37°, as upon this body I had bestowed less labor in fractioning than upon most of the others, on account of the extreme volatility and consequent

* See foot-note on the preceding page.

loss of the substance, by which the quantity had become so much reduced that I could ill afford further loss. In the case, also, of cymole from oil of cumin, and cumole from cuminic acid, in which the boiling-point difference varies only 1°.5 from the common difference of 30°, the want of perfect agreement may be fairly accounted for by the fact that the quantity of cumole at command was too small to admit of continuing the process of fractioning far enough to obtain perfect constancy of boiling-point. In consequence, also, of the quantity being so small, the *determination* of the boiling-point of cumole is less reliable, as this had to be conducted in a test-tube. It came into full ebullition at 148°.4, the temperature rising gradually to 151°.6 (observed temperatures), at which latter temperature it had distilled nearly to dryness. The distillation occupied thirteen minutes in passing over the range of three degrees. The average of the extremes, with the usual corrections for pressure, &c., was taken for the boiling-point. Abel,* who probably operated on a larger quantity, found the boiling-point of cumole to be 148°. It does not appear that he applied the corrections for pressure and the upper column of mercury. I do not doubt that the true boiling-point of this body will be found to be 150°, which would establish the difference of 30° between it and cymole.

I would here remark that this difference of 30° for the addition of C_2H_2 was first observed while engaged in fractioning Pennsylvania petroleum, and the oil from Albert coal, — substances the most difficult to separate, on account of the presence in each of two parallel series of constituents, whose boiling-points lie so near together.

As no one had preceded me in the investigation of these substances, my mind was as far as possible unbiased as to the boiling-points of the constituents of these mixtures. I was, however, aware of the beautiful relation between elementary constitution and boiling-point which Kopp had discovered, and familiar with the fact that the more recent investigations had shown the boiling-point difference among homologous hydrocarbons to be about 22°.5. If there was any one thing which more than another tended to bias me, it was the recent work of Church† on the boiling-points in the benzole series, in which he made the boiling-point difference invariably 22° and a fraction, a number varying but 3° from the theory of Kopp. Soon after the publication of Church's results, however, Kopp‡ accepted the number 22°.5 as about the boiling-point difference in this series, therefore regarding it as one of the exceptional series in which the boiling-point difference is greater than 19°. The work of Church had cer-

* Annalen der Chemie und Pharmacie, 1847, LXIII. 308.

† Philosophical Magazine, 1855, (4.) IX. 256.

‡ Annalen der Chemie und Pharmacie, 1855, XCVI. 29.

tainly the appearance of having been performed with great care, conducting to a beautiful harmony of results. My confidence in his determinations of boiling-points was increased not a little by his alleged discovery in coal-naphtha of xylole, boiling at 126°.2, indicating a more thorough analysis of this naphtha than those which had been previously published. This body, the supposed middle member of the benzole series, had up to that time been regarded as wanting in coal-tar naphtha, although all of the other members, above and below it, were found to be present, — an anomaly not easily reconciled with any plausible theory in regard to the formation of these bodies. In view of these circumstances, therefore, I was naturally led, from analogy, to anticipate that the boiling-point difference among the hydrocarbons from petroleum and Albert coal would not vary much from 20°. Not being able, however, to reconcile with previous facts and theories on this subject, the indications which were being gradually unfolded by my seemingly unerring process of separation, I was compelled to lay aside all bias, and to regard these indications as pointing unmistakably to a much greater difference of boiling-point for the addition of C_2H_2 than had previously been supposed to exist in this class of substances.

Having finally established beyond question the common difference of 30° for the addition of C_2H_2 among the hydrocarbons from Albert coal and petroleum (the third series from petroleum, with the difference of 20°, had not then been reached), I began to surmise that this difference might be found to be common among all other series of hydrocarbons. In this connection my mind naturally reverted to the earlier determinations of the boiling-points of the members of the benzole series, some of which, especially those of benzole and toluole, which had been more studied than the others, indicated strongly that 30° might prove to be the true difference for the addition of C_2H_2 in this series. My confidence in Church's determinations thus began to diminish, and finally I undertook to make a thorough analysis of coal-tar naphtha, the results of which are given in Table 3. As there shown, the boiling-point difference in the benzole series is also 30°, and the number of its members is reduced to four, in place of five, as alleged by Church.

This difference of 30°, thus shown to be so common with the hydrocarbons, is so much larger than the difference of 19° which Kopp had found so frequent in other classes of substances, that the discrepancy cannot be regarded otherwise than as conclusive evidence, if such were wanting, that all liquid bodies do not obey the same law in this regard, but that there are unquestionably those series in which the boiling-point difference for the elementary difference of C_2H_2 may be greater than 19°, of which Kopp has already furnished some examples.

That the difference may also be *less* than 19° in some series receives confirmation from the facts presented in the following tables.

6. *Of the Nitro-compounds derived from the Hydrocarbons of the Benzole Series.*

Name of Substance.	Formula.	Boiling-point.	Elementary Difference.	Difference of Boiling-point.
Nitro-benzole,	$C_{12} H_5 NO_4$	212°.1		
			$C_2 H_2$	13°.8
Nitro-toluole,	$C_{14} H_7 NO_4$	225.9		
			$C_2 H_2$	13.4
Nitro-xylole,	$C_{16} H_9 NO_4$	239.3		
			$C_2 H_2$	
Nitro-isocumole,	$C_{18} H_{11} NO_4$			

7. *Of the Alkaloids derived from the Hydrocarbons of the Benzole Series.*

Name of Substance.	Formula.	Boiling-point.	Elementary Difference.	Difference of Boiling-point.
Aniline,	$C_{12} H_7 N$	184°.6		
			$C_2 H_2$	17°.1
Toluidine,	$C_{14} H_9 N$	201.7		
			$C_2 H_2$	
Xylidine,	$C_{16} H_{11} N$	216.0*		
			$C_2 H_2$	
Iso-cumidine,	$C_{18} H_{13} N$			

In regard to the results presented in the last two tables, it may be remarked, first, that of the difference shown in the table of nitro-compounds, viz. an average of 13°.6, the discrepancy between this and the number 19°, being 5°.6, is so large as to leave no room for reasonable doubt that this is one of those exceptional series in which the boiling-point difference is less than 19° for the elementary difference of $C_2 H_2$. As this series does not appear to have been examined by Kopp, I have taken care to make as accurate a determination of the difference as circumstances would allow. The boiling-points were corrected as usual for pressure and the upper mercurial column. The boiling-points which have already been published of these bodies, so far as I have noticed, appear to have been given in the observed, i. e. uncorrected temperatures. The quantities of nitro-benzole and nitro-toluole which I operated upon were sufficiently large, and of a high degree of purity, presenting perfectly constant boiling-points. The quantity of nitro-xylole, however, was not so large as would have been desirable. Although the boiling-point of this body is doubtless very nearly correct, those of nitro-benzole and nitro-toluole are more to be relied upon; and omitting the fraction, the number 14° may, I think, be safely taken as the true boiling-point difference in this series. Secondly, that the less striking difference presented in the series of alkaloids, being only 2° under the number 19°, cannot reasonably justify the assumption that this small discrepancy of 2° is attributable to impurity of the substances, or to

* Not corrected.

inaccuracy in the determination of the boiling-points, when it is considered that great care was taken to obtain a high degree of purity and accuracy, and when it is considered also that previous observers have made this discrepancy larger than mine. It was on account of the fact that so small a discrepancy would naturally raise a doubt as to the reliability of the determinations, and for the reason that Kopp* has considered this series of alkaloids as agreeing tolerably well with his general law, that special care was taken on my part to arrive at a correct result. I am confident, therefore, that the boiling-point difference here will not be found to vary more than a fraction from 17°. Of the absolute accuracy of the boiling-points themselves I do not speak so confidently, since these depend so much on the accuracy of the thermometer at these high temperatures; but the correction of any errors which may have arisen from this source would not be likely to alter the relation, and the difference between the boiling-points would still remain about the same. This remark applies with equal force as to the reliability of the other boiling-points presented in this paper, especially of those of high temperatures.

It remains now to consider the foregoing facts with reference to the other theories mentioned.

Of the Calculated Boiling-points of Hydrocarbons by Schröder's Theory.

The subjoined tables exhibit the theoretical boiling-points of the above-mentioned hydrocarbons,† as calculated according to Schröder's last theory, in comparison with the boiling-points actually found. By this theory, as already stated, each double atom of carbon (C_2) contained in a body is supposed to influence the boiling-point by 30°, and each double atom of hydrogen (H_2) to influence the same — 10°; from the sum of these influences the number 70° is in all cases to be deducted, in order to find the boiling-point.

1. *Hydrocarbons from Pennsylvania Petroleum.*

1st Series.

Formula.	Determined Boiling-point.	Calculated Boiling-point by Schröder's theory.	Difference between Calculated and Determined Boiling-point.
$C_8 H_{10}$	0°.0 (?)	0°	°
$C_{10} H_{12}$	30.2	20	10.2
$C_{12} H_{14}$	61.3	40	21.3
$C_{14} H_{16}$	90.4	60	30.4
$C_{16} H_{18}$	119.5	80	39.5
$C_{18} H_{20}$	150.8	100	50.8

* Annalen der Chemie und Pharmacie, 1855, XCVI. 24.

† To avoid useless repetition, the hydrocarbons from Albert coal-oil will be omitted in this series of tables, they being considered identical with the corresponding bodies from petroleum.

2D SERIES.*

Formula. (?)	Determined Boiling-point.	Calculated Boiling-point by Schröder's theory.	Difference between Calculated and Determined Boiling-point.
$C_8 H_{10}$	8°–9	0°	8°–9
$C_{10} H_{12}$	37.0	20	17.0
$C_{12} H_{14}$	68.5	40	28.5
$C_{14} H_{16}$	98.1	60	38.1
$C_{16} H_{18}$	127.6	80	47.6

3D SERIES. (*Not completed.*)

Formula.	Determined Boiling-point.	Calculated Boiling-point by Schröder's theory.	Difference between Calculated and Determined Boiling-point.
$C_{20} H_{20}$	174°.9	130°	44°.9
$C_{22} H_{22}$	195.8	150	45.8
$C_{24} H_{24}$	216.2	170	46.2

2. *Hydrocarbons from Coal-tar Naphtha.*

Name of Substance.	Formula.	Determined Boiling-point.	Calculated Boiling-point by Schröder's theory.	Difference between Calculated and Determined Boiling-point.
Benzole,	$C_{12} H_6$	80°.0	80°	0°.0
Toluole,	$C_{14} H_8$	110.3	100	10.3
Xylole,	$C_{16} H_{10}$	139.8	120	19.8
Isocumole,	$C_{18} H_{12}$	169.9	140	29.8

3. *The Homologous Hydrocarbons from Oil of Cumin and Cuminic Acid.*

Name of Substance.	Formula.	Determined Boiling-point.	Calculated Boiling-point by Schröder's theory.	Difference between Calculated and Determined Boiling-point.
Cumole,	$C_{18} H_{12}$	151°.1	140°	11°.1
Cymole,	$C_{20} H_{14}$	179.6	160	19.6

It appears, therefore, that the theory of Schröder finds no support from any one of the different series of hydrocarbons presented in these tables. The discrepancy between the observed and calculated boiling-points, as shown, varies from about 10° to 50° C. This discrepancy is found to increase pretty uniformly by about 10° as we rise from one member to the next higher in the ascending series. In the series of the formula $C_n H_n$, however, the discrepancy is nearly a constant one, viz. about 46°. I would not overlook the fact, that the calculated boiling-point of benzole is absolutely identical with that found by experiment; nor the remarkable coincidence, that the agreement is almost perfect between the probable boiling-point, and that obtained by

* See foot-note on page 167.

calculation for the body of the probable formula $C_8 H_{10}$ in the 1st Series from petroleum. It is obvious, however, that these are merely accidental circumstances, to which no importance can attach.

OF THE CALCULATED BOILING-POINTS OF HYDROCARBONS BY LÖWIG'S THEORY, VIZ. THAT ONE ATOM OF CARBON (C) RAISES THE BOILING-POINT 38°.4, AND ONE ATOM OF HYDROGEN (H) LOWERS IT 29°.2.

Hydrocarbons from Pennsylvania Petroleum.

1ST SERIES.

Formula.	Determined Boiling-point.	Calculated Boiling-point by Löwig's theory.	Difference between Calculated and Determined Boiling-point.
$C_8 H_{10}$	0°.0 (?)	15°.2	°
$C_{10} H_{12}$	30.2	33.6	3.4
$C_{12} H_{14}$	61.3	52.0	9.3
$C_{14} H_{16}$	90.4	70.4	20.0
$C_{16} H_{18}$	119.5	88.8	30.7
$C_{18} H_{20}$	150.8	107.2	43.6

2D SERIES.*

Formula. (?)	Determined Boiling-point.	Calculated Boiling-point by Löwig's theory.	Difference between Calculated and Determined Boiling-point.
$C_8 H_{10}$	8°–9	15°.2	6°.7
$C_{10} H_{12}$	37.0	33.6	3.4
$C_{12} H_{14}$	68.5	52.0	16.5
$C_{14} H_{16}$	98.1	70.4	27.7
$C_{16} H_{18}$	127.6	88.8	38.8

3D SERIES. (*Not yet completed.*)

Formula.	Determined Boiling-point.	Calculated Boiling-point by Löwig's theory.	Difference between Calculated and Determined Boiling-point.
$C_{20} H_{20}$	174°.9	184°.0	10°.9
$C_{22} H_{22}$	195.8	202.4	6.6
$C_{24} H_{24}$	216.2	220.8	4.6

A cursory examination of the last three tables will suffice to show that, so far as regards the hydrocarbons of the formulæ $C_n H_n$ and $C_n H_{n+2}$, the theory of Löwig also has no foundation in fact. That his theory did not hold good with the hydrocarbons of the formula $C_n H_{n-6}$ was observed by Löwig himself, who found that it would place the boiling-point of benzole at 285°.6, i. e. 205° above its actual boiling-point.

* See foot-note on page 167.

OF THE CALCULATED BOILING-POINTS OF HYDROCARBONS BY GERHARDT'S THEORY.

We come finally to test the law of Gerhardt, above mentioned. Inasmuch as this law was specially designed to apply exclusively to the hydrocarbons, — upon the observed boiling-points of some of which it was indeed founded, — we should naturally expect to find this more in accordance with facts than either the hypothesis of Schröder or that of Löwig, both of which were claimed to be of more general application, and were framed more especially with reference to other classes of substances. The facts presented in the following tables will show, however, that this is far from being the case; and that the theory of Gerhardt, as well as those of Schröder and Löwig, so far as these relate to the hydrocarbons, was by no means legitimately drawn from nature, but is altogether artificial.

1. *Hydrocarbons from Pennsylvania Petroleum.*

1ST SERIES.

Formula.	Determined Boiling-point.	Calculated Boiling-point by Gerhardt's theory.	Difference between Calculated and Determined Boiling-point.
C_9H_{10}	0°.0 (?)	—8°.0	°
$C_{10}H_{12}$	30.2	12.5	17.5
$C_{12}H_{14}$	61.3	33.0	28.3
$C_{14}H_{16}$	90.4	53.5	36.9
$C_{16}H_{18}$	119.5	74.0	45.5
$C_{18}H_{20}$	150.8	94.5	56.3

2D SERIES.*

Formula. (?)	Determined Boiling-point.	Calculated Boiling-point by Gerhardt's theory.	Difference between Calculated and Determined Boiling-point.
C_9H_{10}	8–9°	—8°	16°.5
$C_{10}H_{12}$	37.0	12.5	24.5
$C_{11}H_{14}$	68.5	33.0	35.5
$C_{14}H_{16}$	98.1	53.5	44.6
$C_{16}H_{18}$	127.6	74.0	53.6

3D SERIES.

Formula.	Determined Boiling-point.	Calculated Boiling-point by Gerhardt's theory.	Difference between Calculated and Determined Boiling-point
$C_{20}H_{20}$	174°.9	130°.0	44°.9
$C_{22}H_{22}$	195.8	150.5	45.3
$C_{24}H_{24}$	216.2	171.0	45.2

* See foot-note on page 167.

2. *Hydrocarbons from Coal-tar Naphtha.*

Benzole Series.

Name of Substance.	Formula.	Determined Boiling-point.	Calculated Boiling-point by Gerhardt's theory.	Difference between Observed and Calculated Boiling-point.
Benzole,	$C_{12} H_6$	80°.0	93°.0	13°.0
Toluole,	$C_{14} H_8$	110.3	113.5	3.5
Xylole,	$C_{16} H_{10}$	139.8	134.0	6.0
Isocumole,	$C_{18} H_{12}$	169.9	154.5	15.5

3. *Hydrocarbons from Oil of Cumin and Cuminic Acid.*

Name of Substance.	Formula.	Determined Boiling-point.	Calculated Boiling-point by Gerhardt's theory.	Difference between Observed and Calculated Boiling-point.
Cumole,	$C_{18} H_{12}$	151°.1	154°.5	+3°.4
Cymole,	$C_{20} H_{14}$	179.6	175.0	—4.6
Cumo-oil of turpentine,	$C_{20} H_{16}$	155.4	160.0	+4.6

The chief conclusions deduced from the foregoing facts and considerations may be briefly summed up as follows: —

1. That the boiling-point difference for the addition of $C_2 H_2$ in homologous series of hydrocarbons is generally 30° C., which is a much larger difference than has been commonly supposed.

2. That of the five series of hydrocarbons examined, only one series was found exceptional to the rule just stated, and this presented the boiling-point difference of about 20°, which is but little larger than the number 19°, which Kopp found so common with other classes of substances.

3. That certain series of derivatives from the benzole series of hydrocarbons present boiling-point differences, corresponding to the elementary difference of $C_2 H_2$, considerably smaller than the number 19° of Kopp.

4. That the formulæ of Schröder, Löwig, and Gerhardt for the calculation of boiling-points, so far as these may be supposed to relate to the hydrocarbons, are incorrect and purely artificial.

5. That the custom of taking boiling-points with the bulb of the thermometer in the vapor is more liable to lead to an erroneous determination, at least in certain cases, than if the bulb be placed in the liquid.

ON

A PROCESS

OF

FRACTIONAL CONDENSATION.

By C. M. WARREN.

[From the Memoirs of the American Academy, New Series, Vol. IX.]

CAMBRIDGE:
WELCH, BIGELOW, AND COMPANY,
PRINTERS TO THE UNIVERSITY.
1865.

VI.

On a Process of Fractional Condensation; applicable to the Separation of Bodies having small Differences between their Boiling-Points.

By C. M. Warren.

Communicated May 10th, 1864.

It is well known that the process in general use for the proximate analysis of mixtures of volatile liquids, — viz., that of simple fractional distillation, either from a tubulated retort or from a flask with bulbs, as proposed by Wurtz,* — affords but very imperfect and unsatisfactory results, and not unfrequently leads to gross errors and misconceptions, except in those cases in which the boiling-points of the constituents are widely different, or in which some auxiliary method can be advantageously employed.

The want of a more efficient process for effecting such separations has long been recognized. There are numerous natural and artificial products, of the highest scientific interest, — such as petroleums, essential oils, tars, and other mixtures of oils obtained by the distillation, under varied circumstances, of bituminous, vegetable, and animal substances, — of which it may at least be said that we have but very imperfect knowledge, — I might almost say no knowledge, except such as could be derived from the study of very impure materials, — still mixtures of different bodies, — with which, instead of the pure substances sought for, chemists have felt compelled to content themselves, as the best results which they were able to obtain by the means at their command.

In repeated instances, apparently after persevering and protracted efforts, investigators have been forced to assert either the impossibility, or their inability, to obtain, from such mixtures, bodies of constant boiling-point, — a property which is generally received as a test of purity for liquid bodies.

I may here specify a few recent instances of this kind.

* Annales de Chimie et de Physique, 3e Série, XLII. 132.

1. Warren de la Rue and Hugo Müller,* in their paper entitled "Chemical Examination of Burmese Naphtha or Rangoon Tar," after detailing the preliminary treatment by distillation in a current of steam, add that "A further separation of the various products was effected by repeated fractional distillations; but no absolutely constant boiling-points could be obtained, notwithstanding the great number of distillations and the large quantity of material at command. It is true that considerable portions of distillates could be collected between certain ranges of temperature, tending to indicate a constant boiling-point; nevertheless it soon became evident that distillation alone could not effect the separations of the various constituents, and that recourse must be had to other processes." The other processes resorted to were, treatment with sulphuric and nitric acids, either separately or mixed; but still with very imperfect results. This acid treatment, which was first proposed by De la Rue, and subsequently employed by C. Greville Williams,† Schorlemmer, and others, will be further noticed below.

2. Frankland,‡ in speaking of a mixture of the hydrocarbons of the formulæ $C_n H_n$ and $C_n H_{n+1}$ (now generally considered as $C_n H_{n+2}$), which have a difference of 6° to 7° C. between their boiling-points, says, "The separation of two such bodies by distillation alone is impossible"; and suggests that the employment of anhydrous sulphuric acid may accomplish the object by dissolving out the body of the formula $C_n H_n$.

3. And so recently as 1862, Schorlemmer,§ in his first paper "On the Hydrides of the Alcohol-Radicals existing in the Products of the Destructive Distillation of Cannel Coal," remarks that "it was, however, found impossible to obtain a product of constant boiling-point by repeated fractional distillations"; and he also had recourse to the acid-treatment above referred to.

4. Pebal,‖ after an elaborate research on the petroleum from Galicia, in which Wurtz's bulbs were employed, and also Eisenstuck,¶ who made an extended investiga-

* Proceedings of the Royal Society, VIII. 221.

† Philosophical Transactions, 1857, 447.

‡ Quarterly Journal of the Chemical Society, 1851, 3, 43.

§ Journal of the Chemical Society, XV. 419.

‖ Annalen der Chemie und Pharmacie, CXV. 20, asserts the "Unmöglichkeit, das Gemenge durch fractionirte Destillationen zu entwirren."

¶ Annalen der Chemie und Pharmacie, CXIII. 169, says as follows:—"Mit den 5° zu 5° aufgesammelten Destillaten wurde die fractionirte Destillation wieder von Neuem vorgenommen, aber nachdem diese Operation sieben Wochen mit etwas 50 Pfund Steinöl fortgesetzt worden war, erhielt ich doch kein Product von irgend constantem Siedepunkt. Nach diesen Versuchen halte ich es für Unmöglich, das Steinöl durch fractionirte Destillationen allein in Producte mit constantem Siedepunkt, zu scheiden."

tion of the petroleum from Sehnde, near Hannover, also with the use of Wurtz's bulbs, both assert in the most positive manner the impossibility of separating from petroleum, by fractional distillation, products of constant boiling-point.

Such is the general character of the results obtained in the attempts which have been made to separate the constituents of such mixtures by fractional distillation.

The treatment with strong acids, etc., as an auxiliary to the common method of fractional distillation, which is claimed to have given good results in some cases, is open to serious objections in its application to mixtures of unknown substances, as must be readily apparent. The further consideration of this subject is reserved for another occasion, when I shall submit the results which I have obtained by my process in the study of mixtures almost identical with some of those in the investigation of which the acid process has been employed. I shall then be able to show that the results obtained by that process are, to a considerable extent, inaccurate and by no means exhaustive; and that it is still of the highest importance to have a process which shall be generally applicable in all such cases, without resort to any harsh and uncertain treatment.

With regard to the value of constancy of boiling-point above referred to, as a test of purity of a liquid substance, I may here say that, without scarcely lessening the importance of obtaining constancy of boiling-point, before resorting to harsher treatment, in the study of mixtures of unknown substances, I think I shall be able to show, on another occasion, that this property is not necessarily indicative of so high a degree of purity as has generally been supposed; and that a body may have a constant boiling-point, and yet contain enough of a foreign substance to appreciably — and, in delicate cases, seriously — affect the determination of its constitution and of some of its other properties. But in no such case have I yet found that the removal of the impurity by chemical means has essentially changed the boiling-point, — *i. e.*, never to the extent of 1° C. of temperature. I propose, at a future time, to study this question synthetically, operating with pure liquid substances, with the view to determine, in a few cases, how much of a foreign substance may be present, — which would probably be variable in different cases, — without sensibly affecting the boiling-point. A solution of this question would, I think, be of considerable practical value in some instances.*

* Since this was prepared for the press I notice that late experiments by Berthelot go to show the correctness of my conception of the value of constancy of boiling-point, as above stated.

Of the New Process.

The chief distinctive feature of my process, as compared with the common ‹ consists in this, — that the operator has complete and easy control of the temperat of the vapors given off in distillation; and consequently can readily cool these va] to the lowest limit of temperature which the most volatile portion, under the circ stances, is able to bear and retain its vaporous condition. It will be seen at a gla that, under these conditions, the operator has it in his power to secure in any ‹ the very largest possible amount of condensation of the heavier from the ligl vapors. The liquids resulting from the condensation of the less volatile portion course fall back into the retort, while the vapors of the more volatile parts conti to go forward to a cold condenser, descending in the opposite direction, from wl the condensed product falls into a special receiver. In this manner he is abl obtain, in each successive operation, a series of products which shall contain minimum quantity of the less volatile constituents, which a single distillation is c ble of affording.

Of the common process, on the contrary, nearly the reverse of all this is true: operator having no control whatever; being forced to receive the vapors at the t perature which they naturally acquire in passing from the retort, and laden with s proportion of the less volatile bodies as may be carried forward with them.*

* The only apparatus, of which I have any knowledge, which can be regarded as bearing any analogy t own, is that employed in the rectification of alcoholic spirits, on a manufacturing scale. In one of the forms of this apparatus, that of Solimani, to which my attention was first called by a friend, after my pr had been in use more than a twelvemonth, the temperature of a dephlegmator is kept within such limits give alcohol of any required strength more readily than by the common methods. The mode of constructi this apparatus is, however, only adapted to manufacturing purposes, and it could not be utilized in the exact experiments required in scientific research. Either on account of its complication, or some other c the apparatus of Solimani has, I believe, long since been abandoned.

Mansfield (Quarterly Journal of the Chemical Society, 1849, I. 264), observing that "the boiling-poi benzole is the same as that of alcohol of sp. gr. 0.825," remarks that "any of the summary processes of re cation which are practised by distillers in the manufacture of alcoholic spirits, are applicable to the separ of benzole from the less volatile fluids of naphtha"; and, appended to his scientific treatise on coal-tar, u the title "*Of a Practical Mode of Preparing Benzole*," goes on to describe a process for that purpose, w I believe, he had previously patented. It appears that Mansfield did not employ this process in his rese but obtained his benzole, as well as the other less volatile hydrocarbons, in the usual manner, — by si distillation.

In the belief that no process of fractioning at all analogous to mine has ever been employed in scie research, and that I am not in any way directly indebted to any of the devices of my predecessors, I taken no special pains to consider these devices in much detail. I may say, however, that I have foun

In the new process, perfect control of the temperature of the vapors is secured by simply conducting these vapors upward through a worm contained in a bath, *aa*, Figs. 1 and 2, the temperature of which is regulated by means of a separate lamp, *b*, Fig. 2, or by a safety-furnace, *p*, as shown in Fig. 1. The bath may be of oil or water, or of metal for very high temperatures, as the case may require, and is furnished with a thermometer, *t*.

Fig. 1.

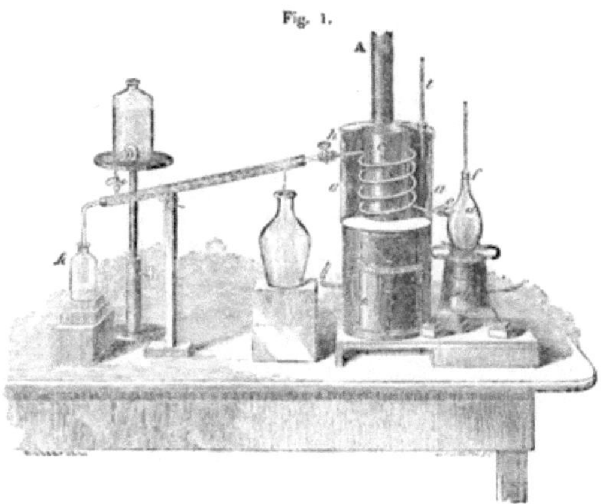

That this bath may be equally adapted for the separation of liquids boiling below the common temperature, an empty vessel, *c*, Fig. 1 and 2, is permanently secured in the interior of the bath by means of straps of metal across the top, to serve as a convenient receptacle for ice or iced water, by means of which a low temperature may be steadily maintained. This interior vessel also serves a good purpose in economizing

record of any one's ever having employed the oil bath and a separate fire to regulate a heated condenser, this being the essential feature on which the superiority of my process is based; adapting it at once to both high and low temperatures, and for the most delicate work.

The employment of bulbs, above referred to, as proposed by Wurtz, is simply a modification of the old process. The bulb apparatus furnishes the same, or, at most, but slightly better results than a simple retort; being no more than equivalent to increasing the height of the sides of the retort itself, without introducing any control over the accuracy of the results; the only advantage gained being, that these results are obtained somewhat more quickly.

Fig. 2.

time, and fuel in heating the bath, as it diminishes the quantity of oil required to cover the worm. It is made to extend to within about three inches of the bottom of the bath, and large enough to fill the greater part of the space in the centre of the coil. The bath and interior vessel are both made of sheet-copper, with joints brazed so that they will bear a high temperature. I generally use, also, copper worms, especially in the earlier distillations, the quantities then operated upon being larger, as such worms are conveniently procured, and not liable to break. In the larger-sized apparatus, the tube of which the worm is made measures ten feet in length and half an inch in diameter. I have tried several lengths of worm and several diameters of tube, but not, as yet, with any special view of determining the precise proportions, in relation to the size of the retort, which would be best adapted to the purpose. There appears, however, to be nothing gained by increasing the length of the worm beyond what is required to reduce the temperature of the vapors to that of the bath. I have in use three sizes of apparatus: the largest has a copper worm 10 feet long and $\frac{1}{2}$ inch bore; the medium size, a worm 5 feet long and $\frac{3}{8}$ inch bore; and the smallest size, for very small quantities, a worm 1 foot 6 inches long and $\frac{1}{4}$ inch bore. Each of these has been found to answer a good purpose. The distillation may be conducted in a glass flask, or more conveniently in a glass retort of the form shown at *d*, Fig. 1 and 2. The body of this retort, as appears in the figure, is of the form of the corresponding part of the common retort; but which, in place of a long neck, has only a short tubulure, *e*, in the side, for escape of the vapors, and another tubulure, *f*, in the top, which contains the thermometer, and through which the retort is charged.

In the larger apparatus the retort is connected with the lower end of the elevated worm by means of a glass tube of about the same diameter as the end of the worm. One end of this tube enters the retort at the lateral tubulure through a perforated cork, and the other end is joined to the end of the worm either by being firmly bound with a strip of cloth thickly covered with vulcanized caoutchouc, — such as is found in commerce, — or by means of a perforated cork, which is made to fit the ends of both tubes as snugly as possible, and then tightly pressed together upon the joint by means of an iron clamp, as shown at *g*, Fig. 2. This clamp is figured on a larger scale at E. As it is highly important that all joints in the apparatus should be perfectly tight, inasmuch as the least leakage, when continued a long time, would cause, in the aggregate, a serious loss of material, I would call special attention to the clamp joint as the best which I have tried. Before falling upon this device I had used exclusively the vulcanized caoutchouc joints, which were found to answer a good purpose, in most cases, except that they required too frequent renewal. I have found the cloth cov with vulcanized caoutchouc preferable to the common caoutchouc tubing. In smaller sizes of apparatus I have the end of the worm itself project far enough f the bath to connect directly with the retort by means of a perforated cork, with the use of an additional connecting tube.

The upper end, *h*, of the elevated worm is brought out through the side of the b at a point about three inches below the top; so that, when working with a low t perature of the bath, the worm may still be completely covered with oil, and also g sufficient space above the worm for the expansion of the oil when higher temp tures are employed. To avoid contaminating the atmosphere of the laboratory v the disagreeable fumes which are given off, in large quantity, from such a mas heated oil, the top of the bath is tightly closed with a sheet-iron cover, from whic small funnel, A, Fig. 1, conducts these fumes to a chimney.

In the larger apparatus, the vapors which succeed in passing through the hea worm are conducted downward into a cooled worm contained in a bath of wate Fig. 2, and the liquid product is collected in the receiver, *k*. The cold bath, *ii*, cont two condensing worms, — one for each apparatus, — and is large enough to conde for both without the necessity of renewing the water. I have represented two ap ratuses combined, as it will be found more economical of time to operate with tw once. In the smaller apparatus, for the table, a Liebig condenser may be convenier substituted for the cold worm, as shown in Fig. 1.

For collecting liquids which boil below the common temperature, when such present, I attach a refrigerator, B, Fig. 2, which is provided with two block-tin c densing-tubes, — one for each apparatus. These are bent in a zigzag form, attached to the inner sides of the refrigerator. The lower ends of the tubes ext through the end of the refrigerator far enough to form a convenient connection w the second receiver, *l*, Fig. 2, which communicates with the first receiver, *k*, by me of the glass tube, *m*.

In order to successfully collect and condense the vapors of such extremely vola liquids as are now under consideration, it is of course indispensable that the appara should be constructed with very tight joints; and for greater convenience, but m especially to prevent breakage, such of the joints as require to be frequently tal apart should be made flexible. A very convenient and perfectly tight joint of t kind may be made as follows: — the short stationary tube, *n*, in the cork of receiver, *k*, Fig. 2, is made with the opening somewhat divergent upward; the enc of the worm is enough smaller than the inside diameter of the upper end of the tu *n*, to leave room for a piece of caoutchouc tube to be drawn over it, and still admit of its being inserted in the end of the tube, *n*; the flexible tube is drawn on far enough to prevent the drops which form on the end of the worm from coming in contact with the caoutchouc; a perfectly tight and convenient flexible joint is now made by pressing the tube, *n*, over the caoutchouc covering of the end of the worm, *o*. The joints of the receivers, *ll*, are made in the same manner.

The vapors which escape condensation in *ii* pass through the receivers, *kk* and *ll*, to the refrigerator B, which contains ice, or a mixture of ice and salt, are there condensed and fall back into the receivers, *ll*; which should stand in a wooden vessel also containing ice or a freezing mixture. The refrigerator, B, is made with double bottom and sides, with an inch space between, which is filled with pulverized charcoal. Being tightly covered, a charge of ice and salt will serve for a long day's operations without renewal. In this manner I have been able to collect, in considerable quantity, bodies boiling nearly at 0° C., and this from mixtures in which such bodies had been quite overlooked by previous investigators.

It will be observed, on reference to Fig. 2, that the larger distilling apparatus is represented as standing in a brick fire-place, with brick-work, CC, a few inches high, built up in front; and a sheet-iron apron, DD, folded above. This is for security against fire in case of accident, either to the retort or hot bath of oil. As arranged, the contents of either or both of these could run out and burn without danger to the operator or the premises, as the brick-work in front would prevent the liquid from spreading beyond the fire-place, and the dropping of the sheet-iron apron would cause an additional draft, and thus insure the passage of the flames into the chimney. Instead of placing the apparatus in a fire-place, where that is not convenient, equal security against accidents may be attained by the use of my safety heating-lamp,* *q*, Fig. 1, to heat the retort, and safety-furnace, *p*, containing a Bunsen's burner, for heating the bath. The bottom of this furnace, and also a large part of the sides, is formed of wire gauze, such as described for the safety-lamp.† The gauze upon the bottom need not be permanently attached to the furnace, but may be simply laid over an opening cut in the stool or board on which the furnace is to be placed; if the furnace be then set upon it, taking care that the joint shall be tight around the edge, nothing more will be required. A strip of vulcanized caoutchouc, about an eighth of an inch in thickness, is riveted around the edge of the opening for the door; against this the door tightly closes, so that no ignition can take place through the cracks which would otherwise remain under the edges of the door.

* American Journal of Science, 1862 (2), XXXIII. 275.

† *Loc. cit.*

For an apparatus to stand upon the table, the safety-lamp and furnace are especially desirable. I have also used them for the larger apparatus, placed upon the floor of the laboratory. As a practical test of the security which they afford, I may relate an incident which happened to myself. I had left the laboratory for a short time, with such an apparatus in full operation; the retort containing nearly a quart of light petroleum boiling below 100° C. Having been detained longer than I expected, on returning I found the laboratory filled with the vapors of hydrocarbons; and, on approaching the retort, found that the caoutchouc joint, connecting the retort with the elevated worm, had failed, and that the larger portion of the liquid had distilled into the room, having been mainly condensed in the upper worm, and conducted thence down the outside of the retort into the safety-lamp. This process was still going on, the lamp being highly-heated from the excess of fuel thus added to it, but no ignition took place outside the lamp. Although this experiment was rather injudicious, it furnishes a valuable test of the efficiency of the safety-lamp and furnace.

Having described the apparatus, I now proceed to give such details of the method of conducting the separations as have been found, in my experience, most efficient and economical of time. In commencing with a crude mixture of unknown liquids, I deem it advisable to operate at once on a tolerably large quantity of material, especially if the constituents are supposed to be numerous, and to omit chemical treatment till after the separations have so far progressed as to indicate the number and species of bodies present, and, approximately, their several boiling-points.

Notwithstanding the precautions taken to avoid loss from evaporation and leakage, I have at times been surprised at the large waste of material which has been made apparent after a long series of operations. When it is considered, however, that the time required to make a complete separation of a very complex mixture of liquids must necessarily be very protracted, during which more or less of evaporation is constantly taking place, it will be a matter of no surprise that the loss is so considerable. The quantity of material required must depend also on the proportions in which the various constituents are contained in the crude mixture, and upon their degree of volatility; but as these cannot be known *a priori*, it may suffice to make a single preliminary distillation of a portion of the mixture, from a tubulated retort, to ascertain the range of temperature within which it distills, noting at the same time the proportions which come over between certain temperatures; as, for example, below 50° C.; between 50° and 100°, etc.; from these data one may judge pretty nearly of the quantity which it will be advisable to take. It is evident that, when very volatile bodies are present, even in considerable proportion, a much larger quantity would be required than if the material were but slightly volatile; as the waste in the former case, from evaporation, would be much greater.

But in many cases it will be found that highly volatile bodies are present only in very small proportion, — e. g. in viscid petroleums like Rangoon tar, and in the products of distillation of some species of asphalt. In such cases, the requisite quantity to be operated upon, to obtain the most volatile constituents in sufficient quantity for anything like a complete study of their chemical relations, would be extremely large, — too large to be conducted in the laboratory, — and one would have to resort to the manufactory for the first distillation. I have dwelt at some length on this point, having experienced the disappointment which one feels, after months of labor, on finding the products insufficient for his requirements, when the expenditure of a little more time, comparatively, might have given double the quantities obtained.

In the first series of fractioning I generally operate on successive portions, of about one gallon each, of the crude material, and take off a fraction for every 20° C. rise of temperature of the retort. These fractions are preserved in well-stoppered bottles, and each carefully labelled with the temperatures between which it was obtained. The fractions for each fresh portion of the crude material, being collected between the same limits of temperature, are added to the corresponding products from the preceding operations, till enough of the crude material has been taken to insure, ultimately, a sufficiency of the pure products.

In the commencement, not only of this but of all subsequent fractionings, when the temperature to which the bath should be raised is unknown, I first bring the liquid in the retort into full ebullition, so that a steady stream of liquid shall flow back from the end of the worm into the retort. I then carefully raise the temperature of the bath until the vapors from the retort pass through the heated worm so freely that the liquid, in condensing from them, shall drop with tolerable rapidity into the cold receiver. In order that this dropping may be continuous, it is necessary that the temperature of the bath should rise *very gradually* as the more volatile constituents of the mixture are taken off; this is easily effected by carefully regulating the flame under the bath.

It is advisable to boil the retort as rapidly as possible without choking the lower end of the heated worm with the returning liquid. As this choking would give rise to additional pressure in the retort, and consequently occasion abnormal elevation of the temperature, and possibly a rush of liquid into the receiver, and thus introduce irregularities in the work, excessive heat under the retort should be avoided. The first indication of choking of the worm is a partial or entire stoppage of the strea liquid which normally flows steadily from the end of the worm into the retort. interruption or unsteadiness of this flow would indicate too rapid ebullition.

As a rule, other things being equal, the greater the difference between the perature of the bath and that of the retort, the slower the products will come and the more effectual will be the separation. I think it possible, however, that earlier fractionings may be conducted so slowly that the loss of time would r than counterbalance what might be gained by more thorough separation, and equally good results may be more economically obtained by more frequent operat somewhat more rapidly conducted.

A striking illustration of the advantage to be gained by this process is presente the fact that, during the first fractioning of a crude mixture, such as American p leum or coal-tar naphtha, for example, the difference between the temperature of bath and that of the retort may sometimes be as much as 35° C., or even more. W as the products become purer, this difference between the temperatures of the and retort proportionally decreases, till finally, in operating on a pure product, temperature of the bath must be brought to within a few degrees of that of the re in order to bring the vapors through. But the amount of this difference is vari for different bodies of equal purity.

These first fractionings must necessarily be quite arbitrary; for, as a general when operating on such mixtures as those just mentioned, neither the thermom nor the quantities obtained for any given range of temperature will indicate decided preponderance of any one substance. On the contrary, the temperature uniformly, and about the same quantity is generally obtained for the same numb degrees of temperature throughout the operation. In other mixtures, in which cer bodies may seem to be present in much larger proportion than others, or in which tl may be a greater difference between the boiling-points of the constituents than in cases referred to, — facts which would be indicated by the thermometer of the re and by the relative quantities of the products obtained, — there might be sometl gained by exercising discretion in taking off fractions according to these indication

In the second series of fractioning, the first or lowest fraction of the preceding se which is large enough to operate upon by itself, is transferred to the retort, and brou into ebullition. The temperature of the bath is then adjusted as above described, the distillation continued, the fractions obtained being placed in their appropriate tles until the temperature of the retort shall have risen to, or somewhat above, point at which the second or next succeeding fraction of the first series may be posed, or has been found by experiment, to boil. This fraction is then added to the residue in the retort, and the distillation is continued as before. In the same manner, I proceed with the remaining fractions of the first series.

All subsequent fractionings are similarly conducted. As the work progresses, however, the fractions are taken for a gradually decreasing number of degrees of temperature, until finally it becomes necessary, for the attainment of absolute constancy of boiling-point, to take off a fraction for every degree, centigrade; and to continue thus to operate on these fractions, each representing one degree of temperature, until the desired end is attained.

The operator will observe that, in each series of fractions, in which each fraction has been taken for the same range of temperature, the difference between the boiling-points of any two contiguous fractions is nearly the same as the difference between any other two contiguous fractions, — in other words, that the difference referred to approximates to a common difference throughout the same series. Once ascertained, this difference serves as a valuable guide in determining with sufficient accuracy when to add the next fraction to the retort. By observing this systematic course, irregularities, from the improper mixture of products, may be avoided, and time thus economized.

After a few series of fractionings, — sometimes after two or three, variable in number, according to the nature or complication of the mixture, — it will be found that some of the fractions are considerably larger than others for the same range of temperature, indicating approximately the boiling-points of the several constituents. But fractions of constant boiling-point, or those, the boiling-points of which cannot be sensibly changed by further fractional condensation, are not obtained, as already mentioned, till after repeated careful fractioning for every degree of temperature. When fractioning for every degree, it is important to use every precaution to protect the thermometer from external influences, and to carefully apply the corrections for variations in the atmospheric pressure. This may even be desirable earlier; but it is of so much importance in the case specified, that, if omitted, the operator would be liable one day to mix products which he had separated the day previous.

In this way, certain larger fractions are obtained, which are not susceptible of further alteration in their boiling-points; but there are yet considerable quantities of liquid in the intermediate fractions, which still continue to change more or less in each succeeding operation. When the fractions of constant boiling-point have once been obtained, if it were not important to test for other bodies in the intermediate fractions, the operation might here be suspended, provided the pure products already obtained should be large enough for the purposes required.

But in my investigations, I have undertaken to prove the negative as well as the positive. I have attempted to carry the process of separation so far, that I might assert the absence of other bodies, as well as the presence of those obtained; and this clearing up of the intermediate fractions has generally been the most tedious part of the work. I have continued to operate upon these by themselves, until they also have become distributed in regular course — no new bodies appearing — among the fractions of constant boiling-point, or to such an extent that the intermediate quantities have become too small to admit of further continuance of the process.

This process has been in constant use in my laboratory during the last three years. In this time it has been applied in the study of petroleums, coal oils, the more volatile parts of coal- and wood-tars, the essential oil of cumin, commercial fusel oil, from corn whiskey, and even to mixtures more complex than either of these. As the result of this long experience, I can say that as regards bodies not decomposed by heat in distillation, I have not yet found a mixture so complex that it may not be resolved by this process into its proximate constituents so completely, that these shall have almost absolutely constant boiling-points. In repeated instances, even from petroleums, I have obtained these constituents so pure, that the contents of an ordinary tubulated retort charged with one of them has been completely distilled off without any essential change of temperature; i. e., not to the amount of $\frac{1}{2}$° C., the thermometer frequently remaining absolutely constant for more than half an hour, a constancy of boiling-point not exceeded by that of distilled water. This state of purity, I think I may safely assert, has never before been attained from such mixtures by any system of fractional distillation.

As I shall soon be prepared to present to the Academy detailed results of the investigations above referred to, I may omit further allusion to them on this occasion.

I would remark, in conclusion, that it seems to me not improbable that this process may ultimately prove to be of great value in the arts. It is not too much to anticipate that, whenever the various constituents of the mixtures referred to shall have been separately and thoroughly studied in a pure state, some of them may be found to possess properties which will give to them great commercial value, sufficient to justify the expenditure necessary to separate them in large quantities.

RESEARCHES

ON THE

VOLATILE HYDROCARBONS.

(TWO MEMOIRS.)

I. NAPHTHA FROM LIME SOAP.
II. NAPHTHA FROM RANGOON PETROLEUM.

By C. M. WARREN AND F. H. STORER.

[From the Memoirs of the American Academy, New Series, Vol. IX.]

Cambridge Press:
DAKIN AND METCALF.
1866.

VIII.

Examination of a Hydro-carbon Naphtha, obtained from the Products of the Destructive Distillation of Lime-soap.

By C. M. Warren and F. H. Storer.

Communicated, August 9th, 1865.

In the winter of 1859, when the supply of coal-oil in the Atlantic States was altogether inadequate to meet the daily increasing demand for that article, and before the discovery of the fact that abundant supplies of petroleum could be obtained by sinking artesian wells in proper localities, it occurred to one of us that a burning-oil, equal to that from cannel-coal, could be readily obtained from the cheap fish-oils of commerce, by saponifying these with hydrate of lime and then subjecting to destructive distillation the lime-salts thus obtained.

In acting upon this conception, several trial experiments were conducted by its author, upon a somewhat extended scale, in the manufactory in New York, which was at that time under his control. These trials were as follows: — In a shallow wooden tub, eight or ten feet in diameter, at the bottom of which was a coil of metallic perforated pipe, for the introduction of steam, there was first prepared a quantity of milk of lime, and to this was added some two hundred or more gallons of commercial "menhaden-oil." This menhaden-oil is manufactured upon the large scale by boiling and expressing the common fish, *Alosa menhaden*, a sort of herring, which is known popularly in some localities as the menhaden. Steam being then blown into the mixture of oil and lime, saponification was effected in the course of a few hours. After the glycerine-water had been drawn off from the finished lime-soap, the latter was shovelled out into a bin and there left to dry. The amount of quick-lime employed having been about 25 per cent. of the weight of the fish-oil, the finished soap was of course mixed with a considerable excess of hydrate of lime. A ten-barrel cast-iron still was in the next place charged with the dry mixture of soap and hydrate of lime, and the whole heated so strongly that the bottom of the retort was finally red-hot. The distillation proceeded quietly and regularly, the matter in the retort exhibiting no tendency to froth or boil over; but in the still employed, which was of the ordinary pot-shape, the operation was somewhat tedious, on account of the difficulty of heating the interior of so large a mass of lime. Portions of the products of distillation also condensed at first in the upper layers of the lime, and were driven off with difficulty. Both these impediments could however undoubtedly have been avoided by employing a common iron gas-retort instead of the still.

As a distillate there was obtained a mixture of hydro-carbon oils, of a dark brown color, and a peculiar, disagreeable odor. In consistency this mixture did not differ much from the crude coal-oil which is obtained by distilling rich cannel-coals. The distillate in question came over mixed with some water, which, however, immediately separated as a layer beneath the oil.

The calcareous residuum in the retort was usually colored more or less strongly with carbonaceous matter.

The crude hydro-carbon oil was rectified by first distilling it in a slow current of steam, then treating the distillate successively with oil of vitriol and a solution of caustic soda in the usual way, and again distilling in steam, as before. The refined product so closely resembled refined coal-oil and petroleum in odor, color, and illuminating properties, that it could hardly be distinguished from these.

The yield of refined, merchantable hydro-carbon oil amounted to 60 % or more of the menhaden-oil from which it was derived. Refined coal-oil was at that time selling for $1 to $1.25 per gallon, while the cost of the menhaden-oil was only 25 cents per gallon. But the discovery of petroleum in Pennsylvania, that is, of the method of obtaining petroleum by boring, of course destroyed the technical value of these results.

The residuum of the first rectification of the crude oil was a thick grease, from which large quantities of a colorless crystalline compound were easily separated; but of this solid matter we have as yet made no examination.

Preparation and Investigation of the Naphtha.

The naphtha which we have subjected to particular examination, and of which alone we propose to speak in the following memoir, was obtained from the crude hydro-carbon oil above described, as follows: After having stood enclosed in air-tight iron tanks during four years, that is, until the autumn of 1863, a part of the crude oil which had undergone no preliminary treatment whatsoever, was subjected to the process of distillation, and fractional condensation devised by one of us, which is described in detail in the ninth volume of the memoirs of this Academy.*

* Warren, Memoirs of American Academy, [N. S.] IX. 121.

Of the crude oil in question, ten separate portions, each measuring 6000 *c. c.* were distilled from a copper retort through the hot condenser, as described in the cited Memoir. The oil began to boil in the retort at about 140° C. and the first portions of distillate passed through the hot condenser when this had risen to about 120°; the temperature of the oil in the retort gradually rising to 250° or more, and that of the hot condenser to 220°, at which point the process was interrupted, and the residue in the retort thrown aside. During this first distillation the temperature of the hot condenser was maintained on the average from 30° to 50° below that of the boiling liquid in the retort. The total amount of distillate, that is, of naphtha, obtained was equal to about 20 % of the crude oil; by far the larger portion of the latter being composed of difficultly volatile substances incapable of distilling over at 220°. The naphtha is a mobile liquid, of light, lemon-yellow color, and peculiarly nauseous odor. As in the crude oil, so here the odor of acetone is noticed among others. But in this connection it will be well to remark that by far the larger portion of the naphtha appears to consist of hydro-carbon oils, the oxygenated compounds, like acetone, &c., which have been noticed by previous observers, being present in altogether subordinate proportion, and merely as impurities, as it were, or contaminations.

This first distillate or naphtha was now repeatedly redistilled, — on an average about seventy-five times, — from glass retorts through hot condensers as before, until portions of constant or nearly constant boiling points were obtained; and until the quantities of material lying between these "heaps" or fixed points had become so small as to leave no doubt of the absence of other bodies. During the progress of these operations, which lasted nearly a year, the more offensive element of the odor of the hydro-carbons, and the odor of acetone also, gradually disappeared in great measure; the yellowish color of the first products also diminished as the work went on, all of the pure hydro-carbons finally obtained being perfectly colorless. Considerable amounts of solid matter also collected in the retorts, especially during the distillation of the bodies of higher boiling points, being formed most probably from the oxidation of impurities with which the crude hydro-carbons were contaminated.

When the process of distillation was completed it appeared that at least sixteen bodies of constant boiling points had been obtained. But up to that time not the slightest clew to the composition of any of these bodies had been observed. So far as had been noticed their odor was unlike that of any bodies with which we were familiar, while the action which some of them had been found to exert upon sodium indicated the presence of substances very different from the hydro-carbons which had previously fallen under our notice.

Trial-analyses were now made of several of these products, from which it appeared that they were really hydro-carbons, though still all more or less impure. The analysis of the body boiling at 81°–82° (uncorrected) may be cited as an example of the results obtained at this stage: 0.2685 grm. of substance gave 0.8849 grm. carbonic acid and 0.2203 grm. water; or carbon 89.87% and hydrogen 9.13%.

These figures point at once towards the members of the benzole series, and in fact the body in question was benzole itself. Upon examination, it was found that even the impure substance analyzed had the characteristic odor of benzole, and that after agitation with a little concentrated sulphuric acid, the odor was identical with that of pure benzole, while, on being immersed in a mixture of ice and salt, the liquid crystallized readily, in the same manner as benzole. This result was particularly interesting to us, since we had not anticipated that benzole or its homologues would be found among our products, though a moment's reflection suggested that the conditions under which the lime-soap was heated were such as might give rise to the production of some of these highly carbonized bodies. Moreover, in pointing out the probable presence of its homologues, the benzole here went far toward accounting for several of our unknown bodies. This presumption was subsequently realized, the presence of each of the four members of the benzole series having been proved: and it may here be remarked that as the final result of our investigation it appeared that of the other twelve bodies, four were of the olefiant series ($C_n H_n$), being probably identical with those recently obtained by A. Wurtz * among the products of the action of chloride of zinc upon amylic-alcohol; that four others were members of another $C_n H_n$ series, isomeric with the above, and identical with those previously obtained by one of us, † from American petroleum, and that the remaining four belonged to that series of hydrides specially studied by Schorlemmer ‡ and by Warren, § whose members boil at degrees the names of which end in "eight" or "nine." ||

In view of the impure condition of our products, as indicated by these preliminary analyses, and by the peculiar action upon sodium,** already alluded to, it was deemed

* Bulletin de la Société Chimique de Paris, 1863, p. 300. † Warren, Memoirs of the American Academy [N. S.], IX. 167.

‡ Journal of the Chemical Society of London, 1862, XV. 419. § Memoirs of the American Academy [N. S.], IX.

|| Isolated members of this series had previously been encountered by Greville Williams, Philosophical Transactions, 1857, CXLVII. 461; and Journal of the Chemical Society of London, 1862, XV. 130.

** When a bit of metallic sodium is thrown into the crude hydro-carbon oil it is at once acted upon, becoming bright and lustrous while bubbles of gas are slowly evolved from the liquid so long as any of the metal remains. A flocculent, viscid, alkaline sediment at the same time separates out, which, on being collected and treated with water, behaves like a highly alkaline soap.

The action of sodium upon the isolated heaps composed of members of the $C_n H_n$ series was similar in kind to its action upon the crude oil, and quite unlike anything which we have noticed in studying bodies obtained from petroleum or any other source. In the case of some of the $C_n H_n$ products in question, it was found to be necessary to boil them repeatedly with sodium best first to subject them to a slight chemical treatment before proceeding to determine their composition. Most of them were consequently treated with a mixture of two volumes of monohydrated sulphuric acid and one volume of water, then washed with a dilute solution of hydrate of potash, — here avoiding agitation which is liable to give rise to emulsions, — then dried over chloride of calcium, or, better, solid hydrate of potash, and distilled repeatedly over metallic sodium before being subjected to analysis. In other cases a treatment with undiluted oil of vitriol was resorted to as will be described further on.

The diluted acid above mentioned was added to the hydro-carbon, by successive small portions, each portion of acid amounting to perhaps one-fiftieth or one hundredth of the bulk of the hydro-carbon, the two liquids being violently agitated together during five or ten minutes, and the acid sediment finally drawn off after having been allowed to settle. As a general rule the first portion of acid became very dark colored and slightly viscid, although the hydro-carbon did not become colored to any extent; the second and third portions of acid behaved in a similar manner, though each was less strongly colored than the preceding, while the fourth, fifth, and sixth portions were only slightly colored. Since the hydro-carbon itself usually began to become colored on the addition of the fourth or fifth portion of acid, the acid treatment was rarely pushed beyond this limit. The caustic potash appeared to exert little or no action upon the hydro-carbons, serving only to remove the last traces of the acid employed. In practice it was found that while the bodies boiling at 35° and other degrees of temperature, the names of which end in five, that is, those of the formula $C_n H_n$ could be obtained in a state of tolerable purity by the treatment just described, the members of the other series required further purification before being fit for analysis, as will appear in the sequel.

Before proceeding to describe in detail the several bodies which we have isolated from the lime-soap naphtha it should be remarked that all statements of temperature refer to the uncorrected indications of ordinary thermometers, and make no claim to special accuracy, excepting when followed by the word "corrected," in which event they refer to the indications of the best Fastrè thermometers, corrected for atmospheric pressure, and for the upper column of mercury by H. Kopp's formula. The method of de-

in order to obtain purity. The more volatile members of this series ceased to act upon sodium much more quickly than those of higher boiling points. The precipitates produced by the action of sodium upon these products, or probably upon impurities contained in them, were white and flocculent, and closely resembled in appearance hydrate of alumina. It is worthy of remark that the heaps composed of members of the benzole series and of Schorlemmer's hydrides did not thus act upon sodium to any appreciable extent. But on the contrary exhibited the same deportment with this metal which we have been accustomed to witness when operating upon these and other products obtained from petroleum, etc.

termining these corrected boiling points being the same as that already described by one of us.* Most of the statements concerning "heaps" and quantities of products obtained refer to the series of distillates,—each representing one degree centigrade of temperature,—which were in our possession at the moment, already mentioned, when the process of fractional condensation ceased to be employed.

Amylene = C_{10} H_{10}.—The most volatile product obtained from the naphtha, boiled at 33.5°, and the fraction collected between 33½° and 35°, persisted, after repeated redistillation, in commencing to boil at 33½°, there being evidently no appreciable quantity of any substance more volatile than this in the naphtha. The quantity of this product was small, the sum of all the final fractions between 33½° and 55°, not amounting to 100 *c. c.* The summit of the heap was at 35°–37°, this fraction amounting to about 25 *c. c.*; the fractions 37°–39° and 39°–41° were also tolerably large, the latter being larger than the former. But above 41° all the fractions were exceedingly small, as was also the fraction 33½°–35.°

The fraction 35°–37° was selected for analysis. After being treated with diluted sulphuric acid, and alkali, as above described, it was boiled upon metallic sodium.

The dark sulphuric acid liquor which was obtained during the purification, became milky from separation of an oil, and evolved an agreeable, fruity odor when mixed with water.

After the purification, the body boiled, in an ordinary retort containing bits of sodium, at 34.5°–35.6° (corrected).

On combustion, 0. 1215 grm. of the substance gave 0.1682 grm. water, and 0.3796 grm. carbonic acid, or

	Found.		Theory.
Carbon	85.18	C_{10}	85.71
Hydrogen	15.30	H_{10}	14.29
	100.48		100.00 .

Hydride of Amyl = C_{10} H_{12}.—The fractions 37°–39° and 39°–41° most probably contained a portion of that variety of hydride of amyl, obtained by Schorlemmer † and by Warren, ‡ which boils at 38.° But the quantity of material at our disposal is so small that we have made no attempt to purify and analyze it.

Caproylene = C_{12} H_{12} and *Hydride of Caproyl* = C_{12} H_{14}. Next above the prod-

* Warren, Memoirs of American Academy, [N. S.] IX. 159.

† Journal of the Chemical Society of London, 1862, XV. 421.

‡ Memoirs of American Academy, [N. S.] IX. 167.

ucts at 35°–41°, a heap was obtained at 64½°–66½,° which, roughly estimated, amounted to about 250 *c. c.* This heap was well defined, the quantities obtained for each degree above it diminishing rapidly towards 70,° while on the other side the fractions fell away to almost nothing at 63.° At 70°–71° was another well-marked though smaller elevation, amounting to about 180 *c. c.* This diminished rapidly on either hand, but especially on the side towards 80.° The product at 70°–71° had an odor like petroleum, quite unlike the odor of acetone, possessed by the fraction 92°–93,° or the odor of the fraction 64½°–65½°, which though hardly to be compared with that of acetone still reminded one of the latter. Each of the fractions between 64½° and 72° was separately treated with diluted sulphuric acid and subsequently boiled over sodium. The sodium was at first acted upon to a considerable extent, even in the cold, but after three or four redistillations this action ceased almost entirely. The dark sulphuric acid liquor from 70°–71° evolved no such ethereal odor as did that from 92°–93°.

The purified fractions between 64½° and 72,° were now all redistilled some eighteen times through Warren's hot condenser, new fractions being taken off for every half degree. The thermometer employed was graduated to fifths of a degree, and the most scrupulous care was constantly exercised, in the belief that the two heaps might be made to coalesce into one. But the longer the distillatory process was conducted so much the more clearly did the two heaps stand out, their summits being respectively at 64°–65° and 67°–68°. About one-half of the material taken for purification wasted away during the operations here recorded.

Allowing for the elevating influence of the second (68°) body, we estimate the true (corrected) boiling point of the first, when pure, to be 65°.

On combustion, 0.1896 grm. of the purified fraction 65½°–66°, gave 0.254 grm. water and 0.5921 grm. carbonic acid; another portion, not weighed, gave 0.2978 grm. water, and 0.7085 grm. carbonic acid, or

	Found.			Theory.
	I.	II.		
Carbon	85.18	85.37	C_{12}	85.71
Hydrogen	14.87	14.63	H_{12}	14.29
	100.05	100.00		100.00

A determination of the vapor density of the hydro-carbon boiling at 65½°–66°, afforded the following result.

Temperature of balance,	18°
Temperature of oil-bath,	128°
Excess of weight of balloon,	0.2965.

Capacity of balloon,	217 c. c.
Air remaining in balloon,	5 c. c.
Height of barometer,	755.4mm. at 19°
Density of vapor found,	3.001.
" " theoretical, ($C_{12} H_{12}$),	2.9046.

The sp. gr. of the liquid was found to be 0.6938 at 0.° A portion of the fraction 67½°–68°, purified as above, and now boiling at 68.5°(corrected), being analyzed, afforded the following result: 0.159 grm. of the hydro-carbon gave 0.2176 grm. water, and 0.4935 grm. carbonic acid, or carbon 84.65 % and hydrogen 15.22 %. Taken in connection with the boiling point of this body, and its petroleum-like odor, the analysis points at once to that hydride of caproyl which boils at 68°–69°, and which has been isolated from coal-oil by Greville Williams,* Schorlemmer, and others.

The method of purification with monohydrated sulphuric acid was here resorted to, in the hope that by this means the caproylene with which the body was supposed to be contaminated might be removed. The action of the concentrated acid, so far as the destruction of impurities is concerned, was apparently feeble; the acid did not even blacken, but only became yellow, though some warmth was evolved, and hence only a single portion of it was employed. But the acid evidently combined with a considerable portion of the hydro-carbon, a certain quantity of a compound much less volatile than the hydro-carbon being formed. After having been decanted from the acid sediment, washed with caustic alkali, and dried over chloride of calcium, and then heated in an ordinary retort, the hydro-carbon began to boil at 72°, the temperature gradually rising, as the distillation proceeded, to 81°, at which point the operation was interrupted and the oily residue in the retort put aside. On redistilling this distillate upon sodium almost all of it came over at 69.5°(corrected).

The last named product was now analyzed with the following result: 0.1111 grm. of the hydro-carbon gave 0.1633 grm. water, and 0.3417 grm. carbonic acid, or

Found.		Theory.	
Carbon	83.89	C_{12}	83.72
Hydrogen	16.38	H_{14}	16.28
	100.27		100.00

It is evident, therefore, that this body, boiling at 68°–69° (corrected), is probably identical with the hydride of caproyl of Schorlemmer, and of Warren; and that the concentrated sulphuric acid did really remove caproylene from the product first analyzed.

* Philosophical Transactions, 1857, CXLVII. pp. 452,461.

Benzole = C_{12} H_6. Next in order was a very decided heap at 80°–81°; the quantities of the degree-fractions falling off immediately to almost nothing upon either side of the fraction in question. The quantity of liquid in this heap was rather less than 200 *c. c.* The odor of this body was that of benzole. When plunged in a mixture of ice and salt, the liquid did not congeal; but after having been treated with a single portion of monohydrated sulphuric acid, it crystallized at once, almost completely, when immersed in the freezing mixture. When ignited upon a wick, it burned with an exceedingly smoky flame, unlike that of the bodies previously described; when the latter are burning, no such abundant flakes of soot are disengaged. In the cold it had but little action upon metallic sodium, there being, at all events, nothing like the action which it exerted thereupon by the C_n H_n bodies hitherto in question.

An analysis of the product obtained by distillation has already been stated. (See p. 180, and No. I. below.) Attempts were now made to purify this impure material by chemical treatment. In the first place it was treated with the diluted sulphuric acid and alkali, and then repeatedly redistilled over sodium. The first portions of the diluted acid became very dark-colored, but the fourth and fifth portions exerted but little action. For an analysis of the liquid resulting from this purification, see No. II, below.

Monohydrated sulphuric acid was then resorted to, a portion of the product purified as above being treated therewith. The first portion of this strong acid blackened very much, a thick, viscid matter separated out, while some heat was evolved and a slight odor of sulphurous acid was manifested. The second portion of acid had but little action, and the third and fourth portions hardly became colored. These last portions of acid, however, caused the hydro-carbon itself to became rather dark-colored, though on adding dilute alkali, this color changed to a light-yellow.

The dark acid liquor resulting from the treatment with concentrated sulphuric acid, on being mixed with water, became turbid, from separation of a sort of tar; an abundance of sulphurous acid was also evolved on this addition of water, even after the acid liquor had stood at rest for a long while. This remark is true as well for all the other bodies which were treated with monohydrated acid, and in no instance did the addition of water to these dark acid liquors give rise to the evolution of agreeable ethereal odors such as were obtained from the product of the action of diluted acid upon the members of the C_n H_n series.

After having been dried over chloride of calcium, the purified hydro-carbon was heated in an ordinary retort containing pieces of sodium. After a small quantity of the hydro-carbon had distilled over, the thermometer in the retort rapidly rose to above its upper limit, 120°, the liquid in the retort became black, and sulphurous acid was evolved. The distillation was at once interrupted and the residue put aside. The distillate, being now repeatedly redistilled over sodium, came over clear at 79.5° (corrected). For an analysis of this sample, see below, No. III.

A second portion of the product resulting from the treatment with diluted acid having been treated, as above, with monohydrated sulphuric acid, the first distillation over sodium was now more carefully watched than before. The retort being heated with a small flame, its contents distilled over freely at first, and without coloration, at 79°; after a while the temperature of the retort rose slowly, and at 87° scarcely anything came over. At this point the distillation was stopped, the liquid in the retort being quite oily, though still light-colored. On redistilling the distillate, upon sodium, it came off at 79.9° (corrected).

The bottle containing the product (No. III.) resulting from the treatment with monohydrated acid, was now immersed in a mixture of ice and salt until the moment when crystals began to form, when it was quickly removed and the still liquid portion of the hydro-carbon poured off, the bottle being inverted and the crystals allowed to drain as they melted until only a comparatively small portion of the solid remained. This last was then subjected to analysis; see below, No. IV.

The quantity of material at our disposal being small, we were unable to carry out any systematic course of purification by crystallization, and a single operation like the preceding could hardly be expected to augment the purity of our product to any great extent. But the tendency of this experiment is none the less worthy of being noted; its result still points in the direction indicated by the preceding trials. Each step in the series of treatments above recorded brings us a little nearer to the pure benzole of which, as we have ourselves no doubt, the product (80°–81°), obtained by distillation, is mainly composed.

I. As has already been stated, 0.2685 grm. of the unpurified hydro-carbon, obtained by distillation and fractional condensation, gave 0.2203 grm. water, and 0.8849 grm. carbonic acid.

II. 0.1914 grm. of the hydrocarbon, after treatment with diluted acid, gave 0.1593 grm. water, and 0.6386 grm. carbonic acid.

III. 0.1485 grm. of the hydrocarbon, after treatment with monohydrated sulphuric acid, gave 0.113 grm. water, and 0.4985 grm. carbonic acid.

IV. 0.1962 grm. of the hydrocarbon, after crystallization, gave 0.1484 grm. water, and 0.6631 grm. carbonic acid. Or

	Found.				Theory.	
	I.	II.	III.	IV.		
Carbon	89.87	90.96	91.55	92.15	C_{12}	92.31
Hydrogen	9.13	9.25	8.48	8.41	H_6	7.69
		100.21	100.03	100.56		100.00

Omitting No. I., these results correspond with the following formulæ: —
II. = $C_{12}\ H_{7.32}$; III. = $C_{12}\ H_{6.67}$; IV. = $C_{12}\ H_{6.57}$, — instead of $C_{12}\ H_6$, as required by theory.

The sp. gr. of No. II. was found to be 0.8697 at 0°, and that of No. III. 0.8882 at 0°.

A portion of this benzole (No. III.) having been converted into nitro-benzole and anilin, there was at once obtained from the latter the purple reaction with hypochlorite of lime. Several portions of this anilin having been heated with arsenic acid, there were obtained in each instance decided manifestations of the color of anilin-red, though the red thus obtained was by no means so brilliant as that subsequently obtained from the toluol-fraction 110°–111° (*vid. inf.*).

A sample of anilin, prepared from a portion of the impure fraction 83°–84°, which fraction had never received any chemical treatment, gave the violet coloration with hypochlorite of lime, but it yielded no red color on being heated with arsenic acid.

Œnanthylene = $C_{14}\ H_{14}$. Above the benzole heap (81°–82°), the quantities of the degree-fractions were very small, until at 90° they began to increase again, there being a prominent heap between 90° and 94°, which amounted to about 300 *c. c.* The summit of this heap was at 92°–93°. On treating it with diluted sulphuric acid, the acid became dark colored, an aromatic odor being at the same time manifested, while a slight odor of acetone, which had previously been present, now disappeared altogether. On adding water to the dark sulphuric acid liquor, after this had been separated from the hydrocarbon, a very penetrating ethereal odor was evolved, while a small quantity of oil, of a reddish color, rose to the surface of the water. After the acid treatment and the subsequent washing and drying, the hydro-carbon was distilled eight times upon metallic sodium, through Warren's hot condenser. The sodium was very strongly acted upon at first, but on the fourth distillation this action had well-nigh ceased. At the close of these operations the summit of the heap was at 93°–94°, this fraction amounting to about 45 *c. c.*, the next fraction (94°–95°), being almost as large (42–43 *c. c.*) The fraction 91°–92° was now very small, the heap only beginning to show itself at 92°–93°, which was equal to 28 *c. c.* The fraction 95°–96° amounted to only about 12 *c. c.*, and the residues, at 96°, were each very small.

Boiled upon sodium, in an ordinary retort, the fraction 93°–94° came over at 94.1°

(corrected); hence, when the quantity of liquid in the fraction 94°–95° is considered the corrected boiling point of the hydro-carbon may be estimated at something less than 95°.

On combustion, 0.1297 grm. of the purified hydro-carbon gave 0.1688 grm. water, and 0.4081 grm. carbonic acid. Or,

	Found.		Theory.
Carbon	85.81	C_{14}	85.71
Hydrogen	14.42	H_{14}	14.29
	100.23		100.00

A determination of the vapor density of the purified fraction 93°–94°, gave the following result:—

Temperature of balance,	= 17°
" " oil-bath,	= 186°
Excess of weight of balloon,	= 0.3845 grm.
Capacity of "	= 219 *c. c.*
Air remaining in "	= 0 "
Height of barometer,	= 757.2mm. at 18°
Density of vapor found,	= 3.4445
" " " theoretical (C_{14} H_{14})	= 3.389

Hydride of Œnanthyl. = C_{14} H_{16}. At 97°–98°, as a summit, was a very well-marked heap, the adjacent fractions, 96°–97° and 98°–99°, being also large, while those next in order fell off gradually upon either hand,—more rapidly, however, above 99° than below 96°. Roughly estimated, the heap from 96° to 100° amounted to about 450 *c. c.*

The fraction 97°–98° having been analyzed before it had been subjected to any chemical treatment, afforded the following result:—

0.2252 grm. of the hydro-carbon gave 0.2913 grm. water, and 0.6964 grm. carbonic acid. Or,

	Found.
Carbon	84 32
Hydrogen	15.19
	99.51

These figures agree with the improbable formula C_{14} $H_{15.2}$.

The fraction 97°–98° was now at once treated with monohydrated sulphuric acid. The first portion of the acid blackened considerably, though the hydro-carbon itself was at first only slightly colored; this blackening was, however, not nearly so decided as was the case with benzole. A portion of viscid matter also separated out and adhered to the sides of the bottle; but only a slight amount of heat was evolved. The second portion of acid blackened like the first, and considerable heat was now evolved, but less of the viscid matter was formed. The third portion of acid was still considerably colored, though much less than the preceding portions. Abundant fumes of sulphurous acid were now disengaged, and, as a very considerable proportion of the hydro-carbon had been destroyed, the treatment with strong acid was here stopped. The hydro-carbon was now washed with diluted sulphuric acid, with chlorhydric acid (which caused the hydro-carbon to assume a beautiful purple coloration, which was at once destroyed on the addition of potash), and with a solution of potash; it was then dried by means of sticks of hydrate of potash. By this time the portion of hydro-carbon operated upon, which originally amounted to 125 *c. c.*, was reduced to 65–70 *c. c.*

On distilling the purified product upon sodium, from a retort connected with Warren's hot condenser, the temperature of the liquid rose to 102°, and nothing came over until the hot condenser had attained a temperature of 94°. When the temperature of the retort had reached 108°–112°, that of the hot condenser being 96°, the contents of the retort became very black, and torrents of sulphurous acid were evolved; the thermometer in the retort then suddenly rose to 140°–145°, and a very violent reaction occurred in the retort. Much water was at this time evolved, a portion of it having condensed upon the upper part of the retort as soon as this had been removed from the fire. The water was evidently generated by the decomposition of a portion of the liquid contents of the retort. But, in spite of the water and of the sulphurous acid already alluded to, a great part of the sodium in the retort remained unacted upon.

From the foregoing it is evident that during the chemical treatment of this hydro-carbon a portion of it combines with the elements of sulphuric acid to form a compound of high boiling point, and decomposable at the temperature of ebullition.

The distillate was at first distributed as five fractions of nearly equal size, each representing two degrees centigrade, between 102° and 112°; but, on redistilling, the first fraction began to boil at 98,° and the last had all come over before the temperature of the retort reached 100.° After the two fractions thus obtained had been twice redistilled, it was found that nearly all of the hydro-carbon had collected again as a heap at 98°–99.° This product was, however, still highly charged with sulphurous acid gas, in spite of the sodium, which had all the while been present; but on being washed with caustic alkali, the odor of sulphurous acid was at once removed. After having been dried with hydrate of potash, the product was distilled upon sodium, in an ordinary retort, from which it came over at 97.8° (corrected).

On combustion, 0.1464 grm. of the purified hydro-carbon gave 0.1897 grm. water, and 0.4144 grm. carbonic acid (I.). Another portion of 0.1168 grm. gave 0.1654 grm. water, and 0.3601 grm. carbonic acid (II.) — or,

	Found.			Theory.	
	I.	II.			
Carbon	84.27	84.08		C_{14}	84
Hydrogen	15.74	15.75		H_{16}	16
	100.01	99.83			100

A determination of the density of its vapor resulted as follows: —

Temperature of balance,	18°
Temperature of oil bath,	150°
Weight of balloon,	0.3795 grm.
Capacity of balloon,	221 *c. c.*
Air remaining in balloon,	3 *c. c.*
Height of barometer,	757.2mm. at 18°
Density of vapor found,	3.5616
" " " theoretical (C_{14} H_{16}),	3.458

The sp. gr. of the liquid was 0.7085 at 0°, and 0.6942 at 17.5°.

Toluole = C_{14} H_8. Next above the hydride of œnanthyl (98°), was a singularly well-defined heap at 110°–111°. This body was more readily isolated — that is to say, brought into such a state of equilibrium that its boiling point was almost absolutely constant — than any of the other hydro-carbons which we have obtained from the lime-soap-naphtha. Altogether, from 109°–112°, this heap amounted to about 440 *c. c.* Its odor was that of toluole.

The fraction 110°–111° was treated at once with monohydrated sulphuric acid. The first portion of acid made the whole liquid dark-colored and became itself very viscid, some heat being evolved. The second and third portions of acid also became dark-colored, as did the fourth, though to a somewhat less extent. The fifth, sixth, and seventh portions of acid were each allowed to act during twenty-four hours, but they appeared to affect the hydro-carbon very little. The hydro-carbon was now very dark-colored, but on the addition of a dilute alkaline solution it cleared up to a light-yellow color. It was dried over chloride of calcium and distilled in an ordinary retort without sodium. After about two-thirds of the liquid had come over colorless, the residue suddenly became black, its temperature rose rapidly, and much sulphurous acid was evolved. The distillate being twice redistilled over sodium, the greater portion of it came over at 111° (corrected) in each instance. The product was, however, evidently still impure, for in each case a small residue of higher boiling point was obtained. The boiling point above given is doubtless too high; but we have deferred any reconsideration of this result until such time as a method of properly purifying our first product shall have been discovered. The impurity of the material in question appeared, moreover, from the following analysis: — 0.1656 grm. of the hydro-carbon gave 0.152 grm. water, and 0.5504 grm. carbonic acid, or

	Found.
Carbon	90.64
Hydrogen	10.20
	100.84

This result indicates that the product still contained some sulphurated compound, which, on combustion in the oxygen constantly present in the tube during the analysis, forms sulphuric acid; the latter condenses in the neck of the chloride of calcium tube and so vitiates the hydrogen determination.

A portion of the product just analyzed was now digested during twenty-four hours with a quantity of concentrated chlorhydric acid, by which it was at once rendered milky. After decanting the acid and washing with water, the hydro-carbon was dried over hydrate of potash, and finally distilled upon sodium. On combustion, an unweighed portion of it gave 0.1679 grm. water, and 0.6345 grm. carbonic acid, or

	Found.		Theory.
Carbon	90.25	C_{14}	91.3
Hydrogen	9.75	H_8	8.7
	100.00		100.00

The liquid which had been treated with chlorhydric acid was now distilled in vacuo. It began to boil at 66°, between which point and 68° a fraction was collected (No. I.). Another small fraction was then taken off above 98° (No. II.).

On combustion, 0.1985 grm. of fraction No. I. gave 0.1765 grm. water, and 0.6572 grm. carbonic acid.

0.2595 grm. of fraction No. II. gave 0.2244 grm. water, and 0.8579 grm. carbonic acid.

	Found. I.	Found. II.		Theory.
Carbon	90.07	90.17	C_{14}	91.3
Hydrogen	9.87	9.60	H_8	8.7
	99.94	99.77		100.0

These results correspond respectively with the formulæ: — I. C_{14} $H_{9.2}$; II. C_{14} $H_{8.97}$; the previous analysis, see above, agrees with the formula C_{14} $H_{9.00}$. The body is doubtless toluole mixed with a portion of one of the more highly hydrogenized substances which occur with it in the crude naphtha.

Attempts to obtain a purer product by first converting portions of the crude fractions 108°–109° and 111°–112° into nitro-toluole led to no useful result, the mixture of nitro-products, etc., obtained being quite unmanageable, at least when in small quantity, as in the present case.

A portion of the product boiling at 111° (corrected) was converted into nitro-toluole and toluidin, and the latter was then heated with arsenic acid, a magnificent product of anilin-red being thus obtained. This toluidin gave no reaction for anilin on being tested with hypochlorite of lime. It may here be remarked that we have in the same way repeatedly obtained anilin-red from toluidin prepared from samples of toluole obtained from coal-tar naphtha by the process of fractional condensation.

Caprylene = $\bar{C}_{16}H_{16}$ and *Hydride of Capryl* = $C_{16}H_{18}$. At 117°–127° there was a large heap, amounting to about 800 c. c. It had two principal summits, one at 123°–124°, the other at 126°–127°, and a subsidiary elevation at 118°–120°; but this last was probably caused by some irregularity in the conditions under which the distillation was conducted, the work of two operators having overlapped at this point. Moreover, as will be seen directly, analyses of the subsidiary heap, after purification, indicated that it, as well as the fraction 123°–124°, belongs to the $C_n H_n$ series.

All of the fractions from 117° to 127° constituting the great heap were treated with diluted sulphuric acid in the usual way, after which the fractions belonging to each of the three summits were separately and repeatedly distilled through Warren's hot condenser; the same thermometers, condenser, and retort being used in the distillation of each of the summits. The relative importance of the fraction 123°–124° was maintained throughout, this fraction being far larger than any of the others. The fractions 125°–126° and 126°–127° also held their own during these redistillations; but the position of the lower, subsidiary summit changed materially, the greater portion of it having finally collected at 121°–122°. It is probable that by continued redistillation this might all have been collected at 123°–124°, or rather that these two heaps could have been made to coalesce at some point between 122° and 124°; but the quantity of material being small, we have made no special effort to effect this result.

Previous to the treatment with acid, th heap 117°–127° had a remnant of the offensive odor of the original crude hydro-carbon oil together with a trace of the odor of acetone; but on the addition of diluted sulphuric acid, an odor like that of mint was developed together with an ethereal odor. The first portions of the diluted acid became dark-colored and rather thick; but the fifth and last portion of acid was but little colored, though still by no means colorless. After washing with a solution of caustic alkali, and drying over sticks of hydrate of potash, it was found necessary to boil the product with sodium during a long time, and to distil it repeatedly from the sediment which formed, before its action upon this metal became in some degree moderate.

The dark sulphuric acid liquor became turbid, as usual, when mixed with water, and evolved an agreeable ethereal odor.

Distilled over sodium from an ordinary retort, the boiling point of the purified fraction 123°–124° was 125.2° (corrected); and that of the fraction 121°–122° was 123.8° (corrected).

On combustion, 0.2278 grm. of the purified fraction 123°–124° gave 0.2994 grm. water, and 0.7114 grm. carbonic acid (No. I.). Another portion of 0.19 grm. gave 0.2504 grm. water, and 0.5917 grm. carbonic acid (No. II.).

Analyses of the purified fraction 121°–122° afforded the following results: 0.1894 grm. of the hydro-carbon gave 0.2466 grm. water, and 0.5925 grm. carbonic acid (No. III.). Another portion, not weighed, gave 0.1685 grm. water, and 0.406 grm. carbonic acid (No. IV.). Or,

	Found.				Theory.	
	I.	II.	III.	IV.		
Carbon	85.16	84.95	85.32	85.55	C_{16}	85.71
Hydrogen	14.62	14.63	14.47	14.45	H_{16}	14.29
	99.78	99.58	99.79	100.00		100.00

A determination of the vapor density of fraction 123°–124° gave the following result: —

Temperature of balance,	22°
" " oil-bath,	178°
Excess of weight of balloon,	0.3843 grm.
Capacity of "	201 c. c.
Air remaining in "	0 "
Height of barometer,	758mm. at 21°
Density of vapor found,	3.9756
" " theoretical (C_{16} H_{16}),	3.873

The sp. gr. of fraction 123°–124° was 0.7396 at 0°; that of fraction 121°–122° was 0.7433 at 0°, 0.735 at 12°, 0.7321 at 15°, 0.7305 at 17°.

After treatment with diluted sulphuric acid, the fraction 125°–126° afforded the following results on being analyzed: 0.1829 grm. of the hydro-carbon gave 0.2432 grm water, and 0.5687 grm. carbonic acid (I.). Another portion, not weighed, gave 0.2398 grm. water, and 0.5647 grm. carbonic acid (II.). Or,

	Found.	
	I.	II.
Carbon	84.80	85.27
Hydrogen	14.76	14.73
	99.56	100.00

From these analyses the improbable formulæ C_{16} $H_{16.7}$ and C_{16} $H_{16.6}$ are derived. The excess of hydrogen, however, indicates the presence of a member of the hydride series, and to obtain this the degree-fractions about 128° were treated with monohydrated sulphuric acid. The first and second portions of acid blackened instantly and much viscid matter was deposited; heat was also evolved. The third, fourth, fifth, and sixth portions of acid each became less black than the preceding portion; but a large proportion of the hydro-carbon disappeared during this treatment. The operations of washing, drying, and boiling with sodium were conducted in the usual way.

On combustion, after this treatment with strong acid, 0.1253 grm. of the hydrocarbon gave 0.1746 grm. water, and 0.3895 grm. carbonic acid. Or,

	Found.		Theory.
Carbon	84.75	C_{16}	84.2
Hydrogen	15.48	H_{18}	15.8
	100.23		100.0

The upper portion of this heap consequently contains hydride of capryl, the true boiling point of which is 128°–129°.

Xylole = C_{16} H_{10}. Between 140° and 144° was a large heap of 840–850 *c. c.*, the well-defined summit of which was at 142°–142½°. Upon either side of this point the size of the degree-fractions rapidly diminished, these being all very small below 140° and above 144°.

The fraction 142°–142½° was treated at once with monohydrated sulphuric acid, the first portion of which became very dark and viscid, some heat being at the same time evolved; the second and third portions of acid also became very dark, though less viscid than the first; the fourth portion of acid became somewhat dark, and the hydrocarbon itself now began to be colored, and the odor of sulphurous acid was perceptible.

After having been washed and dried in the usual way, the hydro-carbon was redistilled through Warren's hot condenser, when it appeared that, by combination of a portion of the hydro-carbon with the elements of sulphuric acid, there had been formed during the acid treatment a quantity of a difficultly volatile compound, which, at a temperature between 150°–160°, becomes black and undergoes decomposition, while much sulphurous acid is given off.

The first portion of distillate from the above, having been washed with an alkaline solution to remove sulphurous acid gas, was analyzed, with the following result: 0.199 grm. of the hydro-carbon gave 0.2226 grm. water, and 0.6403 grm. carbonic acid. Or,

	Found.
Carbon	87.74
Hydrogen	12.41
	100.15

These numbers correspond with the improbable formulæ C_{16} $H_{18.58}$. We entertain, however, little doubt that the substance analyzed is really a mixture of xylole (C_{16} H_{10}), the boiling point of which is at 140°, and of a hydro-carbon, of the C_n H_n series, boiling at 155°, or thereabouts, which will be described directly.

An attempt was made to separate a purer sample of xylole by repeatedly redistilling the heap and collecting apart the portion more volatile than 140°, this being subsequently reworked, together with the small fractions which had previously been left between 130° and 140°. By this means a small heap was finally obtained, the summit of which was 135°–136°. This heap was treated with diluted sulphuric acid, the first portion of which blackened much, the second portion to a less extent, the third still less, and the fourth but little. After washing, drying, and distilling with sodium, in the usual way, a portion was analyzed with the following result: 0.181 grm. of the hydro-carbon, purified with dilute acid, gave 0.1905 grm. water, and 0.5858 grm. carbonic acid. Or,

	Found.
Carbon	88.29
Hydrogen	11.71
	100.00

This result corresponds with the formula C_{16} $H_{12.74}$; the body still containing far more hydrogen than pure xylole. But as this subsidiary heap is probably contaminated with hydride of capryl (boiling at 128°), we have made no further attempt to purify it by treatment with acids.

Pelargonene = C_{18} H_{18}. About 148°–150° was a rather large heap, amounting to some 500 *c. c.* This retained a little of the offensive odor of the crude lime-soap naphtha, but had none of the odor of acetone with which the offensive odor had hitherto been accompanied. It was treated with six successive portions of diluted sulphuric acid. The first portions of acid became very black, but the fifth and sixth portions were only slightly colored. After two or three additions of acid, the hydro-carbon itself became rather dark-colored; but on treating it with a solution of caustic alkali the color changed to a light-yellow. After having been dried over hydrate of potash, the hydro-carbon was repeatedly distilled through Warren's hot condenser, being boiled the while over sodium, upon which it continued to act to a considerable extent for a long while.

At the close of these operations the fractions 148°–149° and 149°–150° retained their former prominence, either of them being more than three times as large as the adjacent degree-fractions; 148°–149° was rather larger than 149°–150°, standing to it in the ratio of 5 : 4.2.

Distilled in an ordinary retort over sodium, the fraction 149°–150°, boiled at 153° (corrected).

On combustion, 0.1499 grm. of the purified hydro-carbon gave 0.1965 grm. water, and 0.4705 grm. carbonic acid. Or,

	Found.		Theory.
Carbon	85.59	C_{18}	85.71
Hydrogen	14.54	H_{18}	14.29
	100.13		100.00

Determinations of the density of its vapor gave the following results: —

	I.	II.
Temperature of the balance,	22°	24.5°
" " oil-bath,	187°	186°
Excess of weight of balloon,	0.5493	0.4873
Capacity of "	239 c. c.	210 c. c.
Air remaining in "	0 "	0 "
Height of barometer,	766.6mm. at 22°	765mm. at 24°
Density of vapor found,	4.557	4.561
" " theoretical (C_{18} H_{18}),	4.357	

Its sp. gr. was found to be 0.7618 at 0°.

Isocumole = C_{18} H_{12} and *Rutylene* = C_{20} H_{20} } At 165°–173° was a very large heap amounting to 1200–1500 *c. c.*; being by far the largest heap obtained from the lime-soap-naphtha. Though perfectly well defined as regards the bodies next above (195°) and below (155°) it, this heap, nevertheless, exhibited no clearly-marked summit, each of the degree-fractions within the above-mentioned limits being about as large as the others, and with the exception of its unusual lateral extension and of a slight depression at the fraction 167°–168° there was nothing in the appearance of the heap to denote any one of its component fractions as the point of culmination, or to indicate the presence of more than one body. The heap in question did, however, really contain two separate substances, being composed principally of a body (C_{20} H_{20}) boiling at 174°–175° (corrected), or thereabouts, together with a quantity of isocumole the boiling point of which is at 170°, as has been shown by one of us.

Analyses of several of the unpurified fractions afforded the following results:— 0.2689 grm. of the fraction 164°–165° gave 0.3038 grm. water, and 0.8264 grm. carbonic acid, or carbon 83.82 %, hydrogen 12.53 %. 0.1345 grm. of the fraction 166°–167° gave 0.1609 grm. water, and 0.4157 grm. carbonic acid, or carbon 84.12 % and hydrogen 13.31 %; another portion of 0.2732 grm. gave 0.3245 grm. water, and 0.8429 grm. carbonic acid, or carbon 84.15 % and hydrogen 13.18 %. 0.1734 grm. of the fraction 170°–171° gave 0.2118 grm. water, and 0.535 grm. carbonic acid, or carbon 84.20 %, and hydrogen 13.55 %.

Despairing of being able to find any central point in this heap, and acting upon the hint furnished by the aforesaid depression, at 167°–168°, we proceeded to purify and examine fractions at each of the extremities. The fractions 170°–171° and 171°–172° were treated in the usual way with diluted sulphuric acid. The first two portions of acid blackened very much; the third, fourth, fifth and sixth also became dark, but each less so than the portion which preceded it. The hydro-carbon itself finally becoming dark-colored, the acid treatment was stopped, and the hydro-carbon, washed with water and alkali, was dried over hydrate of potash and boiled repeatedly upon sodium.

As thus purified it boiled at 174.6° (corrected).

On combustion, 0.1706 grm. of it gave 0.214 grm. water, and 0.5373 grm. carbonic acid, or

	Found.		Theory.
Carbon	85.93	C_{20}	85.71
Hydrogen	13.95	H_{20}	14.29
	99.88		100.00

A determination of the density of its vapor gave the following result:—

Temperature of the balance,	25°
Temperature of the oil-bath,	229°
Excess of weight of balloon,	0.4714 grm.
Capacity of balloon,	208 c. c.

Air remaining in balloon,	0 c.c.
Height of barometer,	769.3mm. at 25°
Density of vapor found,	4.9166
" " theoretical ($C_{20}H_{20}$),	4.841

Its sp. gr. was found to be 0.7912, at 0°.

The fraction 165°–166° was treated at once with monohydrated sulphuric acid. The first portion of acid blackened very much, and heat was evolved, but no very great amount of viscid matter separated; the second portion of acid also blackened very much, but was unusually free from viscidity; the third portion acted much less than the second, and the fourth and fifth portions much less than the third, though considerable heat was evolved throughout. The hydro-carbon at last became strongly colored, and much sulphurous acid was evolved. It was washed, dried, and boiled upon sodium in the usual way.

On combustion, 0.2294 grm. of the hydro-carbon gave 0.285 grm. water, and 0.7264 grm. carbonic acid, or

	Found.
Carbon	86.36
Hydrogen	13.77
	100.13

These numbers give the empirical formula $C_{18}\ H_{17.2}$.

Previous to the above-mentioned examination of the two extremities of this heap, but not until long after the heap itself had been obtained, an attempt was made to hasten operations by working upon it alone; the ten or twelve most prominent fractions of the heap having been selected and repeatedly redistilled, to the exclusion of all other fractions, both above and below, in the hope that products of nearly constant boiling point might thus be more quickly procured. At the commencement of this special operation the common difference between each of the fractions was about one degree, that is, at each successive distillation each of the fractions began to boil about one degree lower than it did in the preceding distillation, and the distillatory process was continued until this common difference had been reduced to one-third of one degree; the portions of distillate more volatile than the selected fraction of lowest boiling point, and of residue less volatile than the selected fraction of highest boiling point, being meanwhile added to the fractions in the old series, now excluded from the distillation, which had been taken off at similar temperatures. It may here be said that this operation was not found to be advantageous, and we do not in any way commend it, at least when applied, as above, to bodies which have already been brought to such a condition that their boiling points are tolerably constant.

As a result of this trial, however, we were led to appreciate more clearly the importance of conducting the entire series of distillations, from first to last, in a systematic and methodical manner, and of avoiding as far as possible interruptions and irregularities of every kind; for we have observed how easily one might fall into error by pursuing the opposite course. Thus, after the prominent fractions composing the heap 165°–173°, had been repeatedly redistilled by themselves, and the products had been finally set aside as completed, our attention was next directed to the intermediate fractions lying between the heap in question and that next below, namely, at about 155°, which fractions had latterly been untouched, excepting for the purpose of adding to the highest among them the most volatile portions of distillate obtained from the selected fractions. It will be observed that, by these additions, the last or highest of the outlying fractions had become quite large, and that the hydro-carbons composing it were undoubtedly mixed in proportions very different from those of the old fractions next below. On being now repeatedly redistilled, together with the old fractions, the position of this factitious heap gradually changed to lower degrees of temperature. This result was of course to be expected, since the accumulated distillate from the special series of fractions would naturally contain much of a comparatively volatile hydro-carbon. This change of position was rapid at first, but soon became less marked, and after a while a sort of temporary equilibrium was attained at 157°–160°, about which point a small heap maintained itself during several distillations. Though this heap was evidently still to be regarded as a mixture, both in view of its previous history and of the fact that it continued all the while to give up considerable quantities of its material at each successive distillation, it was nevertheless thought best to ascertain something concerning its composition, rather than to continue the process of distillation until the heap should be completely destroyed. The propriety of analyzing the compound was, moreover, especially indicated, since there was no apparent improbability that a hydride, homologous with those already described, might be found at 158°–159°. The heap in question was consequently treated with diluted sulphuric acid, precisely as has been described under pelargonene, and again distilled several times through a hot condenser. As before, it soon fell into a condition of equilibrium, — a long flat heap, rising gently to a decided summit at 158°–159°, being constantly obtained. The size of the fractions near the summit remained almost absolutely the same during any two or three distillations, although considerable quantities of the fraction 150°–151° and of residue at 161° were taken off at each successive distillation, and the general behavior of the heap indicated that it was still a mixture.

On combustion, 0.1195 grm. of the purified hydro-carbon gave 0.1348 grm. water and

0.3832 grm. carbonic acid (I.). Another portion, not weighed, gave 0.18 grm. water and 0.5138 grm. carbonic acid (II.).

	Found.	
	I.	II.
Carbon	87.46	87.51
Hydrogen	12.47	12.49
	99.93	100.00

From these results we derive the formula C_{18} $H_{16.4}$. It appears, then, that this spurious heap is composed in great part of a member of the benzole series,— undoubtedly of the one which boils at 170° (isocumole); indeed, the formula last given is much nearer that of isocumole than the one previously derived from an analysis of the fraction 165°–166°. During the redistillation of the intermediary fractions the volatile matter, which, as fast as it was eliminated from the products 165°–173°, had been heaped up at the upper extremity of the intermediary series [namely, at 163°–164°], gradually came forward towards its own proper place at 153°, or thereabouts, and in so doing dragged along with it a quantity of the isocumole properly belonging at 170°, until a point was reached at which the tendency of the isocumole to go back nearly balanced the power of the 153° body to go forward, and at this point a temporary heap of course arose. At the moment of the analysis, this heap had been operated upon so long that the isocumole was largely in excess; but if an analysis had been made of the heap as it existed a week earlier, a different result would undoubtedly have been obtained.

Such temporary adjustments, or, as it were, balancings of the opposing forces exerted by two bodies of different degrees of volatility, are noticed not unfrequently in the course of the earlier series of distillations of a mixture of crude hydro-carbons. Soon after definite heaps first begin to appear, there will be seen for a time, at points about midway between the real, permanent heaps, small temporary elevations, which subsequently disappear again as the distillation progresses. But as at this stage of operations all of the fractions are far from possessing constant boiling points, no question as to the lack of individuality of these half-way heaps can well arise. It is probable that the danger of mistaking a counterfeit for a real heap can only occur by virtue of some such cause as in the instance above cited, or where one of the components of a mixture of two bodies is in large excess as compared with the other. Perhaps the substance encountered by Pelouze and Cahours * at 136°–138°, and described by them as hydride of pelargyl = C_{18} H_{20}, may have been nothing more than a spurious heap, such as

* Bulletin de la Société Chimique de Paris, 1863, pp. 235, 238.

we have just now alluded to; this compound, of P. & C., is in any event unconformable with either of the series of hydrides which are known to exist in petroleum.

It is of course always possible that cases may occur where, from insufficient quantities of material, it will be impracticable to continue the process of distillation until a constant boiling point has been reached; indeed, this inability will in most instances occur, in due course, at either end of every long series of fractions which have been obtained as in the present case from a complex mixture of substances; we would insist only upon the fact that doubts as to the definite character of any small heap will be far less likely to arise when the process of distillation has been carefully and methodically conducted from beginning to end.

With regard to the bodies which we have obtained at or near 140° and 170°, it is no doubt still conceivable that they are not really impure xylole and isocumole, as we suppose, but new compounds, and the observations of Tollens and Fittig,* upon mixed radicals of the ethyl and phenyl series, would seem to strengthen this thought; but in our opinion the weight of evidence is decidedly in favor of the view which places these 140° and 170° compounds in the benzole series. As we understand it, our own experience indicates that the members of the benzole series are peculiarly liable to retain a certain portion of the more highly hydrogenized hydro-carbons so forcibly that these cannot be readily separated by fractional condensation.

Margarylene = C_{22} H_{22}. At 193°–196° was a heap of about 650 *c. c.* Its summit was well defined at 194°–195°, from which point it fell away gradually on either hand through several degrees. It was treated with diluted sulphuric acid in the usual way, the first portion of acid becoming quite dark, and the second, third, and fourth portions each less dark than the preceding. The hydro-carbon itself began to be colored on the fourth addition of acid.

In an ordinary retort upon metallic sodium it boiled at 195.4° (corrected).

On combustion, an unweighed portion of it gave 0.2721 grm. water, and 0.6478 grm. carbonic acid. Or,

	Found.		Theory.
Carbon	85.40	C_{22}	85.71
Hydrogen	14.60	H_{22}	14.29
	100.00		100.00

A determination of the density of its vapor gave the following result: —

Temperature of balance, . 24.5°

* Annalen der Chemie und Pharmacie, 1864, CXXIX. 369 and CXXXI. 303.

Temperature of oil-bath,	234°
Excess of weight of balloon,	0.557 grm.
Capacity of balloon,	213 c. c.
Air remaining in balloon,	0 c. c.
Height of barometer,	765 mm. at 24°
Density of vapor found,	5.471.
" " theoretical,	½ $(C_{22} H_{22})$ 5.325.

Two determinations of its sp. gr., at 0,° gave respectively 0.7902 and 0.7916.

Laurylene = $C_{24} H_{24}$. After the first distillate from the crude lime-soap naphtha had been eight or ten times redistilled, the quantities of residue at 200° were so small in comparison with the large retorts employed that it was found to be impracticable to continue the distillation to 220°, as had been originally proposed; the larger portion of the matter less volatile than 200° which was contained in the first distillate, was consequently set aside as a highly impure residue at an early period. After a while, however, when smaller retorts were employed, the distillation of the products then in hand was carried as high as possible, and a small, very flat heap was finally obtained at 208°–212°.

Although there was still considerable doubt whether this heap had been distilled sufficiently, it was thought best to examine it as it stood. It was consequently treated with the diluted sulphuric acid, and subsequently analyzed, as follows: The first, second and third portions of acid blackened very much, the third portion less than the others, a faint odor of mint being meanwhile developed; the fourth and fifth portions of acid blackened much less than the preceeding, and the sixth was but little colored. The hydro-carbon was then washed, dried, and boiled with sodium, as usual.

The largest degree-fraction of the purified product boiled at 212.6° (corrected.)

On combustion (I.), 0.1481 grm. of it gave 0.1735 grm. water, and 0.4715 grm. carbonic acid. After having been again distilled over sodium several times, it was again analyzed (II.) as follows: 0.1463 grm. of it gave 0.1680 grm. water, and 0.468 grm. carbonic acid. Or,

	Found.		Theory.	
	I.	II.		
Carbon	86.83	87.22	C_{24}	85.71
Hydrogen	13.03	12.78	H_{24}	14.29
	99.86	100.00		100.00

A determination of the density of its vapor gave the following result: —

Temperature of the balance,	25.5°
" " oil-bath,	248°
Excess of weight of balloon,	0.5853 grm.
Capacity of the balloon,	217 c. c.
Air remaining in "	0 c. c.
Height of barometer,	769.3mm. at 25°
Density of vapor found,	5.7314
Theoretical ($C_{24} H_{24}$),	5.8092

Its sp. gr. was found to be 0.8361 at 0°.

We suppose this body to be that member of the $C_n H_n$ series which boils at 215°, but contaminated with some less highly hydrogenized substance. That this contaminating substance is naphthalin we entertain but little doubt, since we have encountered a case almost precisely similar to this when studying the hydro-carbons from Rangoon petroleum, and in that instance were fortunate enough to crystallize out from the hydro-carbon, which corresponds to the one now under consideration, so much naphthalin, that we were able to prove its identity by an analysis and by the examination of its properties. In the case in hand, however, we could obtain no deposit of napthalin on cooling the fractions 202°–203° and 204°–205° in a mixture of ice and salt. It may here be stated that no crystals of any kind separated from any of the products which have been described above, although all of these were maintained during several days at temperatures below 0°.

Mention has already been made, when specially treating of each of these bodies, of the fact that the hydro-carbons boiling at 175°, 195°, and 215° do not readily collect in abrupt heaps at a single fraction, but remain dispersed in nearly equal quantities through a range of several degrees. This comparative flatness of the heaps of high boiling points is in striking contrast with the clearly defined summits of the bodies which boil at low temperatures, that is, below 140°. The constituents of Pennsylvanian and of Rangoon petroleum, which boil at 175°, 195°, and 215°, exhibit the same characteristic flatness; which fact, so far as it goes, would tend to indicate their identity with the corresponding bodies from the lime-soap naphtha. In the same way it may be counted as one item of difference in distinguishing the upper from the lower series of the formula $C_n H_n$. The tendency of these hydro-carbons to form flat heaps undoubtedly explains one part of the difficulty of removing them from isocumole and xylole, to which allusion has already been made.

It has occurred to us that it is not altogether unlikely that the flatness of the heaps at these comparatively high temperatures may be occasioned by the partial decomposition, during distillation, of the hydro-carbons of which the heaps are composed; if such decomposition occur, it would be attended with the formation of small quantities of bodies boiling at lower temperatures than the substance sought for. It should be remarked, however, that this view has been suggested to us, not so much by any observations peculiar to ourselves, as by the consideration of the well-known fact that paraffine and those portions of petroleum which boil at very high temperatures can be broken up by repeated distillation, with formation of much lighter and more volatile oils, — a fact which has frequently been acted upon by the manufacturers of coal-oil for illuminating purposes, and which, when carried out upon the large scale, is technically known as "cracking" the paraffine or heavy oil.

In brief, then, it appears as the result of our examination of the naphtha from lime-soap that this mixture contains: —

Amylene,	$C_{10} H_{10}$
Hydride of Amyl,	$C_{10} H_{12}$
Caproylene,	$C_{12} H_{12}$
Hydride of Caproyl,	$C_{12} H_{14}$
Benzole,	$C_{12} H_6$
Œnanthylene,	$C_{14} H_{14}$
Hydride of Œnanthyl,	$C_{14} H_{16}$
Toluole,	$C_{14} H_8$
Caprylene,	$C_{16} H_{16}$
Hydride of Capryl,	$C_{16} H_{18}$
Xylole,	$C_{16} H_{10}$
Pelargonene,	$C_{18} H_{18}$
Isocumole,	$C_{18} H_{12}$
Rutylene,	$C_{20} H_{20}$
Margarylene,	$C_{22} H_{22}$
Laurylene,	$C_{24} H_{24}$

Or, arranged in homologous series: —

FORMULA.	OBSERVED BOILING POINT.[1]	FORMULA.	OBSERVED BOILING POINT.[1]
$C_{10} H_{10}$	34.5°–35.6°	$C_{10} H_{12}$	About 39°
$C_{12} H_{12}$	About 65°	$C_{12} H_{14}$	68.5°–69.5°
$C_{14} H_{14}$	Something less than 95°	$C_{14} H_{16}$	97.8°
$C_{16} H_{16}$	123.8°–125.2°	$C_{16} H_{18}$	128°–129°
$C_{18} H_{18}$	153°		

[1] With regard to these two series we are still uncertain whether or no the true boiling points may not in the one case be a trifle, say a fraction of one degree, lower than the degrees the names of which end in five; and in the other case be more nearly expressed by the degrees the names of which end in nine than by those which end in eight. These points we hope to elucidate thoroughly at some future time. But with regard to the difference in boiling point of almost precisely 30° C. for each addition of $C^2 H_2$ there can be no room for doubt.

FORMULA.	OBSERVED BOILING POINT.	FORMULA.	OBSERVED BOILING POINT.
$C_{12} H_6$	79.9°	$C_{18} H_{18}$	153°
$C_{14} H_8$	111.°	$C_{20} H_{20}$	174°–175°
$C_{16} H_{10}$		$C_{22} H_{22}$	195.4
$C_{18} H_{12}$		$C_{24} H_{24}$	212.6° [1]

It will be noticed that the observed boiling points of all these bodies go to corroborate the results previously published by one of us.[2] A difference of 30° C. for the addition of $C_2 H_2$ being the rule in each of the series, — with the single exception of the higher $C_n H_n$ series, in which the difference is only 20°, as has been previously stated. See pp. 168, 176 of the memoir cited. It will be noticed, moreover, that in this research we have encountered, for the first time in our experience, the lower $C_n H_n$ series (homologues of olefiant gas), and that its members follow the rule of 30°; hence the addition of still another series to the list of those known to conform to this law.

It is a curious fact that the two $C_n H_n$ series unite at 155°. We are still ignorant whether the body, "pelargonene," which boils at about that temperature, belongs to the lower or to the higher series; or whether, as is possible, it does not belong to both series. In petroleum we have found it as a member of the higher series. Since the two series thus coalesce, or at all events since there is no absolute breach between them, it seems to be proper enough to derive the names of the members of the higher series in accordance with the rules which have hitherto been employed by chemists in designating the members of the lower or olefiant series. In view of the greater simplicity of this course, we have preferred to adopt it, rather than to leave the substances without names, or to attempt to base a system of nomenclature upon the somewhat discordant data concerning diamylene, triamylene, etc., which have been published. Further researches are of course called for before the true character of these new bodies can be definitely determined.

It would be premature, at this time, to offer any speculations as to the precise manner in which the hydro-carbons which we have here examined are formed during the destructive distillation of the lime-soap. But it is important to bear in mind the facts that while in coal-tar naphtha we find members of the benzoleseries, and in coal-oil naphtha and petroleum two series of hydrides and the higher series of $C_n H_n$, we have here in the products of distillation of lime-soap a third naphtha which stands in some respects midway between the other two; for it contains both benzole, Schorlemmer's hydrides, and the higher series of $C_n H_n$, though it is at the same time specifi-

[1] Known to be impure.

[2] Warren, Memoirs of American Academy (N. S.), IX. 170.

cally characterized by the presence of the olefiant series of hydro-carbons, that is, the lower series of $C_n H_n$. A recent examination by A. Wurtz,[1] of the naphtha obtained by distilling a mixture of amyl-alcohol and chloride of zinc, goes to show that in this case the olefiant series is accompanied by that series of hydrides the several members of which boil at 0°, 30°, 60°, 120°, and 150°. We have proposed to ourselves to re-examine this naphtha from amyl-alcohol at an early day, for the purpose of proving whether or no it contains also members of the other series of hydrides (Schorlemmer's) which boil at 8°, 38°, 68°, 98°, and 128°, as well as for the sake of obtaining the paramylene compounds, which we desire to compare with some of the members of our higher series of $C_n H_n$.

As has been stated in the text above, the quantity of liquid contained in each of the heaps was roughly measured. On summing up these several amounts it appeared that there was altogether a total of nearly 6400 *c. c.* of liquid. Of this amount about 0.8% consisted of amylene and hydride of amyl.

3.9% of Caproylene.
2.8% of Hydride of Caproyl.
3.1% of Benzole.
4.7% of Œnanthylene.
7.6% of Hydrate of Œnanthyl.
6.9% of Toluole.
12.5% of Caprylene and Hydride of Capryl.
13.3% of Xylole.
7.8% of Pelargonene.
23.5% of Isocumole and Rutylene.
10.2% of Margarylene.
3.1% of Laurylene.

With regard to this table, it must be understood that it refers only to the quantities of liquid contained in the actual heaps, and does not include the numerous small fractions lying between the heaps. It is offered merely as an approximative indication of the relative proportions in which the several hydro-carbons were obtained. In the present condition of chemical science there can be of course no thought of attempting the quantitative analysis of a crude naphtha like the one now under consideration. Indeed, it has been to ourselves a matter of surprise and gratulation that we have been able successfully to effect the qualitative separation of the hydro-carbons from a mixture so extremely complex as this. The actual isolation of fifteen or sixteen different

[1] Bulletin de le Société Chimique de Paris, 1863, V. 300; compare Bauer, Sitzungsberichte der math. naturwissen. Klasse der Akademie zu Wien, 1861, vol. XLIV. part II. p. 89.

hydro-carbons, belonging to four distinct series, and all boiling within a range of 180° centigrade, is a result in obtaining which we feel amply repaid for all the time and labor which this exceedingly tedious research has cost us. Certainly no more stringent test of the efficiency of the process of "Fractional Condensation," as contrasted with the old methods of distillation, need for the present be required.

Boston, August, 1864.

IX.

Examination of Naphtha obtained from Rangoon Petroleum.

BY C. M. WARREN AND F. H. STORER.

Communicated August 9, 1865.

SEVERAL years since, Warren De La Rue and Hugo Müller[1] attempted to determine the chemical composition of the petroleum from Rangoon. But the results obtained by these distinguished chemists were exceedingly unsatisfactory.

De La Rue and Müller operated upon the large scale, having started with a stock of several tons of the crude petroleum; but in so far as concerns the hydro-carbons, which, as they admit, constitute the chief part of the naphtha, these observers confess their inability to separate the mixture into compounds of fixed boiling points.

So soon as the method of separating volatile hydro-carbons by fractional condensation had been successfully employed by one of us,[2] the desire naturally arose to apply this method to the elucidation of problems which the best chemists of the day had failed to solve. The labors of De La Rue and Müller at once occurred to us as furnishing an extreme instance, and it was determined to test the new process with materials which, as these chemists had shown, could not be unravelled by the old processes of analysis. With this view a sample of native Rangoon Petroleum was obtained, in Jan. 1862, from Price's Patent Candle Co., of London, it being well known to chemists that this firm was at that time constantly importing the petroleum in question. The sample received from Price's Co. amounted to "five imperial gallons;" it was contained in a well-secured vessel, and was accompanied by a certificate of the company to the effect that the petroleum was in the condition in which it is imported into England, — that is, "just as we receive it from Burmah."

The package containing this sample remained in our possession unopened until the autumn of 1863, when the investigation now to be described was commenced. Upon examination the petroleum was found to be a thick, greasy matter, not sufficiently

[1] Proceedings of the Royal Society of London, VIII. 221; or Phil. Mag. 1857, [4.] XIII. 512.

[2] Warren, Memoirs of American Academy, [N. S.] IX. 121.

liquid to admit of being poured from the can which contained it, when the temperature of the air was 25° C.; but, upon being heated, it flowed readily at 30°–33°, and became perfectly fluid at 38°–40°. The color of the mass was yellowish-green. It emitted the odor common to the purer varieties of native petroleum; though its odor was but slight and in no wise offensive. The specific gravity of this native petroleum was 0.875 at 29°.

Four separate portions of the crude petroleum, each about 5600 *c. c.*, were distilled in a common copper retort without the interposition of any hot condenser. A few drops of the liquid began to distil over at about 140°–150°, and the process of distillation was continued until the temperature had reached 270°–300°. The distillate obtained amounted, all told, to a little more than 7000 *c. c.*, or 30.46% of the crude petroleum.

The volatile product, or *naphtha*, thus obtained was now subjected to the process of distillation and fractional condensation, as described in Vol. IX., p. 130, of the Memoirs of this Academy. This naphtha began to pass through the hot condenser at about 125°, the liquid in the retort then boiling at about 165°. During a dozen or more operations the distillation was carried up to 260°; afterwards, as the quantities became smaller, only up to about 250°. The naphtha contained only a very small quantity of easily volatile products, nothing having been collected, in a second cold receiver surrounded with ice, either during the preliminary distillation from the copper retort or during the first series of fractional distillations.

Fractions of the naphtha were taken off for every ten degrees of temperature at first, then for every five degrees, then for every two degrees, and, finally, for each single degree, — by far the larger part of the work having, of course, been done in fractions of one degree. The greatest care was constantly exercised in order to lessen as far as possible the loss by evaporation of the more volatile products. It is, however, impossible to avoid a great waste of these matters. With the same regard to economy of liquid, the size of the glass retorts and of the worms employed was reduced to the lowest practicable limit.

After the distillatory process had been continued until products of definite boiling points had been obtained, or until, in the lack of this, the amount of liquid in each fraction had been so far reduced that there was no longer any hope of isolating pure substances in that part of the field, a survey of the work indicated that there had been obtained seven well-defined heaps[1] between the temperatures of 170°[2] and 250°; but

[1] For definition of this term see the preceding Memoir, p. 179 of this volume.

[2] All statements of temperature, when not followed by the word "corrected," refer to the indications of ordinary thermometers. Corrected temperatures are those taken in the manner described in Vol. IX., p. 143 of the Memoirs of this Academy, and corrected for atmospheric pressure, and the upper column of mercury in accordance with H. Kopp's formula.

that below 175° the quantities of liqiud had become so small that no definite results could there be obtained. It is true that several elevations existed in this range of small fractions, but to these we will refer hereafter.

It should here be mentioned that we had not been long at work upon this naphtha from Rangoon petroleum, before the conviction was forced upon us that we had started with an insufficient quantity of material. Application was therefore made in the winter of 1863–4 to Price's Patent Candle Company for a supply of the naphtha such as was formerly prepared by them by distilling Rangoon petroleum upon the large scale, but to our regret we learned that the naphtha in question was no longer manufactured by the company, and that it was out of their power to furnish us with any of it. In spite of this, and in fact while the negotiation was pending, we continued to work upon our naphtha as before, being animated by a determination to learn how much could be done with the process of fractional condensation when this is applied to so small a quantity of volatile material as that at our disposal.

Each of the isolated heaps of liquid was now worked by itself, over sodium, until this metal was no longer acted upon, after which the most prominent fractions were analyzed and otherwise examined, as is stated below. It should be noted that neither the crude petroleum, nor the naphtha, nor the finished heaps were ever subjected to the action of any chemicals other than this distillation from sodium which has just been alluded to.

Rutylene = $C_{20} H_{20}$. The heap at 170°–176° amounted to about 120 *c. c.* Its summit was very clearly defined at 172°–173°, this fraction being twice as large as those at 171°–172° or 174°–176°, and half as large again as that at 173°–174°.

The fraction 172°–173° boiled at 175.8° (corrected).

On analysis, 0.2036 grm. of it gave 0.255 grm. water, and 0.6421 grm. of carbonic acid. Or,

	Found.		Theory.
Carbon,	86.00	C_{20}	85.7
Hydrogen,	13.75	H_{20}	14.3
	99.75		100.00

Determination of vapor density: —

Temperature of balance,	12.5°
" oil-bath,	223°
Excess of weight of balloon,	0.5745
Capacity "	242 *c. c.*
Air remaining in "	0 "
Density of vapor found,	5.086
" " theoretical ($C_{20} H_{20}$),	4.841

Its specific gravity was found to be 0.823 at 0°.

Heap at 187° = $C_n H_n$. Immediately above the rutylene heap there was noticed a well-defined tendency toward persistency at 180°–184°, and upon finally working these fractions by themselves, it was found to be impossible to reduce them below a certain size, little or nothing coming off at 180°, and there being no residue worth mentioning at 185°. The summit of this spurious (?) heap remained constant at 182°–184°.

The fraction 182°–183° boiled at 187.4° (corrected).

On analysis, 0.234 grm. of it gave 0.289 grm. of water, and 0.736 grm. of carbonic acid. Or,

	Found.		Theory.
Carbon,	85.77	C_n	85.7
Hydrogen,	13.68	H_n	14.3
	99.45		100.0

Its specific gravity was found to be 0.8356 at 0°.

Margarylene = $C_{22} H_{22}$. Between 186° and 193° was a heap amounting to about 215 *c. c.* the summit of which stood out boldly at 188°–190°.

The fraction 189°–190°, which, by the way, was of precisely the same size of the 188°–189°, boiled at 195.9° (corrected).

On analysis, 0.1407 grm. of it gave 0.175 grm. water, and 0.4469 grm. carbonic acid. Or,

	Found.		Theory.
Carbon,	86.64	C_{22}	85.7
Hydrogen,	13.79	H_{22}	14.3
	100.43		100.0

A determination of vapor density resulted as follows:—

Temperature of balance,	13.5°
" oil-bath,	249°
Excess of weight of balloon,	0.5697
Capacity "	231 *c. c.*
Air remaining in "	0
Height of barometer,	759mm. at — 2°
Density of vapor found,	5.478
" " " theoretical ($C_{22} H_{22}$),	5.325

Its specific gravity was found to be 0.8398 at 0°.

Laurylene = $C_{24} H_{24}$. Between 200° and 214° there were three distinct summits amounting respectively to about 125 *c. c.*, 150 *c. c.*, and 150 *c. c.* These summits were well defined, particularly the lower one, the true boiling point of which was found to be 208.3° (corrected); the second summit boiled at 214.6° (corrected), and the third at 219.5° (corrected).

On analysis, the following results were obtained; No. I. refers to the fraction which boiled at 208.3° (corrected); No. II. to that boiling at 214.6°; and No. III. to that boiling at 219.5°. 0.1845 grm. of No. I. gave 0.2121 grm. water, and 0.5885 grm. carbonic acid (*a*); a second sample of 0.1326 grm. of No. I. gave 0.1525 grm. water, and 0.4235 grm. carbonic acid (*b*.); 0.1387 grm. of No. II. gave 0,1654 grm. water, and 0.443 grm. carbonic acid (*a*); a second sample, of 0.1433 grm., of No. II. gave 0.1728 grm. water, and 0.4552 grm. carbonic acid (*b*); while 0.194 grm. of No. III. gave 0.2407 grm. water, and 0.6106 grm. carbonic acid. Or,

	Found.					Theory.
	I.		II.		III.	($C_{24} H_{24}$)
	a.	*b*.	*a*.	*b*.		
Carbon,	86.99	87.10	87.09	86.60	86.83	85.7
Hydrogen,	12.79	12.82	13.27	13.40	13.87	14.3
	99.78	99.92	100.36	100.00	99.70	100.0

These figures accord with the formulæ I. (*a*) $C_{24} H_{21.19}$, (*b*) $C_{24} H_{21.20}$:— II. (*a*) $C_{24} H_{21.95}$, (*b*) $C_{24} H_{22.28}$:— III. $C_{24} H_{23.00}$; and point clearly to the presence of some substance less highly hydrogenized than laurylene. In a subsequent paragraph it will be shown that this disturbing element was naphthalin. That the naphthalin should have given rise to the formation of three heaps is a matter of no surprise in the present instance, since unfortunately the work of two operators happened to overlap at this very point. One obtained the greater part of the naphthalin, the other most of the laurylene; while between the two a spurious heap[1] was formed.

A determination of the vapor density of Nos. II. and III. gave the following results: —

	II.	III.
Temperature of balance,	12.5°	13°
" " oil-bath,	256.5°	262°
Excess of weight of balloon,	0.6247	0.6238
Capacity "	228 c. c.	226.5 c. c.
Air remaining in "	0 "	0 "
Height of barometer,	759mm. at — 2°	748.6mm. at 3°
Density of vapor found,	5.980	6.061
" " theoretical ($C_{24} H_{24}$),	5.809	5.809

The specific gravity of No. I. was found to be 0.8654 at 0°; that of No. II. to be 0.8548 at 0°; and that of No. III. to be 0.8453 at 0°.

Naphthalin = $C_{20} H_{8}$. In the course of the winter it happened that the temperature of the apartment in which the products from the Rangoon naphtha were kept, fell to 1° or 2° below zero, and remained at that point during several days. It was then

[1] See this volume, p. 200.

noticed that an abundant crop of crystalline plates had separated out in the fraction which boiled at 208° (corrected), and the fraction next above, namely, 209° (corrected). The quantity of these crystals was large as compared with the amount of liquid from which they had been deposited. After they had been removed from the liquid, a second crop of crystals was obtained from the same fractions, by cooling them in a mixture of ice and salt. These crystals were specially abundant, as before, in the fraction 208° (corrected); but no crystals were obtained, by the treatment with ice and salt, from any of the neighboring fractions, or from any of the fractions in the heap at 214.6° (corrected). Nor were any crystals deposited during the continuance of the cold weather from any of the other products which we have obtained from the Rangoon naphtha. The crystals from fractions 208°, 209° (corrected), were allowed to drain and were then pressed gently between folds of filter paper so long as any oil could be thus removed from them. During these operations the crystals remained unchanged; excepting in so far as they developed the unmistakable odor of naphthalin, Like those of pure naphthalin from coal-tar, the crystals were not very soluble in cold spirit, but on warming the spirit they dissolved in the same manner as crystals of pure naphthalin. In cold ether they dissolved in the same way as the crystals of naphthalin, and crystallized out again like naphthalin; a portion of the crystals in each case, that is, both the crystals from Rangoon naphtha and those from coal-tar, sublimed into the upper part of the test-tube in which the solution was effected, and were deposited there in the well-known characteristic plates. The crystals from fraction 208° (corrected) melted at 74°. A portion of them having been maintained during some time at a temperature slightly superior to 90°, a sublimate of the characteristic plates already alluded to was deposited upon the cold upper part of the tube above the source of heat.

On analysis, 0.167 grm. of the crystals first deposited from fraction 208° (corrected) gave 0.1015 grm. water and 0.5729 grm. carbonic acid. Or,

	Found.		Theory.
Carbon,	93.53	C_{20}	93,75
Hydrogen,	6.70	H_8	6.25
	100.23		100.00

Cocinlyene = $C_{28}\,H_{28}$. The last heap in our series was at 226°–234°, the summit of it being at 229°–232°, each of the fractions 229°–230°, 230°–231°, and 231°–232 being very nearly of equal size, though each was considerably larger than any others in the heap. The fraction 230°–231° was a trifle larger than the others. The quantity of liquid in the whole heap 226°–234° amounted to about 325 *c. c.* Above 234 the quantities of liquid in the degree-fractions fell away to almost nothing; there is evidently no compound present between 234° and 250°.

The fraction 230°–231° boiled at 232.75° (corrected).

On analysis, 0.2871 grm. of the fraction 230°–231° gave 0.3541 grm. water, and 0.91 grm. carbonic acid. Or,

	Found.		Theory.
Carbon,	86.38	C_{26}	85.7
Hydrogen,	13.69	H_{26}	14.3
	100.07		100.0

In determining the vapor-density of this substance the balloon was filled with an atmosphere of carbonic acid[1] after the introduction of the liquid. The following result was obtained: —

Temperature of balance,	22°
" " oil-bath,	274°
Excess of weight of balloon,	0.6863
Capacity "	233 c. c.
Air remaining in "	0
Height of barometer,	760.5 m. m. at 21°
Density of vapor found,	6.4225
" " theoretical (C_{26} H_{26}),	6.2940

The specific gravity of the fraction 230°–231° was found to be 0.8445 at 0°.

The attempts which we have made to isolate the constituents of that portion of Rangoon naphtha which is more volatile than the hydro-carbons above described, were unsuccessful; the quantity of naphtha boiling at temperatures lower than 175° having been so small that it could not be thoroughly analyzed by the process of fractional condensation. After protracted efforts to separate these volatile hydro-carbons from one another by means of a diminutive apparatus, we were at last reluctantly forced to abandon the attempt, and to acknowledge our inability to obtain satisfactory results from such small quantities of the complex material.

Indeed, the quantity of volatile naphtha at our disposal was so small that although at the last it was divided only into fractions of wide range, each of them representing three or more degrees of temperature, these portions in several instances soon became too minute to be operated upon at all, even in the smallest practicable apparatus. But since these volatile products had been subjected, first and last, to a large number of distillations and fractional condensations, each of the fractions finally obtained must have

[1] In a previous attempt to determine this vapor-density in the usual way, without employing carbonic acid, the mixture of air and vapor in the balloon took fire with a slight explosion, the temperature of the oil-bath being then at 321°.

been tolerably well purified from all substances, excepting those whose boiling points are not widely different from its own. We have, therefore, taken pains to analyze some of the more prominent among the fractions into which the volatile portion of the naphtha had been divided, in order to learn whether there might not thus be obtained a general idea of the composition of this part of the naphtha.

The following is a record of the analyses in question, — all statements of degrees of temperature here referring to "corrected" boiling points: —

I. One portion (*a*) of the fraction 98°–109°, this being the most volatile[1] of all the products which we have obtained from Rangoon petroleum, gave 0.3294 grm. water and 0.771 grm. carbonic acid; another portion (*b*) gave 0.4533 grm. water and 1.0673 grm. carbonic acid.

II. 0.194 grm. of the fraction 121.6°–123.5° gave 0.2589 grm. water and 0.6022 grm. carbonic acid.

III. 0.2987 grm. of the fraction 142.3°–144.3° gave 0.3799 grm. water and 0.9416 grm. carbonic acid.

IV. 0.1583 grm. of the fraction 151.6°–153.7° gave 0.2048 grm. water and 0.4952 grm. carbonic acid; another portion (*b*) gave 0.1346 grm. water and 0.3245 grm. carbonic acid.

V. A portion of the fraction 154.7°–155.7° gave 0.2002 grm. water and 0.491 grm. carbonic acid.

VI. 0.1554 grm. of the fraction 158.8°–159.8° gave 0.1986 grm. water and 0.488 grm. carbonic acid.

VII. 0.1714 grm. of the fraction 164°–165° gave 0.2174 grm. water and 0.5422 grm. carbonic acid.

VIII. 0.1899 grm. of the fraction 172.3°–173.8° gave 0.2398 grm. water and 0.5992 grm. carbonic acid.

Reducing these results to per cents., we have

	I.		II.	III.	IV.	
	a	*b*			*a*	*b*
Carbon,	85.18	85.27	84.64	85.97	85.34	85.59
Hydrogen,	14.82	14.73	14.85	14.13	14.40	14.41
	100.00	100.00	99.49	100.10	99.74	100.00

	V.	VI.	VII.	VIII.
Carbon,	85.79	85.65	86.23	86.04
Hydrogen,	14.21	14.16	14.06	14.01
	100.00	99.81	100.29	100.05

[1] It should be remembered, in this connection, that De La Rue and Müller, by operating upon large quantities of the petroleum, obtained products boiling as low as 50°.

From these analyses the following formulæ are derived: —

I. $(a) = C_{14}\ H_{14.62}$; $(b) = C_{14}\ H_{14.51}$. II. $C_{16}\ H_{16.86}$. III. $C_{16}\ H_{15.78}$. IV. $(a) = C_{18}\ H_{18.23}$; $(b) = C_{18}\ H_{18.19}$. V. $C_{18}\ H_{17.9}$. VI. $C_{18}\ H_{17.86}$. VII. $C_{18}\ H_{17.54}$. VIII. $C_{18}\ H_{17.89}$.

It will be observed that the fractions Nos. I. and II. are largely composed of hydrides, — doubtless those of œnanthyl and of capryl, which boil at 98°, 120°, and 128°, — though still contaminated with hydro-carbons belonging to one or both of the $C_n\ H_n$ series, or possibly even with toluole. Fraction No. III. is probably a mixture of xylole, the foregoing hydrides, and members of the $C_n\ H_n$ series, as before. The composition of fraction No. IV. indicates the probable presence of hydride of pelargonyl, boiling at 150°. Fractions Nos. V., VI., VII., and VIII. are probably composed for the most part of pelargonene ($C_{18}\ H_{18}$) contaminated with a little isocumole ($C_{18}\ H_{12}$).

The comparatively small proportion of hydrogen found in the fractions which boil in the vicinity of 140° and 170° (the boiling points of xylole and isocumole), goes to corroborate the opinion of De La Rue and Müller,[1] that Rangoon petroleum contains members of the benzole series, and is perhaps all the more pertinent in view of the fact that we have ourselves isolated naphthalin from the petroleum, as has been already stated. It is of course conceivable that the naphthalin alone may have contaminated the fractions in question, as well as the definite heaps which have been previously described, the analysis of all of which indicate the presence of a little less hydrogen than is contained in pure $C_n\ H_n$. But this conception seems to us improbable; the composition of fractions 142.3°–144.3° (No. III.) and 151.6°–153.7° (No. IV.), in particular, would appear to invalidate it. We may here say that on the whole our results have very much weakened the opinion, which at one time seemed to us to be not altogether improbable, that the benzole-homologues obtained by De La Rue and Müller might have resulted from the action of nitric acid in removing hydrogen from the more highly hydrogenized hydro-carbons, and might not have been contained in the native petroleum.

As the result of our examination thus far, it appears that the naphtha from Rangoon petroleum contains: —

Rutylene = $C_{20}\ H_{20}$	boiling at about	175°
Margarylene = $C_{22}\ H_{22}$	" " "	195°
Laurylene = $C_{24}\ H_{24}$	" " "	215°
Cocinylene = $C_{26}\ H_{24}$	" " "	235°
Naphthalin = $C_{20}\ H_8$.		

Also, probably, Pelargone = $C_{18}\ H_{18}$, boiling at about 155°, and members of one or both of the series of hydrides; it being a fair presumption that we have had in our hands the Hydrides of Œnanthyl, of Capryl, and of Pelargonyl. Our experiments also indicate the probable presence of Xylole and Isocumole.

[1] Proceedings of the Royal Society of London, VIII. 225.

Boston, June, 1865.

www.ingramcontent.com/pod-product-compliance
Lightning Source LLC
Chambersburg PA
CBHW031958230426
43672CB00010B/2196

* 9 7 8 3 3 3 7 3 7 4 3 1 0 *